52ND STREET:
THE
STREET
OF JAZZ

52ND STREET:
THE STREET OF JAZZ

(Originally published as
THE STREET THAT NEVER SLEPT)

by ARNOLD SHAW

Foreword by ABEL GREEN

A DA CAPO PAPERBACK

To my beloved wife
Ghita
a rare, remarkable woman

Library of Congress Cataloging in Publication Data

Shaw, Arnold.
    52nd Street, the street of jazz.

    (A Da Capo paperback)
    Reprint of the 1971 ed. published by Coward, McCann &
Geoghegan, New York, under title: The street that never
slept.
    1. New York (City)—Streets—Fifty-second Street.
2. Jazz music. I. Title. II. Title: The street that
never slept.
[F128.67.F5S5 1977]   874.7'1   77-23547
ISBN 0-306-80068-3

ISBN: 0-306-80068-3
First Paperback Printing, August 1977
Second Paperback Printing, December 1983

This Da Capo Press paperback edition of *52nd Street: The Street of Jazz* is an unabridged
republication, with the exception of several minor additions and a postscript to the introduction, of the first edition published in New York in 1971 under the title *The Street That Never
Slept.* It is reprinted by arrangement with the author.

Published by Da Capo Press
A Subsidiary of Plenum Publishing Corporation
233 Spring Street
New York, N.Y. 10013

Contents

Foreword:
America's Montmartre

by ABEL GREEN

Bourbon Street, Beale Street, Rush Street, The Strip, Sunset Boulevard, Central Avenue, Market Street, Haight-Ashbury, Sankt Pauli, the West End, the Kurfürstendamm, Pigalle, Montparnasse, the Via Veneto, need little identification. They automatically conjure up the smells and the sounds.

New York has had its renowned 42d St., Broadway, Lenox Avenue —and 52d St.

Where Hamburg's notorious Reeperbahn waterfront is a sprawling complex of bawdy boîtes, and Paris' Butte, from Place Pigalle along Boulevard de Clichy, is an even larger spread of tourist traps, none was so compact and as diversified in its excitement and its assorted sounds, madcapades, variety talents, gastronomy and jazz mania as 52d St. in its hey-heydays. But the accent was dominantly on music. Truly "the street that never slept," it is fitting that music man-*cum*-composer Arnold Shaw should be the one to capture the mood and modes, manners and mores of that madcap Manhattan street.

Arnold Shaw has run the Tin Pan Alley gamut. He is also a long-hair songsmith, but his milieu has been definitely pop. As a professional manager for major music pubberies, he has known the economic travail of "the No. 1 plug," the more a hardship if the song proved to be a "dog." Himself a composer, he has ambivalently known the creative pains of the tunesmith and the commercial publisher. As an historian, he seemingly retained the vivid and affectionate memories of 52d St. that are reflected in this book. With detached photographic recall he has recorded a vivid segment from an era of wonderful nonsense which spawned some truly wonderful music.

It may be apocryphal but probably true that one young man, more than slightly under the influence, staggered up the stairs of one of those 52d St. town houses, passed the upstairs speakeasy to the further upstairs illicit-gambling room, and declaimed to one and all that he just had to see once again the room where he was born and spent his preteens until the family apparently took a capital gains and sold it for more alfresco purposes.

What might have gone on upstairs was more vividly echoed and reechoed on the street level with much musical fanfare. Its lasting musical legacy reflects a nostalgia for a street that never slept. Shoddy, bawdy and boozy, it was never lacking for humor and tempo. Its rhythm was in tune with the times. And the times were serene for all its scofflaw pattern.

The 1970's have spawned a wistful desire for nostalgia. Whereas in the late sixties it was called camp, the sentiment of the seventies is genuine, viz., *No, No, Nanette, et al.* "I Want to Be Happy" was the way of life on "The Street That Never Slept."

Introduction

In 1948, when *Metronome* magazine ran a historical, if premature, obituary on 52d St., it noted: "Even today, when you leave a musician and say, 'See you on The Street tonight,' he doesn't have to ask you which street you mean." For that matter, in 1948 and for a score of years before then, neither did the average cabdriver. If you flagged a taxi in NYC and asked to be taken to *The Street,* you would be driven, without giving a number or avenue, to 52d between Fifth and Sixth avenues.

Not only to musicians but to night people generally—to the spenders, to Ivy League collegians, to the sophisticates of any age, to people of the theater, and to jazz fans the world over—The Street was known as a swinging place between 1934 and 1950.

This book is the story of that midtown Manhattan block, a monochrome of five-story brownstone buildings in whose drab and cramped street-level interiors—once known as English basements—there were more clubs, bars, bistros and boîtes than crates in an overstocked warehouse. Known in its heyday as Swing Street or Swing Alley, The Street actually included the block past the elevated on Sixth Avenue, now Avenue of the Americas. The clubs on this westerly block are part of our tale, but they were always like the back of the orchestra in a theater.

Why the block between Fifth and Sixth should have attained its undeniable notoriety and nostalgia cannot be easily answered. In a sense, 52d did not differ from all the other midtown blocks of Victorian brownstones. It was as narrow as any of its undistinguished neighbors. But it did have a number of things going for it.

In the Prohibition era, for no readily accountable reason, it had a larger concentration of speakeasies than any of its neighbors—and these became nightclubs or restaurants after Repeal. Among these Judas-hole establishments, four were pivotal in setting up The Street. 21 early brought glamor, high society, top politicians, and with these, columnists who spread the fame of The Street. At No. 57–59 Tony's attracted the literary and theater set of the famous Algonquin Round-table. At No. 33 Leon & Eddie became home for the tourists, cloak-and-suiters and show biz folk who couldn't make it at 21 or Tony's. And Joe Helbock's Onyx, originally an in spot for studio musicians at No. 35, triggered the awareness and influx of the public through its song hits.

From a musical standpoint, 52d St. is the story of three major jazz styles. It came into existence as small-combo Dixieland (hot jazz) of the speakeasy era developed into the big-band swing of the New Deal thirties. Attaining its apogee in the years of World War II, it began to decline as swing gave way to small-combo modern jazz, bop and cool. By 1936 it was known as Swing Street, and the following year Sammy Cahn and Saul Chaplin wrote a song, "52 St.," in which it was eulogized as "the place where the swing cats meet," even though few of the name bands could or did play the cramped clubs. In its flourishing decade (1935–45), The Street served as the launching pad for more singers, more hit songs and more instrumentalists than any of the country's entertainment centers—Rush Street in Chicago, Bourbon Street in New Orleans, Beale Street in Memphis, and Central Avenue or The Strip in Los Angeles.

"On 52d St., you could walk through the history of jazz," says pianist Marian McPartland, long a Hickory House habitué. "In several hours, nursing a few drinks, you could travel musically from New Orleans up to Harlem and bop."

Viewed sociologically, 52d St. is the story of how Harlem came downtown—not only its music and dances, but its chicken and rib joints and its talented people. The Street embodies the struggle of black singers and musicians to gain their rightful place in white society. There were, of course, many white people for whom The Street proved a pathway to public recognition—Woody Herman, Charlie Barnet, Buddy Rich, Dave Tough, George Shearing, Joe Mooney, Joe Marsala, Wingy Manone, Louis Prima, Lili St. Cyr, Jack White, Eddie Davis and others.

But in an important sense, 52d St. is the street of Art Tatum, Billie Holiday, Coleman Hawkins, "Hot Lips" Page, Roy "Little Jazz" Eldridge, Teddy Wilson, Fats Waller, Erroll Garner, Eddie Heywood, Billy Daniels, Slim & Slam, "Stuff" Smith, Leo Watson, Mary Lou Williams, Dizzy Gillespie, Charlie "Bird" Parker, Mabel Mercer, Maxine Sullivan, Sarah Vaughan, Count Basie and a host of other inspired black performers.

These men and women lived through the period when, accepted and admired as performers, they had to withstand segregation and even physical attacks. They had their friends in the John Hammonds, Joe Marsalas, Milt Gablers, Charlie Barnets and other ofays. And they had their problems with prejudiced New Yorkers, Southern servicemen and the Manhattan police. The Street provided employment and a showcase for their talents, opening its doors a little more quickly than the rest of Manhattan's midtown restaurants, hotels, theaters and even movie palaces.

"Fifty-Second Street was a mother," says Dizzy Gillespie, the noted bop trumpeter. "I say mother—and I don't mean motherfucker, though it was that, too."

Many think of the jam session as the earmark of The Street's exciting aesthetic. Most clubs featured such sessions at one time or another, and they were a tremendous audience draw. But 52d St.'s power lay in something else, though it was something allied to the jam session. It became known as "sitting in." As in a jam session, a man who *sits in* plays music that is unrehearsed, improvised and spontaneous. But the difference is that he invades a place where a set group of musicians is in residence at union rates. He comes for the sheer love of playing, for the stimulus of exchanging ideas with others, for the pleasure of speaking and communicating through his instrument.

"Sitting in" implies a freedom of movement, a body of shared feelings and a camaraderie that tended to disappear with the rise of bop and with the stringent enforcement of union regulations against free play. It was also based on a rare community of interests between performer and audience that placed *communication* and *expression* on the same level as *entertainment*. When the adventure worked, all three phases were present at a peak of excitement.

If you will countenance the comparison, in the heyday of 52d St. jazz enjoyed the integrated interplay of listeners and performers that marked the theater of the Elizabethans and Greeks and the art of painting in the Renaissance. Forced on people generally by the exigencies of worldwide depression, this togetherness gave The Street its vibrancy and, in an oft-repeated phrase, "made every night into New Year's Eve."

"52d St. was total friendship," says noted composer-arranger Alec Wilder. "It was the last time that an American street gave you a feeling of security and warmth and the excitement of musical friendship."

The spirit of spontaneous improvisation and rapping together carried over into areas other than music—into the Celebrity Nights at Leon & Eddie, where almost anyone could get up and do his thing, and in the raucous comedy of Jack White and Club 18. The Street embodies the story of American humor, particularly the types known as "bait the audience" and "deflate the bum." The latter is still quite evident in the work of Jackie Leonard, Don Rickles and other stand-up comics. But no one today picks on audience members as Jack White and his associates did—though celebrities and important people still seem to be fair game for David Frye and other satirists.

As a wee-hours-of-the-morning syndrome, The Street brought to a peak of expressiveness the torch ballad and balladeer, a type of heart-break song and performer largely gone from the pop scene. Billie Holiday (earlier Helen Morgan and later Judy Garland) exemplified the intensity and vulnerability of the style. Mabel Mercer presented the cooler, more sophisticated side in her crystalline, supper-club soliloquies. There were also the "after-hours" eighty-eighters like Tatum and Garner and Guarnieri, who explored the " 'round about midnight" moods instrumentally. Soft and intimate, running the emotional gamut from longing and world-weariness to a "one-for-my-baby, one-more-for-the-road" gaiety, the style flowered in the smoky, cramped quarters of 52d St.'s "upholstered sewers," as Earl Wilson termed them.

The Street also produced and attracted zany characters, as well as evil men and women. There was the club owner who sang songs standing on his head and the many masters of double-talk and jive like Harry "the Hipster" and "The Neam." The shadow of the Mob hovered over many clubs and created an aura of sin and danger that attracted even as it repelled. Eventually, under the impact of emotions and opportunities loosed by the war, cheap entertainment, the shoddy practices of club owners and the expansive plans of New York realtors combined to bring the downfall of The Street. Although insiders and outsiders were writing its obit in '48, The Street lingered a tawdry tenderloin of clip and strip joints into 1960. In the period of its decline, exotic dancing by broads frequently characterized as "fat, flabby and fortyish" became the major commodity—and 52d St. became part of the decadent story of American sex and drugs. Although stripping and burlesque humor had always been a phase of The Street's existence, now they served not as entertainment but as bait for the fast buck.

Walking today from Fifth to Seventh Avenue, and gazing up at the tidy towers of aluminum and glass, no one could possibly imagine what a nighttime whirl of exciting sounds, gifted performers and enthusiastic audiences The Street once was. Of all the clubs, only the Iron Gate still stands. Until March of 1971 Toots Shor could, perhaps, be counted as a survivor too, even though his Temple of Palship was long on 51st St. His location at No. 33 had been the address of Leon & Eddie, where he once served as a daytime manager. But neither elegant 21 nor sports-oriented Toots Shor's gives any real clue to The Street, where jazzmen, comics, song pluggers, strippers, pushers, prosties and a variety of characters nightly paused for a wee-hours-of-the-morning snack or snifter at Reilly's Tavern, Mammy's Chicken Koop, Pic-A-Rib or White Rose bar. For a feeling of The Street That Never Slept, one should hike over to 54th St. near Seventh Avenue, where some of the old-time Dixieland jazzmen blow nightly at the still-extant Jimmy Ryan's and where the man who was the "Doorman of The Street" still operates as he once did.

I have elected to tell the story of The Street through a double device. The chapters are built around the clubs whose very names— Onyx, Famous Door, Kelly's Stable, Three Deuces, etc.—recall the glamor that was 52d St. The Tapes are the subjective reminiscences of men and women who were part of the life of The Street as club owners, performers, songwriters, trade-paper reporters or record producers. These reminiscences are taped interviews from which I have merely eliminated myself as the questioner.

I was myself part of The Street from the early forties, when I functioned as advertising and publicity director of the "Big Three"—Robbins, Feist and Miller Music corporations—at 799 Seventh Avenue, on the southeast corner of 52d and Seventh Avenue. Although I had been to many of the clubs as a listener, it was at this time that I began entertaining the idea of writing a book. Through the years I made periodic surveys of changes in The Street and was able to photograph major developments like the tearing down of Jimmy Ryan's and the Famous Door. From 1957 into 1966, as the general professional manager of Edward B. Marks Music Corporation, I had an office at 136 West 52d, directly over the Hickory House, where I frequently ate lunch and rapped with the late John Popkin and his longtime publicity agent, Joe Morgen.

Of one of The Street's unforgettable performers, Frank Sinatra said: "It is Billie Holiday, whom I first heard in 52d St. clubs in the thirties, who was and still remains the greatest single musical influence on me." "Lady Day" and "The Voice" (who never appeared on The Street) typify its significance in American entertainment.

—ARNOLD SHAW

Postscript, 1977

In 1972 I flew to New York to meet with the Director of the Urban Improvements Program of the City's Parks Council. My purpose was to interest the Mayor Lindsay Council in an idea generated by jazz critic Leonard Feather. Reviewing my book in the *Los Angeles Times*, Feather had suggested that the sidewalks of 52d St. be repaved and like Hollywood Boulevard, display medallions with the names of the great performers who made it the Jazz Mecca of the world.

With the Parks Council tentatively approving the idea but lacking funds, I formed a committee to raise the $20,000 required to repave 52d St. between 5th and 6th Avenues, also to secure permissions of landlords on the block and of related city agencies. Arnold Gingrich, publisher of *Esquire*, I. Robert Kriendler of the 21 Club, and Abel Green, editor of *Variety*, all now deceased, were members of the committee, which failed to find a city resident to spearhead its activities once I returned to my home in Las Vegas. But it is a project that should be revived and completed.

Making 52d St. a "living" landmark of the city's musical history is hardly as urgent a matter as some of its troubling problems. But it might contribute to a revival of the aura the city once had when nighttime on its streets was a time of joy, excitement and even romance—when one of the great thrills was to watch dawn breaking over the silent streets as one walked home, body aglow and head athrob with the rapturous music of the 52d St. clubs.

Las Vegas, Nevada
March 10, 1977

1. Speakeasy Street

Sometime in the early thirties, before Prohibition was repealed, there was a spirited argument at Jack & Charlie's 21 about the number of speakeasies on the block. In the interest of the social sciences, if not in his capacity as a gentleman boozer, humorist Robert Benchley offered to do a tally. Benchley chose Jack Kriendler, one of the founder-owners of 21, to accompany him.

Together the two drank their way west up the odd-numbered side of 52d to Sixth Avenue, where elevated trains thundered by. Back down the even-numbered south side they went to the corner of Fifth Avenue, where an imposing, if unattractive, brownstone castle stood. The results of the survey might have been lost to posterity since both investigators seemed to lose track of things. Being a writer, however, Benchley scrawled in a small notebook the names of the speaks at which they paused. Several days later, when he had recovered from the night's research, his notebook revealed the not quite legible names of no fewer than thirty-eight Judas-hole establishments.

It was a situation that provoked an outraged dowager still occupying one of the brownstones to put a sign under her bell: "This is *not* an illicit resort!" The "not" was so frequently obliterated that the lady revised the copy: "This is a *private* residence. Do not ring!"

Through the first two decades of the twentieth century, 52d had been a quiet, expensive residential thoroughfare. Its five-story brownstones served as town houses for the city's well-to-do families and social elite. Such illustrious and aristocratic names as Rhinelander, Hofstadter, Baruch, Bishop Potter, and White (head of the U.S. Steam Company) were associated with it.

Even the Prohibition Amendment was slow to affect the area. But in 1925, six years after its passage, 52d had its first speakeasy—established, it is said, by one Jean Billia in a brownstone converted from a millionaire mansion into a multiple dwelling. How a socialite residential street thereafter became a spiderweb of speaks might be a subject for speculation.

To students of New York real estate, the answer is simple: rising land values, increased taxes and upped rents. As business invaded Midtown Manhattan a movement started toward Long Island and Connecticut—recall *The Great Gatsby*—and multiple dwellings superseded private residences. The new or old owners could command higher rentals from illicit speakeasy owners than ordinary apartment dwellers, or even from the kept women who occupied many a brownstone apartment in the twenties.

It is possible to find a more formal marker for the beginning of The Street than the establishment of the first speak. Put it down as December 10, 1926. On that day the New York City Board of Estimate passed a resolution lifting the residential restrictions on the brownstones between Fifth and Sixth avenues. In actuality, the resolution permitting business rentals was passed by the board seven days earlier. But Mayor Jimmy Walker requested a week's delay to permit consideration of a similar rezoning proposal for 55th St. Opposition to the latter was led by the Rockefellers who, it was reported, wanted to limit business rentals to the Radio City complex they were planning. The Rockefellers lost their fight. In the resolution on rezoning 52d, the board also rezoned 55th St.

Eventually, it was the real-estate interests and Rockefeller Center that transformed "the nocturnal heart of America," as *Variety* editor Abel Green characterized The Street in 1937, into a daytime conglomerate of banks and business skyscrapers. But as Green points out, The Street was itself "the illegitimate offspring of Rockefeller Center and Radio City." Rockefeller purchases of buildings between 48th and 51st streets for the Center forced clubs like Tony's, Jack & Charlie's and John Perona's to relocate in the 52d St. area. In fact, the growth of The Street in the thirties seemed to parallel the growth of Rockefeller Center. As the RKO Building, now the American Metal

Climax Building, Radio City Music Hall, RCA and British buildings opened in '32 and '33, so clubs began to proliferate on The Street.

Other things happened before 1926 to shatter the quiet and roil the high-society elegance of 52d St. On New Year's Eve, 1923, as a gay party broke up in the apartment of a Mr. Frank Carman, one of his guests discovered that half a million dollars' worth of her jewelry had disappeared. When the newspapers began digging into Mrs. Irene Schoellkopf's loss, it developed that Carman, a rather attractive young man, had no visible means of support. Apparently, his "work" consisted of escorting women generally older than himself to the theater, to parties, etc. Suddenly, old-time residents of the street were compelled to face up to the fact that some of the thick-walled brownstones housed gigolos, kept ladies, if not high-priced prostitutes, and even a high-echelon mobster. It was discovered that Eugene Moran, a bodyguard of gambler Arnold Rothstein, had lived with his mistress in the very brownstone where the Schoellkopf robbery occurred. Moran had been burned to death during a gang war with Jack "Legs" Diamond, and shortly afterward, his mistress's body had been found in the Harlem River, weighted with lead. The movement away from the street began to develop impetus.

Fifty-second Street west of Sixth Avenue also had its moments of tough notoriety. In 1912, at Eighth Avenue and 52d, there was a ballroom known as the Arbor Dance Hall. (It survives today as a rock discothèque.) On election night of that year, the Dave Hyson Association threw a "racket"—in the lingo of the time, a party or dance. Hyson was neither a celebrity nor a poltitcian. He was just a waiter in whose name the racket was thrown in order to evade excise taxes and sell liquor after hours.

Among those who attended was the wife of racketeer Owney Madden, from whom he was temporarily separated. Sometime during the evening Madden showed up with his usual retinue of hangers-on and bodyguards. To get a better view of his estranged wife's cavorting, he wandered by himself up to the balcony of the hall. What he got was six slugs. He had been followed to the Arbor Dance Hall by members of the Gophers, bitter enemies of the Hudson Dusters, as Madden's gang was called. Madden surprised everyone by recovering from the many bullet wounds, though they left him with injuries that required operations years later.

The gang war between the Gophers and Madden's Hudson Dusters, as well as other racket wars, was a minor skirmish compared with the bloody hijackings and wanton killings of hoodlums, bootleggers and rumrunners of the speakeasy era. When the Prohibition Amendment became the law of the land on January 17, 1920, it energized a postwar sense of lawlessness and immorality that made even average citizens glory in defiance of the law. Among its minor effects, the Eighteenth Amendment and the enforcing Volstead Act brought an end to what has been called the cabaret era in American entertainment—just as Repeal transformed the speakeasy era into the nightclub era.

Through the first decade of the twentieth century, New York Society (capital *S*) supped at home and made merry in its own private ballrooms. The 400 came to be a symbol of the Society because that was the number of celebrities and socialites that could be accommodated in arbiter Mrs. Astor's ballroom at 350 Fifth Avenue, later the site of the Waldorf-Astoria Hotel. But this private mode of dining and entertaining came to an end around 1910, when the brothers Bustanoby began serving gourmet food to the accompaniment of music for dancing.

Soon, making an entrance at Bustanoby's or at Martin's became as important as being invited to Mrs. Astor's ball had once been, or later being seen at a Broadway opening or the opening of the Metropolitan Opera season. Bustanoby's Café des Beaux Arts was at Sixth Avenue and 40th St.—John Perona, later the owner of El Morocco, worked there as an immigrant youngster—while the dancing rooms, where one could turkey-trot, bunny-hug, grizzly-bear or one-step, were entered at 39th St. Louis Martin's Café de l'Opéra was at Broadway and 42d, with a gilded, mirrored ballroom and cabaret above a spacious restaurant. Nearby, Churchill's, one of Broadway's gaudier lobster houses, was soon converted by owner Captain Jim into a cabaret. The performance of music at Shanley's lobster palace, whose entrance was just behind the 43d St. corner of the no-longer existent Paramount Theater, prompted Victor Herbert to initiate the lawsuit that resulted in the formation of ASCAP.

Reisenweber's three floors of dance halls were just below Columbus Circle on Eighth Avenue. Here, in 1916, New Yorkers first heard Nick La Rocca and the Original Dixieland Jazz Band in the two-beat style that later became a staple of Jimmy Ryan's and other 52d St. joints.

And then there was Rector's in a long, low yellow building beneath a luminous griffin, on the east side of Longacre Square. Perhaps because of the showy patronage of "Diamond Jim" Brady, the gaudy cabaret became a symbol of the unconventional life and morals of the Gay White Way, as Broadway began to be called. In the same year as *The Girl from Rector's* (1909), another play, *The Easiest Way,* ended with a flag-waver worth a million in publicity. Deserted by her Wall Street lover after she has given up her true love, Laura Murdock asks her black maid to doll her up, and as the curtains descends, she announces: "I'm going to Rector's to make a hit and to hell with the rest!"

From Rector's, theatergoers of the 1910's wandered east to Jack's at 43d and Sixth Avenue for a late-night or early-morning drink. Opposite the new Hippodrome Theater—where the great Houdini, manacled in a locked trunk, escaped from the trunk after it had been lowered into a huge swimming pool—John Dunstan's bar had enough pull (today they say "juice") with Tammany politicians to stay open into dawn. It was Dunstan who performed the symbolic act that announced the end of the cabaret era. The night that Prohibition went into effect in 1920, he allowed his patrons to snack and guzzle into the wee, wee hours. Then, as dawn was breaking over the quiet streets of Manhattan, he locked the door and tossed the key into the gutter. Without liquor to sell, he could not pay the enormous rent. Neither could Rector's, which was supplanted by the Café de Paree.

"The Speakeasy Era," columnist Louis Sobol wrote later, "was a sizzler for excitement, danger, larceny, romance, intrigue—and murder. . . . Along drab side streets of New York, dark and guarded doors opened into a spreading world of soft lights, seductive scents, silken music, adroit entertainment, smoke and laughter—of perfection of food and services, of wines and liquors of first qualities—and, of course, the big thrill was that we were all doing something unlawful."

In the unlawful atmosphere, murder could take a senseless shape, as it did one night at Porky Murray's, a 52d St. speak near the Guild and Alvin theaters. When the bartender asked several argumentative boozers to quiet down, guns blazed and three corpses were found on the floor—the bartender and a man and a woman. The couple had criminal records. But no motive for the mayhem was uncovered, except high spirits and hot tempers. Porky Murray paid for the burial of his bartender.

Of all the "unlawful" establishments on 52d, none could vie in elegance or snob appeal with Jack and Charlie's 21, which opened its doors on January 27, 1930—almost four years before Repeal. And no one joined the national game of beat the booze hunters with more zest than its owners, or displayed greater ingenuity in the apparatus they devised to outwit Andrew Volstead's underpaid and potentially larcenous agents.

Tape 1 . . . JOHN HAMMOND

Long before 52d St. became known to New York taxi drivers as The Street, twin mansions on the west side of Fifth Avenue between 51st and 52d gave it an imposing approach, if not an air of expectant promise.

Built of brownstone, like the facing rows of five-story buildings that lined the street, the mansions were erected in 1881 by William Henry Vanderbilt of the steamship-railroad dynasty founded by Commodore Cornelius Vanderbilt. Among some of The 400, to whose sacrosanct circle the upstart Commodore and his family were not admitted, the brownstone palaces were sneeringly characterized as Hodgepodge House. But other members were not unimpressed by the sixty foreign sculptors, seven hundred American laborers and the $3,000,000 used to erect the mansions.

During the cabaret era the mansion on the southwest corner of 52d and Fifth Avenue was occupied by a granddaughter of the doughty Commodore, the wife of William D. Sloane, treasurer of the home-furnishings firm W. & J. Sloane. Mrs. William Douglas Sloane, later Mrs. Henry White, was the grandmother of the man who has been called "the most important of all jazz writers" and "the most effective catalyst in the development of jazz."

The coincidence of John Hammond's early familial contact with The Street (while it was still the locus of wealth and social prominence) and his later musical association with it (through artists whom he sponsored) makes him an inevitable starting point of the 52d St. story.

"My first memory of The Street," he told me, "was of Grandma's house, the twin Vanderbilt mansion on the corner, where DePinna's department store was later situated. The numbers were 2-4-6 West Fifty-second. Back in 1915, when Grandfather William D. Sloane was still alive—he died that year—I remember being taken there on Sunday afternoons. The grand old mansion had a drive-in, built originally for carriages. A marble-floored entry led up a marble circular staircase to the receiving parlor.

"What fascinated me as a four-year-old boy was an Aeolian organ. Three years later I discovered it was a player organ. You could not only listen to recitals by Archer Gibson, organist at Saint Bartholomew's, who was brought over from the Park Avenue church for private Sunday night concerts. You could also put in a perforated roll, as in a player piano, and have a marvelous time pumping the pedals. Not really! The player mechanism was activated electrically. But there were all kinds of stops that you could manipulate manually and that altered the volume and sound. It was quite exciting for a small boy to insert a roll and then hear this monster thunder forth wonderful music.

"As I grew older, it became a ritual to go to Grandma's for Sunday night dinner and concerts. Togged out in a well-pressed blue suit, I would be driven down Fifth Avenue—we lived further uptown—in a Brewster or Pierce-Arrow. My grandmother preferred a Rolls-Royce. But we never had one. My father, a lawyer who died in '49, and my mother, a fine, amateur pianist, who just recently died at ninety-five, considered the Rolls ostentatious.

"I was interested in jazz by the time I began attending Hotchkiss prep school in 1925. It was a taste I developed through listening to phonograph records. I had quite a collection even then. While at Hotchkiss, I was permitted to come down to Manhattan from Lakeville, Connecticut, every other weekend for a viola lesson. My teacher was on Tieman Place, just south of 125th Street on Riverside Drive. I would take the Harlem division train to 125th Street and ride the crosstown trolley to the West Side.

"I shall never forget the shock of excitement I experienced in 1927. As the trolley ground its way past Seventh Avenue, I saw on the marquee of the Alhambra Theater: THIS WEEK IN PERSON, BESSIE SMITH. I had all of Bessie's records, a collection I assembled by prowling around Harlem shops. You couldn't get Bessie Smith downtown, even though she was known as Empress of the Blues. Records by black people (Race Records) were simply not sold in 'respectable' stores like Landay's or the Plaza Music Company.

"I couldn't wait to hear Bessie in person. She later became an indelible part of my experiences on 52d St. In '27 she was at the peak of her power and talent—and I don't think that I have ever heard

Left to right, John Hammond, Count Basie and Billy Eckstine at the Yacht Club on 52d St. during a Celebrity Night in the early forties.

blues singing that moved me more than those forty minutes at the Alhambra Theater in Harlem.

"When I was at Yale, from '29 to '31, I used to come down from New Haven almost every weekend, not only for my viola lesson, but to play in an amateur string quartet. Afterward, I would wander around Harlem, visiting the night spots. I got to know them all—The Stable, Hole in the Wall, Saratoga Club, Savoy Ballroom, and many others, all gone—that made Harlem the jumpingest part of town. Also the only place where you could really hear live jazz.

"The first downtown jazz joint I found was the Stork Club. That was when it was in a brownstone, across the street from what is now the Barbizon-Plaza Hotel on 58th and Sixth Avenue. Prohibition was then in force, and the Stork was a speakeasy, where Sherman Billingsley served fancy food and Eddie Condon played two-beat Dixieland. I was a very puritanical young man. I didn't drink, I didn't smoke, and I was a devoted reader of the liberal *New Republic*. I went to the Stork because it had a piano player who was a god of mine. I didn't go to hear the Blue Blowers, as Condon called his combo. I went to listen to Joe Sullivan.

"The cellist of our amateur string quartet was Artie Bernstein, who later became Benny Goodman's bass player. I hung out with Artie, among other musicians. Since there was practically no jazz to be heard downtown, Artie and I used to spend our time in Harlem after we finished playing quartets. We spent much of our time at Smalls' Paradise.

"Before I knew Artie, I used to go to Ed Smalls' place to hear Charlie Johnson's wonderful band. He opened there while I was still a student at Hotchkiss, and he was there even after I began writing a jazz column for *The Gramophone*. Artie and I were particularly fond of Elmer Snowden's Band at Smalls'. He figured later on 52d St. at the Club Samoa. I got to know Snowden even before he came to Smalls'. I heard him first at a little Harlem joint, The Bamboo. The men he had with him at Smalls' were an exciting group—Chu Berry, Big Sid Catlett on drums, Dickie Wells on the trombone, Red Allen on trumpet and Howard Johnson, who later was Duke Ellington's first alto sax.

"In 1931 I started writing about jazz. No American publication was then interested in the subject. Startling but true. I had a sister who was living in England, and she made contact for me with *The Gramophone*, a very staid periodical that covered the worldwide record scene better than any publication before or since. They had me cover the New York jazz scene, particularly Harlem. A year or so after I began writing for *The Gramophone*, I switched to *The Melody Maker*. They paid me five guineas a month (about twenty-six dollars) to cover the jazz scene with emphasis on black musicians.

"Out of these contacts and activities came a very wonderful association with the English Graphophone Company, now part of EMI. Because I wrote about American jazzmen, Edgar Jackson, who produced records for English Columbia, introduced me to its head. When Sir Louis Sterling asked if I'd be willing to record some American jazzmen for the English market, I jumped at the opportunity. I gave him a list that included, as I recall, Fletcher Henderson's band, Joe Sullivan, Coleman Hawkins, Benny Carter, fiddler Joe Venuti and others. One person I was really anxious to record was a young clarinet player from Chicago—he happened to be white—who had made many records as a sideman but never with a band of his own.

'I didn't then really know Benny Goodman—that was his name—

and I was making commitments over my head. Nevertheless, I signed a contract with English Columbia in September, 1933, to produce something like one hundred sides for English Parlophone, as well as English Columbia. The series was to be called Rhythm Style Series.

"Among other provisions, the contract called for the delivery of eight sides by an All-Star Band to be formed by Benny Goodman. On my return to the United States late in September of '33, I sought out Goodman. I knew from my musician friends that he hung out at a speakeasy called the Onyx on 52d St. I went up there a little petrified because I knew Goodman only slightly from casual meetings at the Woodmansten Inn, where he had led Russ Columbo's band. After I introduced myself, I told him I had a contract for him to record at Columbia. He bluntly told me, 'You're a liar.' When I protested, he informed me that he had just talked with Ben Selvin, who was then head of American Columbia's recording department. 'Selvin told me that they were broke,' Goodman said, 'and that they had no budget for recording us.'

"Well, American Columbia was then in bankruptcy. As part of the Grigsby-Grunow Company that made Majestic radios, they had gone broke in 1931 and were operating on a budget that had no provisions for anything except surefire pop hits. I explained that I was representing English, not American, Columbia; that they had *not* been hit as hard by the Depression; and that there was still a market for jazz among British record buyers. I explained that we would record in the American studios and that the discs would be released here if American Columbia paid a royalty to the English company. I talked and talked. I think that my enthusiasm, plus the possibility of an American release, may have persuaded him.

"By this time I had become a good friend of Joe Helbock, the bartender who owned the Onyx. The place had a piano. But it did not have any regular entertainment. Not during the speakeasy days anyway. Musicians would simply drop in and jam for their own amusement. They came from studio jobs at the nearby broadcasting studios —CBS and NBC. Billingsley's Club was now at 51st between Park and Madison, not in a brownstone but in a lovely building. Eddie Condon would drop in after he finished working at The Stork, as would a Harlem group known as The Spirits of Rhythm.

"It's always been ironic to me that Sherman Billingsley, one of the most prejudiced people that ever operated in the American entertainment scene, really had his first big music hit with a black group, The Spirits of Rhythm.

"Though Prohibition had been repealed during 1933, places could serve only 3.2 beer. It wasn't until sometime in 1934 that clubs were once again able to serve hard liquor legally. Until then, 52d St. didn't really exist, musically speaking. Liquor income made it possible for them to begin booking name attractions. By late '34 and early '35 the clubs were vying with each other for acts that would bring in the crowds. Soon The Street was a lively, and what a lovely, scene of all kinds of music—all of it music with a beat.

"My most intimate association with 52d came in 1938 at the Famous Door. I had brought the Count Basie band to New York two years earlier and had been responsible for converting a nine-piece, territorial Kansas City band into a thirteen-piece commercial band. In 1937 Basie had had a big record on Decca with his 'One O'Clock Jump.' But outside Harlem, there were still few places where a Negro band could play in New York. Though we were a big Northern metropolis, we had a complete color bar. And when a Negro band played in a downtown club, Negro patrons could not get in.

"The Basie band was then managed, as it still is today, by Willard Alexander, Benny Goodman's manager and then a vice-president of Music Corporation of American (MCA). Alexander was terribly anxious to get exposure for Basie in midtown Manhattan. But in addition to the color line, there was the problem of the Mob. Even in the days of Fiorello La Guardia, who really fought the Mob during his mayoralty, the clubs were not free of their influence and control.

"Willard Alexander was quite friendly with the two guys who owned the Famous Door, Al Felshin and Jerry Brooks. Felshin's brother was business manager of the *Daily Worker* and Al had a sort of social conscience. It was a tiny place that couldn't seat more than ninety. Most important, it was summer and there was little business.

"Felshin and Brooks had little to lose in booking Basie. And Willard felt it would be good exposure if he could get a CBS wire to pick up 'remotes' several times a week. The hangup was air conditioning. You couldn't get people into a club during New York's hot, humid nights, and Felshin and Brooks didn't have the cash to air-condition the joint. Well, I agreed to put up the money. It was to be a loan. And one of the conditions was that I was to be permitted to

The Count watches the Basie band blues singer Jimmy Rushing at his favorite pastime. The Famous Door opened doors for both.

Down Beat

bring Negro friends into the club to hear Basie. Until then, you never saw a black face at the tables or even at the bar of the Door.

"Of course, Basie was a sensation—a total and absolute sensation. I don't think that New York had ever heard a jazz band quite like this ever before—and, perhaps, since. He had sidemen like Lester Young, Dickie Wells, and Jo Jones on drums, Walter Page's marvelous rhythm section with Freddie Green on guitar, and those wonderful saxophones of Earl Warren on first alto and Herschel Evans and those great horns of Buck Clayton and Harry 'Sweets' Edison. There were stars all over that band. And little Jimmy Rushing sang the blues and Helen Humes the ballads. The music was just miraculous. Drinks were cheap. Food wasn't bad and you could get a dinner for two-fifty. Of course, nobody made much money. It was with Basie in 1938 that 52d St. got its reputation as the jumping-off place for jazz in New York.

"But 52d St. had already become the downtown home of great Negro jazz. I recorded Billie Holiday and Teddy Wilson for Brunswick, and we got both of them on The Street, at the Onyx, around '35–'36. The Three Deuces had Art Tatum, as well as The Spirits of Rhythm and John Kirby and Maxine Sullivan.

"And all this time, there was the Club Samoa next door to the Door. It was a burlesque strip joint. But what bothered me was that it was nonunion. I was a militant unionist and a member of the Newspaper Guild. And there were always pickets in front of the door. It used to kill me because one of my favorite musicians had the trio at the joint. Elmer Snowden was the same banjo-guitarist who had played uptown at Smalls' Paradise in the early thirties. He had gotten into some kind of scrape with the Musicians Union and he worked as a scab. It was painful. The other thing that sticks in my memory about the Samoa was a name prominently displayed on the club's electric sign. Perhaps it was done to aggravate the union for the owner's name was Henry Fink. He was the author-composer of that old tearjerker 'The Curse of an Aching Heart.' Naturally, the union was quite determined not to give in to Fink's finks. And so was I, despite Elmer Snowden.

"When The Street went downhill, it slid in the direction of the Samoa. Strippers instead of jazzmen. G-strings instead of guitar strings. But at its peak, there was one club after another where you could hear fine black music played with an irresistible beat every night of the week.

"As I think back, I believe that it was Bessie Smith, along with Basie and Billie Holiday, who endowed The Street with such rich memories for me. Back in 1936, my good friend Milt Gabler of the Commodore Record Shop started something called the United Hot Clubs of America. It was loosely modeled on the Hot Club of France and dedicated to perpetuating great jazz performances on wax. Occasionally, it presented jazz in live performance.

"In '36 I persuaded Milt to sponsor a Bessie Smith concert. Curiously, it also took place at the Famous Door. Bessie had once played at Connie's Inn when it moved downtown to where the Latin Quarter was later situated, on 48th St. between Seventh Avenue and Broadway. It was for only two nights, and she flopped. In 1928 she had been in a Broadway revue at the Belmont Theater, and that lasted only three nights. But that Sunday afternoon at the Famous Door! I don't think that anyone who was there will ever completely forget the rich sounds and emotions that poured out of this woman's—I was about to say 'throat'—but Bessie's blues came out of her entire body and soul.

"That was what I meant when I later wrote: 'To my way of thinking, Bessie Smith is the greatest artist American jazz ever produced. In fact, I'm not sure that her art did not reach beyond the limits of the term 'jazz.' She was one of those rare beings, a completely integrated artist capable of projecting her whole personality into music. She was blessed not only with great emotion but with a tremendous voice that could penetrate the inner recesses of the listener.'

"In the year after her appearance at the Door, Bessie was in that fatal automobile accident that took her life. It happened just as I was about to leave for Mississippi to bring her back to New York for some new recording sessions. That Sunday afternoon in February, 1936, was the only time she appeared on The Street. But it was an unforgettable experience for those who heard her—and many who were not present talk about it as if they were. It was one of The Street's great moments."

2. Jack & Charlie's 21

It was a long day at the 21 Club, then known as Jack & Charlie's 21, in 1932 when the doorman sensed that the two portly gents seeking admittance were federal revenue agents.

Bootleg liquor was then selling at an all-time high as stockbrokers and their clients vended Jonathan apples on street corners—when they were not leaping from upper-story windows. Through the country, banks were going down like ninepins in a busy bowling alley. But in George White's *Scandals,* they were singing "Life Is Just a Bowl of Cherries"; Bert Lown and his Biltmore Orchestra were nightly playing "Bye, Bye, Blues"; and Bing Crosby was urging folks to "Wrap Your Troubles in Dreams and Dream Your Troubles Away."

Tall buildings were shooting up around Manhattan as small stores were closing down—the new Waldorf-Astoria Hotel on Park Avenue and the Empire State on Fifth, where the Waldorf had originally stood—and the Rockefellers watched the rise of their first skyscraper in Radio City, the RKO Building on Sixth Avenue. The *Scandals* also featured a blasé ballad, "The Thrill Is Gone," as two white sluts falsely accused nine black boys of rape on a freight train near Scottsboro, Alabama. Americans were avidly reading William Faulkner's sensational potboiler *Sanctuary,* which also concerned a faked rape.

Listeners from coast to coast were charmed by a fat girl singer who greeted them, "When the moon comes over the mountain," while others chose the "Groaner" *cum* toupee who arrived weekly "when the blue of the night meets the gold of the day, buh-buh-buh-boo." Radio City Music Hall opened with a seating capacity of 6,200 while neighborhood movie houses resorted to double features in a vain effort to bolster sagging attendance figures.

The doorman at Jack & Charlie's did not squirm when he sensed who his prospective diners were. With the reserve that was an early earmark of the luxurious 52d St. speakeasy—it was one of 32,000 that sprang phoenixlike from the ashes of the 15,000 saloons shuttered by the Prohibition Amendment—he proceeded to check their reservations over the intercom. At the same time, he pressed a secret vestibule button that sounded an alarm at the bar upstairs. There were four such buttons in the vestibule so that the doorman could not miss giving an alarm, no matter where he stood.

While he delayed the entry of the two agents, waiters hurriedly gathered all the visible glasses and bottles and placed them on the bar. At the touch of a concealed button, the bar top slid into a recess in a wall. Glassware and illegal liquids were tipped into a chute that sent them hurtling, not into the city's sewer or into a shattering cellar grate (as has been erroneously reported), but into a specially constructed sandpit that absorbed the telltale liquid evidence. The bar button simultaneously cut off the current operating trick doors in the cellar, where bootleg liquor was stored.

Once inside the tavern-styled club, the federal agents proceeded at a leisurely pace, searching all through the night and into the following day. Eventually, they descended into the cellar. Here, their thoroughness peaked. After nineteen hours they departed wearily, unconvinced but unrewarded.

As they suspected, there was a huge cache of prewar booze. It was stored behind a massive, masonry door that seemed part of the cellar walls. The agents had tapped walls throughout the club and particularly in the cellar. They had, perhaps, noticed—but had no reason to suspect—a small hole near the floor of the east cellar wall. Through this hole, a slender iron rod could be inserted to flip a switch—when the current was not shut off at the bar upstairs—that caused the masonry door to swing back. More than 5,000 cases of liquor were

21, in 1933, when Jack and Charlie refurbished No. 17 for 21 Brands, Inc. Jack Kriendler looks out the window of No. 19.

concealed in the cellars of 17 and 19 West 52d (not 21), both shuttered buildings owned by Messrs. Kriendler and Berns.

The raid could have been unwittingly triggered by George Jean Nathan, then the country's most influential theater critic and an editor of the iconoclastic *American Mercury*. Returning from Europe in '32, a Presidential election year, and queried about his political preferences, Nathan told shipboard reporters: "Jack and Charlie of my favorite speakeasy would make the best President and Vice President. The speakeasy makes money and the customers and owners are happy. In what other business is that true?"

The friendship of Jack and Charlie dated back to the years when both their families, Austrian Jews, lived on Manhattan's Lower East Side. They were cousins. Mama Kriendler, who served as midwife to augment Papa Kriendler's pay as a welder, delivered a brother of Charlie—Jerry Berns, now H. Jerome Berns, sixty-two-year-old vice-president and secretary of the corporation. There were four girls and four boys in the Kriendler ménage.

"We lived in a five-room walk-up," recalls H. Peter Kriendler, sixty-three-year-old managing director, "on the fifth floor of a tenement. To get warm, we had to stand around the stove. To keep cool, we had to sleep on the roof or fire escape. We spoke Yiddish almost as much as English, and we were a tough lot then." *Fortune* magazine recently characterized them as "highly polished, civilized and urbane."

With Papa a victim of the wartime flu epidemic of 1917, they listened to Mama, who kept reminding them when they came home from a street fight minus a tooth, fingernail or clump of hair: "They can't take away what you've got in your head." I. Robert Kriendler, youngest of the four boys and now president of the corporation, is a graduate of Rutgers and a member of its Board of Trustees. H. Peter, who inherited brother Jack's love of the West but also enjoys opera in the East, is a member of the New York Bar, having graduated from CCNY and Brooklyn Law School. Maxwell, an officer of the related but separate 21 Brands and a frustrated opera singer, holds a degree in law from St. John's. Jack, the oldest and born John Karl Kriendler, went to Fordham University but opened a speakeasy instead of getting his degree.

To support himself at Fordham, Jack worked in his uncle's saloon. Summers, he and cousin Charlie Berns labored on the Borscht Circuit in the Catskills. In 1922 they opened The Red Head, a tiny basement speakeasy in Greenwich Village, then developing as a bohemia of arts and letters. Much of the real estate in the area was owned by the Strunsky brothers, who also operated some night spots. After Lenore Strunsky married Ira Gershwin, brother George Gershwin could occasionally be found playing the piano in a small joint, Three Steps Down, not far from The Red Head, on West Eighth Street.

The cashier of Jack and Charlie's first joint venture was Mark Hellinger, the tabloid columnist, later a film producer, after whom the Broadway theater is named. Another associate was cousin Bill Hardy, later operator of Manhattan's Gay Nineties Club. Fire or purchase of the land by the city for the independent subway line forced them to move from Fourth to Eighth Street. They called their new Village speak Club Fronton. A larger place than their first den, it drew a wider clientele than the coterie of Village artists, writers and reporters who nightly squeezed into The Red Head.

Perhaps because of this clientele, Kriendler had an inspiration. By the time he and Berns opened the Puncheon Grotto on West 49th, his master design was to develop a twentieth-century coffeehouse that would provide a feeling of Old World grandeur for the notables of the

New World. Before long, Jack Kriendler was known around town as The Baron, a man whose interest in sartorial elegance (cutaways, tails, sable-lined overcoats, etc.) is reflected in the three changes of clothes that all 21 execs practice today. Before long, the Grotto was catering to celebrities like artist Peter Arno, millionaire Jock Whitney, tastemaker Lucius Beebe. "In snob appeal, distinction of clientele and the preparation of Steak Diane," Beebe said years later, "21 is tops" and the service is "the most perfect of any restaurant in the world."

In 1929, when Jack and Charlie were forced out of their 49th St. location by the Rockefeller expansion of Radio City, they were determined to buy their own building. The brownstone at 21 West 52d attracted them because it maintained their midtown locale, boasted a wrought-iron grille gate similar to the one at the Grotto, and because of the good omen that 21 was just half of 42, the Grotto's address on 49th.

To insure their being the classiest of the classy, Jack & Charlie's 21, as it was called when the impressive gates swung open in January, 1930, employed the simplest of formulae—high prices. Today's figures provide an index. In 1971 minimum cost of a drink is $1.65 sans tip. Hamburger lunch for two: $14 sans tip. A more ambitious lunch: $25 to $50. Dinner for two: $30 to $75. In addition to the waiter, there is a headwaiter and a captain who expect a minimum of $1 each, which could climb for the latter to $10 for a complex service. One dollar per bottle of wine is an average tip for the sommelier. In the private suites on the upper floors, lunch begins at $17 a person, not including cocktails, wine or tips. With a present-day capacity of 466 diners—136 on the street floor, 200 on the second and 130 in the private rooms above—21's annual gross is about $4,500,000, or an average of $15,000 a day.

Despite its affluence, no credit cards are honored, and the management seldom, if ever, picks up checks. Sole exception is the noted artist Marc Chagall who receives no bill because he gives his food order to Pete Kriendler in the form of a sketch. Even press people do not eat on the cuff. "Oddly enough," columnist Louis Sobol observed, "during the Great Drought, there was one club that barred columnar gentlemen. That was 21. And it wasn't until after Prohibition had died that I found my way into the place. The theory was that if anything happened—if some gentleman out of town were out with some other gentleman's wife—it would be the duty of a conscientious columnist to make due report thereof."

Charge accounts are available to longtime patrons, who also enjoy the privilege of being able to cash checks. (Incidentally, this special service was the family's explanation of $180,000 in cash found in Jack Kriendler's apartment and safety deposit box after he died suddenly of a heart attack in 1947.) Several years ago the Secretary of Treasury under President Eisenhower signed the check after completing dinner. The waiter returned with a polite request for cash. Only after George Humphrey established that he was the Mr. Humphrey whose signature appeared on new U. S. currency was the charge honored. The story is told of another guest who, when his effort to sign was rebuffed, handed a noncommittal waiter a $10,000 bill. The management had the change wheeled up on a silver trolley.

Because of its insistence on cash, 21 has had limited experience with deadbeats. But at least one has publicly proclaimed his indebtedness. "I would like to be buried in 21's cellar," artist-author Ludwig Bemelmans wrote columnist Leonard Lyons, "with Kriendlers standing by in dark suits, each holding a burning candle in one hand and in the other, my large unpaid bills."

The additive to high prices, not surprisingly, is food and liquor of unimpeachable quality. The one conviction Jack and Charlie suffered as violators of the Volstead Act—this occurred before they set up shop on 52d St.—helped establish the superiority of their cuisine. "The prosecution analyzed the liquor," Charlie Berns, late head of 21 Brands, recalls, "and they admitted in court that it was first-class. Editorials in all the big papers asked why we had been convicted when joints selling rotgut were left alone. We paid the fine and the legal fees out of the increased business." And that business came increasingly from the rich and the renowned.

One of the biggest boosters of 21 was Mayor James J. Walker, whose mere presence brought a flow of lawyers, politicians, judges and businessmen. Walker liked the Grotto on 49th and moved with it to 52d. His reign as mayor ended in the third year of Jack & Charlie's presence on The Street—in the very year, in fact, of the famous raid.

Jack and Charlie, both of whom had infallible memories for names, faces and personal preferences in food and tables, went out of their way to dance attendance on the influential and the powerful. Masters of the craft of friendship, they provided personal services that ran to extremes where important customers were involved. The moment their first shipment of oysters arrived each season, they were on the phone to Governor Nelson Rockefeller, who is partial to the mollusks. Not too long ago, when the late General David Sarnoff of Radio Corporation of America was recuperating from a series of mastoid operations, 21 delivered specially prepared dishes to his hospital bedside twice a day.

For other esteemed patrons, 21 secured hard- or impossible-to-get hotel suites, confirmed airline reservations and tickets for Broadway hits. During the bank holiday in 1933, it lent harried customers more than $25,000. Later, when apartments were hard to find in Manhattan, it found them. In emergencies, it has been able to get hospital beds for desperate clients. And once it went so far as to arrange for the funeral of a customer at Saint Patrick's Cathedral.

To insure privacy for its customers, 21 relied on the unflagging loyalty of a large staff. It may be a showcase in which the rich, powerful and famous are on display—"a Tiffany's window on society," in *Fortune* magazine's apt phrase. But the management and a long-lived staff—more than 20 percent of the present personnel of 287 are members of the restaurant's 21-Year Club—display a rare sensitivity and discretion in handling delicate situations. Bob Kriendler describes this aspect of 21 policy as "our protective feeling" and notes that everyone connected with the club is keenly aware that "we do not talk about our patrons. We never divulge who dined with whom." But top management makes a point of knowing who likes whom and who would prefer to avoid whom.

While the management makes no secret of its concern about name people, it has always placed a high valuation on decorum. Prexy Kriendler thinks of the late Humphrey Bogart in this connection. "Bogie ate here frequently," Bob recalls. "He was an absolute gentleman. But he'd leave here and minutes later create a ruckus at El Morocco or The Stork. Was it that he respected us or sensed the dignity and discipline of our atmosphere? We never once had a problem with him." But they did have a problem not too long ago with Hollywood agent Irving P. Lazar, who broke a glass on the bald pate of producer Otto Preminger.

As an aspect of decorum, dress has proved a stumbling block even to luminaries. Darryl Zanuck was refused admission when he showed up in a turtleneck. More recently, writer Rex Reed was barred for lack of a tie. "But this is Bill Blass," he argued. The receptionist was unimpressed that Blass is the chic fashion designer.

In his restaurant guide, Craig Claiborne, dining-out connoisseur of the New York *Times,* has said of the management of 21: "They soothe and smooth the pelts of their best customers more than any restaurant in New York. They're wonderful hosts, quietly spoken, beautifully manicured and groomed. But an unwary customer can be thoroughly uncomfortable." He adds: "They're just not very democratic."

When Jack and Charlie moved into 52d St. in 1930, having redecorated their brownstone to give it the woody look of an English tavern, their next-door neighbor at No. 23 was the Madison Lewis family. "They were friendly and discreet," Bob Kriendler notes. "When slightly confused customers of our establishment rang their bell by mistake, the butler courteously apprised them of their error. Neither he nor any member of the family ever said anything that would endanger the security of Jack and Charlie's."

Within a year after they became part of 52d St.'s speakeasy milieu, the two entrepreneurs were doing so well that they purchased No. 19. By 1932, the year that Jimmy Walker resigned as mayor, they also owned No. 17. Both buildings were kept dormant, except for their cellars. After Repeal in 1933, when Jack and Charlie secured the franchise to import Ballantine Scotch, No. 17 was refurbished to house 21 Brands, Inc. Two years later, No. 19 was joined to No. 21, and the small, straight bar on the street floor's west wall was moved to the east wall, where it assumed the semielliptical shape it still holds.

It was not until ten years later that the club finally assumed the form and size of today. By then (1945) the older members of the Madison Lewis family had passed away and the younger members were following the trend of Manhattan socialites to the ex-urbs of Westchester, Connecticut, and Long Island. 21 Brands purchased and moved into the stately residence at No. 23, whose Old-World façade remains as it was at the turn of the century. At this point No. 17 was added to No. 19 and No. 21, giving the club the space of three brownstones and permitting the enlargement of the crescent-shaped bar to a 60-foot arc.

Some of the club's steady clientele prefer the quieter and more intimate atmosphere of the upstairs dining rooms, Jackie and Aristotle Onassis among them. The competition for "territorial rights" is most intense in the bar area. Here, celebrities come to be seen, and aspiring celebs to rub shoulders and be noticed. As you enter the bar at lunch, Mrs. Stephen Smith, Nick Biddle and Millie and Bob Considine might be sitting at the three tables facing the entry. At dinner these same tables are frequently occupied by ex-columnist Louis Sobol and Punch Sulzberger of the New York *Times* clan and were once occupied by the late John O'Hara. After dinner, one might encounter Anita Louise, Sherman Fairchild or Joan Crawford, a longtime habitué.

To your near right, an unobtrusive wall table is the favorite dinner spot of the families of both Benson and Henry Ford II. On your left, dinner guests might number Alfred Hitchcock, opera star Licia Albanese, John Jacob Astor, Winthrop Rockefeller, or socialite-sportsman Dan Topping. Luncheon diners in the bar area frequently include RCA prexy Bob Sarnoff, actress Helen Hayes, millionaire toymakers Louis and David Marx, actor Hugh O'Brian (when he's in town), noted architect Charles Luckman of Beverly Hills, and Ralph E. Ablon, chairman of the Ogden Corporation that almost bought 21.

Though the bar area at the most easterly wall is not too many feet removed, it is viewed by insiders with the same distaste as the center-field bleachers in Yankee Stadium. "Siberia" is the inside term. But comic Alan King always picks it because he wants everybody "who sees me sitting here to know I'm real secure." Sometimes a diner is assigned to Table 34. In 21 code, it's the bum's rush.

In the bar area there are two inconspicuous memorials to late patrons. A gold *H,* imbedded in the paneling near the east end of the bar, was placed there by drinking friends of Harold Klem, a vice-president of U.S. Trucking Corporation, whose capacity was legendary. Over table three, a small bronze plaque placed by the management reads: "Robert Benchley, His Corner, 1889–1945."

As oft repeated as the tale of Benchley's effort to tally the speakeasies on the street is the story of the night that he left the club, only to come charging back claiming that there were elephants outside. It was almost 2:00 A.M., and he had, of course, put away a few jiggers of liquid refreshment. "All these elephants," he cried, "clumping along. And would you believe it, they didn't make a sound!" When friends stepped outside to reassure him, there were no elephants. But the following day's tabloids carried photos showing a herd of elephants outside 21. Associated with Ringling Brothers Circus, they were being moved across town to Madison Square Garden. And they did not make a sound! To avoid disturbing sleeping Manhattanites, their feet had been wrapped in gunny cloth.

Apart from clientele, cuisine and service, 21 has always been a matter of trappings. Outwardly, it still has the appearance of a turn-of-the-century New Orleans mansion. The tall wrought-iron grille fence preventing access to the fused brownstones has its complement in decorative iron grillwork that serves as housing for a second-floor balcony. Daily locked and unlocked by the club's chief steward, the double gate in the fence is flanked by cast-iron jockeys attired in the colors of well-known racing stables.

Jack Kriendler began collecting these colorful hitching posts when they were still in the shape of little black boys. 21 patrons contributed so many that they line the steps of the exterior brownstone stoop leading up to the balcony and stand shoulder to shoulder along the balcony itself. Today they no longer possess black countenances. To please stable owners, who compete for the honor of occupying the flanking positions at the entry to the club, the jockeys are still rotated. Though it is not generally known, 21 is in the business of selling these jockey hitching posts.

Inside, other special accoutrements add to the rich decor and give 21 the feeling of a private club rather than a public restaurant. Once hung with pewter mugs, antique pistols and symbols of Old World dining, the bar area is today decorated with models of planes, ships, railroad cars and other means of transportation. The switch occurred several years ago when the airlines presented models of their aircraft to celebrity wateringholes. The second-floor dining room is graced by English Sheffield sterling silver, recently valued at $250,000. All through the club, one encounters paintings, drawings and bronzes with a distinct Western flavor. The collection was started by the late Jack Kriendler, an East Side boy who loved the American West and who became enamored of the artistry of Frederic Remington, one of the great interpreters of the life of the American cowboy.

After 21 moved to 52d, Jack became known as Two-Trigger Jack when he was not being called The Baron. In addition to the Remingtons, his purchases included a $10,000 silver saddle, as well as a dude ranch out West. Whenever he could, The Baron spent time in the

Tucson-Phoenix (also Palm Springs) area, riding the old cowboy trails, attired in costly Western garb. Opera-lover Pete Kriendler took up where his brother left off. A trustee of the Whitney Gallery of Western Art and of the Buffalo Bill Association, both of Cody, Wyoming, Pete has helped expand the Remington art collection started by his brother. The taste that created 21 has yielded a collection valued by the Ogden Corporation, when it was negotiating to buy the club, at no less than $750,000.

In 1968 the Kriendlers-Bernses became interested in selling 21 because they feared that the death of a member of the two families might create insuperable estate problems. But they were also greatly concerned that the character of the club and their control remain unchanged. By accident they discovered that two of their regular patrons had negotiated a deal with similar objectives on their own premises. Charles Luckman had sold his million-dollar Beverly Hills architectural firm to Ogden Corporation through its president, Ralph Ablon. And so conversations began between Kriendlers-Bernses and Ablon at dinners for which the Ogden president paid handsomely. Eventually, after nine months of negotiation, there appeared to be a deal, and details were announced in the press in April, 1969. For their stock, Bob Kriendler, Pete Kriendler, cousin Jerry Berns—each of whom owned 30 percent—and nephew Sheldon Tannen, owner of 10 percent, were to receive a total of $10,000,000 in Ogden stock.

The sale was to include not only the trappings of silver and art but two subsidiaries: Iron Gate Products, importers of delicacies like reindeer meat from Lapland, hazel hens from Manchuria, etc.; and 21 Club Selected Items, Ltd., importers of cigars and smoking accessories. It was not to include 21 Brands, a separate corporation, headed since 1936 by Charles A. Berns, the Charlie of Jack & Charlie's. Grossing more than $5,000,000 annually, 21 Brands is a public corporation listed on the American Stock Exchange, with 53 percent control in the hands of the Kriendlers-Bernses. Nor was the sale to include Bob Kriendler's invaluable collection of autographed first editions, now almost thirty-five years in the gathering.

In October, 1937, Bob Kriendler was an apprentice to the basement stewards at 21. "One day word came from above," he recalls, "that Mr. Jack wanted to see young Bob, meaning me, immediately. Donning a tie and jacket, I raced upstairs.

" 'Get over to Doctors Hospital,' Mr. Jack said. 'Go to Mr. Gene Fowler's room and deliver a bottle of our best scotch from our private stock.' Mr. Jack added: 'His doctors don't want him to drink, so the nurses won't be of any help. Otherwise, Fowler would not have called me. But you get it to him.'

"Off I went carrying a fifth of our most expensive scotch in a brief-case. The nurses were suspicious. But at an opportune moment, I slipped the bottle under Fowler's blanket. A short time after he left the hospital, a messenger delivered a book to me. It was Fowler's *Salute to Yesterday,* and in the flyleaf he had written: 'To my timely young friend Bob Kriendler who rushed into the battle with a bottle, and thereby saved a life.' It was dated October, 1937.

"That was the beginning of my collection of autographed first editions. It now numbers several hundred volumes by outstanding writers of the day, some of whom were and are regular customers.

"Two or three years after my trip to Doctors Hospital, John Steinbeck and Ernest Hemingway and their wives dined at the club. Steinbeck had just published *Grapes of Wrath,* and I wanted his autograph. But I found him difficult to approach. So I asked Hemingway, who was a 21 regular, for his help. Steinbeck balked, despite Hemingway's intervention.

" 'You know I don't like to autograph my books,' Steinbeck protested.

" 'Do it anyway,' Hemingway insisted.

" 'What am I going to say?' Steinbeck asked.

"Joking, Hemingway said: 'Say something scatological.'

"So Steinbeck took the pen I offered him and wrote in the flyleaf: 'To Bob Kriendler, Scatologically, John Steinbeck.'

"Some years later, when an anthology of his writings appeared, Steinbeck responded to my request for his autograph with less urging. In *The World of John Steinbeck,* he wrote: 'Bob—It's a little tiny world as we both know—*pas de merde*. John Steinbeck.' I need not mention that the French words mean 'no shit.' "

From the start, the Kriendlers and Bernses have operated counter to an oft-voiced tenet of American business. Instead of eschewing nepotism, they favor it. They claim that it works for them. And they note that the top echelon has long consisted of three brothers of co-founder Jack Kriendler; a nephew, Sheldon Tannen; and two

21

21 in 1971.

Bernses, co-founder Charlie and brother Jerry. (Charlie Berns died at sixty-nine in Palm Springs in 1971.)

"But the back of the house," Bob Kriendler advises, "is also populated with an assortment of relatives: brothers-in-law, uncles and cousins."

However, when the sale of 21 to Ogden fell through in September, 1970, Bob announced that the executive group was being augmented with the addition of Bruce Snyder, John Fleming and Terrance Dinan, none of whom sounded like *mishpocheh*.

Catering to celebrities, the Kriendlers and Bernses have become celebrities in their own right. And 21 is not only the longest-lived nonmusic club but the only joint that helped make The Street a legend that remains a living legend on The Street today.

Tape 2 . . . SHERRY BRITTON

"I came to Leon & Eddie's in March, 1941," Sherry Britton recalls. "I was not yet sixteen, although I had worked three years in burlesque. On the third night, I had words with the club's headwaiter and was fired. Hugo apparently thought that he was paying me a compliment when he told me: 'My wife thanks you when I come home at night.' Despite my years in burlesque, I was rather naïve, and probably to compensate for the strip act, I was quite prudish. When I asked Hugo for an explanation, he gave it without mincing words. I slapped his face.

"I was immediately summoned to the office of Eddie Davis, who gave me a lecture on the value of a headwaiter compared to a stripper. Quite upset, I pleaded for the chance to finish the week. When Eddie declined, I lost my temper and bluntly told him what he could do with his job. It was my first use of vulgarity. Fortunately for me, though I did not know it until later, Eddie was hard of hearing. After we had some more words, he relented and agreed that I could stay on to complete the week. I worked the following week, the week after that, and the weeks stretched, so that I remained steadily at L & E for seven and a half years. During that time I took only one vacation, and Lili St. Cyr was brought in as a sub.

"I used to strip down to an itsy-bitsy G-string and nothing else. Not even pasties. I did this even during the dinner hour when lots of children were in the audience. Please remember that this was March, 1941. But my body was so perfect and I did it with such good taste that no one ever thought of complaining—quite the opposite!

"L & E outlived most of the places on The Street because they offered unusually good food, outstanding service and great big drinks. And the place had warmth. Leon, who acted as host, knew how to make customers feel wanted and at home. Both he and Eddie never forgot the name of anybody who came in more than once. They remembered birthdays and anniversaries. They made a point of recalling the occasions on which customers came to the club, where they sat

Leon & Eddie

Sherry Britton, featured stripper at Leon & Eddie from 1941 to 1949.

and what they ate. To keep 'the family,' as they called their regulars, together, they maintained an enormous mailing list of more than twenty thousand active names. And they worked at it keeping it up-to-date. It was so precious to them that once when a customer dropped dead in the club, Leon turned to his partner after the initial shock had worn off and said absentmindedly: 'Let's not forget to take his name off the mailing list.'

"Sunday night was a dead night at many clubs. But not at L & E. It was Celebrity Night and the place was generally jammed. You never knew who would show up. And most of the future celebrities did. At nineteen, Alan King had the poise of a star. At another Celebrity Night, Jerry Lewis overwhelmed everybody by the way he took a heckler apart. Cut the guy to ribbons but managed to be hysterically funny at the same time. Eddie Davis was pretty effective in squelching hecklers, though he seldom had to contend with them. 'The next beer you order,' he would say, 'have them put a head on you.' Or: 'I never forget a face, but in your case it would be easy to make an exception.'

"We gave three farewell parties for Dean Martin. He was always going to Hollywood. But unlike Bob Hope, who sang 'Thanks for the Memory' and hit in his first film, Dean kept coming back.

"The one vacation I took in seven and a half years came in 1944 as the result of a remark made by Mike Todd. An agent who was trying to promote me for a show brought Todd into the club. At the end of my act, Todd's only comment was: 'She needs a nose job.' I hurried to a plastic surgeon and had my nose bobbed. It took several weeks before the swelling and discoloration disappeared. Then I waited expectantly for another audition. It never came. I never saw or heard from Todd again.

"Molly Berns, the wife of Charlie of the 21 Club, was more persistent. I got to know her because, occasionally, she or Jack Kriendler would invite me and Eddie to entertain in the private, upstairs dining rooms. Like all good Jewish mothers, she was always ready to play Dolly. The first time I met her, she wanted to know why a nice Jewish girl like me wasn't married. And the second time, she told me she had a nice rich socialite bachelor for me. Thereafter, every time I saw her it was a struggle to avoid being dragged over to a table where she knew there was an eligible bachelor.

"Like 21, Leon & Eddie's was then known as one of the few clubs not dominated by the Mob. I remember one evening when several very tough-looking guys asked to see Eddie. It soon became apparent that they had not come to eat or see the show. Eddie sat down to talk with them. It was a very brief conversation. And to make sure that they understood him, Eddie signaled his headwaiters. There were seven of them, and they were as adept in removing undesirable customers as boning a flounder. Within seconds, the mobsters who had sought in were muscled out.

"Eddie was quite hard of hearing even then, as I came slowly to realize. Once somebody was commenting on a ball game and said something like: 'This nut thinks that Gehrig was a better hitter than Babe Ruth. How do you like that?' And Eddie responded: 'I feel fine, thank you! How do you feel?' It became a catchphrase around the club. Anytime someone wanted to suggest that something didn't make sense, he'd say: 'I feel fine, thank you! And how do you feel?'

"Eddie was a surprising man in many ways. In the club or away from it, he never touched a drop of liquor or smoked. Leon did the drinking for him. Eddie had a fabulous memory, not only for people's names and faces, but for hundreds of songs and parodies. And, curiously, to turn to another part of his anatomy, he had the most beautiful legs you ever saw on a man.

"As a gag, we occasionally had contests in the club to pick the man with the most attractive pair of legs. Women served as judges and they only saw the legs. Eddie always won. At my suggestion, they introduced the gimmick into the only show he ever played, *Glad to See You*. Unfortunately, he broke his collarbone during the out-of-town tryouts and was replaced by Eddie Foy, Jr. At one point he made a recording, 'I'm the Laziest Guy in Town,' backed with 'I Guess I'll Have to Change My Plans.' It was no more successful than his trips to the Coast on a picture deal.

"While Eddie was a great showman, in some strange way his medium was not records, not films, not Broadway musicals, but simply Leon & Eddie's. Despite all the tremendous performers who appeared at the club throughout the years, I don't think there was anybody who had his power over an audience. They simply adored him. He always did a long act—close to an hour. And he'd go on three times an evening. He always had to beg off.

"Many of his parodies were on the blue side. Things like 'I'm the Great Doctor Proctor,' a takeoff on headshrinkers, or 'The Virgin Sturgeon,' or the story of the country girl who had them 'Comin' 'Round the Mountain.' But his concern about his family clientele and out-of-towners led him to use *double-entendre* material rather than explicitly sexy or four-letter stuff. His parodies were tinted blue, not a deep purple, and he had an innate feeling for where to draw the line. After several of these off-color songs, he'd do a torch ballad like 'She's Funny That Way' or a tearjerker like 'Melancholy Baby'—and there wouldn't be a dry eye in the joint.

"I did the last Celebrity Night. I can never forget the date—April 11, 1954. I remember so many things as a result of it—like Sinatra's comeback in that film, Eddie Fisher singing 'Oh! My Papa,' and so many other things. But strangely, I can't remember what happened that Celebrity Night. I can't forget the feeling I had inside me. Only a few people knew what was coming, for they never made any announcement. Went through the evening as if it were just another night. But when it was over and they locked up, a chapter in entertainment history was closed. Just a few hours after the last applause had died down, the wreckers were there with their crowbars tearing down the place.

"Of course, by that time Leon was gone. They broke up in '49. And it couldn't have been easy for Eddie to do it all alone. But I think that the closing had something to do with the times. A year or so after the war, a lot of the black-market money that made things swing dried up. People seemed to tire of going out as they did during the war, and nightclub attendance sagged.

"I went back for two months in 1952. I had left just about the time that the active partnership broke up. For a while in '52, every night seemed to be New Year's Eve again. But Eddie, who had a testy streak, would berate old customers for having stayed away. By this time his old material didn't seem to register as well as it had and he somehow lacked interest in finding new stuff. Although the club eventually went broke, I hear that they sold the property for two hundred and fifty thousand. Like Leon, Eddie moved to Florida, though he settled in the Fort Lauderdale area.

"I'd rather remember the years when business was booming. Then every night was literally New Year's Eve at L & E. The weirdest things seemed to happen. Like one night a man who was obviously not well came in with his wife and a nurse. You could see that he wanted desperately to get into the spirit of things. The two women tried to hold him back. But after a time, the wife relented and the nurse gave a reluctant okay to his dancing a bit. He couldn't have been on the floor for more than a minute. It was enough. He just dropped dead.

"The nurse rushed to the phone for an ambulance when she saw her patient collapse. But it took some time in coming. In the meantime, it was show time—and I had to go on. Of course, attendants quickly moved the prone figure to the side of the room and surrounded him with chairs so that he could not be seen by the audience. Even those people who had seen him fall didn't know that he was dead. But I knew. And from the raised stage, I could see him as he lay among the chairs. I can never forget the feeling I had, dancing and stripping as he lay there lifeless. The weird thing was that I could see his wrist-watch, with the second hand sweeping around. It was so incongruous. His watch seemed alive. And there he was, alive one minute and an inert chunk of matter the next. I kept trying not to look. But my eyes kept returning to that sweep hand on his watch. . . .

"Strange things were always happening at L & E. But somehow I can't help thinking of this weird thing—probably the most bizarre of all—whenever I think back to that wonderful, exciting time."

3. Sherry, Shenanigans, and the Saloon Caruso

"They named a chair after Morris," he sang, "and a town after Morris and a hotel in New York, the St. Morris. Every Sunday on the air, he's in everybody's hair—who calls for Philip? Morris!"

The singer was not named Morris, but Eddie. From 1928 through 1953 on 52d St., he sang parodies of well-known songs and special lyrics to familiar melodies—many with topical payoffs like the reference to the Philip Morris cigarette ad, delivered by a midget barker with a mammoth voice and as popular in the thirties as Alka-Seltzer's recent "spicy meat ball" commercial.

Some of Eddie's parodies were slightly off-color. Like the tale of the three sisters, Faith, Hope and Charity. Two went to the big city to make good. "Scotch and sofa" did not hurt their ambitions. Having accumulated a bundle, Faith and Hope went back home to show off. But their sister had an even bigger bundle than they. Her explanation: "Charity begins at home."

His name was Eddie Davis. He was known as the Saloon Caruso and Super Songman for the stay-up set. In 1928 he and Leon Enken opened a tiny speakeasy on 52d St., where Club 18 was later situated and where today one enters the towering Esso Building. It was a cellar speak that could at best accommodate forty thirsty patrons, and it cost the pair less than $1,000 to set up. The hooch was not in the same league as that served across the street where Jack and Charlie opened their club two years later or at No. 57–59 where Tony operated. But it had Davis' showmanship and Enken's big-jawed, business acumen.

Having weathered the speakeasy era and its larcenous revenuers, Leon and Eddie moved to larger quarters on the north side of the street just west of 21. They settled at No. 33, where their bouncers included Joe Marsh, later proprietor of the Spindletop Steak House, and Toots Shor, who ran a four-story world-famous restaurant at the identical address in the sixties. Everybody called their cabaret-restaurant Leon & Eddie's, but the vertical three-story sign, long a landmark of the block, just read Leon & Eddie. (Legend has it that a speakeasy run by Jimmy Durante became the Club Durant—no terminal *e*—for fiscal considerations.)

From the start, L & E worked to develop a family or tourist club, rather than a swinging "in joint." This orientation is apparent in a chartreuse-colored, orchid-adorned souvenir program that "New York's Number One Restaurant & Cabaret," as typed on the cover, presented to patrons. No menu was to be found in the multicolored sixteen pages crammed with photographs of celebrities. There were full-page bios of Leon, described as a "king-size combination of Lou Costello and Fiorello La Guardia," and of Eddie, recipient of the New York *Mirror*'s Medal of Honor as top nightclub entertainer of 1940. There were reprints of a column that Davis wrote in 1941 as a sub for vacationing Walter Winchell and the *double-entendre* lyrics of "She Came Rolling down the Mountain," a saucy song made famous by Eddie. No fewer than two full pages were devoted to photographs of a dozen places of interest in "New York—The World's Most Famous City." L & E was the only 52d St. spot listed in *Gotham Life,* New York's hotel guide.

L & E were content to leave the smart set to Tony's, the hep and hip crowd to the jazz joints, and high society and the heavy spenders to 21. Like the Latin Quarter later, they sought to keep their prices within reach of the middle-class pocketbook and to attract average rather than night people. And they were not tarred with the odor either of the Mob or clipping, even though they early featured a stripper. The partners worked assiduously at developing a clientele of regulars and repeaters, including out-of-towners, who would feel that L & E was their dining room away from home. In their heyday they boasted a mailing list of 400,000 names developed entirely from their own clientele. They were among the first restaurateurs to cultivate the practice of sending birthday cards to customers. "They really stressed family," stripper Sherry Britton notes. "Family in the sense of people who would come to celebrate important personal occasions. In the many years I performed there, it used to shake me up to be invited out by a young man who first came to the place as a teen-ager. That's how long people continued coming to Leon & Eddie."

L & E managed to attract people who otherwise had taken to heart Police Commissioner Grover A. Whalen's warning of 1930: "Gangdom is in control of the nightclubs. All decent people will shun such places." Reviewing the killings at the Hotsy Totsy Club that provoked the commissioner's statement, columnist-author Robert Sylvester concluded: "In 1929 you could be murdered just for being in a nightclub." L & E succeeded in creating an atmosphere and image that made customers of those who might have been uneasy about going to other clubs.

By 1936 L & E was said to employ as many as 165 people, with a break-even running expense of $10,500 a week. Nevertheless, in that year its gross exceeded this nut by 50 percent, and Leon and Eddie, according to *Variety,* each were able to take a $45,000 dividend above their regular drawing accounts. *Variety* editor Abel Green adds that the weekly nut included substantial payments to Moses Polakoff, "their mouthpiece and 10 percent partner, as well as to a former newspaper gal who came through with a bankroll at a crucial period."

Although the club presented many interesting performers through the years, its incomparable drawing card was Eddie Davis himself. Four times a night, he went on for 40 to 60 minutes. Boasting a repertoire of more than a thousand songs, he reportedly never repeated a number during an evening. A Harry Richman rather than a Harry Lillis Crosby, he could put over a song better than most trained singers. His nightly audience provided ample proof. While the early shows attracted out-of-town tourists and Seventh Avenue cloak-and-suiters, the last show generally brought in performers who had finished their own stints. In the course of a week, columnists might spot Crosby, Sinatra, Ethel Merman, Betty Hutton, Bob Hope, Dorothy Lamour, Jack Dempsey, Gregory Peck, Darryl Zanuck, and even George Jean Nathan. For the edification of this in crowd, Davis would do a variation of his Paean to Morris that went: "They named a plan after Morris and a chair after Morris—and a hotel in New York, the St. Morris—and when I'm looking for a booking and I want to know what's cooking, who sends me to William? Morris!"

"If Joe E. Lewis is the comedian's favorite comedian," columnist-author Louis Sobol once wrote, "Eddie Davis is the No. 1 singing man with the stars of the nation." Sobol recalls an evening when he brought author Jim Tully to the club. They arrived as the waiters were placing chairs upside down on the tables. Tully, who was leaving the city next day, was so disappointed at having missed Davis' act that Sobol pleaded for just one song.

"Eddie couldn't resist the appeal," Sobol wrote in *Along the Broadway Beat*. "He sat there at our table. Without piano accompaniment, he sang 'Melancholy Baby,' then 'Night and Day,' 'Body and Soul' and, finally, half a dozen ribald ditties. The sun was breaking through little clouds when we left and Tully said: 'When I get back to California, I am going to write the best novel of my life about this big, lovable Saloon Caruso.' "

Apart from Davis, L & E had at least one other thing going for it. Mention the name of the club and an image is immediately conjured up of the audience draw known as Celebrity Night. This was held on Sundays. Despite the designation, you did not have to be a celebrity to do your thing. Through the years, the number of would-be celebs greatly outweighed the name people who appeared. You just had to have the guts to get up and take the gaff. There were auditions but the unexpected happened frequently.

One Celebrity Night, Franklin Delano Roosevelt, Jr., mounted the stage and simply talked for an hour. He did not make jokes but merely delivered a speech about things on his mind. Stripper Sherry Britton, who was present, recalls that at first the audience was just polite. "But then it became entranced," she says. "I can't remember what he talked about and I don't know how the men reacted. But by the time he was through Junior had conquered every woman in the club. He just had to wave his little finger."

Like jam sessions, Celebrity Nights were improvisational training grounds for performers, particularly comics. It would be difficult to name a comedian who did not make at least one appearance. Jackie Gleason, Alan King, Jerry Lewis, Joey Adams, Jackie Leonard, Henny Youngman, B. S. Pully—all tried their jokes at a Celebrity Night. One evening, after he had told a few and was sitting down, Milton Berle remarked that he was coming back the next evening to see how Joey Adams, then on the regular bill, would do with his

Jack E. Leonard, one of today's top comics who, early in his career, made the scene at a Leon & Eddie Celebrity Night.

RCA Records

material. Adams jumped up. "I wouldn't steal any of your jokes," he shouted. "Think I want Bob Hope to sue me?"

For managers, agents and publicists in the entertainment field, Celebrity Nights were as much of a godsend as they were for L & E's entrepreneurs, who got the performers for free. Barbara Belle, who once managed Louis Prima and singer Fran Warren, recalls: "If an artist didn't have it, you found out. And if they did, it was a great way to start a lot of good talk. Celebrity Nights brought out the pros and the press. Around 1946, Fran Warren wanted to step out on her own. She had been singing with Claude Thornhill's band and was on his best-selling record of 'A Sunday Kind of Love,' a blues ballad I wrote with Prima and two other songwriters. On the strength of that vocal, we managed to sign her as a solo singer to M-G-M Records. One of her first sides was 'For Heaven's Sake,' a song by Don Meyer, Elise Bretton and Sherman Edwards, composer-lyricist of *1776*. But there it was. We hit on a Celebrity Night to get her out of the crush of new singers at the starting gate. The day and week after she appeared, Fran was all over the columns and music trade papers. It was a good beginning."

Before Joni James had her first noisemaker also on M-G-M Records—a cover of Hank Williams' "Cheatin' Heart"—L & E connoisseurs heard her at a Sunday night shindig. For baritone Alan Dale, Celebrity Night brought concrete results on three different occasions. On his first appearance, a friend of Carmen Cavallaro touted him so highly that he became the bandleader-pianist's vocalist. It was Cavallaro who gave Dale, son of an Italian comedian, his professional name. Another appearance led to his joining trombonist George Paxton's band for a two-and-a-half-year run. Still later, Ray Bloch, conductor of the *Ed Sullivan Show,* helped Dale get a Signature Records' contract after he heard him at a Celebrity Night.

L & E was a very publicity-conscious club. It welcomed offbeat *shtik.* "One evening," Eddie Davis recalls, "zany millionaire Tommy Manville told our reservations man that he was going to arrive in a hansom cab—you know, the kind that's drawn by a horse and can still be rented outside Central Park on 59th St. Photographers were waiting when he drove up. But I had dreamed up the idea of having him ride the horse directly into the club. This was possible because there were no steps. The floor of the lobby and dining room were level with the street.

"When I asked the old Irish driver to unhitch his horse, he was hesitant—but only until I put a fifty-dollar bill into his hand. With an assist, Manville managed to mount the refugee from a glue factory. Dressed in an elegant tux, he not only entered the club, but we had him ride the horse completely around the dance floor. The crowd loved it. So did the AP and other wire services whose pictures and stories appeared on front pages from coast to coast."

Some years earlier, customers entering the club found a young calf cavorting about. It was a surprise birthday gift for Frank Parker, then the high-tenor vocalist of the Jack Benny radio show. Parker was always depicted as a fumbling moon calf. As he entered the club after the show's coast-to-coast broadcast, he was handed a feedbag. The calf made a dash for the food—and landed himself and Parker in the following day's picture newspapers.

Other animals contributed to L & E renown. There was a kangaroo about whom Eddie Davis wrote me: "He was in an animal act engaged by Leon while I was on vacation. When I returned, a 'Welcome Home' was arranged at the airport, with a band, the kangaroo and his animal trainer. As they tried to get the animal into a position for picture taking, he reared up on his tail, which is like an iron pole, and kicked forward with his hind legs. He just missed giving me a hernia.

"Another act Leon brought in while I was away was Rosita Royce and her doves. For a finale, she would release about twenty birds at once. Can you imagine the dinner show with people eating and the doves flying wildly around the room? Leon was an Ed Sullivan before Sullivan when it came to animal acts. Once during my vacation, agents submitted two acts: one was a bird act known as La Monte's

Cockatoos; the other, an up-and-coming comic named Billy De Wolfe. Leon bought the cockatoos."

When the hula caught on as a dance and the country became Hawaii-conscious, L & E built an outdoor Pago Pago Room in the rear of the club at a cost of $20,000. Boasting windstorm and rain effects, it was a strong tourist attraction and yielded many column items. But after a time, the novelty wore thin.

The Glass Glamor Tank, the new publicity gimmick, was a novel act in the summer of 1938. Anticipating the water ballets of Billy Rose's Aquacade at the 1939 World's Fair, L & E had five girls splashing around in a tank, which, in the words of a *New Yorker* observer, "was hardly big enough for a middle-sized guppy."

"Not so," says Eddie Davis. "I bought the tank from an old circus sideshow. It held seven tons of water and had two thick panes of glass so you could see inside. To increase visibility, I borrowed a dozen klieg lights from the Capitol Theater. We hired five chorus girls that could dive and for a glamorous name, Helen Wainwright, 1936 Olympic diving champion. I had to convince her husband that she would be safer with us than in an office with a lecherous boss. Signing her was headline news.

"It was a hot summer and we advertised a dollar-fifty dinner, plus the girls in the tank. One girl would smoke a cigarette through a tube. Another would eat an apple, banana and grapes. The girls did front-overs and back-overs, and Helen performed with her beautiful, waist-long hair. For the big finale, I made a rattling-gun barker's announce-ment from behind the bandstand, the band struck up 'Anchors Aweigh,' and the girls dived in one side and the other in rotation. It was maddening, with the water splashing over customers who fought to sit close to the tank. When the lights came up, they found them-selves in an inch or more of water. It was the biggest act in New York that summer, with my show following in the inside room."

One of the weirder bits of publicity involved stripper Lois De Fee, who was more than 6 feet tall and built like an Amazon. Suddenly, Miss De Fee up and married a midget. Nobody ever reported what came of the curious union. But it certainly made copy—and jokes. At one point, the club made Miss De Fee its bouncer, another space grabber. Whether the owners took the appointment seriously or not, Miss De Fee was proud of her priority as the first and only female bouncer. One night, the brother of a rather well-known comedienne became boisterous. Miss De Fee approached the gent, who was her match in size and muscle, and urged him to quiet down. No self-respecting drunk is going to take such a request without wanting to know who made it. "I'm the bouncer," Miss De Fee replied with authority. The gent did not hesitate. "Well, then bounce!" he announced, and landed a blow that flattened Miss De Fee. The incident did not make the papers.

Once typed "The Eiffel Eyeful" by Walter Winchell, Miss De Fee supposedly started as a bouncer at the Dizzy Club, across the street from L & E. When she was hired away, her well-developed mammary glands "helped to give the owners of L & E," she later observed, "the idea for a sweater girl gimmick. My job was to walk through the club wearing tight slacks and a sweater, with LEON sewed over one breast and EDDIE over the other. I used to wonder what would've happened if the bosses had taken in another partner."

Eddie Jaffee, longtime Broadway publicist, remembers L & E as a club that somehow brought out the clowning side of people. "One night," he recalls, "Marlon Brando was barred because he came dressed in a T-shirt like the one he wore as Stanley Kowalski in *A Streetcar Named Desire*. It rankled Brando, who happened to be living in a nearby brownstone. L & E had a movable roof, which they could open in the warm weather for ventilation. One night, when Brando had, perhaps, imbibed a little too much, he made a fast trip to Central Park's bridle path with a bucket. Socony ads were then featuring the Flying Red Horse. Brando went up to the roof of the building adjoining L & E, and as he hurled the contents of the bucket onto the club's open roof, he shouted: 'Watch out for the Flying Red Horse!' "

"I don't know where Eddie Jaffee got that story," Eddie Davis comments. "It never happened. Brando did live in a brownstone two doors away at No. 37, as did comedian Wally Cox. I do know that our doorman Walter, who was the best-known and liked on the block, used to watch their motorcycles. Nobody would have dared destroy L & E property or upset the club's normal functioning, believe me."

Brando's jest is, perhaps, understandable in light of the atmosphere radiated by L & E's decor. Over the entrance to the club, you were greeted with a jocular paraphrase of Earl Carroll's well-known slogan: "Through these portals, the most beautiful girls in the world pass out!" Inside, in place of drawings of female nudes found in many clubs and speaks, the walls were covered with tongue-in-cheek murals.

The bantering legend over the swinging doors into the kitchen read: "Through these portals pass the most beautiful waiters in the world!" And on the back wall, separated by a series of saucy murals, Leon and Eddie were shown thumbing their prominent noses at each other.

Through the quarter of a century of its existence, L & E presented a considerable number of future stars. Lennie Hayton led the house band for a time. The first midtown appearance of The Revuers, a comedy-singing quartet that included Judy Holliday, was at L & E. Slim Gaillard, the "Cement Mixer" man, early presented his novelty musical act. And there was the man who, for three years from 1940 on, quietly played luncheon-cocktail piano. Nothing in Harry Gibson's behavior suggested the excitement he would cause after 1944. While at L & E he gave three lightly attended concerts at Town Hall. At the recommendation of Herman Chittison, a fellow pianist, he was apparently being considered for a Juilliard scholarship when he left L & E. Then, in 1944, as the hip sounds of bebop began invading The Street, L & E's studious pianist suddenly became Harry "the Hipster" Gibson and did an act at the Three Deuces, Spotlite and Downbeat clubs, cigarette drooping from his mouth, in which he sang original songs replete with double-talk and jive.

To suggest that Eddie Davis had fathered the Hipster would hardly excite the Saloon Caruso. Yet there can be no question that during his years as L & E's luncheon-cocktail pianist, Gibson had taken a course from Professor Davis in showmanship, the art of parody, and how to put over a comedy song. Eddie doubtless takes greater pride for his part in "siring" the man who ran a celebrated restaurant at his old address. Toots Shor, incidentally, was not really a bouncer, as many reports have it. From 1932 for about four years, he was L & E's daytime manager at a salary of $50 a week.

When did Barnum meet Bailey? The oft-repeated story is that Leon and Eddie met in Atlantic City in the mid-twenties when both were working as waiters. "It's an honorable profession," says Eddie Davis, "but I never was a waiter. We did meet in Atlantic City. Here's how it happened. I started singing in the Army—got the bug from my older brother, Phil, who was a blackface comedian with Al Fields' Minstrels before he went into vaudeville. After I was mustered out, some Philadelphia friends opened a beautiful café (the word 'nightclub' had not yet arrived). They asked me to be MC. I used to help the headwaiter in recognizing VIP's, and on busy nights I helped out in seating people. Guess that's how the story about my being a waiter started.

"But if you look at the pink-colored program of the Club Cadiz on Chestnut St. in Philadelphia, you'll see that the show was billed as 'Eddie Davis, Master of Ceremonies, EDDIE DAVIS and his gang.' I sang duets with Helen Schroeder, a moonfaced gal on the bill. She's better known as Helen Kane—she married Joe Kane of the Ohrbach department store family on NYC's Union Square—who became famous as the Boop-Boop-A-Doop Girl. Before that happened, a J. J. Shubert scout got her a part in a so-so Shubert musical, *A Night in Spain*.

"In the meantime, an agent booked me as MC into the Folies Bergère in Atlantic City. 'Will sing any song you ask of him,' wrote the *Official Atlantic City Guide* of July 31, 1927. Clayton, Jackson and Durante were then appearing at the Palais Royal a block away, and Leon Enken was the headman at the velvet rope. That's how Leon & Eddie first met.

"When the summer was over, I was booked into the Everglades on 48th St., just west of Broadway. I was supposed to be a two-week headliner, but I stayed for two years. Across the street from the Everglades was the Parody Club, where Clayton, Jackson and Durante were appearing. One day, Leon, who was their headwaiter wherever they went, invited me to go into business with him. Although I had offers from Chicago and points west, I liked New York. When the Everglades and Parody closed for the summer, Leon and I rented a spot at 18 West 52d. A few doors from us, at No. 8, another speakeasy called the Wing Club attracted all the pioneer aviators of the day: Wiley Post, Clyde Pangborn, Russell Boardman and George Halderman, who flew Ruth Elder nonstop across the Atlantic. One night George asked me whether I would like to have breakfast in Florida the next morning. I said: 'Excuse me while I make a phone call for the man in the white coat.' All the rest of the patrons at our end of 52d St. were society."

For two decades from 1928, Leon and Eddie worked together. It was a fruitful association. By 1937 *Variety* editor Abel Green named L & E as the top grosser of America's Montmartre, as he liked to call The Street. Citing a figure of $15,000 a week, he placed it ahead of 21, the Onyx and the Yacht Club, in that order. "The year before L & E broke up," Eddie notes, "we had a beautiful place in Palm

Beach. We put eighty thousand dollars into it. To get out after one year, I gave Leon my interest for one dollar. The following year [1947] we came to a parting of the ways by my choice."

After Leon and Eddie split up, Enken tried to make a go of it in Palm Beach, though he still retained his piece of the New York club. The Florida place did not last long, but Enken remained in the resort area until his death in 1964. On 52d St. L & E lasted a scant five years after Enken's departure. On August 1, 1953, shortly after its silver anniversary, it filed a petition in bankruptcy.

By then 52d St. had been steadily going downhill for a number of years. When the tall L & E sign came down in April, 1954, nobody could pretend, despite the continuing presence of Jimmy Ryan near Sixth Avenue and Hickory House near Seventh Avenue, that The Street had any future in show business. The parking lot that took over and remained until Toots Shor moved his restaurant from 51st was a dismal portent.

Tape 3 . . . JOE HELBOCK

"I was on 52d St. before Leon & Eddie's," says Joe Helbock. "I was there before 21 came over from 9th St. in 1930." As founder of the original Onyx, "the Cradle of Swing," Helbock may justly claim to be the father of The Street, or perhaps even the grandfather, since he was seventy-seven years old on October 18, 1971.

"I was bootlegging on The Street in '27–'28, when the Aquarium was near Sixth Avenue," he recalls. "That was a speak with a tank of fish behind the bar. The Wing Club was a hangout for aviators. And Tony's was the smart speakeasy. Catered to Dorothy Parker and her crowd, Bob Benchley, Noel Coward, Monty Woolley and Tallulah Bankhead. I liked musicians and tried to make a home away from home for them.

"Before I came to 52d, I had a telephone service on 49th, where Radio City is now. Had two kids running. Billy Leavitt, my partner, and I made deliveries too. We printed up cards that just said Joe & Bill and gave a phone number. No address. It just said: Any Hour. The kids carried the stuff in paper bags. But we used briefcases. Most of the time I was too busy aging the stuff. [Chuckling and his eyes twinkling slyly.] I could age a bottle between the time you called and the boy went out with the delivery. Bottles sold for eight to twelve dollars.

"Remember Pearl White? She was a big movie star in the days of the silent pictures. She lived across the street at 18 West 49th. She'd spend all night drinking at the Park Central Casino. Before she'd go upstairs, she'd yell across the street, 'Hey, Joe.' And I'd bring a bottle up to her. She became a nun.

"We got mixed up in a murder. It was a famous case. Dot King murder. We sold her booze. She was kept by some rich guy. They found my number in her book. Musta thought I was a boyfriend or something. It just said 'Joe.' But 49th was a quiet street. Brownstones like 52d. John Perona, who made it big with El Morocco, had a place near us."

The move into bootlegging was an easy transition for Helbock, who worked in "pharmacies" from the time he left school at the age of fourteen. "At that time," he observes, "pharmacies sold medicine and pills only as a last resort. And we didn't sell alcohol for rubbing either.

"My first job was in the Murray Hill section of Manhattan. One of our best customers was Teddy Roosevelt. He'd come in the morning after the night before to get a hangover drink like a Bloody Mary. I worked at a very popular drugstore on Broadway at 43d St. The pills got kinda dusty in that place, too. Every clerk had a tuxedo. We were polite bootleggers. And when the day's errands were over, we would drop around to see Ziegfeld's *Midnight Frolics* at the Amsterdam Roof on 42d.

"I got acquainted with many celebrities at this store—also at another 'pharmacy' on 79th and Broadway. Personalities like Babe Ruth, Will Rogers, Marilyn Miller and Jimmy Walker. You know, Jimmy had a lot to do with the success of Jack and Charlie's 21. He hung out at their place on 49th. He'd come in with Bob and Alfred Newman. Alfred later went out to the Coast and won all those awards for his movie scores. Walker was mayor when they opened on 52d and a lot of the city's big politicians came to Jack and Charlie's because that was his hangout.

"I became friendly with Jimmy Dorsey around '25, and we lived together for about a year in a sublease in the Des Artistes on 67th and Central Park West. We had wild parties there. I remember one that Jimmy threw for Bette Davis the night before she left for Hollywood. Her first husband was a trumpet player. Jimmy was my best man when I got married in '28, just about the time I opened the Onyx. I was with Jimmy the night before he died in '57. He said: 'Joe, if there's anything you need, just let me know.'

"I was pretty chummy with Paul Whiteman—Pops, as his musicians called him. Palled around with him and all the guys in his band. They hung out at a speak on West 53d St. That was where the Ninth Avenue el came east and turned onto Sixth Avenue. Plunkett's was just west of Broadway, a dark, narrow, little joint. It was hard to pass guys standing at the bar. I used to go there with Jimmy Dorsey and Roy Bargy—he was Whiteman's pianist. I guess the Onyx put Plunkett's out of business. All the musicians came over once we got going."

Helbock was born in the Bronx in October, 1894. His memory goes back to the years before World War I, when somebody called Gene Sennett opened a cabaret on Westchester Avenue in the Bronx. "The place that Sennett picked," he notes, "was originally a stable. It was where the Seven Santini Brothers got their start. The old man went into business with one horse and wagon. When he moved out, Sennett converted the stable into a cabaret and used singing waiters. Jack White, who was then a bricklayer, hung around the place and clowned with a guy who became a stooge for Willie and Eugene Howard. I can't remember the name of the joint or of the stooge.

"When I was fourteen, I used to hike into Harlem across the 138th St. bridge on Saturdays. The Jenkins Orphanage Band of Charleston, South Carolina, gave free concerts at the Harlem YMCA on 135th St. I heard jazz bands at Barron Wilkins' on Seventh Avenue and 134th. I once heard Jim Europe's great Negro band, but that was in a parade on Fifth Avenue. When I came out of World War One, I went to hear Duke Ellington at the old Kentucky Club on 49th and Broadway.

"Remember that bad flu epidemic during the war? I think it was the worst they ever had in this country. It hit me while I was in a camp in South Carolina. When I recovered, my hair started falling out. I've been kinda bald since then. But it hasn't hurt my memory."

Helbock stated that he launched the Onyx in 1927, not in '29–'30, as has been reported. The walls were alternating stripes of black and silver, not black. The bar had a black top, not black and white. "My partner then was Fred Hoetter," Helbock said. "He and I couldn't decide on a name. The only decent piece of furniture in the place was the black-topped marble bar. So we picked Onyx. I can't remember the name of the guy who owned the building at No. 35. But I do know that he was in trouble with the government. When he died, the tax boys got a writ to open the grave and verify that the corpse was really the deadbeat they were after. He was charging us seven hundred dollars a month. Can you imagine! Seven hundred a month back in the late twenties! And for a one-room, call it a room-and-a-half apartment in the rear of a walk-up. The roomers in the building were paying a hundred dollars a month and less.

"On the street floor, some guy tried to open a 'club.' He wasn't there a month when the cops walked in. It was terrible. They wrecked the place. I guess he refused to pay off. But even when you paid the local cops, you'd sometimes be raided by the feds. Then you had to take care of the agents so they'd change their testimony before the commissioner. To make sure that he'd allow it, you had to take care of him, too. Crazy days, they were! You stayed in business only if you had enough money and the right connections. I had a couple of pretty good connections. One was a deputy police commissioner, an old friend from the Bronx. With the right connection, you got the word of whom to pay and how much.

"Sometimes you got help from the law. I once saw Johnny Broderick, the famous Broadway detective, give Legs Diamond the beating of his life. This friend of mine, Bob Lynch, opened a speak on 51st St. I knew him from the days when he was a singing waiter at Sennett's in the Bronx. He had a nice place over one of those garages that used to be on 51st between Sixth and Seventh.

"One night I get a call from Lynch. 'What am I going to do, Joe?' he asks. 'Legs Diamond is here and he's messing up the place and chasing all my customers out.' I said to him: 'Why don't you call up Broderick? You can always get him outside of Lindy's.' Well, he got Broderick on the phone and Johnny was there in minutes. He gave Diamond the beating of his life. Must of knocked him down a dozen

Stuff Smith's Gang in action at the Onyx. Left to right, Mack Walker, Bob Bennett, Jonah Jones, Stuff Smith, Cozy Cole.

Down Beat

times. When he came to, Broderick told him: 'Look, if I find you anywhere from 42d St. to 59th between Fifth Avenue and the North River, you'll get worse than you got tonight!' My friend never had trouble again, not with Legs anyway. Diamond was really a phoney. He was only tough when he had half a dozen of his goons with him. Johnny Broderick operated as an independent. This was his territory, and nobody, not even hoods, were going to muscle in.

"We started with some pretty good talent at the Onyx, and the Onyx started some pretty big careers. Performers like Art Tatum and Maxine Sullivan and Joe Sullivan and the Spirits of Rhythm and John Kirby and Louis Prima and Stuff Smith. Now, Stuff was a very talented man but not easy to handle. After he made such a splash at our place, he had a chance to appear in a movie. I wasn't going to stand in his way, even though he hadn't played out his contract with us. I let him go, but he was supposed to come right back after the shooting. Well, once he's in Hollywood, he gets talked into appearing at the Famous Door out there. Prima had the place, and Red Colonna, Jerry's brother, ran it.

"When I started hollerin', he says, 'We'd like to come back but we don't have any money.' So I sent him six hundred dollars. A couple of days later, he showed up, but the rest of his band was still out in Hollywood. It cost me another thousand to bring them in. Then the Famous Door made a squawk to the union. The windup is that after we had him back, he wasn't nearly as big as in his first appearance.

"I was the first to have Art Tatum. He played in the speakeasy for nothin'. I gave him all the beer he could drink—half a dozen bottles a night. Tatum was playing in some club up in Harlem. Jimmy Dorsey and I went up to ask him to the Onyx after Repeal. Offered him fifty dollars a week. It was big money in those days—a lot of money.

"Jimmy Dorsey was a happy drinker. Tommy always looked for trouble. One night during the speakeasy days, Tommy was around until closing time. I got him into a cab to take him to the Taft. For no reason at all, he gets into an argument with the cabdriver. He wanted to pull him outa the cab. The cop on the beat was a friend, Paddy Flood, light heavyweight champ of the police department. Tommy started giving him abuse. He would have been taken in if I didn't know Paddy.

"There was a lot of clowning in those days. I have a record that the boys made one night at a regular recording session. They called it

'The Onyx Club Review.' They just had copies made for themselves. On one side, there's 'Have a Little Dream on Me,' done in a very funny style. On the other side Joe Venuti does 'Pagliacci' after Manny Klein, the trumpet player, introduces him in Yiddish. Joe comes back at him with a big argument in Italian.

"I think that Venuti was one of the funniest men that ever lived. As good a fiddler as he was, he coulda been just as great a comedian. And when it came to practical jokes, you had to be on the lookout. Once the Whiteman band was playing the old Hippodrome. The preceding act was one of those circus things, with a white horse trotting around a ring. Venuti happened to be in the wings as the horse was waiting to go on. He took his violin bow and began gently sawing on the horse's penis as if it were the strings of his fiddle. When the animal finally trotted out on stage, the audience saw this long, pink thing hanging between his legs. The horse was in no mood to go through his act, and people were laughing so hard they weren't much interested in acrobatics.

"After Carl Kress, the guitarist, became my partner in the Onyx, I began getting accused of everything in the world. You know we had this fire at the end of February, 1935. My partner of those days collected the fire insurance and went out to Denver. A few months later, I reopened the club with thirty-two hundred dollars Kress give me. Well, I paid him back the thirty-two hundred and gave him about forty-five thousand dollars on top of that. Was that a bad return on his money? He was not a working partner, after all. But the stories that went out about me! They had my wife so upset, I didn't know what to do. The joint didn't last too long after I got out.

"A lot of music business people hung around the Onyx. I remember Rube Bloom, the guy who wrote 'Soliloquy,' and Johnny Mercer. Jerry and Harold Arlen came in frequently. Jack Robbins, the publisher they called Mr. Music, was always around. So was Lou Levy, the manager of the Andrews Sisters. Jack Bregman was another publisher, and the guys from Santly Joy, who wound up with the publishing rights to 'The Music Goes 'Round.'

"Red McKenzie was a great singer. Too bad he never made it. I don't know, he had a certain way about him, that he used to get disliked by everyone he knew. I can't explain what it was. He was originally supposed to go with the band that Bob Crosby took over. In fact, he was the one who brought the band up to the Rockwell-O'Keefe office. But he wound up on the outside.

"I liked Red. He was a strange man. Can never forget this story that a bartender told me. He was with Red when he died. Red kept trying to tell this guy not to forget. But he seemed to forget what he wanted the bartender to remember. Finally, he got it out. Once he got some money from Gordon Jenkins, the arranger-composer of *Manhattan Tower*. He wanted the bartender to tell Jenkins, if he saw him, that he always meant to repay that loan."

4. "The Music Goes 'Round"

"I'd heard the boys speak of the Onyx," wrote Paul Douglas, a top radio announcer in 1938 and, later, the well-known actor, "but as far as I could make out, it was exclusively for the profession. One night, however, George Troop, who played plenty of trombone for Henry Theiss, took me to Helbock's place. George did the answering when the slot in the door opened, and we were in a crazy madhouse. The wicker chairs, the tables, the bar, the pounding piano, the phonograph, were overflowing with musicians, eating, talking, arguing, explaining, lying and drinking. From behind the bar, shaking a whiskey sour, his bald pate reflecting a hanging light, Helbock gave me the once-over and said hello.

"A hundred messages in his head, orders for drinks coming up, the phone to answer, his teeth troubling him, Helbock presided over his nuthouse with great élan."

This was the Onyx when it was on the parlor floor in the rear of the brownstone at 35 West 52d. "You got in by going down a couple of stone steps," Willie "the Lion" Smith recalls, "to a basement door that was always open." They were known as English basements in those days. "After you walked down a short hall, you came to a dark staircase and climbed one flight to another hallway. It was so dark that you couldn't see behind or in front of you. You'd knock at this doorway with silver paint all over it. A guy would look at you from a peek hole in the door."

Joe Helbock adds: "When you said, 'I'm from 802,' we put the rug out." Some writers have reported that the password was "Benny Goodman" or "Bernie Hanighen." Though the clarinetist and the songwriter-record exec were both members in good standing, it was the number of the New York Musicians Local that was the Onyx's password. And appropriate, too, considering the number of tootlers frequenting the joint.

Later dubbed "The Cradle of Swing," the Onyx launched 52d St. as a music thoroughfare and helped make it the foremost jazz street in the world. The first magnet to draw the general public to The Street, it remained *hot* for more years than any other club, with the possible exception of the Famous Door, which also started as a musicians' in spot.

Having spent considerable time with saxophonist Jimmy Dorsey and others at Plunkett's, a musicians' speak on West 53d, Helbock was aware that they liked to conduct business not from offices but in bars and cafés. Even today a number of midtown restaurants fulfill a similar function, among them, Charlie's Tavern on West 52d and Jim & Andy's on West 47th St. Helbock, who greeted friends "Hi ya, toots," before the salutation was a commonplace, provided a central place where musicians could pick up phone messages (before the days of answering services and exchanges), lounge between shows, meet for business confabs, and receive mail they did not want sent home. Musicians were delighted to have a place where they could park their instruments without fearing thievery.

After hours, the boys came to jaw, juice and jam, playing the kind of music they could not play on their jobs. "It never ceased to amaze me," Helbock says, "how they would come in complaining about how some leader kept them for rehearsals ten minutes longer than expected. Then they would stay in my place playing all night long—for free."

Paul Douglas has left this vivid account of how jamming developed: "Dick McDonough dragged me over to the phonograph to hear 'something terrific by a guy who knows how.' Nobody was startled when the machine began to grind out the London Symphony recording of Delius' 'First Cuckoo in Spring.' When it was finished, Joe Sullivan sat down at the piano and began to run through 'Three Little Words.' Nobody thought 'Three Little Words' incongruous after Delius. . . . 'Big and Little T,' Jack (trombone) and Charles (trumpet) Teagarden, sat in to show what they had in mind. Benny Good-

Jimmy and Tommy Dorsey played (and fought) as the Dorsey Brothers until 1935. They both jammed on trumpet at the Onyx.

man, who at that time had one clarinet and one program, joined in with the stick. Each man had his turn to throw the theme around while the others made background. The lid began to lift, and the boys fell into the groove, and the crib was rockin'. By the time Big T had done a hundred and sixty bars, Tommy Dorsey had arrived and had been handed T's sliphorn. Manny Klein had Little T's trumpet, Carl Kress was fingering McDonough's guitar. By mutual consent, each man took the lead and took the melody apart, developed, embroidered, made it his own. Roy Bargy was at the piano, Bunny Berigan blowing the trumpet, Frankie Chase alternated with Bud Freeman on the tenor sax."

Freeman, who was part of the Austin High School musical gang in

Chicago and is a member today of the Greatest Jazz Band in the World, has said: "When we wanted to play music for ourselves, we went to 52d St. In those days, I was making a busy living playing with Ray Noble—Rainbow Room, recordings, concerts and films with Amos and Andy. But the only time I had fun, musically speaking, was in the clubs on The Street. You know 52d was not the Broadway kind of street they showed in that corny movie named after it. It was really an esoteric street, even if some of the joints were owned by questionable people. Jazz was not a paying proposition, as it became for a time after Benny Goodman made it. So 52d St. clubs like The Onyx, The Door and later Jimmy Ryan's played an extremely vital role in the history of jazz—almost as important as Harlem, which moved downtown. It was a place where you could let off musical steam."

And when Helbock finally locked up the joint, somebody would say, "Let's go uptown for some yardbird and strings," lingo for fried chicken and spaghetti. The guys would crowd into cabs and chase up to Harlem—there to continue jamming and drinking at Dickie Wells' on East 136th St., Yeah Man, Smalls' Paradise, Clarence Robinson's, Clam House, Ye Old Nest, Ubangi Club, Breakfast Club, Pod's and Jerry's on West 133d—and other joints where you sometimes had to go down a flight of stone steps into a tenement basement and clamber over a pile of coal. Though Helbock did not play an instrument, he traveled with the boys. When guitarist Eddie Lang, who left Whiteman with Bing Crosby, suddenly died after a tonsillectomy in March, 1933, Helbock drove a carload of the Onyx crowd down to Philadelphia for the funeral.

There were a few outsiders who gained admittance to the inner circle. Such a pair were the W. B. Armstrongs of Orange, New Jersey, whose liquor tabs more than equaled their feeling for the music. Helbock recalls how they suddenly stopped coming and then one night a long-distance call came from Hollywood. It was Armstrong apologizing for their absence and asking a favor: Would the boys jam a bit for him and his wife?

"So I put the receiver down," Helbock noted, "and I asked the boys to play a bit. About an hour later I realized that the phone was off the hook. But there were the Armstrongs listening. It cost him more than drinkin' in my place all night. But I coulda kept the phone off the hook for the rest of the evening so long as the music was going."

*   *   *

With all the homemade entertainment, Helbock had no need to employ musicians. Somebody like Joe Sullivan, Frank Signorelli, Roy Bargy, Milt Raskin, Arthur Schutt, Charlie Bourne, Walter Gross, Willie "the Lion" Smith, or Art Tatum was always noodling at the corner upright. "The great Tatum played the speakeasy as a guest four or five times," Helbock recalls. "Jimmy Dorsey and I used to go up to Harlem to a place called Percey, a second-floor flat, and stay there until eight or nine in the morning. Then we'd drag Art down to the Onyx to play for the boys."

After he had warmed himself with a life-size shot of Prohibition gin—Tatum drank everything in one gulp and never seemed to get drunk—he proceeded to produce the effortless music that won him such accolades as "Tatum—no one can imitatum" and "No one can overratum." Sometime later, when Fats Waller spotted the almost-blind pianist in the audience of the Yacht Club, where he was the featured performer, he announced: "I just play the piano. But God is in the house tonight." Such giants of the classical concert world as Vladimir Horowitz and Sergei Rachmaninoff came to hear Tatum and went away from The Street overwhelmed by his prodigious technique, the fecundity of his invention and the beauty of the harmonic tapestries he wove.

Although Art Tatum worked most clubs on The Street and became one of its most consistent drawing cards, many remember him from his appearances at the Onyx both in its speakeasy days and after Repeal. Tatum was basically an after-hours pianist, a type of musician that, like jam sessions and sitting-in, disappeared with the tightening of union regulations and licensing laws. Tatum's talent was so much a matter of infinite invention—endless variation achieved through decorative fill-ins, dazzling arpeggios and rich chording—that a dusk-to-dawn performance provided the ideal exposure.

With his phenomenal technique and stamina, he was also a man for the cutting contests that once were a regular feature of Harlem and Chicago rent parties. The after-hours scene was a natural setting for dueling, resulting in such apocryphal tales as that of the contest when Tatum bested cocky Bud Powell by playing with his left hand everything that Powell played with his right—and immediately after Powell had completed a sequence.

Coming to New York from his native Toledo, Ohio, in 1932—he

served as accompanist to singer Adelaide Hall—Tatum inevitably gravitated to Harlem. If the Onyx had not been a musicians' hangout, there is some reason to believe that he would not have ventured into midtown. Even there the shading was almost all white, the accepted color of musicians working at CBS (52d and Madison), NBC (711 Fifth), Radio City and in the pits of Broadway theaters.

It was not until sometime in 1933 that Helbock put a steady pianist on his payroll. To Dennis Patrick Terence Joseph O'Sullivan, better known as Joe Sullivan, fell the honor of playing the cocktail hour for pay. But Willie "the Lion" Smith disputes this and claims priority. "The Lion got in the habit," he reports, "of stopping by Helbock's joint and giving the piano a workout once in a while. One day Joe said: 'Lion, why don't you stop by every day around five and I'll give you a little salary for your trouble?' *That deal* [the Lion emphasizes in italics that somehow recall Jelly Roll Morton's *I discovered jazz in 1902*], the engagement of the Lion for the cocktail hour in 1930, was the beginning of 52d St. as 'The Cradle of Swing.' "

The Lion adds: "Helbock's got to be quite a meeting place for famous musicians, especially piano men. . . . There was one guy who used to hang around and mystify everybody, as he was not a professional musician. He was Martin Block, who later became the most famous disc jockey in radio with his *Make-Believe Ballroom* record programs." By the time Sullivan was padding the ivories for a pittance the clientele of the Onyx had widened to include celebrities outside the broadcasting and recording studios—men and women in motion pictures, radio, baseball and the theater. In 1933 Helbock also employed the digital skills of Charlie Bourne, as well as the Lion. Tatum did not attain the status of a paid performer until after Repeal, when he served as intermission pianist on the first "legal" bill.

Tatum went on to become one of The Street's brightest stars, with a following that brought him the highest salary paid to any performer. In the forties he seemed to favor the Three Deuces and the Downbeat. He was in great demand at private parties. Host Sam Weiss of the Onyx recalls taking Tatum to a shindig at George Gershwin's penthouse on 103d and Riverside Drive, where he received a $100 bill for performing during the sixty minutes that were his intermission time at the club.

Occasionally during intermission, Tatum would ask a friend to walk him over to Hanson's drugstore at 51st St. and Seventh Avenue.

Second from left, Phil Moore, and far right, Art Tatum, when he was headlining at the Downbeat.

(His vision was limited to about 25 percent in one eye.) A paperback bookshop now occupies the Hanson corner—it's part of 1650 Broadway, a concentration of music biz concerns. The drugstore was a gathering place, not unlike Schwab's in Hollywood, of theater people, celebrities, and hopefuls. As the Hollywood columnist Sid Skolsky made the Laurel Canyon Schwab's his hangout, so Winchell and other Broadway columnists regularly poked around the 51st St. pharmacy.

Tatum always took a seat at the L-shaped counter, not at the tables in the rear. When the counter was crowded, he would ask someone to drop a handful of coins on the marble top. Then, as people stared in astonishment, he would demonstrate the acuteness of his hearing by identifying each coin on the counter.

With the prodigality that characterized his keyboard pyrotechnics, Tatum lived, drank and died. He frequently stayed awake for days at a time, playing steadily, except for catnaps. He also slept in long stretches, though, according to Harlem tavern keeper Tom Tilghman, he awoke instantly when one of his hands was touched. He was only forty-six when he died of uremic poisoning in 1956. Of 46 pianists queried two years after his death, 30 named Tatum as their favorite pianist. He was one of The Street's legendary giants.

*　　*　　*

When the Onyx opened as a legitimate club on February 4, 1934, it became the pioneer jazz club of 52d and a major launching site for swing. Hoagy Carmichael has not forgotten that he just missed being a co-proprietor. "There was a musicians' speakeasy on 52d St.," he later wrote, "that was a hangout for me and Bix [Beiderbecke], an upstairs smelly place where, if you sat long enough, you could meet all the jazzmen that were around New York, or hunting a job, or passing through. . . . The bartender asked me to put up a thousand clams to help him start a place across the street when Prohibition ended . . . I finally reneged and lost the opportunity of being the co-proprietor. Red McKenzie and the Spirits of Rhythm opened—and The Street was on fire."

The legit Onyx located at No. 72 on the south side, near the corner of Sixth Avenue. On the street level, a few steps down, it had a second floor with rest rooms, and this served as a lounge with an intermission pianist. Large paintings adorned the walls—one of Mildred Bailey, already known as the "Rockin' Chair" lady after the Hoagy Carmichael song that was her theme, and the other of her boss, Paul Whiteman. Pops, as he was nicknamed by Mildred, was a potent figure on the recording-broadcasting scene and one of the few commercial bandleaders who had an ear for virtuoso jazz sidemen. A large number of these were habitués of the Onyx.

The aura then pervading the midtown night scene was still one of Prohibition violence, though the day of peepholes, barricaded doors, warning buzzers and broken-nosed bouncers was over. Texas Guinan was dead, a victim of surgery in the month before Repeal was voted. But her "Hello, sucker!" was still ringing in the night air and only "big butter and egg men," as she termed conspicuous spenders, could enter clubs without worrying about the check. Not all the spots had bloody histories like the Hotsy Totsy, where ten bystanders were eliminated to avoid their possible testimony about a gun battle involving mobster Jack "Legs" Diamond.

The ebullient Guinan spots were backed by the Mob, notably Owney Madden, as were sad-eyed Helen Morgan's hideouts. In fact, no popular speakeasy seemed devoid of hoodlum associations, backing or control, regardless of whether a top performer's name like Club Durant or Club Richman appeared on it. The Onyx had had the good fortune to be an in-group spot—and for some unaccountable reason, the hoods generally let the musical fraternity alone. By the same

Leo Watson, scat singer with the Five Spirits of Rhythm, brought crowds to the Onyx.

Down Beat

token, what the Onyx had going for it as a legitimate club was a built-in clientele.

Just before the Onyx turned legit—Utah put the Repeal Amendment over at 32½ minutes past 3, Mountain Time, on December 5, 1933—Helbock featured a novelty instrumental group called the Five Spirits of Rhythm: three tipples (adolescent guitars that sounded like ukuleles); a paper-wrapped suitcase that served as a drum and was played by Virgil Scroggins with brushes or whisk brooms; and scat singer Leo Watson, who had a whalelike mouth and could vocally produce a trombone sound indistinguishable from the real thing.

A "bit of Harlem" to whites, they represented the high inventiveness of black musicians—the inventiveness of poor blacks who had created the brownie bass out of an overturned metal washtub and a broom handle and who developed jazz out of the unschooled and untrained handling of traditional European brass instruments and marches. The Spirits of Rhythm swung before swing was a commonplace word.

"Once Jack Teagarden gave Leo Watson a trombone," Sam Weiss recalls. Later a successful music publisher, Weiss served without portfolio as a host at the legit Onyx. "Watson mastered the instrument in record time. But he preferred to pretend he was playing one, moving his arms as if he were manipulating a slide. Teagarden—he was Big T because he was a Texan in size and on his instrument—came to listen to Leo. So did Tommy Dorsey, one of the great sliphorn players of all time. Arrangers came to copy his hot licks. Leo was also a great scat singer. You know, the style Satchmo popularized with his record of 'Heebie Jeebies' and Ella Fitzgerald developed as a jazz stylist. Watson introduced a lot of Negro jive talk into pop music.

"52d St. came alive because of the Onyx, and the Onyx began booming after Repeal because of the Spirits of Rhythm," Weiss concludes. "It's interesting that The Street started with an all-black bill. The great Tatum was the intermission pianist. Soon white people could see and hear the top black performers without having to go to Harlem. The Street was a showcase for Negro talent, but it paid less for Negro talent than white. And Negro artists not only started The Street on its way to fame but made it largely what it became."

By the time the Onyx had modulated from a speakeasy into a licensed club, the Spirits were a sextet. The sixth member was Ernest Myers, a bass player whose serious mien contrasted sharply with the rollicking music and comic antics of his colleagues. Myers kept the group together, although it was comparatively short-lived considering the excitement it generated on The Street and on the radio—the *Rudy Vallee Show* and others.

Opening night in February, 1934, Helbock threw a monster bash. Everybody who could blow joined in the spirited all-night jam. But the public was somewhat slow in coming; Helbock's liquor license was delayed. Shortly after the freebooting party of February 9, Tommy Dorsey, who had a sardonic sense of humor, sat around needling Helbock to lower the rope so that the nonexistent crowds could come in. But the public was not long in showing. Soon there was a nightly clamor for Spirits of Rhythm favorites like "My Old Man" and "Dr. Jekyll and Mr. Jive." A takeoff on the Mills Brothers by Wilbur Daniels was also an audience rouser by the Mad Monks of Rhythm, as they came to be called.

"Because they were such good entertainers, the Spirits attracted the squares," said Sam Weiss. "The musicians and jazz critics came to hear Art Tatum. The Spirits were a noisy bunch like the crowds they drew. Tatum had to be heard. That's why when Art went upstairs to the lounge for Charlie Bourne's 'Take Five,' the musical people would crowd the lounge. All the top singers of the day came to hear him— Lee Wiley, Bea Palmer, Mildred Bailey—also longhairs like Leopold Godowsky."

If Tatum and Leo Watson started The Street on its historic jazz journey in '34, it was two cutups, brass men Mike Riley and Ed Farley, who spread its fame far and wide. On the evening of February 28, 1935, however, the music was apparently so hot that after the joint closed, a fire broke out and the club burned to the ground. It was just a year since it had settled at No. 72. The Spirits of Rhythm were forced to seek another location. For a time they worked the Coin de Paris, then came back to The Street at the Famous Door, but failed to generate the jubilation of their Onyx appearance.

The Onyx did not reopen until five months after the conflagration. When it did, on July 23, 1935, guitarist Carl Kress was Helbock's silent moneyman. A five-piece combo structured by William "Red" McKenzie provided the entertainment.

"Red was the singer's singer," Sam Weiss observes. "Lee Wiley was the female counterpart. McKenzie, who came from St. Louis, took Bing's spot in the Whiteman Orchestra when Crosby took off as a single-o with guitarist Eddie Lang. Red originally led that history-making jazz group, Mound City Blue Blowers, singing and playing, of all things, a toy kazoo. For the Onyx reopening, he built a combo around Ed Farley, trumpet, and Mike Riley, trombone, who were cutups as well as good musicians. Red was a much more talented man than others who went much further, and he knew it. He was also a good promoter. But he had a way of alienating people that I could never figure."

In Jack Egan's memory, "1935 was a swinging summer at the Onyx. The cats would drop around after they'd finished their regular chores and sit in with the McKenzie-Riley-Farley combo. The most remarkable case was that of Tommy Dorsey, who was then working at the Glen Island Casino, off Shore Road in New Rochelle. It was a drive, but Tommy made it night after night. I drove that old Buick of his. And I can never forget how he would sit in the car outside the club, listen until he could identify the tune and key, and then go marching in playing his horn. What made him do it? After all, he had just been playing his horn for hours. I guess that sitting-in permitted a certain kind of freedom, a give-and-take between musicians that was absent when they played from charts. And there was something about The Street, something in the atmosphere. I can't find the words. But it was there."

Came the fall and one historic night, if you hark to legend, Riley pretended to have a problem playing his trombone or, perhaps, a battered French horn. Comedy routines were then an adjunct of jazz performances. (Remember those crazy pictures that jazz bands took, with each horn pointed in a different direction, some musicians crouching animal-fashion, others lying on the floor or piano?) Legend has it that a half-drunk dame taken in by the Riley dumb show commented on how difficult it must be to play the instrument.

"No, ma'am, not really," Riley reportedly replied. "You just blow in here." He pointed to the mouthpiece. "You press the middle valve down. And the music goes 'round and around." His fingers followed the coils of the horn. "And it comes out here." He pointed to the instrument's bell. Sidekick Farley was supposedly so amused by the routine that he soon improvised the music for the novelty song that thereafter became internationally famous as "The Music Goes 'Round and Around."

The first record company to sense its potential was the fledgling Decca label, launched by Jack Kapp a year earlier, in August, 1934. With the American economy still in the grip of the world-crippling Depression, Decca's first year had been an edgy one.

"At the office in New York," E. R. Lewis of British Decca (he financed Kapp) later wrote, we had a pleasant enough waiting room. There the unfortunate creditors used to wait. Whilst demanding to see Rackmil, the treasurer, they little knew that he had probably left by the baggage elevator and was lunching with Stevens (another executive) and me at the Hickory House, where in those days you could get a first-class lunch, including London broil, for seventy-five cents, and for eighty-five cents a cocktail was thrown in."

Recording the song with its co-writers gave Decca its first big best seller. The Riley-Farley opus was a "rocking-chair hit"—in the lingo of music business, a song and recording that allowed song pluggers and record salesmen to sit back in their chairs and rock. "It had an astonishing sale for those days," Lewis observes, noting that the record went over the 100,000 mark. And he adds: "Surprisingly, not by Bing Crosby." Der Bingle was the first artist signed by Kapp and did, in fact, become Decca's Elvis Presley. But it was "The Music Goes 'Round" that set the new company on its notable course.

That New Year's Eve, pianist Teddy Wilson was working at the Famous Door. He has not forgotten that on his way home every street drunk he encountered was gargling the song's infectious strain: "Oh-ho-ho . . . Oh-ho-ho . . . and it comes out here." I, too, remember hearing it the same night at every New Year's Eve party and on every corner. It was like an echo that followed you around through the night and into the quiet and deserted streets of New Year's Day, 1936. To the Riley-Farley recording, Barry Ulanov in his *History of Jazz in*

Mike Riley demonstrates his trombone in a music store shortly after "The Music Goes 'Round" became famous at the Onyx.

America attributes the epic accomplishment of "inaugurating modern jazz in general" and, more specifically, the period now known as the swing era.

"The Music Goes 'Round" performed another, if less formidable, function. It first drew the attention of the general public to The Street. As its popularity grew and word of its origin was circulated by the columnists, people began flocking to 52d St. For a period during '35–'36 the Onyx—like the Peppermint Lounge during the twist craze—could not accommodate the hordes that descended on it. So great was the popularity of the song that Riley and Farley were quickly booked into the New York Paramount, rushed out to the Coast, and by February 29, 1936, *The New Yorker* was carrying a review of a new film hastily titled *The Music Goes 'Round*.

"Harry Richman's little valentine," critic John Mosher observed, "to a song that may be described as a pop melody of its period . . . includes a suitable rendering of the celebrated ditty and shows its creators, Messrs. Farley and Riley." Unimpressed by additional tunes created by a trio of songwriters or by a stale plot, Mosher was overwhelmed by the reaction to the Farley-Riley ditty. "The audience actually joins in," he noted, "and sings and sings away when it comes to the title tune."

While the song was still enjoying its notable success, a Chicago songwriter named Red Hodgson began making claims that he was its author-composer. He contended that the two bandsmen had appropriated it when a girl he dispatched to New York auditioned the zany novelty for them. Guitarist Eddie Condon, who was part of the McKenzie-Riley-Farley combo at the Onyx, later gave support to Hodgson's claim. He recalled that a girl had appeared at one of their rehearsals "and began talking about a gag she had heard in Chicago, something called 'The Music Goes 'Round and Around.' She sang it for the boys." And he added: "We played the chordal structure of 'Dinah' for background and Riley tried it out."

But even before Condon's account, one could have noted a curious discrepancy between the label credits on two recordings of the song. Sometime after Eddy Reilly (*sic*) and their Onyx Club Boys recorded the tune for Decca, Tommy Dorsey and his Clambake Seven cut it for Victor. In the time that elapsed between the release of the two discs, the song lost two *a*'s and gained one writer. The Decca label reads: "The Music Goes Around and Around (Reilly-Farley)" while the

Victor label credits: "The Music Goes 'Round and 'Round (Hodgson-Farley-Riley)." Since then, Hodgson's name has appeared on all sheets and recordings of the song, whose accepted title is "The Music Goes 'Round and Around."

It is now known that the song was, in fact, devised by Red Hodgson when he was playing trumpet in Ernie Palmquist's band on the Pacific Coast. The year was 1931, and it was then called the "Orange Song" because Hodgson not only graphically described the movement of sound through a horn but ate an orange at the same time. He was still performing the novelty tune as his specialty when he joined Earl Burtnett's band in Chicago. Vocalist Ruth Lee brought the song from Chicago to Riley and Farley at the Onyx.

Among other effects, "The Music Goes 'Round and Around" broke up the McKenzie band. One night Riley had guitarist Eddie Condon fired for openly displaying his disdain for the duo's antics. Red McKenzie thereupon took a walk. To play jazz, Red and Eddie joined trombonist George Brunies at the Famous Door. By then the Onyx combo had turned into a comedy vaudeville act. Everybody squirted seltzer at everybody or tried to tear their clothes off. They even resorted to pie throwing, with trumpeter Manny Klein, the busy radio musician, supplying lemon meringues.

Glen Gray and the Casa Loma Band were appearing at the New York Paramount Theater when the Riley-Farley song became the talk of music business. A visit to the Onyx convinced Gray that he should add it to his show. Being an ethical man, he called upon songwriter Sammy Cahn to write some special material making it clear that he first heard "The Music Goes 'Round" on 52d St. Within days, Cahn had another and more involved request from Gray. The managing director of Paramount had also visited the Onyx and decided to bring Riley and Farley in as an extra added attraction. Gray was worried that once the duo did the song on stage, the Casa Loma Band would fade into the scenic flats.

"There was good reason for his concern," says Sammy Cahn, whose Academy Award songs include "Call Me Irresponsible," "All the Way" and "High Hopes." "That song was dynamite. Riley and Farley were bound to take the play away from Casa Loma, just as years later a kid called Sinatra took the play away from the Goodman band, and on the same stage! I couldn't sleep trying to figure a gimmick that would save the day for Glen. I was worrying myself sick until I happened to walk into an instrument store on 48th St. to see a friend, Chubby Goldfarb, who later became a top manager. When I left, I had the idea that I knew would do in Riley and Farley.

"The following day I received a call from Glen Gray. 'The New York Band Instrument Company just delivered a Tally-Ho horn to us,' he reported. 'What's it about?' I told him: 'That's gonna be your answer to Riley and Farley,' and it was. The piece of business I devised yielded one of the great memories of show business for me.

"Here's what we did. When Riley and Farley finished their song and the audience shouted for "More!" Glen would ask the audience: 'How about having our Pee Wee Hunt do a chorus?' As the audience applauded, Pee Wee came down from his chair to the apron of the stage. Just as he started to sing, he would pick up the Tally-Ho horn, which was lying out of sight. You know, this is a long, straight horn, without valves, that royal pages once used for blowing fanfares.

"The band began playing the song in minor and Pee Wee would sing: 'I blow in here . . . But the music can't go 'round . . . Who-who-who, Who-who-who . . . Who made this horn?' The next verse went: 'There are no valves to push down . . . And the music can't go 'round . . . Why-why-why, Why-why-why . . . Why was I born. . . .' Well, if you think that Riley and Farley wowed the audience! Pee Wee stopped the show—absolutely stopped it. He had to do a repeat and he always went off with the audience screaming for more. Casa Loma did not have to take a back seat to Riley and Farley."

But as the zany duo left for the Coast to appear in the film named after the song, the Onyx faced the same troubling question as Glen Gray. Who could top their drawing power or at least attract a large enough audience to keep attendance up?

Owner Helbock was keenly aware that once Repeal had eliminated the great allure of the speakeasy—the chance to buy an illegal drink—entertainment was the only key to a successful nightclub operation.

Tape 4 . . . "THE ONYX CLUB REVIEW"

The word "underground" was not used in those days. But records were occasionally made and circulated among musicians and their friends. Trumpeter Manny Klein, one of the most active New York studio men in the early thirties, and equally busy on the Coast since then, has one of the few copies extant of "The Onyx Club Review."

"We were trying to cut this corny waltz," Manny recalls. "Sometime around 1931. The musicians were top men: Tommy Dorsey, Jimmy, Artie Schutt at piano, Charlie Margulies and myself on trumpets, Joe Venuti fiddling—and Victor Young conducting one of his fine arrangements.

"It was a simple song. But we wasted one master after another. In those days, there was no tape and no splicing. If someone made a boo-boo, it blew the master and we had to start all over again. We kept blowing them. Finally, Victor said, 'Let's play it through. Play the worst you can. And let's get all those clinkers out of our systems.'

"And so we started with an off-key fanfare. Young announced: 'The Onyx Club Review.' And we played it flat as first-grade students. Will Osborne improvised some lyrics and sang like Rudy Vallee with a cold in his nose: 'Have a little drink on me, my boy. . . .' Someone let out a belch. 'At the Onyx Club with me, my boy. . . .' Another belch. Brunswick made copies for all the boys. It wasn't really a review, but it gave us a laugh."

Sam Weiss: "Big instruments—I'm not talking about those you play—were a big thing in those days. Wilbur Daniels of the Spirits of Rhythm was a very handsome man with a rep for having a really long tool. But so did Joe Venuti, who was a short man. Well, one night at the Onyx, Ben Bernie began gabbing about Daniels' equipment. Paul Whiteman, who was at a nearby table—all the tables were nearby— got into the conversation. And soon they had a bet going. When they saw Daniels heading for the men's room, they took after him. Nobody said anything to him. They just looked. Afterward, Whiteman turned to Ben Bernie and paid off without a word."

*   *   *

Manny Klein: "There were a lot of cathouses on The Street. One evening, when Pops was feeling no pain, one of the boys began talking about the 'beautiful cats' in the house across the street. He hadn't been on the subject very long when Whiteman stood up and invited everybody to go as his guest. About twenty guys didn't need a second invitation. The Onyx emptied in no time flat. Those girls didn't know what hit them when we came charging in. And Pops, like the big shot in a Western movie buying drinks for the boys, shelled out the green for everybody."

Gordon Jenkins: "I was just twenty-three when I arrived in New York from St. Louis. I soon found my way to the Onyx. And before long, I was a steady habitué, to use Johnny Mercer's felicitous phrase. It was awe-inspiring being in a place that had such an aura of New York and moving among names that looked so big to me then—name musicians I had heard about. But everybody was friendly. During an evening, you'd buy the band a round. They'd buy one for you. Then the house would pour for everybody. I've never had that feeling of camaraderie again.

"My great thrill was the Spirits of Rhythm. I got such a kick out of them, I went there night after night. Leo Watson was an amazing performer and singer. Well, once when I was giving a cocktail party, I splurged and hired the group. I was living in Jackson Heights, Queens. They arrived an hour or so before starting time and immediately began warming up. I was so excited about having them to myself, I didn't wait for the guests to arrive. I began serving food and keeping their glasses filled. Of course, I was sampling the stuff myself. In fact, I sampled so much that I can't remember a thing about the party. I don't know who came or what happened. All I do know and remember, with a great feeling of warmth, is that I had the Spirits of Rhythm to myself for part of an afternoon.

"One night, as I was heading for the Onyx, a cat from my hometown, St. Louis, walked in. I figured he'd prize the chance of meeting New York musicians and I took him along. The bandstand was pretty crowded when we arrived, with some top guys sitting in. You'd think that my St. Louis pal would be impressed by the caliber and prominence of the cats. But, oh, no. In fact, he was soon putting some of the guys down.

"Not even the presence of Red McKenzie, who joined us, stymied my friend. He continued rapping the guys. Finally, Red couldn't take it: 'He's such a smart ass,' he said. 'Why don't you let him blow a little?' Eagerly, I followed Red's lead: 'I'd sure like to hear him play.' With that, my pal suggested that we go to his hotel so that he could pick up his horn. The moment we returned, he got up on the bandstand. If we expected him to fall on his prat, we were in for a shock. He played the greatest tenor sax you could imagine. When he started going, the other cats almost dropped their saxes. By the time he got off the stand everybody was asking about him, and several contractors wanted his phone number. You could make your reputation that fast in those days—if you were good enough. And Forrest Crawford did. The name probably won't mean anything to anybody because he flew in and out of the music scene pretty fast. But no musician who was in the Onyx that night has forgotten it."

Tape 5 . . . JOHNNY MERCER

In 1946 John H. Mercer, born in Savannah, Georgia, won an Oscar for his lyric to Harry Warren's tune, "On the Atchison, Topeka and Santa Fe." He has since won three additional Academy awards for his lyrics to "In the Cool, Cool, Cool of the Evening" (music by Hoagy Carmichael), "Moon River" (music by Henry Mancini), and "Days of Wine and Roses" (music by Henry Mancini). Possessing one of the largest catalogs of hit songs, Johnny has also been a record executive, composer and hit singer.

"The first time I visited 52d St.," he recalls, "I went to the Onyx. My impression is that it was with Jerry Colonna, who was then a trombonist. I had met him and his wife through Dick McDonough, who played guitar with Red Nichols and liked to share his friends with me. I was a young singer with the Paul Whiteman band, about twenty-two years old. About all I remember from that visit is that I met Artie Shaw.

"About six months later, or maybe a year, the Onyx was across The Street. And that's where I really began to come around quite often. I was working with Whiteman at the Biltmore Roof. We played from seven to nine and again from eleven to two. Usually in the two off-hours, between nine and eleven, we'd go over to the Onyx en masse. My wife and I were young marrieds, and we'd sometimes spend those two hours hopefully wishing that somebody would buy us a drink. That's how I met Joe Helbock, also his partner, who was a dignified man with glasses and looked like Otto Harbach or Tommy Dorsey. That's when I heard the Spirits of Rhythm and Stuff Smith and his group.

"When Gordon Jenkins came to New York, he was an arranger for Isham Jones. A most gifted musician, he understood much more serious music than most of the guys did and had a great feeling for jazz. But he was really a country bumpkin about a big city. Champagne and things like that were brand-new experiences. He had one meal that he seemed to eat constantly—boiled beef with thick, brown gravy and mashed potatoes, and he'd pour ketchup all over it. The city really went to his head. You can hear it in *Manhattan Tower.* And he wore tails and began drinking cocktails. He was the cutest guy, a good friend, and a fine composer. We wrote 'P.S. I Love You' together.

"That same year I wrote 'Pardon My Southern Accent.' It was 1934 probably, and there was much more magnolia in my speech than you hear now. Matty Malneck, who played fiddle with Whiteman, did the music. We also did 'Goody-Goody,' which Benny Goodman recorded, and 'Eeny Meeny Miny Mo,' which I introduced in the film *To Beat the Band* and recorded with Ginger Rogers. Fred Astaire introduced 'Eeny Meeny' on the air. Most people don't realize that Fred was a rather good songwriter and that he wrote the music of a number of big songs. In this period I wrote 'I'm Building Up to an Awful Letdown' with him.

"Gordy and I always met at the Onyx, where I also frequently spent time with Bernie Hanighen. Wrote 'My Old Man' with Bernie. I wish he hadn't quit writing. The middle part of 'My Old Man' is written around a riff developed by the Spirits of Rhythm. I think that ' 'Tis Autumn' was written the same way. A lot of tunes were built on riffs that jazz bands and soloists of those days improvised. I think Bernie built 'Man' on Leo Watson's style of singing. The words just went along.

"Hanging around the Onyx, I met one of my closest friends. Frank Cavett was then an assistant director at Paramount out on Long Island. Later he came out here to Hollywood and wrote 'Going My Way' and some other things for Cecil B. De Mille. He put one of the things I wrote with Bernie in a movie. That bit of business was transacted at the Onyx.

"The Onyx was pleasure and it was business and it was music. For laughs we went to Club 18. I remember Marlene Dietrich was there one night, wearing a great big floppy hat. Jack White came up with some putdown like: 'Doesn't that look like an old Caruso record?' Everybody got into the act, including the two waiters and even the colored boy in the men's room. The gags were as funny and came as fast as in *Laugh-In* today. Jack White indulged in slapstick. But he was the kind of comic who attracted people like Dashiell Hammett, the great detective writer of *The Maltese Falcon* and *The Thin Man.* People—and drunks—of intelligence like that. One of the waiters

used to call himself Dr. Frisbee Donegal. He looked a bit like Durante
—had a great big nose. He'd come out with a Band-Aid on his face.
The other waiter, a fat little guy, would yank the Band-Aid off, and as
Donegal was screaming with mock pain, he'd say: 'Well, let's see what
number won the turkey.' They were wild.

"I loved Jimmy Ryan's simply because of Jimmy. As a lyric writer,
how could I help liking him. Jimmy could quote the verses of hundreds of songs, verses that I'm sure the lyric writers had themselves
forgotten. He was one of the few guys who had a real feeling for
Dixieland jazz, and he held out for it long after many cats considered
it old hat.

"By the time I got to Whiteman it was '32–'33. Paul held a series of
contests called 'Pontiac Youth of America.' I won the one held in
New York, which entitled me to sing on one of his weekly radio
programs. That's when I first met Mildred Bailey and Red Norvo.
They could see that I was scared to death, and they both went out of
their way to boost my confidence. About a year later, Whiteman hired
me as a band vocalist. I got to know the Rockin' Chair Lady and Red
pretty well. Theirs was a great musical partnership. Their marriage
had its funny and sad moments.

"Almost everybody you knew in the entertainment field gravitated
in those days to 52d. That's where you found all the new attractions.
That's where you first heard Frances Faye and the new people coming up.

"My introduction to Billie Holiday was through Dick McDonough.
One day he said to me: 'There's this melody of mine. I call it 'Riffin'
the Scotch.' This girl's gonna sing it and I need a lyric fast.' Well, I
went home and wrote a lyric I called 'I Jumped Out of the Frying Pan
and into the Fire.' When I met Billie, in 1933, she was quite a pretty
girl. But there was something about her—not just the torchy quality
of her voice—that made you want to try to help her. 'Out of the
Frying Pan' was one of her first records. Benny Goodman and his
orchestra—it was not his big swing band—got top billing. Billie was
credited with the vocal. It was not a hit.

"I saw Billie occasionally after that. Colored people didn't really
come down to 52d as customers. They came as entertainers. White
musicians went up to Harlem as customers. The line of demarcation
was not yet abolished, as it is now, where everybody goes everywhere.
Fifty-second Street was then mostly for the white, young musicians,

though the clubs did present colored entertainers. But if you wanted to hear Ellington or Fletcher Henderson, you had to go up to Harlem after hours. It was safe and it was fun. Everybody'd have a few drinks and go home. Then Harlem got dangerous—and the entertainers moved downtown. Or they moved and then it got dangerous.

"Now The Street is so changed. There are lots of great, glistening buildings, and it's so clean. In the old days, particularly on warm nights when the clubs had to keep their doors open, you'd hear one band, and after a few feet, another. It was a crazy quilt of sounds.

"For somebody of my age, there was and is no other neighborhood like The Street. For the kids of today, probably the pubs on Second and Third avenues are the equivalent. Fifty-second was the focal point of jazz for the influential musicians of the time. When they weren't playing, they wanted to listen. That was their idea of fun, especially with guys that shared their enthusiasm. They liked to meet every new guy who came into town and might be more proficient on their instrument, say, like Peck Kelley, the legendary pianist from Texas—he never showed, of course—or Albert Ammons or Meade Lux Lewis with a fresh-sounding style. And the great names and the new all came to The Street. . . ."

5. Stuff and Swing

In November, 1936, FDR swept the nation for a second term with a landslide electoral vote. The following month Edward VIII renounced the British throne for "the woman I love" in a worldwide broadcast, later released on Brunswick Records. And at the beginning of '36 a Buffalo fiddler named Hezekiah Leroy Gordon Smith opened at the Onyx and once again made jazz history for the club and The Street.

Stuff Smith, to give him the handle by which he is known, was an unorthodox violinist, whose quintet included two other virtuoso performers: Jonah Jones (in a derby) on trumpet and, shortly after the opening, Cozy Cole on drums. Born in Ohio in 1909 and reared in Cleveland, Stuff had taken fire from the jazz fiddling of Joe Venuti, first of a rare breed that included the great Eddie South. Working with a microphone hidden under his fiddle (in the lapel of his jacket), he produced jazz that struck many as tough barrelhouse rather than lilting swing. In addition to his assets as a musician, Stuff was a talented songwriter and a natural clown who reminded one of Fats Waller. Instead of wearing a cocked derby as Fats did, Smith appeared in a battered black stovepipe that rested rakishly on the back of his head.

Convinced of Smith's skill as a fiddler but uncertain of how the public would react, Helbock limited table reservations for the opening on February 3 to musicians. To dress up the occasion, he imported Paul Douglas, then a prominent radio announcer and jazz buff, as master of ceremonies. Helbock's intuitions were sound. Smith was an absolute sensation to the in crowd. The word of mouth spread. And the SRO rope went up.

Manager Willard Alexander has a vivid memory of the occasion. Before he began managing bands—Goodman and Basie, among others—Alexander was a violinist. He had been mesmerized by the fiddling of Joe Venuti in the Whiteman band. But when he heard Stuff, he was, in his words, "completely swept away. I was really shaken up by what that man could do with four strings and the same horsehair bow that I once dragged across those strings."

Songwriter-pianist Hoagy Carmichael was also left with an unfor-

Down Beat

Stuff Smith's Gang pose in 1936, after their stint at the Onyx made them famous.

gettable memory: "When Stuff got the feeling, he would change his fiddle bow to an inverted position so that he could saw all four strings at once. Then he'd start pumping four beats to the measure while Jonah and the others did their work. One chorus would lead to another. It was a welling thing that led to pandemonium and a breaking point at about the fifteenth chorus. A brainwashing delight!"

When it came to the public, Stuff had other strings to his bow. As with Farley and Riley, it was a song—several, in fact—that brought him national renown and helped make sellouts of his club appearances. In the month of his Onyx debut, he recorded a nonsense novelty. His own "I'se a Muggin' " at first went over bigger in the club than on a Vocalion record. It seemed to require the visual pantomime of which Smith was a master. But as the popularity of the number grew in the club, Vocalion was moved to rerecord it. The second version, with Cozy Cole instead of Johnny Washington on the hides, did better.

But by then another novelty number written by Smith had taken off on a Vocalion disc. "You'se a Viper" boasted a rare vocal by trumpeter Jonah Jones. To hear both of these performed by the writer-originator, crowds once again crammed the club. They came also to watch Stuff and Jonah in a hilarious version of "Truckin'," a song and dance introduced at the Cotton Club. ("You'se a Viper" was in the same tradition as Cab Calloway's '34 hit, "Reefer Man." A viper was a marijuana smoker. But as a result of Stuff's song and the use of the expression in a comic strip of the day, it came to have a broader and rather humorous connotation.)

New York's summer heat did not interfere with business at the Onyx. But Stuff had a complaint. On the basis of his representations to the Musicians Union, Local 802 filed a complaint against a booker-manager of Consolidated Radio Artists charging that he took excessive commissions from Smith. This was a problem that troubled many black artists, though not all were ready to take the offensive as Stuff did.

Stuff also raised his voice in at least one less acceptable situation. In October, '36, Helbock booked Billie Holiday. Although she had bombed in her first appearance on The Street a year earlier at the Famous Door, now Lady Day seemed a winner. Stuff started by complaining that she was on too long and insisted that she do no encores. Shortly after a rave appeared in one of the columns, he went to

Helbock and demanded that she be fired. He was then in the third month of a new six months' deal negotiated by Helbock because, as *Down Beat* pointed out, during the summer slump of '36, the hot fiddler "had doubled his earlier attendance record and was well on the way to breaking the Riley-Farley record made during the previous Christmas season." Although Helbock liked Lady Day's work, he had little alternative. She was still an in-group stylist with a dedicated but small following. And so Billie had to swallow a second defeat on The Street, this one made more bitter because it was the result of her growing acceptance.

Into 1937 Stuff continued to be solid box office. But by April, when the Onyx had moved from No. 72 to larger quarters at No. 62, *The New Yorker* opined that "Stuff and the boys are getting a little arty and smirking, and should be slapped down." However, Louis Sobol in the New York *Journal-American* felt that Stuff caused "pulchritudinous young women to let their hair down, as they rose from their tables, to the consternation of sedate escorts, and plunge into wild, uninhibited dances."

After recording the "Onyx Club Spree" on Decca in May, Stuff left for Hollywood to appear in a Walter Wanger movie *52nd Street,* which fared little better than the Riley-Farley film. Some reviewers characterized it as a "fair to middling musical" while the more critical suggested that it was "neither good musically nor good narrative but a spottily diverting hodgepodge."

While Stuff occupied the Onyx bandstand, the club sponsored an off-52d St. concert that was the brainchild of an enterprising song plugger, Charlie Ross. On Sunday evening, May 24, 1936, it presented at the Imperial Theater what was described as "New York's first . . . Swing Music Concert." Now, the Benny Goodman band had already broken through at the Palladium Ballroom in Los Angeles (August, '35) and he had been dubbed the King of Swing during a subsequent eight-month stand at the Congress Hotel in Chicago. But swing was still an enigmatic concept, as articles by the editor of *Variety* and Paul Whiteman in the concert's silver-covered souvenir program made clear.

Editor Abel Green offered explanations by four top musicians to demonstrate that "none seem able to define just what it is." Mike Riley said: "It's jam, but arranged." Red McKenzie said: "It's an

evolution of Dixie. It's carefully conceived improvisation." Red Norvo
said: "It's not just the old-style jazz. . . ." And Wingy Manone said:
"It's a livelier tempo; you know, it's swingy like."

Whether or not the concert clarified the audience's understanding,
it was an exciting assemblage of the day's top jazz artists and groups.
Opening with Joe Venuti's fourteen-piece band, it closed with Glen
Gray's Casa Loma Band, both typical swing aggregations. But the
bulk of the program consisted of strange combos like a guitar duo
made up of Carl Kress and Dick McDonough; a saxophone sextette
led by Frank Chase; and Artie Shaw's String Swing Ensemble, a string
quartet with added drums, guitar and clarinet.

The largest number of groups were small combos playing what
might be described as Dixieland or New Orleans jazz. The instrumentation of three groups was close to the traditional front line,
clarinet, trumpet, trombone, and rhythm: Louis Armstrong and
Band, Original Memphis Five, and Red Nichols and his Five Pennies.
A group sent by Paul Whiteman followed this instrumentation, except
that it also included two saxophones. Other groups that played freewheeling, two-beat Dixie but with variant ensembles were: Wingy
Manone and his New Orleans Jam Band, Bob Crosby and his Or-
chestra, Bunny Berigan and his Swing Gang (courtesy of Club 18),
Tommy Dorsey and his Clambake Seven, Adrian Rollini and his Tap
Room Gang, Red Norvo and his Swingtette (guest star, Mildred
Bailey), and Stuff Smith and his Onyx Club Band.

Jazz historian Charles Edward Smith thought that Red Norvo
"saved this pretentious concert . . . from ignominy." But the sur-
prise hit of the shindig was Artie Shaw and his String Swing Ensemble.
The audience was so enthusiastic that the group had to play an encore
—and all it could do was repeat "Interlude in B Flat," composed by
Shaw for the occasion. It was the only piece the *ad hoc* group knew.
Until then, Shaw had been merely a busy studio sideman. (The later
rivalry between Shaw and Goodman may have had its inception in Al
Goodman's band when the two occupied chairs in the reed section.)
By the time Artie left the platform, agents were backstage waving
contracts at him. Several months later, he was fronting the first of his
big bands in Manhattan's Hotel Lexington.

No one remembers who actually appeared at the long, long concert.
Not even the three radio celebrities who acted as masters of ceremonies: Ben Grauer, courtesy of NBC; Budd Hulick, courtesy of

Colonel Stoopnagle, his partner in one of the day's most popular comedy teams; or Paul Douglas, courtesy of CBS and then announcer of the pioneer radio jazz program, *Saturday Night Swing Club.* But in "Oh, Say Can You Swing," a piece Douglas later wrote in defense of the new jazz, he recalled the concert in these words: "If they had let one more person into the Imperial Theater that Sunday night of May in 1936, he would have found himself in my lap, for there wasn't another unoccupied inch in the house. They were crowding the orchestra pit, jamming the aisles, and swarming twenty-deep in the back. I was nervous as I walked out on the stage. . . . As the house grew still and sat up expectantly, I took my prepared speech from my pocket, hung it over my finger, and set it in motion with a push. The spotlight caught the speech; a white toy, doll's swing, rocking through the air. Swinging. A couple of thousand eyes focused on it, and the roar that went up told me that my message had been received and that New York's first swing concert was under way."

Douglas concluded his 1938 verbal toast to swing by taking issue with the wishful thinkers who were then announcing its death. (Shades of today's premature pallbearers of rock!) "If swing is dead," he wrote, "every college campus is a morgue, and its respective pallbearers, the Dorseys, Goodman, Bob Crosby, Raymond Scott and Duke Ellington, will gross a couple of million dollars this year for attending the wake."

Sam Weiss, who handled the tickets, confirms that the concert was an absolute sellout. Weiss remembers that composer-arranger Gordon Jenkins sat in the front row with his feet on the rail over the orchestra pit. And Jenkins has a happy memory of an "evening when you felt that things were happening. It was like the beginning of an era, and the swing era did begin about that time." Excitement ran so high that no one left the theater until the Casa Loma Band had sounded its last big, brassy chord. It was two and a half hours after the curtains had gone down in all the other Broadway theaters. The crowd pouring out on dark 45th St. was a harbinger of the college-age hordes that were soon jamming ballrooms around the country.

Despite the attendance, the concert was apparently a financial bust, due to fees demanded by the Musicians Union for the long list of performers. But it was an historic occasion for both the Onyx and The Street. Neither then nor later did the club present any of the era's name bands. It did, however, introduce many of the swingiest combos, and it did help to sell the new style through the showmanship of its performers. It earned the sobriquet The Cradle of Swing and contributed mightily to The Street's recognition as Swing Lane or Swing Street. Actually, fewer than half a dozen of the day's big bands appeared on The Street: The bandstands of the brownstones and the cramped confines of the tiny clubs were hardly made for the blast and blare of fifteen instrumentalists. Fifty-second Street was more hospitable to the subtle swing of small combos like Red Norvo, Bunny Berigan and John Kirby—and there was enough Dixieland being played so that The Street bounced with the beat. It was at this time (1936) that editor Abel Green of *Variety* announced: "West 52nd Street, New York, is the capital of the swing world. The addicts sit around entranced, in an ultramodern jazz coma, as the boys cut their didoes at the Onyx Club, the Famous Door and the Hickory House."

While Stuff fiddled at the Onyx, Louis Prima was playing pretty for the people at the Famous Door, and Wingy Manone, his New Orleans *landsman,* was flying them to the "Isle of Capri" via the Hickory House. With the coming of spring, New Yorkers also began barreling to suburban spots like the Riviera at the New Jersey end of the George Washington Bridge, where they danced to the Latin-inflected swing of Enric Madriguera; to Ben Riley's Arrowhead Inn at Riverdale Avenue and 246th St., where Irving Conn's Orchestra held forth; and to Glen Island Casino, off Shore Road at New Rochelle, where Charlie Barnet opened on Memorial Day. And if they just wanted ocean breezes and fresh seafood, there was a deluxe shore dinner at Lundy's in Sheepshead Bay to be had for $2.75. For those who stayed in town weekends and were looking for a pickup, liquid and sociable, there was the newly opened bar in the Hotel Astor— gone in 1969—at Broadway and 44th St.

In the year that George Gershwin died of a brain tumor and John Ford's *The Hurricane* stirred up a tidal wave of South Sea escapism in song and films, the Onyx had a new hit song and record, also star, to bring crowds to its door. By then its walls were a dark blue and it had moved "just five drinks to the east of the old spot," as Jack Egan put it in his *Down Beat* column. Opening night in April, '37, brought out the faithfuls of the music scene, also "vivacious Yvonne King, carrying a box of Kleenex—cold or no cold, Onyx openings must be attended."

John Kirby with Leo Watson and his Spirits of Rhythm at the Onyx in 1937. Left to right, Billy Kyle (piano), Charlie Shavers (trumpet), John Kirby (bass), Pete Brown (alto sax), Leo Watson (at mike), O'Neil Spencer (drums), Buster Bailey (clarinet).

Stuff was still the main attraction, working in front of a giant-size Charles Peterson candid of himself and Jonah Jones. Within a month, however, he was on the way to the Coast for the filming of *52nd Street*. To take Smith's place, Helbock installed a group whose leadership was in question for several months. As late as July, 1937, when the club permitted dancing for the first time in the late hours—how did they manage on the napkin-sized floor?—an advertisement read: "The Onyx—Cradle of Swing—presents John Kirby with Leo and his Spirits of Rhythm featuring Buster Bailey & Frank Newton."

Although many credited Fletcher Henderson's ex-bassist, John Kirby, with forming the group—from a unit playing the Brittwood on Harlem's Lenox Avenue—*Down Beat*'s John Hammond identified Leo Watson as the leader. However, Hammond also described Watson, who had only recently taken up drums, as "the band's only musical liability . . . he gets in everybody's way." He recommended that Big Sid Catlett be sought as a replacement; but it was the Spirits' original drummer, O'Neil Spencer, who soon took over. Business remained just so-so even after members of the band tried to hype it with a record. Led by Frankie Newton, the Uptown Serenaders, as they called themselves, recorded an original Newton instrumental. "The Onyx Hop," released by Variety Records, was not too interesting in itself nor did it stir interest in the club.

It looked like a cold summer for the Onyx until Helbock hired a Pittsburgh vocalist named Marietta Williams as his intermission act. Marietta appeared under the name Maxine Williams. But after she made a recording under the aegis of Claude Thornhill, that was changed.

Two of Miss Williams' most popular numbers were "Brown Bird" and "Trees," a well-known setting of Joyce Kilmer's poem. She did both of these with a swinging lilt. Some of the big bands were then beginning to swing the classics. When Thornhill caught her, at the urging of Ina Ray Hutton's pianist, who had heard her in Pittsburgh, he hit on the idea of having her swing two Scottish folk ballads. The seven-piece group with which Maxine Williams recorded "Annie Laurie" and "Loch Lomond" was a combination of Frankie Newton's and Claude Thornhill's band. But the Vocalion disc carried the credit line "Maxine Sullivan and Her Orchestra." And so Maxine Williams, born Marietta Williams, became Maxine Sullivan—a proper name for a singer of a Scottish song—and brought new fame to the Onyx.

By the fall of '37 it was Maxine Sullivan *and* John Kirby who were the sensation at the club. Rumor has it that Frankie Newton was briefly part of a triangle. His chair at the Onyx was soon filled by Charlie Shavers, and shortly thereafter, Maxine became Mrs. John Kirby. It was a happy marriage musically and domestically from '37 into '41, and at the Onyx into the spring of '38. Even before they left the club, they became co-stars of an NBC network show with a wee reminder of her Scottish hit. The program was called *Flow Gently, Sweet Rhythm*.

"Loch Lomond" also brought controversy into Maxine Sullivan's life. In April '38 Ella Logan charged in a front-page *Down Beat* story, MAXINE COPIED ME! Miss Logan contended that she was the first to swing old songs and waxed furious that the record companies had, by their action in recording Miss Sullivan, conveyed the impression that she was the originator of the concept. Some months later, Miss Sullivan, who is an unusually frank and unpretentious person, observed that she had never claimed to have originated the idea of popularizing Scottish ballads and denied that she was a swing vocalist.

"The characteristics which I consider most important in singing,"

John Kirby's great Onyx Sextet, here on the *Duffy's Tavern* radio show. Left to right, O'Neil Spencer, Buster Bailey, Charlie Shavers, John Kirby (behind bar), Billy Kyle, Russell Procope.

she told *Down Beat,* "are the way in which I hit notes—softly and without effort; a relaxed feeling at all times; and a feeling for what I am singing. Most of all, I like to take sad numbers with a simple melody, changing the notes to fit the soft, straight manner—strict tempo vocalizing and without jive."

The controversy about swinging the classics spread beyond Miss Logan and Miss Sullivan, though "Loch Lomond" probably was the catalyst. Even before Ella Logan made her charge, Station WJR of Detroit cut Tommy Dorsey off the air in the middle of a swing rendition of the Scottish ballad. Two days later, WGAR of Cleveland and KMPC of Beverly Hills announced a ban on swing versions of all old-time tunes. The former offered a list of the songs that could not be swung: "Comin' Through the Rye," "Annie Laurie," "Love's Old Sweet Song," "I Love You Truly," "Darling Nellie Gray," "Drink to Me Only with Thine Eyes," "Last Rose of Summer," "Juanita," "Sweet Genevieve," Brahms' "Lullaby," and "Loch Lomond." WNEW of New York and WTMJ of Milwaukee countered that the public should "get what it wants."

John Kirby, whose renown grew with Maxine Sullivan's, was a

youthful but serious-looking man. He had an unhappy face or, at least, a tense one. The music of his sextet was neither. It was in spirit and style like the white tails in which they performed—and it swung. To jazz *aficionados,* the Kirby Sextet—Russell Procope (alto), Buster Bailey (clarinet), Charlie Shavers (trumpet), O'Neil Spencer (drums), Billy Kyle (piano) and Kirby (bass)—came to represent the acme of small-band precision. More disciplined than The Street's freewheeling Dixieland combos, its lead choir (clarinet, alto, trumpet) produced a light-textured, less raucous and less contrapuntal type of jazz. Kirby's thin-sounding bass contributed lilt rather than drive. And though it was just a sextet, it worked with deft arrangements devised by trumpeter Charlie Shavers, a major figure after '42 in the Tommy Dorsey band. Kirby, whose outlook had been shaped by the discipline of working with Fletcher Henderson and Chick Webb, was a demanding leader. His sextet had the polish and precision of a trio or quartet like the Benny Goodman small combos. Two of the sextet's most popular numbers were composed by Shavers: "Pastel Blue" and "Undecided," the latter a hit in a lyric version recorded in the fifties by the Ames Brothers and Les Brown.

Lionel Hampton liked to sit in with the Kirby group. Most of their arrangements were really too tailored to invite slambang improvisation. But Hampton, who was playing vibraphone with Benny Goodman at the Pennsylvania, would come uptown after an evening's work and get behind the drums. "He loved to beat the hides," Jack Egan, Onyx p.a., recalls, "and this was a chance to talk it over with a group whose jazz spoke to him."

During much of 1938 the Onyx was able to maintain its box office with the help of Mr. and Mrs. Kirby. Stuff Smith returned from the Coast to demonstrate that he still had a following on 52d St. But his May booking did not save him from going bankrupt the following month. When Maxine headed for Hollywood and a film appearance, the Onyx found a sub in Thelma Carpenter, the winner of an amateur-night contest at the Apollo. She was just sixteen and had attained her full height of 4 feet 11½ .

"That was the greatest experience I could get anywhere," Miss Carpenter said recently. "A little later John Hammond discovered me and put me with Teddy Wilson's band at the Famous Door. Between sets I could go hear Lee Wiley at the Onyx—man, she was pure honey!—or Mabel Mercer at Tony's, and there were a half dozen others at clubs all within walking distance. You just can't get that kind of musical education anymore."

When Coleman Hawkins, the legendary tenor saxist, returned from Europe after a five-year stay and formed a band, Miss Carpenter became the vocalist. For two years after that, she was on the road with Count Basie. Then came her East Side period. Looking back, she says: "I got too chichi for my own good. I had diamonds on and furs, and only people with diamonds and furs could appreciate me." Her comeback began in 1968 when she became Pearl Bailey's understudy in *Hello, Dolly* and played the title role more than one hundred times. Now active on many fronts, she reminds one in her petite compactness of Maxine Sullivan, whom she succeeded at the Onyx in 1938 and who is also enjoying a resurgence. Outstanding in her interpretation of Ethel Waters' songs, Miss Carpenter is more of a supper club singer than the swinging Miss Loch Lomond.

In September, 1938, a gossip column carried a blind item: "One of the first inhabitants of 52d St. left his silent partner holding the bills when he skipped with the bankroll this month." It was not accurate. But there had been a hassle between Helbock and guitarist Carl Kress, his silent partner. Kress was left with the ownership of the club.

Helbock tried to find a new spot for himself. He fought Kress and others in the courts in a vain effort to regain control of the Onyx name. In June, 1939, having lost a court test, he opened a spot on the site of the old Club 18. Within a month he closed the Key Club, as he called it, ostensibly to install air conditioning. But the place never reopened. By early '41 he was tending bar at the Copacabana. Later that year he was at the bar of the Riviera on the bluffs overlooking the Hudson River. Some years later he began tending bar at a manor house in Metuchen, New Jersey, where he remained into the sixties.

Though the Onyx's direction was downward after Helbock's departure, Carl Kress was able to keep its doors open for more than a year. Kress experimented with a combo led by trombonist Jack Jenney, and booked combos led by two of The Street's steadiest tenants, Oran "Hot Lips" Page and George Brunies. The John Kirby band returned briefly in the fall of '38 sans Maxine Sullivan, who was on the Coast filming in Parmount's *St. Louis Woman*. (Maxine was supposed to swing a famous song from Shakespeare's *Twelfth Night* but instead did a musical setting by Hoagy Carmichael for "Blow, Blow, Thou Winter Wind" from *As You Like It.* The Hays Office of the movie industry rejected the *Twelfth Night* song on the ground that it contained the word "mistress.")

Kirby was back again in March, '39, alternating with a new Spirits of Rhythm combo. Business seemed good. But as the summer was drawing to a close "the doors were closed suddenly one night and the Kirby band, which had been drawing rave notices, is biding its time in the recording studios, awaiting a possible engagement in Chicago's plush Pump Room." *Down Beat* concluded: "The Onyx has ended a hectic career."

But in September Kress reopened with the most interesting booking of his stewardship. The appearance of the Jimmy Mundy Band represented one of the few times a big band played The Street. Count Basie had been the first in the summer of '38. Mundy was an outstanding arranger, whose charts were in the books of Goodman and Basie. The musicians in his group included six other arrangers who helped create a library in record time. The band was so well received among jazz *aficionados* that it looked as if Mundy might follow in the footsteps of Larry Clinton, Glenn Miller and other arranging bandleaders. The hopes were short-lived as the Onyx found itself unable to sustain the payroll of a big band. With the termination of the band's booking went Mundy's future as a batoneer.

As Kress brought in a small combo led by alto saxist Pete Brown, the troubles of the club multiplied rapidly. After two weeks of so-so business, Brown took his combo back to Harlem, where it had been playing. In desperation, Kress booked a group known as Kenny Watts and his Kilowatts. It was the move that permanently tipped over the "Cradle of Swing." Overnight the Musicians Union threw a picket line around the club, locking out the patronage of the group that had been the Onyx's mainstay. Neither Mundy's band nor Brown's combo had been paid in full. But the immediate provocation for the pickets was that the Kenny Watts group was in trouble with the union.

Curiously, Joe Helbock, who was back at the club as bartender after his Key Club folded, defended the Onyx management. In a statement to *Down Beat,* he emphasized that he "only worked there" and was not involved in Onyx ownership. Regardless of whether or not the union's action was justified, it finished the club. The second phase of the Onyx's existence came to an untimely end in the final week of

1939, just before one of Broadway's biggest New Year's Eve celebrations.

For more than two years there was no Onyx on The Street. In 1942, after a court battle with Helbock, several new entrepreneurs appropriated the name and opened a club on the north side between Jimmy Ryan's and Tony's. The tale of the new Onyx at 57 West 52d is part of the story of bop, the modern jazz style in whose spread it played a large role.

The location at 62 West remained vacant for over a year and then suffered the ignominious fate of harboring a strip joint with a South Sea island decor, Club Samoa. "Ouch!" Jack Egan commented in *Down Beat*. The Onyx's other two locations housed clubs more in keeping with the traditions of the "Cradle of Swing." No. 72 became the site of the Three Deuces while No. 35, the original location, became the address of the first Famous Door.

Tape 6 . . . MAXINE SULLIVAN

Edging sixty, Maxine Sullivan is physically an attractive embodiment of the subtle jazz style that made her world-famous in the late thirties. Her hair is a soft gray, but her chin line is as firm and clean as her melodic line on "Loch Lomond." And she is still as slender and compact as her understated improvisatory style.

Maxine lives in the east Bronx on Ritter Place, a short, seedy block rising steeply from Prospect Avenue. The house in which Maxine spent her years of retirement and brought up her daughter, Paula, has two white columns. They are only one-story columns. But they knife out on a street of dilapidated houses. Inside, there are exposed beams in a large living room, whose size is obscured by a Hammond organ and an enormous grand piano.

The piano dominates the room. Completely covered with gold leaf, it has angels of Victorian vintage flying all over the gilt. Although it came out of a Connecticut attic, the relic comes to life when Cliff Jackson sits down at the keys. Maxine Sullivan has come to life, now that her daughter is married. She is once again swinging the old classics. And having mastered the valve trombone, she also is now playing flügelhorn.

"I came to New York in 1937—June, 1937," Maxine said. "I had been singing at a little place in Pittsburgh called the Benjamin Harrison Literary Club for about a year. Most of the bands that came through Pittsburgh came by after work. The club had a chef that made good barbecued ribs and chicken. I was working there with a piano player named Jenny Dillard. Obie, a waiter who was a jazz fan and who went into New York often, liked my singing and went out of his way to bring musicians up to hear me.

"When Ina Ray Hutton's band played Pittsburgh, she invited me to look her up in New York. So I saved my money for about six months and took the Sunday excursion to New York. I didn't tell anybody I was going and figured that if nothing happened, I'd be back to work on Monday night. How ambitious can you be? I was innocent enough to figure that things would happen that fast.

"When I arrived in New York, the band happened to be playing at

Maxine Sullivan at the Onyx. Pete Brown (left) and Buster Bailey.

the Paramount Theater. I managed to reach Gladys Mosier, Ina Ray
Hutton's pianist, who suggested that we stick around for a while. I had
come, of course, with my accompanist, Jenny Dillard. We didn't know
what to do. But fortunately Jenny had a brother with a large apartment at 409 Edgecomb Avenue in Harlem. Mardo Brown was an old
Cotton Club performer, a twirler or something, who had a good
baritone voice.

"I also had a letter of introduction to somebody at Mills Music. A
sister of George Heller—you know the Heller theatrical family—Shirley Heller used to come up to the Harrison Club in Pittsburgh. She
had written a letter to somebody named Pincus, who was in charge of
acts. I went to the Mills office on the third floor of the Brill Building at
49th and Broadway. But after waiting for quite a while one day, I left
without seeing anybody.

"In the meantime, Gladys Mosier introduced me to Claude Thornhill, the bandleader-arranger. He was sufficiently impressed so that I
signed a contract with Thornhill and Mosier. Funny thing was that
they took me to the Onyx on a Wednesday night to audition. The
Onyx was then at No. 62 West. Two nights later, I began working as
the relief act. You see, it did happen overnight! But I was frankly too
inexperienced to know what a fantastic thing had happened.

Don Frye at the later 54th St. Jimmy Ryan's.

Davis Quinn

"Getting back to the Shirley Heller introduction. Apparently I arrived before the letter to Mr. Pincus at Mills. But after I opened at the Onyx, Sidney Mills of Mills Music, who came in frequently to hear John Kirby and the Spirits of Rhythm, kept telling Joe Helbock that he had this girl singer coming in from Pittsburgh. One night Helbock asked him, 'Is she as good as this new girl I've hired?' Sidney Mills said: 'Oh, sure, she's better than Marietta Williams.' I was singing under my real name. Helbock laughed: 'Williams is from Pittsburgh,' he said. 'She's the girl you've been expecting. She was up to your office and couldn't get to see anybody.'

"Actually I hadn't been hired by Helbock. When I auditioned, he was in California trying to get Stuff Smith to come back to the club. It was Carl Kress, Helbock's silent partner, who put me on. When Helbock returned, he wasn't too pleased, told Kress he needed a new singer like a hole in the head.

"John Kirby was then just beginning to form his group. His was like an interim booking until Stuff Smith returned. Kirby had Don Frye on piano, Buster Bailey on clarinet, Frankie Newton on trumpet, Pete Brown on alto sax, and Leo Watson to play drums. Later, Billy Kyle, Charlie Shavers, Russell Procope and O'Neil Spencer joined.

"I was just doing intermissions at that time with Jenny Dillard. Meanwhile, Claude made arrangements of 'I'm Coming, Virginia,' 'Blue Skies,' 'Annie Laurie' and, of course, 'Loch Lomond.' The idea of swinging those two Scottish tunes came from the fact that Tommy Dorsey had just had a hit with 'Song of India.' Many bands were hunting for traditional classics that they could do with a beat. For the adapter of these things, it was a pretty good deal, since they were in the public domain and the adapter collected like a composer. Of course, I didn't know about such things then. I recorded 'Loch Lomond' for twenty-five dollars.

Claude Thornhill, who helped launch "Loch Lomond" at the Onyx.

"Claude was an arranger for Kostelanetz. Through him we did a couple of transcriptions for the British Broadcasting Company. Since I had these arrangements—really little sketches—I did 'Annie Laurie' and 'Loch Lomond.' At the Onyx both these numbers were scoring with the kids who were flocking into the club. By this time I had graduated to the band.

"A curious thing happened right at this time. Some woman who played the carillon came over from England and was interviewed by *The New Yorker*. When the interviewer asked what she was planning to do while she was here, she said she had to hear ' "Annie Laurie" and "Loch Lomond" as sung by a Maxine Sullivan,' whom the magazine added, 'she had heard God knows where.' They didn't even know I was around! Joe Helbock grabbed onto that. Took a picture of me, blew it up, and put it outside the club. He sent a letter to *The New Yorker,* and the following week I had a profile in the magazine. After that, 'Loch Lomond' took off like wildfire—and in 1970, I'm still doing 'Loch Lomond.'

"I did go through a period when I just didn't want to do the song. But even now, if I don't do it, they don't know who I am. It's the only record I had that was a big hit. Later, I recorded the tune for another label, and I do get royalties on this, so I know how far it's traveled. It's known all over the world. A short while ago, I went down to the *David Frost Show*. I rehearsed a number of songs. Time ran out. And what did I get to do? 'Loch Lomond.'

"I went to see *Purlie* right after it opened. There's a girl in it with whom I appeared in the fifties in a show called *Take a Giant Step*. I had not seen her in years. I went backstage. When she saw me, she couldn't think of my name but she said, 'Ah-ah-ah . . . "Loch Lomond"!'

"After the song became big, John Kirby and I had a program on CBS, *Flow Gently, Sweet Rhythm*, for about two years. After we went our separate ways, I traveled as a single and was featured on bills where they had some of the big bands. I did several jazz radio programs and theaters with Benny Goodman. I worked with Henry Busse, Johnny Long, Glen Gray. When I returned to New York, I settled at an East Side club, Le Ruban Bleu. I was there every season for six years. I worked the Village Vanguard for four years. I kept performing for some twenty-odd years.

"And I'm still around. In 1965 Tommy Gwaltney, who used to play clarinet with Benny Goodman, opened Blues Alley. I was then retired, just working at that school across the street from this house. One day he called and asked me to come down to Washington, D.C., to work. I thought he was out of his mind. I'd been away so long, I was sure nobody remembered me. But there's a disc jockey in the Washington area named Felix Grant, who really knows his jazz. Seems that he played an old recording of mine, 'If I Had a Ribbon Bow.' Tommy liked it so much that he decided he wanted me to come down.

"I explained to him that I was working at a school and that I couldn't come down at least until the summer. Sure enough, as we approached the summer he called and said, 'You open July twelfth.' I decided to get myself together. I picked up my music case and the handles fell off. I hadn't touched the music that long.

"But I opened and was I surprised! A lot of the old-timers who knew me showed up—I don't know from where. The reviews were good. Maybe there's a little starch left in the old girl yet.

"You see, one of the reasons I retired was that my daughter was going to junior high school. I decided that I'd better stay home and look after her. But by 1965 she was a pretty big girl, about ready to graduate from nursing school, and I was going to be left here with nothing to do.

"I don't have to worry too much about getting an act together. There seem to be enough people around who want to hear my old things. I was invited out to Denver to do the jazz festival that Dick Gibson presents each year. I got a standing ovation. Dick Gibson was then forming the World's Greatest Jazz Band. I went to the Riverboat when I got back to New York to hear its debut. Dick Gibson invited me to sing some songs. I did, and Bobby Hackett, who was there, asked me to work several gigs with him.

"The crowds were terrific. Everybody wanted to know where I had been. Then Bobby invited me to open with him at the Riverboat on January third, that was 1969. I was with him for eight weeks. In the meantime, the World's Greatest Jazz Band returned to the city and I went into the Downbeat with them for another eight weeks. All '69, I was busy.

"Bob Wilber, who played with the World's Greatest Jazz Band, had a recording session. He was going to do the music of Hoagy Carmichael. At his urging, Bill Bordon, the producer for Monmouth-Evergreen, came down to the Riverboat and listened to me. As a result, I did five vocals on the Wilber album of Carmichael songs.

"That album did so well that Bordon asked me to do an LP of my own. I did it with Wilber and a rhythm section. Mostly the old songs that I wanted to do. There seems to be a renaissance of jazz. For a time, music sounded like so much camp. But the kids that have stuck with it have discovered that there's more to singing than just hollerin'.

"I went back to the Onyx after I made a picture and traveled around the country. I appeared there with the John Kirby group. Then I worked next door at the Famous Door with Fats Waller. But I did most of my recording with the Kirby band.

"A musician called Lou Singer did a number of things for me. 'If I Had a Ribbon Bow' was his. I recorded 'Molly Malone' and 'Who Is Sylvia?' Singer did quite a bit of Kirby's arranging, especially transcriptions of the classics. They were off the beaten path. When they did a pop tune, they hardly sounded different from any of the more popular swing bands. But when they swung 'Anitra's Dance' or the Schubert thing, they had something that was theirs.

"I really enjoyed myself when I was working. But when Paula moved into that delicate teen-age period, I thought that she was more important than the music. I became active in the Parent-Teacher Association in the school across the street—that was where Paula was going. I wound up being president. Later, I became secretary of the East Bronx Community Council. Just before I came back into show business in '65, I was chairman of the School Board in this district. Most of my time was spent as a school aide, helping patrol the halls, assisting in the school cafeteria, occasionally lending a hand in the classroom. Here, as elsewhere in the city, the schools are over-crowded. It's difficult to keep the kids under control, classes are too large.

"The kids had no idea of who I was. My real name is Williams and that's how I was known. Toward the end, one of the music teachers played a record of mine for the classes. Then the kids would come up to me and want to know whether I was in show business. The school library had an anthology of Negro performers in the theater, and there was a picture of me with Louis Armstrong. We appeared in a show together, *Swingin' the Dream,* a takeoff on *Midsummer Night's Dream.* The kids found it and brought it to me. From then on, the secret was out.

"After that, they asked whether I would sing at a graduation exercise. I was actually scared to perform. I didn't think the kids would go for what I had to offer. But I took Cliff Jackson, who can beat sense into any box, and we went across the street. I did 'Ac-Cent-Tchu-Ate the Positive' and 'Loch Lomond,' of course. The kids seemed to like it.

"Call it second chance or second time around. I'm having a ball. I've even picked up a flügelhorn. In March, 1970, I did a gig with the World's Greatest Jazz Band at the Hotel Pierre. I sprung the surprise on them. I played Basin Street Blues on horn with the band. Now I've got an extra piece of luggage to carry around with me. I picked the horn up by myself. I was playing the valve trombone for a while. But it's too big and I'm so little. And it was kind of hard to carry around.

"I first decided I was gonna play a horn about ten years ago. My last engagement before I retired was in Honolulu. I saw a girl who sang and blew a trumpet. Let's face it. After you've done three or four songs, if you want to stay up there longer you've got to do something else.

"I didn't want to play the slide trombone because that's too much like a circus act. And the trumpet seemed to be too hard. I thought of hitting those high notes and my eyes popping out. Then I remembered that Billy Eckstine once played the valve trombone. Cliff Jackson was then working downtown at Lou Terrazzi's, and I asked him whether he wouldn't stop in at Manny's—that's a great instrument store on 48th Street, the musician's block before the Rockefellers put up those skyscrapers.

"Vic Dickenson, who lived not too far from here on Stebbins Avenue, gave me a mouthpiece. And a friend of Cliff's began giving me lessons. He lived a few blocks away and I used to go over there, carrying the horn in a Gravy Train bag.

"I took the horn with me to an Art Ford shindig once. But I wasn't about to touch it. I was chicken. For the last number, the Red Stewart band did a jam session on 'S'posin'.' Tyree Glenn picked up the horn and handed it to me. We were on television and I had no choice. When I managed to get through the song, the eyes of all those cats got real big. I also played the horn at a jazz festival out in Long Island. But John Wilson of the New York *Times* caught me and said he wished I would stick to singing. That was not too happy.

"Yet I took it with me on a gig with J. C. Higginbotham, Buck Clayton and some of the fellows. I didn't have a hard case, and we were traveling in cars. When we arrived, the bell was smashed. Carrying that thing around in a cloth case was bad enough. In a bigger, hard case, I just wouldn't have been able to make it. So I put it away.

"Last year I decided that I was going to get this flügelhorn. They're not easy to find. When I was down in Washington working at Blues Alley, I found one in Alexandria through Tommy Gwaltney. It's not an easy instrument, but I like the sound. I practice a lot. I can play a nice melody and get a nice tone. Bobby Hackett doesn't play a lot of high notes. And, of course, if I can ever get close to Bobby Hackett, boy, that'll be it. And so I guess I've got myself a new act.

"And I'm still singing of course. I don't try to make a big production. If I sing two choruses, I sing the melody in the first. The second time around, I do a little improvising and an ending. And that's it. I don't have too many new songs in my repertoire because people keep asking for the old ones.

"I like to sing things that you don't hear too much. For some reason, I dread competition. Peggy Lee, Ella Fitzgerald, Carmen

McRae—that's my league. I think that my new albums are doing all right insofar as staying in the league with the girls.

"The fact that I have new record albums out is very good. People know you're around. It may give club owners some ideas. It takes time. I did the Newport Jazz Festival in '69 with the Greatest Jazz Band. That was the year that was. They had some problems up there. I don't think it was a good idea to mix rock and jazz. The kids that like rock are not going to stand still for the kind of jazz that we do. And the people who like our type of jazz are not going to come out for something where they can't hear what's going on. Also, things seemed to get out of hand. The whole atmosphere that goes along with rock is just unhealthy. I hate to say that. I hate to doubt anything. If the kids are having fun, better for them. But the atmosphere about these things sort of frightens me a little bit. . . .

"Well, that's their bag and I've got mine. I'm still on 52d St. It was a good place and I think there's a place for it today."

6. Swingin' at the Famous Door

It was the night after the Onyx, then located at No. 72, burned down. The Famous Door, situated at the Onyx's original location (No. 35), quietly opened its portals. As far as the owners of the Door were concerned—studio and theater musicians—the Onyx had gone out of existence for them long before the flame-filled evening of February 28, 1935.

"It was all right," said Lennie Hayton, today an Oscar-winning composer-conductor and then a prime mover in the establishment of the Door, "until the Onyx moved downstairs and brought in the Spirits of Rhythm. By the time we got to the club after our radio shows, the Spirits had the place jammed. Even if you got in, it was no place to unwind and relax."

"It was a hangup," says Harry Bluestone, an accomplished fiddler in Hayton's Ipana Troubadours, "to get a table and, sometimes, just to get in."

After the "demise," that is, the public capture of the Onyx, the musicians congregated briefly at the Jam Club on West 48th St. Actually the Grill of the Knickerbocker Hotel, the Jam Club existed for about a week. Neither the hotel nor one-armed trumpeter Wingy Manone, who started the Jam, bothered to get a liquor license. For five swinging nights in December, 1934, the musicians packed the joint. "Man, we really blew up a breeze," Wingy later wrote in his autobiography *Trumpet on the Wing*, "and swung it right down to the bricks." But on December 12, there was a large padlock on the door.

The police were not impressed by Wingy's explanation of the club's failure to get a liquor license: "Hell, we don't open until midnight."

Wingy was also involved, as a musician and not as an administrator, in the effort to maintain the Casino Deluxe as a musicians' hangout. Unfortunately, the owners of the Casino, situated at the old location of the Onyx but on the ground floor, did not see eye to eye with Wingy. They wanted paying crowds rather than jamming cats. Manone quickly departed and set up shop at the Hotel Piccadilly, opening what he dubbed Ye Piccadilly Grille Jam Room. It was at this time that Lennie Hayton and/or his manager, Jack Colt, got the idea of taking over the Casino Deluxe's lease and maintaining it as a musicians' club by having the cats themselves own it.

The investors were mainly musicians associated with the Ipana Troubadours on the *Fred Allen Show* or later with the Lucky Strike *Hit Parade,* two of the shows conducted by Hayton. (The famous *Hit Parade* went on the air April 20, 1935.) Violinist Harry Bluestone, trombonist Jack Jenney, trumpeter Manny Klein, bassist Artie Bernstein and trombonist (later comic) Jerry Colonna each contributed $100. So did Jimmy Dorsey, Glenn Miller and arranger Gordon Jenkins. Hayton and Jack Colt added $1,000 apiece, creating a fund of $2,800. The Famous Door opened on March 1, 1935, to the strains of Louis Prima and his New Orleans Gang playing "Way Down Yonder in New Orleans," their theme song. Seating only fifty-five, it sold scotch at 55¢ a shot, whiskey 50¢, and beer 35¢ a brimming glass. In the view of columnist-author Robert Sylvester: "This is how Swing Street was born." In the view of many New York studio musicians, this was how "a club of our own" was born.

There was an actual *famous door* inscribed with the signatures of well-known musicians and personalities. But it was *not* the outside door nor was it in use anywhere in the club.

"You went down a few steps to enter the building," says Sam Weiss, who was a host, as he had been at the Onyx. "A walk down a dark, narrow hallway took you to the club entrance on your left. The bandstand was to your right and the bar to your left. *The* famous door rested on a small platform near the bar. It was an ordinary door signed originally by the guys who put up the loot for the club. Celebrities added their signatures as time went on." Wingy Manone claims that he went to a New York lumberyard, bought and shellacked the door that was used for this purpose.

Four years after Louis Prima's arrival in New York, Benny Carter (left), Coleman Hawkins (second from right), and Roy Eldridge (right), all masters of their instruments, cornered Prima at the Hickory House and, for a publicity joke, dismantled his horn to see what made it swing.

Down Beat

Not too long ago, Sidney Mills, a New York music publisher who is part of the Mills Music family, revealed that his father was the proud possessor of the door. Long a resident of Beverly Hills, California, Irving Mills does, in fact, have a door with the signatures of many celebrities. However, this is not the 52d St. *famous door* but the portal of a Hollywood club with the same name, once situated at Vine and Willoughby streets, where Louis Prima played immediately after he left the 52d St. club. No one knows what happened to the 52d St. door.

Prima, who founded the Pacific outpost after a six-month sojourn at the original Door, was born in New Orleans in 1912. A professional musician by the time he was seventeen, he came to New York in 1934. In the "Crescent City" he made his reputation playing at the Sanger Theater and the Shim Sham Club in the Vieux Carré. "In those days," he says, in his hoarse-voiced Southern-inflected style, "the old French Quarter was a swingin' place and the Shim Sham was the swingin'est. I got to know many people from the New York recording and publishing scene."

Almost immediately on his arrival in the Big Apple, as Manhattan was known to musicians in the swing era, he began cutting records for Brunswick and Vocalion. One of the first sides was "Let's Have a Jubilee," a phrase he popularized. The song was by W. Alexander Hill and Irving Mills, who published it.

According to some reports, he was tapped for the Famous Door at the suggestion of Mills, who had heard him in New Orleans. In Prima's memory, the invitation to "this little fun joint for musicians" came from Manny and Dave Klein, whom he met one day while he was walking on The Street. His salary was a stupendous $60 a week, while the four members of his New Orleans gang each received $40.

"The Door was an instantaneous success," Prima recalls. "Winchell started boosting it, Sobol, Sullivan, and all the top columnists. Soon we had a radio show called *Swing It*. That came from the Door. Like they now say, 'Go, man, go!' The expression 'Swing it!' came up with us. Ours was the first swing combo to get the full coast-to-coast treatment. We didn't broadcast from the club but from the CBS Studios at 52d and Madison. We played head arrangements. Paul Douglas, who later became a fine actor, was our announcer.

"I was fortunate in having Pee Wee Russell with me—the most fabulous musical mind I have known. He never looked at a note. But the second time I played a lick, he'd play along with me in harmony. The guy seemed to read my mind. I've never run into anybody who had that much talent. But he drank too much. We tried to get him off it. In fact, I had Red Colonna, Jerry's brother, room with him when we settled in Hollywood."

Later, Eddie Condon, with whom Pee Wee worked at the Onyx, also tried to limit Russell's intake. The gimmick was to keep the Chicago clarinetist from leaving the club between sets. It did not prevent Pee Wee from imbibing. Only an alley separated the Onyx from Reilly's bar. A window in the men's room of the Onyx opened on the alley. And Reilly's bar had a back door opening on the alley. Russell's countergimmick was to take off the moment another member of the combo embarked on several improvisatory choruses. Through the window, across the alley, into Reilly's, down a double—and he was back in time to join the ensemble. As the evening wore on, the liquid refreshment slowed Russell down. But it took Condon some time before he caught on.

When he performed, Russell frequently screwed up his face as if he were in pain. But on occasion he made faces that were involuntarily comical—the right eye shut and the left eye looking upward in search of a note.

"So many great people started on The Street," Prima continued, "like Ella Logan and Martha Raye. To me, Martha was a great singer with a natural feeling for improvisation. But after she made that one picture, she couldn't help being a comedienne. Like Colonna, who was a fine trombonist. If she had stuck to singing, she woulda been a great one. Funny thing, I was in her first movie, *Rhythm on the Range,* a Bing Crosby picture. She boffed them with her performance of 'Mr. Paganini.'

"You know when we started at the Door, Guy Lombardo was big, Wayne King, and that corny kind of stuff. It was The Street that made all of us and changed the sound of pop music."

In Sam Weiss' memory, "Prima broke The Street wide open. He was entertaining and funny. And we had great relief piano players, first Teddy Wilson and then Joey Bushkin. The Door took the play away from every club on The Street, and Leon & Eddie next door wound up with the overflow. I always remember how well we did because of this free-lancer who acted as our doorman. We called him Yiz'll because we didn't know his name, also because he used to tell the crowds trying to get into the club: 'Please don't block the sidewalk. Yiz'll have to keep moving.'

"Martha Raye and Louis became very close in this period. She copied his playing style in her singing. But don't minimize his appeal to the dames. Somehow the word got around that he was rather well fortified, and there were a lot of tables just bulging with females."

Eddie Davis of Leon & Eddie once told a reporter: "You could hear them breathing all the way down The Street!" The reaction of jazz connoisseurs was hardly as enthusiastic. "Prima persists in playing identical solos night after night," John Hammond wrote in *Down Beat,* "and indulges in certain tricks that become a bit tiresome after a while. . . . The night is saved by the magnificent clarinet of Pee Wee Russell."

But Prima's showmanship and ebullience, his jive patter and good humor, drew the jewels-and-orchids set. "When he shouted, 'Let's have a jubilee,'" Sam Weiss comments, "a lot of those sex-starved dames would practically have an orgasm. I think they thought he was shouting, 'Let's have an orgy,' in that hoarse, horny voice of his."

Apart from Prima's appeal, the Door had another accidental advantage, as Joe Helbock pointed out in discussing the fire that destroyed the Onyx the night before the Door opened. For the first five months of its existence, the Door had no competition from the one club that had drawn crowds to The Street. In fact, part of the musical confraternity that made up the Onyx's original clientele was now involved in the ownership of the new club.

The Door's healthy business may have pleased the investors, but it soon was a headache to the many musicians who had hoped for a club of their own. Within weeks of the opening, *Down Beat* commented on how "Park Avenue nitwits have loused up the jams at the Door" and noted that the cats were beginning to flock to Adrian's Tap Room in the Hotel President. Wingy Manone, who had given up Ye Piccadilly Grille Jam Club, worked with Adrian Rollini to make his West 48th St. room the new jam joint.

In a desperate attempt to save the Door for the musicians and for jamming, the owners appointed a master of the jams and designated Thursday night after 2 A.M. as Jam Night. Manny Klein, who had grown up as one of Red Nichols' Five Pennies and was then busily trumpeting on a score of network radio shows, took on the chore and proved effective. For a time, Benny Goodman came over from NBC after rehearsals of his first big band on the Ken Murray *Let's Dance* show. Tenor saxist Bud Freeman, then playing with Ray Noble in the skyscraping Rainbow Room, joined the jams. One memorable evening, Tommy Dorsey put down his trombone, and brother Jimmy his alto sax, and both demonstrated what they could do on borrowed trumpets. But it was just a matter of time before the musicians felt crowded out, as they had once felt at the Onyx.

Manager-owner Jack Colt had a different worry. In midsummer the Onyx reopened with a combo built around the zany duo of Farley and Riley. And the fall season brought competition from Hickory House, whose main attraction was Wingy Manone, then riding high with "Isle of Capri." When Prima asked for a considerable increase—Red Colonna wanted him to go to the Coast to start a Famous Door—the management of the 52d St. Door turned him down.

By September a new combo headed by trombonist George Brunies succeeded Prima. A native of New Orleans like Prima and Manone, Brunies had played with the New Orleans Rhythm Kings and with pioneer Jack "Papa" Laine and had made records with the legendary Bix Beiderbecke. As a result of working with showman-clarinetist Ted Lewis ("Is everybody happy?"), he had developed various comic routines, including the trick of manipulating the trombone slide with his foot. Nevertheless, his leadership lasted for only three weeks, during which trumpeter Max Kaminsky ceded his chair to Bobby Hackett and Hackett's vibrancy yielded to Bunny Berigan's emotionalism.

Even briefer was the stay of Billie Holiday, for whom the Famous Door represented her first gig outside Harlem. Teddy Wilson, applauded in *Down Beat* as "the big thrill of opening week," served as her accompanist. "They slew the musicians," *Down Beat* reported, "and those who love hot and blue music, but the Park Avenue crowd which supported Prima didn't like her." What is, perhaps, even more surprising—considering that the Door was run by musicians—is that she was not permitted to mingle, occupy a table, or even sit at the bar. Between frustrating sets, she had to endure the aggravation of sitting upstairs in the foyer just outside the club's toilets.

This was where Max Kaminsky found her one night during her 52d St. debut. "What are you doing here all alone?" he asked. He remembered that he had seen her up in Harlem a few years before, singing and waiting on tables at the Alhambra Grill. "The fact that I had heard her uptown," he wrote later in his autobiography, "made us good friends because she was a colored girl downtown in the white section and she felt good knowing I knew about Harlem." Kaminsky goes on to tell of "the unaffected sweet sadness of her voice" and how it could make you "ring with joy as well as sorrow." He notes also that the only ones who went to nightclubs at the time were "people with money, mostly society people and celebrities of the sports and show business worlds, not the general public or the expense-account society."

Apparently, they were not entertained by Billie's tortured style. "She was taken off the stand on September 12," *Down Beat* reported, "after four nights of work and probably won't be back." It was a curious debut but the jazz magazine erred somewhat in its observation. Billie went on to become one of The Street's biggest draws.

Another and more auspicious debut was made at the Door on September 29, 1935, when Red Norvo's Swing Sextet sans Mildred Bailey opened. Although he and the Rockin' Chair Lady had been married for several years, they did not appear together on The Street until 1938—and then at the Door. (They first joined forces musically in 1936 at the Blackhawk in Chicago, where their appearance led to their being dubbed Mr. and Mrs. Swing. Married in '33, when they were both with Paul Whiteman, they were divorced in 1942. Red continued making records with Mildred even after he had married trumpeter Shorty Rogers' sister, Eve. Mildred died in 1951 at the age of forty-four.)

Red dished out a subtle type of swing that appealed more to jazz buffs than The Street's swingers. Lacking both drums and piano, his small combo—clarinet, tenor trumpet, guitar and bass—made music whose soft, sinuous sound was set by his xylophone lead. Not surprisingly, he was the first performer to compel acceptance of the mallet-played instrument in jazz. "We were the first small jazz band," he adds, "to use riffs and arrangements, and not play raucous Dixieland." But comic routines and pyrotechnical displays à la Riley and Farley were then drawing crowds to the Onyx rather than the Door. It was the intoxicating period of "The Music Goes 'Round." As the members of the general public thinned, the musicians came drifting back to the Door.

Norvo's vis-à-vis was Roy Eldridge, who is regarded as the key trumpet stylist of the thirties, as Louis Armstrong was of the twenties, Dizzy Gillespie of the forties and Miles Davis of the fifties. Eldridge's group, the Delta Four, also lacked piano and drums. But Little Jazz, as he was called, played with a high-pitched, frenzied drive that made his trumpet-clarinet-guitar-bass quartet sound bigger than it was. Something of the sound is preserved on a Decca disc, "Swingin' at the Famous Door," recorded in the closing days of 1935. The date was A & R'd by trumpeter Wingy Manone, who succeeded Red Norvo at the Door when Norvo replaced Manone at the Hickory House. In actuality, the Delta Four on the Decca disc was, with the exception of Little Jazz, made up of musicians from Manone's Hickory House combo.

The opening months of 1936 found short-lived trumpeter Bunny Berigan fronting a band at the Door. Manone was back at the Hickory House. Berigan has frequently been compared to another white Midwestern jazz maker, Bix Beiderbecke. Like the legendary "Young Man with a Horn," Berigan parted his hair dead center, was an alcoholic and died prematurely of pneumonia. He was thirty-three at his death, Bix twenty-eight. Like Bix, Berigan possessed a lovely lyrical gift, but a more dramatic style, evident on his best-known recording, Vernon Duke's "I Can't Get Started." By the time that his silver-voiced horn was being heard at the Door jam sessions were once again in vogue.

"Eddie Condon and Joe Bushkin were in Bunny's band, too," Max Kaminsky recalls, "and on Sunday afternoons all the other jazzmen in town would drop in and jam with them." The jamming was not done in the club proper but in a room upstairs. It was not as casual as Kaminsky suggests but relied in part on the administrative know-how of Milt Gabler, owner of the Commodore Record Shop on 42d St. and organizer of the United Hot Clubs of America.

The most memorable of these jam sessions occurred on a cold Sunday in February, '36. No one present has forgotten the event, and many who were not have nevertheless reacted in print to its magic. The occasion was the only appearance on The Street of the great Bessie Smith. "The Empress of the Blues" was then past her really short-lived recording prime. (Except for a comeback session in 1933, arranged by John Hammond of Columbia for whom she made all her 160 sides, she had stopped making records in 1930. And the November 24, 1933, session with Frankie Newton's combo—Benny Goodman played clarinet on "Pigfoot"—actually proved her last.)

"Bessie came in upstairs," Robert Paul Smith reported in *The Record Changer*. "She came in and planted those flat feet firmly on the floor, she did not shake her shoulders or snap her fingers. She just opened that great kisser and let the music come out." According to Eddie Condon, who was a member of Bunny Berigan's backup combo, she sang "Baby, Won't You Please Come Home?" "Mama's Got the Blues," "I'm Wild about That Thing," "The Gin House Blues," "Dirty No-Gooder's Blues," and what may be regarded as her theme and possibly the most moving of her recordings, "Nobody Knows You When You're Down and Out." Although some writers have stated that Ella Fitzgerald was present but declined to face comparison with the Empress, Condon reports in his autobiography that Mildred Bailey was in the audience. Invited to sing after the Empress had completed her stint—jazz critic George Avakian recalls that Bessie did not even take off the cheap furs she wore—the Rocking Chair Lady refused to break the spell.

When she walked out of the Door that Sunday afternoon, Bessie was in her early forties. Not more than nineteen months later, on the eve of John Hammond's departure for Mississippi to bring her to New York for a nostalgic record session, she was in the fatal automobile accident memorialized in Edward Albee's one-act play *The Death of Bessie Smith*.

(Incidentally, Mamie Smith—no relation—who started the blues recording craze of the twenties with her disc of "Crazy Blues," appeared on The Street at the elegant Town Casino in 1936, shortly before the former speakeasy at No. 9 West folded. A Harlemite, Miss Smith was accompanied by the Beale Street Boys. In later years,

Jimmy Ryan's played host to another legendary blueswoman, Bertha "Chippie" Hill, who sang at a '48 Town Hall memorial concert for Bessie Smith and, two years later, was herself killed in an auto accident.)

There was irony in the life of the Famous Door. The week before Joe Helbock presented the Swing Music Concert at the Imperial Theater, the club that contributed to the rise of the new jazz style closed its doors. Bunny Berigan performed at the May 24, 1936, concert, but the Famous Door was, in the words of the late George Hoefer, "conspicuous by its absence." A June, '36, *Down Beat* story indicated that the club had been "forced into bankruptcy by four creditors," food and liquor merchants who were owed $2,000. In a study written in the late sixties, Hoefer traced the Door's bankruptcy to the involuntary neglect of the club by its musician-owners. Most of them had to travel, and some, including Lennie Hayton and Manny Klein, moved to Hollywood.

Columnist-author Robert Sylvester offers a different and rather sinister explanation. Contending that "muscle and music simply do not mix," he attributes the demise of the Door to hoodlums. According to Sylvester, owner-manager Jack Colt turned at one point to a big-shot hood to save himself from a minor mobster, who demanded a piece of the action. After he had helped Colt out of his difficulty, the big shot himself stayed on as a silent partner and, in a short time, enlarged his share and control. The end was in sight when the new boss began cutting the liquor, padding checks, and creating "a general air of danger and tension"—a situation which, in Sylvester's opinion, tolled the bell not only for the Door but eventually for The Street itself.

Although some of the investors have no memory of hood pressure on the club, Sam Weiss provides a partial confirmation. "The attitude of the mobsters," he told me, "certainly the big-time mobsters, was to let the musicians alone. They were gentlemen, too, when it came to the girls. Never bothered them. But occasionally there'd be a young punk who'd get ideas. Obviously, he couldn't muscle into an operation controlled by the big boys. So he'd go after a Jack Colt or a Louis Prima.

"Both of them were annoyed at one time by a small-time hood. Never knew his name. But he'd come into the Door and make them both nervous just by sitting around. After a time, Colt got a friend or a relative to have a talk with somebody whose name was something like Johnny Irish. One evening Irish came into the place when the punk was around. 'Just tell him Johnny Irish wants to talk with him,' he told me. When I gave the punk the message, he looked over to where Irish was sitting, turned pale, dropped some money to cover his tab and ran out. We never saw him again. But I think that one of the things that made Prima go out to the Coast with Red Colonna was this mobster thing. He didn't want to get involved, and he was smart enough to be scared about not getting involved. So he left."

Publicist Eddie Jaffee adds a bit of ancillary evidence. He tells the story of a mobster named "Pretty Boy" Amberg who, when he came to the Door, "insisted on a table where he could sit with his back to the wall. Apparently he had good reason for his caution. Eventually, they found him dead in a burning car on a Brooklyn street, reportedly in retaliation for some shooting in Dave's Blue Room—when it was on Seventh Avenue near 52d. After someone introduced Prima to Amberg, Pretty Boy would feel insulted if Louis didn't come to his table and sit with him. Amberg made Prima nervous, but he'd have to go over because Amberg would begin to make things unpleasant for his waiter.

"Once Amberg showed Louis the picture of a girl on whom he was sweet—Donna Drake, who later achieved stardom on the screen, and who was then a close friend of Louis'. Things came to an unanticipated head one afternoon when Prima answered a knock at his hotel door and found Amberg outside. Pretty Boy wanted to kill some time gabbing. While they were talking, Amberg spotted a framed picture of Donna on Louis' dresser. It had an inscription like, 'To my dearest Louis.' For a tense moment, Prima lost his breath. But thinking quickly, if not desperately, he handed the frame to Pretty Boy and apologized for not having given it to him sooner. 'Donna gave it to me one night at the Door to give to you,' he explained. By some good quirk of fate, the mobster's first name happened to be Louis, too."

Columnist Louis Sobol tells of an evening when Prima somehow failed to play a tune requested by Amberg and, for his oversight, was belted by Pretty Boy as he came off the bandstand.

None of the Door's investors remembers receiving any return on his investment, though a number point out that the club did enjoy a period of affluence. Some have memories of a cashier who decamped about the same time that a sizable sum disappeared. Sam Weiss recalls that several years after the demise of the Door, he and Lennie Hayton had occasion to visit the no-longer-existent Strip hotel, Garden of Allah. There behind the desk, they spotted the missing cashier. For several moments they considered calling the police. But since the man was working as a desk clerk, they concluded that he had not fared too well and decided to forget the matter.

Even before the alleged disappearance of funds, the club suffered a dry spell after its initial prosperity. It occurred about the time Bunny Berigan was on the bandstand. Prima had been an audience spellbinder and drawn crowds. Berigan was a musicians' musician. And the competition of the Onyx, first with Riley and Farley and then with Stuff Smith, did not help. "I don't care what it takes," Lennie Hayton told a meeting of the investors. "So long as Bunny is around, the club stays open."

It did but not for long. On May 10, 1936, just a year and a half after its promising opening, the original Famous Door permanently closed its portals. Before long, instead of hot jazz and spicy swing, Italian delicacies were being devoured on the premises, as the Café Maria took over the spot. But the club had contributed too much to jazz history for the name to disappear forever from The Street. It was not until December, 1937, however, that there was a new Door, sans the inscribed names, on 52d.

"We still owned the name," Lennie Hayton told me, "and we considered taking action to prevent its being appropriated. But it seemed too involved and I guess we were too busy with other things. Perhaps that's the ultimate story. The need for the Door disappeared when many of us moved to the West Coast."

But while the Door was swinging, unexpected things happened, and unbilled performers occasionally contributed to making it a legend. Manny Klein, one of the Door's investors, tells the story of a night when Artie Shaw insisted on playing alto sax. "He was one of the great clarinet players," Klein observes, "but his original instrument was the alto. And he was a fantastic lead alto. Benny Goodman was not. But this never satisfied Artie, who wanted to outdo Benny as a clarinetist. This was not so easy. As a stylist, maybe. But as a technician, hardly. However, this is the story of Artie and his alto. On this particular night, it was Jimmy Dorsey's playing that annoyed Artie, or Archie, as we used to call him. He kept shaking his head. Finally, he

Artie Shaw.
RCA Records

got up and said: 'Are you coming?' I stared at him: 'Where are we going?' He motioned with his hand: 'To get my horn.' So I drove him up to his apartment, somewhere on Central Park West in the 90's. When we returned to the Door, he got on the stand—and he played! You never heard such sax playing in your life. He was a demon! But that was Artie Shaw, a *meshuggener* (crazy man) if there ever was one. I roomed with him once. He's been married so many times that you might think he was a swinger—a real-gone guy with the broads. But what do you think he did at night? He kept me up—believe it or not—with his typing. He was writing some stories. I stood it for two nights and then moved out. But that was Arthur Arshawsky."

To Sam Weiss, the fate of the original Door, as well as the Onyx, encompasses the story of The Street. "Musicians made 52d," he says. "They brought the radio crowd, the music publishers, the talent-agency execs, the theater people, the advertising guys—and, finally, the college kids, the society set, the cloak-and-suiters and the public. Name musicians made The Street into glamorville, with the help of the columnists. But as the public rushed in, the musicians walked out. And when the musicians took a powder, the public wasn't there. It's funny. By themselves, the musicians couldn't provide the business to keep any club in business. But they wanted out, as the public came in to provide the finances."

Tape 7 . . . RED NORVO

Among jazzmen who are still active, Kenneth Norville, better known as Red Norvo, was one of the steadiest tenants on The Street. His close competitors are pianist Marian McPartland and clarinetist Joe Marsala, both of whom played the Hickory House for many years. While Red worked the steakery in the first year of his appearance on 52d (in 1935) and as late as 1944, his initial gig and long-lived association was with the Famous Door.

Now in his sixties, Red is still an active and masterful performing-recording vibraharpist. He switched to this blood relation of the xylophone in the early forties, having spent years demonstrating that the percussion instrument could swing. Before Red, the xylophone was dismissed as a novelty instrument, and Red himself did a vaudeville act (in his twenties) in which he played "Poet and Peasant" overture at breakneck tempo and simultaneously did a tap dance. Red came to The Street via the Paul Whiteman Orchestra through which he also met, married and struck up a fruitful musical partnership with Mildred Bailey.

"Contrary to a number of jazz historians," Red notes, "I left Whiteman in 1932. Or rather his settling at the Biltmore Roof in New York made it impossible for me to continue with him. Being a Midwesterner, I did not have a New York union card and could not take a steady job without waiting a year. Mildred did not leave at the same time, contrary to what these same historians have written. I could freelance and make records, and I soon did. 'Hole in the Wall,' the first side I cut, had Jimmy Dorsey on sax, Artie Bernstein on bass and Fulton McGrath on piano. Between '33 and '35 I was able to record with my own Swing Septet and Octet on Columbia, using young unknowns who later became top musicians and name bandleaders."

Benny Goodman, who played bass clarinet on one of these dates in '34, notes in his autobiography: "Swing was only a word that musicians used then, and it wasn't until later in the same summer that the first record came out with the word on the label (it was something called 'Red Norvo and His Swing Septet,' a result of a date Red had at Columbia)." Today, these '33–'35 sides are jazz collectors' items.

"In our first date on The Street," Red recalls, "we followed Louis Prima into the Door. It was an unusual group in several respects, as was our Hickory House combo. We were the first small band that didn't play Dixieland. Also the first that worked without drums and piano. We had Dave Barbour on guitar, Pete Peterson on bass, and a 'front line' of Don Cook (clarinet), Stewie Pletcher (trumpet) and Herbie Haymer (tenor). You can see why everybody began talking about 'soft, subtle swing.' We got a great sound, light and swinging. And the xylophone was pretty much of a surprise to people interested in jazz, even though I used it as early as 1930 or thereabouts when I recorded 'Moon Country' with Hoagy Carmichael.

"Fifty-second Street had an ear for fresh sounds and welcomed new ideas. And it wasn't like playing for the folks from Beardstown, Illinois—that's where I was born. In a club like the Door, you were playing for cats who knew what it was all about. Any night you could spot faces like Benny Goodman, Dorsey, Teagarden, John Kirby— you name them. And when they liked what you did, it was very satisfying. But we also had the society kids that generally went to the Stork Club—the debs and college crowd—crossing Fifth Avenue to hear us. And when we were at Hickory House, a lot of theater people came in to hear us. I remember Henry Fonda, Martha Scott, others.

"One night a couple came into the Door, and the guy kept saying, 'Play "Dance of the Octopus." ' That was a record I made which got me kicked out of Brunswick. Jack Kapp thought it was too modern. Brunswick had sold it to English Decca however. When John Hammond went to see his sister in London—later she married Benny Goodman—he brought back a batch with him. This guy at the Door had bought the record in London. And he recognized my name. It was Reggie Gardner, who was in a show at the Winter Garden with Bea Lillie. They brought in Johnny Hyde, the agent, and he used to try to get us little extra things like parties and such.

"After that we enlarged the group, added a drum—Maurice Purtill —for dancing, and went over to Jack Dempsey's. That was when he was still on Eighth Avenue. They had a great room in back of the restaurant. Eddy Duchin and his wife-to-be were nearly nightly visitors. They were romancing at the time. That spring he was playing all the big college dances—up at Yale, Harvard—and he took us along. We'd play a jazz set. Jazz was just beginning to take hold then.

"Mildred Bailey worked The Street only once. It was at the Famous

Door in the year that Basie made the big splash on The Street. We were in there around Christmastime for about a month. That's the first and last time she played 52d—and that was where we stopped working together. She really didn't play very many clubs in New York. There was Le Ruban Bleu when Jacoby had it on 56th St. near Fifth Avenue, over Theodore's Restaurant—you went up a flight of stairs. Later she worked the Blue Angel when Jacoby moved there. In between she sang at Café Society Uptown, never Downtown. That was it.

"For me 52d St. was like home plate for years. We'd go up to Boston, do dates out in Rock Island, play Chicago, and in between, The Street. We played the Famous Door when Linda Keene was the vocalist. Around '43 I had a group that was pretty hot: Shorty Rogers (trumpet), Eddie Bert (trombone), Hank Kahout (piano), Clyde Lombardi (bass), Specs Powell (drums) and Aaron Sachs (clarinet). It was getting difficult to hold onto sidemen, so many were being drafted. I remember the kidding that Leo Guarnieri took. He was badly underweight and looked like a physical wreck, especially when he stood next to his bass. He had a novel trick—used to play 'Nola' by hitting himself on the head. Later, possibly in '44, I had a group with Remo Palmieri on guitar.

"I recently saw Erroll Garner in New York. He said: 'Long way.' He opened at a place called Tondelayo's on The Street. They had two pianos. Billy Daniels was there later. We used to run down there to have a drink. And he used to run up The Street, listen to every other group, and sit in with as many as he could. There was a lot of motion on that street. No street like it.

"After Eve and I moved out here to the coast, I went back for a date in New York. The Street had a lot of striptease by then. I worked with Ellington at Bop City over The Turf—you know, in the Brill Building, the songwriter's hangout, at 49th and Broadway. One night this guy came in to see me and asked me to play the Black Orchid. It was located near Tony's. Lennie Tristano, the pianist, was leaving, and the owner said: 'If you'll bring your group in, I'll go partners with you.' [Laughing.] If a guy is gonna give you half of a club, there's something wrong. I didn't do it.

"A number of the 52d Streeters are now out here on the West Coast. One night Eve and I went into a restaurant and this guy jumped up and grabbed me. It was Artie Jarwood, who owned several clubs on The Street. He has since made a big success in the clothing business. He has a big layout in Palm Springs. I've never seen him there, although I've played the Rim Rocks frequently. Used to be Romanoff on the Rocks. But it was taken over by Milton Kreis, the Hollywood druggist, who changed it to Rim Rocks.

"Nemo has been out here for years. Owns a gas station in the Valley, I hear. He sure was a crazy man in the days of The Street. He'd do a Cotton Club review in ten minutes. How Mildred and I met him is a very funny story. We went down to Florida with a great Broadway character, Johnny O'Connor. Big horse-player. He built Fred Waring into a million-dollar attraction. Mrs. O'Connor remained with us in Florida after he returned to New York. One day, when the three of us were sitting at a poolside table, this guy suddenly appeared out of nowhere and asked: 'Do you know Jack Bregman?' I turned and said: 'Why, yes, I know Jack Bregman.' [He was a music publisher.] This guy said: 'I'm his cousin.' So Mildred said: 'Any friend of Jack Bregman is a friend of mine. Sit down.' It was Henry Nemo. He had come down to Florida with a show that went kerplunk. It ended up with us driving him back to New York. He wasn't as wild then as he became later. Mildred later introduced many of his songs: 'Don't Take Your Love from Me,' ' 'Tis Autumn' and others.

"A lot of the cats have become Europeans. Ben Webster is living in Copenhagen. Don Byas went over in '44 with Don Redman and never came back. 52d St. was like Europe in the way jazzmen were treated. They were respected for talent.

"We were one of the first bands on The Street—we were at the Famous Door when Riley and Farley were at the Onyx. But earlier that summer, a bunch of us went to Maine. There were some great musicians—Eddie Sauter and others. It was a fiasco, the worst panic in the world. As I was walking The Street after we got back, Jack Colt approached me. He wanted me to bring a combo into the Famous Door. I had never been a leader before and didn't know whether I could be. But I got talked into it.

"I never worked Jimmy Ryan's. But Jimmy and I were drinking buddies. Mildred and I used to go up to his apartment in that brownstone next door, climbing those long, steep flights. It couldn't have been more than the fifth floor, but it sure left you out of breath. After we climbed up one night, Mildred said: 'No wonder you do so well with the chicks. They haven't the strength to say no!' Jimmy knew the

Red Norvo, left, with George Shearing's group (Don Elliott, Shearing, Chuck Wayne, Tal Farlow). At one time Farlow was Norvo's guitarist.

lyrics of all the show tunes. We used to go into the club after it closed. There'd be Ella Logan, Sinatra, and other singers who'd try to show Jimmy up. But he was an encyclopedia of the verses of show tunes.

"Around 1935 Mildred and I had a home in Forest Hills, Long Island. Benny Goodman, whose band was then playing at the Roosevelt Hotel—on the same stage where Guy Lombardo appeared—came to a party at the beginning of June. Teddy Wilson, who was working up at the Savoy in Harlem, was also a guest. After a time, they began jamming together. A cousin of Mildred's named Carl Bellinger, who was an amateur drummer, joined in. 'Right there,' as Benny later wrote in *The Kingdom of Swing,* 'was the beginning of the Goodman Trio.' It wasn't but a month later that Benny cut those first great sides with Teddy and Gene Krupa.

"John Hammond frequently came to our house—and Mildred and I used to go to his elegant home on East 91st off Fifth Avenue. He used to have musicales there. He himself played in a string quartet, and that's where Benny played Mozart for the first time.

"Not long ago I was down in New Orleans. Played that new Royal Sonesta Hotel in the French Quarter. Big, beautiful place. To the guys, the Quarter looked like 52d St. Well, it is like The Street was after the striptease joints started coming in. Pete Fountain and Al Hirt still have jazz clubs. But Bourbon St. has more girlie joints than jazz. You know [laughing], after all those banks and tall buildings took over 52d, I had trouble finding The Street. If I came along Fifth Avenue, I knew I had to turn at De Pinna's.

"I used to have a lot of great pictures of The Street. They may be in an old trunk I left at the Hotel Woodward in New York. It's at 55th and Broadway. Not long ago I saw a bellboy who is now the bell

Card advertising Red Norvo's 1944 appearance at the Downbeat Club.

captain. There had been a fire at the hotel, and he thought the trunk might be lost. He found it. But it turned out to be the wrong trunk.

"1944 was the last time we appeared on The Street. We were at Hickory House at the beginning of the summer, just before Joe Marsala came in. Then we moved to the Downbeat—Billie Holiday was on the bill and, I think, Coleman Hawkins—and we were there until the end of the summer, maybe into early fall. After that The Street was a place to visit but not to gig."

Louis Prima and his New Orleans Gang (Pee Wee Russell, clarinet; Frank Pinero, piano; Garrett McAdams, guitar; Jack Ryan, bass).

Down Beat

7. The Big Bands and the Famous Door

Louis Prima and his New Orleans Gang opened the new Famous Door at No. 66 just as he had the original Door at 35 West. The intermission pianist was the great Art Tatum. The new owners were a duo named Al Felshin and Jerry Brooks, who simply appropriated the name. Brooks, the short one, was a compulsive gambler. One day he pawned his partner's overcoat to make a big bet. When they were closing the club, burly Felshin could not find the garment. At first he thought that it might have been stolen. But then a suspicion crossed his mind. Unable to get a direct answer from his associate, he hung Brooks on a coat hook until his partner confessed.

Prima had then just returned from Hollywood, where he had been the main attraction at a Famous Door for almost a year. As he tells it, a few nights after he arrived at the film capital in September, '36, he had wandered into a club on Vine Street and Willoughby owned by Gene Austin. It was named Blue Heaven after the Walter Donaldson ballad that transformed Austin from an unknown vocalist into a celebrity. His Victor recording of the song, introduced by Eddie Cantor in the *Ziegfeld Follies of 1927,* was one of the earliest multi-million record sellers.

"I got to talking with Austin," Prima recalls. "When I told him that Red Colonna and I were looking for a club location, he just turned the lease over to us. He said he was tired of the grind. Three days later, we had a new sign over the entry and Hollywood had its Famous Door. No connection with the 52d St. joint.

"It was a small place," Prima continued, "so small you couldn't get *out* when it was crowded. It was a fun joint. All the Hollywood stars came—and we got everybody up to do something. Like we had a number called 'The Love Bug.' After several choruses, I would point to somebody in the audience, and he had to sing a chorus. He could make up his own words. Everybody got into the spirit of the thing. While I was there, I wrote 'Sing, Sing, Sing.' Jack Robbins, the rumba-dancing music publisher, heard me do it one night. 'That's mine!' he said, and went out and got that great Benny Goodman recording. We had a jubilee. But I was glad to get back to 52d St. There was something about that Street. I can't find the words. It always reminded me of old Bourbon Street in New Orleans. But it was more than just music. It was a feeling that it gave you. . . ."

The Door presented many interesting combos and a number of important artists. Ella Fitzgerald made one of her few appearances on The Street during the second anniversary of her success with "A-tisket, A-tasket," the nursery rhyme she cut with the Chick Webb band in 1938. Mildred Bailey's only Street appearance was at the Door in December, 1938, provoking *The New Yorker* comment: "The Famous Door is one of the smallest and smokiest places on 52d St. But, then, it's practically impossible to be a devotee of hot music and fresh air at the same time. Anyway, there is Red Norvo's band and Mildred Bailey's leisurely singing; the relief outfit is John Kirby's, moved from the Onyx next door. You can't ask for much more in a room that size." (Quite a number of cats remember seeing Red, hat-less and breathless, trotting Mildred's dachshunds along windy 52d that December.) When the Basie band was booming at the Door, pretty Hazel Scott was the unobtrusive intermission pianist.

The singular contribution of Famous Door II was, in fact, bringing the sound of the big bands onto The Street. It was an audacious undertaking, considering its shoe-box size and dollar-bill bandstand. There was no sweat about combos like Red Nichols' or Irving Alexander's Ragtime Band. (This was the Alexander of Kelly's Stable who later ran Door III and the Three Deuces.) But when it came to swing aggregations like Charlie Barnet's band, Woody Herman, Teddy Powell or Andy Kirk, the bandstand looked like the famous Marx Brothers' stateroom. It was the great band of Count Basie that launched the big band era on 52d in the summer of 1938.

"For two years," said Willard Alexander, who still handles Basie, "we couldn't stir up the excitement that transforms a working band into a name band. In fact, we couldn't book Basie into any of the big Eastern clubs. I don't think it was color line, since Cab Calloway, Armstrong, Ellington and the Mills Brothers all played the big rooms. Maybe he wasn't hooked up with the right auspices.

"Admittedly, he was not too well known, except among *aficionados* who dug Kansas City swing. His music was ahead of its time. It was wham but not loud. He had drive but he didn't blast. He had a bouncing beat but he didn't pound. Yet next to Benny Goodman, whom I also handled, he was nowhere. Incidentally, Goodman contributed much to Basie's upswing. He played numbers like the Count's 'One O'Clock Jump' and credited Basie on network shows like the *Camel Caravan.*

"By the summer of 1938 there seemed no place for Basie to go. Then I got the idea of putting him on 52d St. It was crazy. The clubs couldn't accommodate a big band on their stands, and they were so small, fourteen men would blow the walls out. But being desperate, I went to the two guys who ran the Door—Al Felshin, big and tough, and Jerry Brooks, little and tough. It was the beginning of the summer, and they had no air conditioning and no business. They were desperate enough, so I managed to get them over to Steinway Hall on 57th St. to hear the band. Once they heard Basie at the Nola Studios, they were talking like it couldn't be done but they sure wanted to do it.

"The hangup, of course, was the club's lack of air conditioning. With difficulty, they could seat sixty people. But can you imagine what it would have been like without air conditioning in New York's summer heat and humidity? When I was convinced that Felshin and Brooks really wanted Basie, I stuck my neck out and offered to get the money to install a cooling unit.

"Now, John Hammond, who found the Basie Band in Kansas City and helped build it, believes that he put up the twenty-five hundred dollars needed to air-condition the joint. Some time ago, I met him and Mrs. Hammond at a party and she asked: 'Willard, who did advance the money for that loan? Was it John or was it you?' At that point, I simply said: 'Whatever John says is all right with me.' But the fact is that neither John Hammond nor Willard Alexander put up that dough. It was Music Corporation of America (MCA) of which I was then a vice-president. There are several ways in which this can be established. Perhaps the most interesting has to do with the collection of the loan after Basie hit pay dirt.

"And how he did hit! He was a resounding smash from the moment

Count Basie's band turns on the college crowd at the Famous Door. Left to right, Count Basie, piano; Freddie Greene, guitar; Jo Jones, drums; Buck Clayton, trumpet; Ed Lewis, trumpet; Harry Edison, trumpet; Dickie Wells, trombone. Present but not visible are Lester Young, tenor sax; Herschel Evans, sax; Dan Minor, trombone; Earl Warren, alto sax; and Jack Washington, baritone sax.

Down Beat

he struck the first opening chords on the piano—splank-splank! The lines began forming and it was SRO the entire time. That rhythm section of his—Freddie Greene on guitar, Walter Page on bass, and Jo Jones on drums! And the stars in his sax section—Lester Young and Herschel Evans on tenors, Earl Warren on alto! And where could you find a more exciting brass choir—Buck Clayton and Harry Edison on trumpets, Benny Morton and Dicky Wells on the trombones! All these men were star soloists. But there was no band that played with the coordination and precision of Basie's. Those guys didn't just play together. They used to breathe together. That's what gave the band its fantastic punch, no matter how softly they played. And that's what brought the crowds to the Door. In that small space, fourteen men playing as one! You could feel the pulsations inside you. We had a CBS wire, and soon people all over the country were sitting in on the birth of a great big band."

Irving Lazar, who ran interference for MCA at the Door, recalls a colorful detail regarding the broadcasts: "Because Basie didn't want to hold back—it would have ruined his sound over the air—the entire audience had to get up and stand outside the club for the thirty minutes. Since it was summertime, it was no real problem. But that

was the procedure throughout the engagement. Come broadcast time and the audience was asked to nurse their drinks on the sidewalk."

Jazz historian Charles Edward Smith was among those who cannot forget "Count Basie's fourteen men playing 'King Porter Stomp' with such steam that the leader's hands dropped off the piano and he sat listening to them with a slight, incredulous smile that reminded me of Fletcher Henderson's in the same kind of situation."

According to Willard Alexander: "Although the Door did tremendous business all through Basie's stay, collecting the loan from Felshin and Brooks was another matter. And here's where you'll find the proof that MCA put up the loot for the air conditioning.

"Just about this time, Sonny Werblin and I gave a start to a new agent. Today, he's one of Hollywood's top literary agents. He's short and bald. But they don't call him Swifty for nothing. He's one of the sharpest agents on the film scene. I mean Irving P. Lazar. One of his first assignments at MCA was to get our money back from Felshin and Brooks.

"And it was a tough one, let me tell you. Even Brooks was bigger than Lazar. As for Felshin, he could put Irving into one of his pockets. And they were tough babies. You had to be to run a club in those days. But Swifty was tough, too. He used to show up on Saturday nights—after they had Friday and Saturday receipts in the till—and he used to grab, but I mean *grab,* as much money as he could. Finally, MCA had its money back—I don't think we ever got all of it—and Count Basie was launched as one of the big, new name bands of 1938.

"After Basie, other bands clamored to get into the Door. And it became a lucky room for a number of bands—Charlie Barnet's, Woody Herman and even mousy Teddy Powell."

To Willard Alexander's account of how Swifty maneuvered to get the money back from Felshin and Brooks, Irving Paul Lazar adds: "Somebody tried to stab me while collecting the money, and I had to go to the hospital for a few stitches in what was then a much flatter belly."

Of course, there is the not remote possibility that Felshin and Brooks secured loans for their air conditioning from *both* John Hammond and MCA without either being aware that the other was shelling out. This would account for Hammond's assertion that he funded the installation of the Door's cooling system.

The Basie band made one other appearance at the Door, in August, 1939. A *New Yorker* critic observed that he was "half blown out of the place by the brass section." In 1939 Artie Shaw caused a riot in Buffalo by walking out in the middle of an evening and bewildered show biz by leaving the band business entirely. It was the year that Ella Fitzgerald took over the Chick Webb band at his death. Becoming a semimonthly, *Down Beat* chose Red McKenzie as the second in its "Immortals of Jazz" series and asked editorially: SHOULD NEGRO MUSICIANS PLAY IN WHITE BANDS? The answer from white musicians was a resounding NO! It was not fair, they said, for blacks to replace white musicians when there was so much unemployment. Considering that there was greater unemployment among black musicians, someone should have noted the irony. But Benny Goodman hired Fletcher Henderson to succeed Jess Stacy at the keyboard, "daring to do," according to the trade paper, "what no other bandleader has successfully done before."

The year 1939 was also when debonair Charlie Barnet made it big. It was his runaway recording of Ray Noble's "Cherokee," cut in July, that established the band. But the booking at the Door in February was such a noisemaker that Bluebird began putting out a new Barnet

Charlie Barnet, who also played the Famous Door, posed for this gag shot after his successful recording of "Cherokee."

Down Beat

disc every week. Among these were the famous "Pompton Turnpike," "The Count's Idea," "The Duke's Idea," and "The Wrong Idea." A putdown of the day's Mickey Mouse bands, the last mentioned was subtitled, "Swing and Sweat with Charlie Barnet," a none-too-subtle takeoff on "Swing and Sway with Sammy Kaye." Jazz historian George Simon calls Barnet's "the blackest white band of all" and feels that he was bypassed when name bands were being chosen for commercial network shows "because of his liberal attitude on the racial question [especially liberal for those days]." Before the Door booking, Barnet featured such black jazzmen as John Kirby and Frankie Newton and, afterward, performers like Lena Horne, Trummy Young and Oscar Pettiford.

Scion of a wealthy New York family, Barnet resisted efforts to make him a corporation lawyer. At sixteen he led his own band on an ocean liner. Although his sax style was at first influenced by the roar of Coleman Hawkins in the Fletcher Henderson band, he soon became a devotee of Johnny Hodges' singing lyricism. A Duke Ellington fan, he not only modeled his arrangements on Duke's, but when he built a fallout shelter in the jittery postwar period, stocked it with as many Ellington discs as cans of food. When he lost his library in the fire that destroyed Hollywood's celebrated Palomar Ballroom, the Duke reciprocated by sending scores from his own library.

Barnet never attained the renown of Miller, Goodman, Dorsey or Artie Shaw. But he ran Artie a close second when it came to wives. He had six against Shaw's eight. Although he was well enough known as early as 1936 to play the famed Glen Island Casino, where he introduced the Modernaires, his move into the big time is, perhaps, best described in a *Down Beat* headline: GETTING OFF—THE FAMOUS DOOR WAY.

Woody Herman's break at the Door came also in 1939, immediately after Barnet's appearance and several years after he formed The Band That Plays the Blues. Built around sidemen from the famous Isham Jones Band, Woody's was a cooperative band that spent three years "scuffling," to use his word. Woody had begun paying dues as a lad of fourteen when he joined the Myron Stewart Band and played a roadhouse near Milwaukee, his hometown. As he progressed through high school, he played clarinet and tenor sax with the Joey Lichter Band. Then came four years with Tom Gerun in whose band he worked alongside Virginia Simms (later Mrs. Kay Kyser) and saxophonist Al Morris (later Tony Martin). After almost a year with Harry Sosnik, whose harpist was Adele Girard (later Mrs. Joe Marsala) and arranger was Dave Rose (later composer of "Holiday for Strings"), Woody joined Isham Jones. The decision of Jones, composer of "It Had to Be You" and "I'll See You in My Dreams," to retire from band business led in 1936 to the formation of the first Herman band.

Just before Jones dissolved his band, Herman recorded a jump instrumental, "Fan It," with the Isham Jones Juniors for Decca Records. The Juniors were a small jazz combo within the big band like the Woodchoppers later in the Band That Plays the Blues. That Woody's first outfit should have found a home at Decca was natural. Unfortunately, Jack Kapp used it as a house band to cover the current hits of other bands. Not until April, 1939, was Woody able to cut a disc that tapped the band's identity. "Woodchopper's Ball," a jazz instrumental he wrote with flügelhorn player Joe Bishop, sold well at first, then stopped, started selling again, and stopped again. Decca was compelled to keep rereleasing it, so eventually it aggregated an impressive total without ever breaking as a hit.

"It gave us a little muscle, however," Woody observed, "when we went into the Door—a springboard for us, as for Basie and Barnet. After that we played the Paramount Theater on Times Square for the first time. That was big time in 1940. On the road after that, we did business, something we attributed to the audience we developed through remote broadcasts from the club.

"A funny thing happened with one of our broadcasts. Though it has no musical significance, the incident provides a clue to the character of the clubs and the times. Our announcer was a cocky guy who always arrived almost as we were going on the air. This particular evening, he came trotting in with no time to spare. He was wearing a hat and a coat, and since he was late, he went sailing past the hatcheck girl. He was too much in a hurry to pay attention to her 'Your hat and coat, sir.' But Felshin, one of the owners, spotted the brush. Perhaps he didn't recognize the announcer. But it didn't matter. There was a lot of bread in the hatcheck concession and one freebee could set a bad example. Besides, there really was no place for a winter coat at those things they called tables. Before the announcer could reach our bandstand, Felshin and a waiter were there. Maybe he tried to brush them. They were on top of him in no time flat, and as they used to say in those days, he 'got punched out' but completely! We went on the air without him."

The Teddy Powell Band, a solid dance combo but hardly as note-worthy as the others, also enjoyed a '39 debut at the Door. The critical reaction was good for a new band. In fact, two years later, *Metronome* chose it as "The Surprise of 1941." But when he under-took a one-night tour after the debut, Powell found that the audience was not there. "I thought with the Famous Door buildup that I'd clean up on one-nighters," he told George Simon. "But I sure learned a lesson. It can't happen that quick."

By the time he appeared at the Door for a second engagement the learning process had cost Powell more than $30,000. And misfortune attended the June, 1940, booking. At that moment the Door featured Andy Kirk and His 12 Clouds of Joy, as well as Powell. It was a short-lived engagement for both. Adhering to the era's tradition of quiet closings that left creditors hunting for the owners, Felshin and Brooks bolted the door one evening and simply did not reopen the next day. Apparently, representatives of the Musicians Union were on their tails about owing money not only to Kirk and Powell but to Ella Fitzgerald for a May date and to Red Nichols. Nightclub business was suffering one of its frequent contractions—and the Cotton Club folded the same week as the Door.

Powell worked to reopen the Door, and by August 15 *Down Beat* announced that the action would begin on Labor Day. But the holiday came and the Door remained shut. Finally, on September 25, it did reopen. Reports had it that business was good and that musicians and jazz fans were flocking back. Shortly after New Year's, 1941, it was revealed that Powell had merely been the front man for a group that included Milton Pickman, his manager, and Phil Howard, to whom he had ostensibly sold his share. The reign of Felshin and Brooks was over. But it was not until late 1941, under an entirely different management, that the club seemed to develop a new momentum that kept it going for several years.

Curiously, if not prophetically, within weeks after the closing of the Door in 1940, Benny Goodman, who had inaugurated the name band era and set the pace for more than five years, broke up his famous band. Goodman was suffering from sciatica and went into Mayo Clinic after the band's final engagement at Catalina Island, California, in the summer of 1940. But even then the band business was beginning to feel the advance tremors of World War II that ultimately finished it and ushered in the era of Sinatra and the big baritones.

Tape 8 . . . Woody Herman

Woodrow Charles Herman has the distinction of having led, not bands, orchestras, groups, or combos, but herds. There have been many: The First Herd, 1943–46, incorporated such maverick talents as Neal Hefti, Ralph Burns, Flip Phillips and Billy Bauer. They helped make Woody's band the most talked-of assemblage of 1945. Then there was the herd known as the Four Brothers, 1947–49, whose famous reed section included Stan Getz, Jimmy Giuffre, Zoot Sims and Al Cohn. The Third Herd won the *Metronome* poll in 1953.

Herman reminds one of Dorian Gray. He has never aged musically. Only his history has added years. He has done this by constantly surrounding himself with fresh young talent. Although he has not had a recording that equaled the renown or sales of "Woodchopper's Ball," cut the year of his Door debut, he has an enormous catalog of recordings on Decca, Capitol, Columbia, Verve, Phillips, Cadet, and Fantasy.

"My memories of The Street go back to at least three years before we played the Door," Woody observes. "In 1936 my wife came in from the Coast, we got hitched, and spent our honeymoon on 52d. I had just started the band, and we were rehearsing at the Capitol Hotel nearby. The management gave us a free rehearsal hall. In the evening, my new missus and I would just roam The Street, going from the original Door to Jack White's across the street, up the block to the Onyx, where John Kirby was playing, back down to the Yacht, and over and across to Leon & Eddie's.

"I wanted to hear all the contemporary sounds. It was such a gay and happy place, and such an exciting and fabulous time. There were little French restaurants all over the block where we'd stop in between listening. And Reilly's bar was a spot where you'd run into all the cats who were playing on The Street, as well as those who weren't.

"I remember one night when a cab came roaring down the block and braked to a fast stop in front of the Onyx. Two guys hopped out, threw the ignition keys to the doorman, and ran into the club. It was Charlie Barnet and Lucky Millinder. They had stolen the cab! Snatched it while the hackie was grabbing a sandwich or something.

Woody Herman (left) and his wife, and Mel Tormé (second from left) visit Dizzy Gillespie at the Spotlite in the mid-forties.

They were screaming with laughter when they ducked into the club. But the poor hackie who came running after his cab was not. He had blood in his eyes.

"Pincus was the doorman. You know, the little, short guy with the oversized cap and long coat, who worked every club on the block. He always had a twinkle in his eye and he managed to quiet the hackie down. Then he went inside and came out with a couple of bills. Barnet had paid off, and the hackie rode away smiling. Those were crazy days.

"After six weeks of rehearsing and our honeymoon on 52d, The Band That Plays the Blues made its debut at Roseland Ballroom in Brooklyn. Then we moved to Roseland in Manhattan. It was on Broadway between 51st and 52d, where the back of the City Squire Motor Inn rests today. What a grind! We wanted to play jazz and the blues, but we had to play for dancers only—foxtrots, rumbas and waltzes. From there we went on the road, where presumably you could really make some bread. The hinterland wasn't any better than Roseland when it came to repertoire. I'll never forget one hotel—I think it was in Texas—where the manager sent a note: 'You will kindly stop playing and singing those nigger blues.'

"It's hard to forget the owners of the Door. Brooks was small and short, looked like a jockey. Felshin weighed over three hundred pounds—he was a giant. When the guys in the band bugged me for an advance on their so-called salaries, I used to go to Brooks. But he could be as hard as his partner. The Door gave you exposure and publicity, no real bread. Probably Felshin and Brooks didn't take out very much either, considering the size of the joint. But they'd put me through such a grilling when I bucked for a bit of bread that I never wanted to approach them.

"I remember also an MCA agent named Irving Lazar, who had some kind of beef with them. At least once I saw them trying to stop him from taking loot out of the till. Even though he was the smallest, he seemed more than a match for them. Lazar was having such a hard time with them that he came to me. He wanted desperately to bring something back to his office. He asked me to sign with MCA, which I couldn't do since we were signed to GAC (General Artists Corporation). He was a determined little guy. I'm sure he got the money— and, believe me, that wasn't an easy thing to do with Felshin and Brooks.

"Actually we played The Street only twice and both times at the Famous Door. I think it was within a period of a year and a half. In between, we started to move and began playing theaters. When we went into the Paramount after the first Door date, Bob Hope was the star of the stage production. He had just broken all theater records in Chicago. But Broadway was another story. The theater's business seemed to depend on the film. And we had *The Magnificent Fraud*. It really was a magnificent turkey. For years afterward, whenever I ran into Hope, he'd always greet me with *'Magnificent Fraud.'* He tried to make a joke of it but it really bugged him. And it didn't help us either. But The Street did."

Tape 9 . . . Benny Carter

"Versatile" is a vague epithet until it is applied to Bennett Lester Carter, born in New York City in 1907 and a resident Hollywood composer-arranger-conductor since the mid-forties. Star alto soloist of the Fletcher Henderson band in the late twenties, he had his own outfit in 1933 and his own sextet with luminaries like Dizzy Gillespie in 1941. By the mid-fifties he had composed, arranged, played, and/or was seen in such films as *The View from Pompey's Head, The Snows of Kilimanjaro, The Five Pennies* and *The Gene Krupa Story*. As a recording instrumentalist, he may be heard performing on trumpet, clarinet, trombone, piano and alto sax, his major instrument. Always an analytical man, he is currently in the forefront of those composing and arranging for films and TV.

In the period when swing was catching on both as a word and style, and some antagonism was developing between proponents of hot jazz (Dixieland and New Orleans) and big-band swing—the schism never went as deep as that between bop and Dixie—Carter refused to talk about swing as "having replaced jazz or followed it." As he put it: "A lot of musicians use the word 'jazz' to denote something that's old-timey and corny. As I understand it, though, 'jazz' means what comes out of a man's horn, and 'swing' is the *feeling* that you put into the performance. . . . So even if 'jazz' and 'swing' as words do mean two separate things, as musical elements they're very often combined in one performance.

"I went to Paris in 1935, after which I lived in England for a while working for the B.B.C. as staff arranger, and made tours of Holland, Belgium and the Scandinavian countries. I came back to the U.S.A. in 1938, on the *Normandie,* and Eddie South was on the boat too. I don't know whether it's the same on all ocean liners, but on this French Line, the bar stayed open twenty-four hours, and Eddie and I took full advantage. We floated right along with the ship. I think that we could have gotten back without it.

"As soon as I got back to New York I led a big band for a couple of years. Then in 1941 I went into Kelly's Stable, near Seventh Avenue, with a sextet. That was quite a show. On the same bill with us was the

Versatile Benny Carter played Kelly's Stable in the early forties. He is shown here with his trumpet, alto sax and clarinet at a recording session in 1951.

Down Beat

Nat King Cole trio, Art Tatum working as a solo, and a swinging blues singer known as Miss Rhapsody. There were three partners running that place—George Lynch, Ralph Watkins and Irving Alexander. I found all of them rather easy to deal with. I was sort of able to get along with most everybody.

."After the Stable engagement we went into the Famous Door, like overnight. The clubs were always having these panics. Thinking of the Famous Door, I remember I had a sextet that included Dizzy on trumpet and Jimmy Hamilton on clarinet and reeds. Between sets, and before the gig began, we usually congregated, with some of the other guys who were playing on The Street, for a libation at the White Rose Bar, around the corner on Sixth Avenue. It's hard to forget the free food and the double drinks.

"Dizzy was not quite as flamboyant a personality then as he became later. Frankly, I never knew why they called him Dizzy. As we all know, he's dizzy like a fox and he has a tremendous sense of humor, probably even then it was a bit unorthodox. But you know he has a really good business head.

"The Door gig wasn't a long one. But our original term was extended when Helen Humes, who had been singing with Basie, came in with Willie Bryant. Helen was singing a thing with a topical slant that always got a big rise out of the audience. Governor Talmadge of Georgia was in the news quite a bit then. Helen sang something she Called 'Gov. Talmadge Blues.' It had a popular line that went: 'Eugene, Eugene, what makes your head so hard?'

"I don't think I ever really got into the spirit of The Street," Benny concluded. "Although there was a lot of jamming going on, and a lot of the guys were always sitting in, I found myself concentrating more on the big-band concept and was doing a lot of writing and arranging with this in mind, as well as for singers and other bands."

Benny went out to California in 1943 with a big band to appear at Billy Berg's Swing Club for an eight-week engagement, during which time he was offered some film work by Twentieth Century-Fox. This led to other assignments in the movie world, and after a few trips back and forth between the coasts, he eventually decided to settle in Hollywood. California's gain was 52d St.'s loss.

8. Hickory-Broiled Steaks and Jazz

In 1944 clarinetist Joe Marsala wrote a heartbreak ballad, "Don't Cry, Joe." Subtitled "Let Her Go, Let Her Go, Let Her Go," it stirred rumors that the seven-year-old marriage of Marsala to his attractive harpist, Adele Girard, was on the rocks. The so-called autobiographical character of the song contributed appealing overtones to a tender melody. Sinatra recorded it. But a disc by the orchestra and chorus of Gordon Jenkins became one of the year's best sellers.

Like the announcement of the death of Mark Twain, the bust-up portended by the ballad was slightly premature. Today, twenty-seven years later, the Marsalas—Adele, attractively silver-haired, and Joe, still a crewcut—boast one of the longest-lived marriages in music business. And the Hickory House at 144 West 52d, where the union was contracted and where Joe and Adele played house for the better part of a decade, eventually became the longest-lived jazz club on The Street. Opening in 1933 when only the Onyx was around—21 and Leon & Eddie don't count in this classification—it remained in steady operation under the same ownership (with some minor changes) for roughly thirty-five years.

John Popkin, born Zelig Pupko in Vilna, Lithuania, in 1895, was the co-founder who remained with the steak house for its entire history. Arriving in the United States on a cattle boat in 1907, Popkin was a fishmonger, a Postal Telegraph messenger (Eva Tanguay's personal runner, no less), a United Cigar Store salesman, a men's clothing model, an auctioneer, a boxer, a duck raiser—then the only Jew in the business—and a perfume manufacturer. During Prohibition, he owned a speakeasy on 44th St. between Broadway and Eighth Avenue. It was known as the Little Club. Then, and throughout his career as a restaurateur, Popkin was an inveterate, irrepressible and, as they say in sporting circles, "degenerate" gambler. According to Joe Morgen, his long-standing press agent: "John would bet you a thousand dollars any hour on whether the next passing car had an even- or odd-numbered license plate."

Popkin had not completely recovered from the stock market crash that helped destroy his perfume business when he rented the site of the future restaurant in 1933. The high-ceilinged, cavernous loft then housed a used-car salesroom. He and his partners picked Hickory House as the name of the new restaurant to emphasize the wood over which they broiled steaks—2-foot logs transported from farms at Cornwall-on-Hudson and Durham, Connecticut. They installed a huge fireplace of white brick in the rear, stained-glass windows in front, and crude, large, heroic paintings of sports figures on the high walls. (Later The Street was to have three other restaurants with a strong men-and-sports aura: Gallagher's, Toots Shor and Manuche.) Hickory House was the most commodious of all the 52d St. spots in which jazz could be heard. Except for 21, it had the largest bar, a 50-foot ellipse that seated seventy-five people. The bandstand was in the center on a raised platform as high as the bar itself and covered with a wooden canopy.

"In November, 1934, after I'd bought out my partners," Popkin told Whitney Balliett of *The New Yorker,* "I got the idea to bring in jazz. So I hired Wingy Manone who had the Marsala brothers with him and Eddie Condon."

Joe Marsala told jazz critic Leonard Feather: "After we had been at the Hickory House about a year, Jack Goldman [Popkin's partner] said to me one night: 'I can't understand how people like this jazz music. There's one guy over there who must really love it. He's been in here every night. I told him: 'Jack, that's Eddie Condon, you've been paying him a salary!' " Regardless of whether Popkin still had partners, Hickory House was one of the earliest 52d St. spots to feature jazz, and the oldest to keep jazz sounding on The Street.

According to Wingy Manone, it was a trip to the South that cost Jack Goldman his piece of Hickory House proprietorship. "He became interested in a piece," he says, with a glimmer of a smile, "and it also cost him a boat he owned. But he found me and I gave him the idea for the circular bar with the bandstand in the middle. It was a big attraction and so were we. By the time we started there in '35 I had that hit record of 'Isle of Capri.' "

Manone had made the record while he was playing at Ye Piccadilly Grill on West 45th St. In actuality, he was not too happy when Harry Gray, musical director of American Record Company, gave him the corny British tune to record. But he was not ready to turn down a recording date. As he tells it, he was so upset by the choice of song that he took a long walk. When he reached the corner of 57th St. and Seventh Avenue, he could no longer restrain his irritation. Throwing the sheet of music to the ground, he muttered out loud—much to the amusement of some passers-by—"Oh, Capra, what you're doing to me!" Then he suddenly realized that he had stumbled upon the switch that might lift the song out of its cliché groove. He hurried to the Onyx, where he enjoyed listening to "Scat" Leo Watson and the Spirits of Rhythm. Through a long night and much liquid refreshment, he ostensibly labored over the song. But by daybreak he had his version of the song "collared," to use his lingo. When he recorded the tune for Vocalion on March 8, 1935, it was drummer Ray Bauduc who suggested the release that he employed on "Oh, Capra." Later, he attempted a transformation of "By a Garden Wall," singing it "By a Tea Garden Wall."

Born around Mardi Gras time in February, 1904, in New Orleans, Manone did a lot of bouncing around before he scored with "Oh, Capra." At ten he lost his right arm in a street car accident, thereby acquiring his colorful cognomen and providing the situation for an oft-repeated humorous story. At Christmas one year, hot fiddler Joe Venuti, whose reputation for practical jokes is legendary, sent Wingy a single cuff link.

Learning his instrument "from the colored boys up the river," as he puts it, Wingy eventually rode the freights to Chicago. Neither the New Orleans Rhythm Kings in the "Windy City" nor the Original Dixieland Band in New York encouraged him about the future of jazz, though George Brunies of the former group helped him get a three-week gig at the Valentino Inn in Chicago. In half a dozen years of bouncing around, he played with the Scranton Sirens, a job that was short-lived because of his limited reading ability, and worked with

Blossom Seeley and Benny Fields, who were vaudeville headliners. At one point he even played with Chief Blue Cloud, who required that he dress in Indian regalia. Of Wingy's reading ability, drummer George Wettling, who worked with him at Hickory House in the spring of '37, recalls his looking at a tune in six flats and exclaiming: "Man, that signature looks like a bunch of grapes to me!"

While he was in the Midwest, Wingy met clarinetist Joe Marsala, who grew up in the "Windy City" and with whom he got a job during the Chicago World's Fair of 1933. Together they worked in a spot called The Brewery, just outside the fairgrounds of the Century of Progress exhibits. When the World's Fair gig ended, Wingy followed Marsala to Florida, where the clarinetist was working dance marathons. Marsala had gone south on the urging of another Chicagoan, a "dancer" whose name was Frankie Laine and who occasionally sang a song so that marathon viewers would throw coins. Despite Marsala's friendliness, Wingy had only limited luck in finding gigs, and on the urging of Jack Goldman, decided to head for New York. Before he had gone south, he had encountered the Mound City Blue Blowers whose members (Red McKenzie, Eddie Lang and others) had recommended that he try the "Big Apple."

"He had no money for train fare," Marsala recalls, "so he went to an Army and Navy Store and bought one of those outfits that engineers wear. He had his trumpet and a great leather belt with which he was going to strap himself in. The way he explained it to me: 'You get in between the mail car and the first car because nobody ever goes through there.' I don't know how he ever managed it, what with the trumpet and everything and his having only one hand. But I'd swear when the train pulled out, I saw him wave at me! Not long after he hit New York, he made his hit record of 'Isle of Capri'—covering a disc by Xavier Cugat—and from then on, things started swinging for him."

But before they did, there was Plunkett's, a bar on 53d St., about four doors off Broadway, across the street from the old Arcadia ballroom. A tiny place that could not accommodate more than thirty boozers, it was frequented by New York's studio, pit and dance band musicians. It led to Wingy's becoming acquainted with the Dorsey brothers, Frank Signorelli, Red Nichols, Miff Mole, Benny Goodman, Artie Schutt, Frankie Trumbauer, Bing Crosby, Harry Barris, Phil Napoleon, Joe Venuti, Manny Klein, Al Rinker, Eddie Condon,

Lennie Hayton, Mildred Bailey, Paul Whiteman (with whom many of the foregoing worked), Vincent Lopez, Jerry Colonna, Phil Harris (then an active drummer), B. A. Rolfe and Adrian Rollini.

Contact with the last-mentioned led to one of Wingy's first consequential Manhattan gigs. At Rollini's Tap Room in the basement of the Hotel President, Manone fronted a quartet consisting of the same men he thereafter led at the Hickory House: Sid Weiss on bass, Carmen Mastren on guitar and Joe Marsala on clarinet. The combo may be heard as part of the seven-piece group that recorded six tunes for Victor as Adrian and His Tap Room Gang. The added members were Rollini on vibes and bass sax, Putney Dandridge on piano, Sam Weiss on drums, with Jeanne Burns handling the vocals.

In *Trumpet on the Wing,* his autobiography, Wingy displays no reticence in asserting that he started 52d St. on its way to jazz fame. "Little places started opening all over The Street," he writes, "because we were such a success." Success he was. But it just so happened that the success of the Spirits of Rhythm at the Onyx antedated his booking at Hickory House, as did the appearance of his New Orleans compatriot, Louis Prima, at the Famous Door.

As Wingy tells it, when publisher-manager Irving Mills offered him a managerial contract, he signed without bothering to read it. When he finally did so at the urging of Joe Marsala, he discovered that he had unknowingly signed a lifetime deal. Aware that Mills was deathly afraid of gangsters, he had Marsala dress up in the black overcoat and fedora that were then recognized as mobster garb. Together, they went up to Mills' office, where Manone introduced Marsala as a cousin who had just blown in from Chicago to take care of some business for the Mob. Mills apparently took the hint and promptly tore up the contract. Some nights later, when he visited Hickory House, Mills realized that he had been the victim of a ruse.

Nevertheless, when Manone participated in the Swing Concert sponsored by the Onyx at the Imperial Theater, late in May, '36, his sextet appeared "courtesy of Irving Mills and Hickory House." As leader of the New Orleans Jam Band, he still spelled his name "Mannone." In the fall of the year, he departed the steak house on a vaudeville tour. "The Hickory House manager told me," he avers in his autobiography, "I could always have the job. So I took those vaudeville dates and I left Joe in charge of the band. When I came back, Marsala's name was outside and Wingy was out. I didn't blame Joe. He was a good boy and I was glad to see him get ahead."

Like Manone, who played other 52d St. joints, among them Kelly's Stable and Famous Door, Joe Marsala is remembered for his work at Hickory House. His tenure at the Popkin steakery exceeded Manone's by quite a number of years. Marsala's father was an amateur valve trombonist, who worked in the sugarcane fields of Baton Rouge, the cigar factories of Tampa, and finally, as an employee of Montgomery Ward in Chicago. In the "Windy City" the Marsala family lived near the Oak Street record shop of the Kapps who later founded Decca Records. They had black neighbors with whom they willingly shared necessities during the Chicago race riots of 1918. At one time, Joe played in a 10-cents-a-dance hall with a trio whose pianist was David Rose, later the composer of "Holiday for Strings."

After working with Wingy at Hickory House, Marsala played at a short-lived club named after Red McKenzie. It was located at 54 West 52d St. in the fall of '36 and early '37. "We used to get a percentage of the take," Marsala recalls. "Each of us generally received seventy-five cents a night. When we got a dollar twenty-five, it was good!"

One night Marsala put a sub into McKenzie's and picked up $75 playing a society party. Returning to McKenzie's, which remained open until 4 A.M., he blew about $50 drinking with Tommy Dorsey. "When we got our percentage, it was a dollar twenty-five again," he recalls. "We were getting thirty percent, so that we should have split at least fifteen dollars more on my tab alone. When I beefed, the owner said: 'You're not supposed to get a percentage on the money you spend.' There was a sign out front with a picture of me. I went and kicked the thing out of its frame and said 'Good-bye.' "

Not long afterward, he was invited to bring his own combo into Hickory House. In typical Marsala style, he explains: "Musicians used to work sitting down in those days, and I think the reason they made me the leader at McKenzie's must have been that I was the only one who stayed sober enough to stand up." From McKenzie's, Marsala took Joey Bushkin on piano and Eddie Condon on guitar. He added Ray Biondi on fiddle, creating a rather novel instrumentation for a jazz combo of the mid-thirties. He wanted Bunny Berigan on trumpet but had to give up the idea when Berigan chose to go on the road with Benny Goodman.

Red Allen at the 54th St. Jimmy Ryan's.

"Suddenly, I thought of Red Allen," Marsala notes. "Nobody had an integrated band on 52d St. or anywhere else. We didn't ask the bosses. We just brought Red in. We had no trouble, although a lot of newspaper people told us that it wasn't going to work. When Red had to leave to rejoin the Mills Blue Rhythm Band, we had another colored trumpet player, Otis Johnson."

Still later, in 1937, Marsala used clarinetist-soprano saxophonist Sidney Bechet in his Sunday jams. Bechet had just left Noble Sissle after a ten-year run. "Herman Rosenberg—he was a good friend," Bechet reports, "he brought me to the Hickory House. . . . So I used to work there nights sometimes, but mostly it was Sundays from four to eight; that was when they had their jam sessions."

Leonard Feather, to whom Marsala described some of these developments, commented: "In the thirties Joe Marsala was responsible in his quiet and unpublicized way for more attempts to break down segregation in jazz than Benny Goodman—and he didn't have John Hammond to push him."

Writing in *Down Beat,* John Hammond thought that the Marsala-Condon combo represented "superlative music making" and felt that Red Allen brought out the best in Condon, whom he then rated as "greatest rhythmic guitarist in the country." Condon, one of The Street's regulars until he settled in Greenwich Village, first at Nick's (Rogatti) and then in his own place, was one of the jazziest personalities of the time. On April 9, 1936, he was operated on for acute pancreatitis. His was only the sixth case of its kind in the history of

Polyclinic Hospital, and the mortality rate was known to be extremely high. As he was receiving a preliminary blood transfusion, he told the nurse: "That must be Fats Waller's blood. I'm getting high." Asked before the operation whether he had false teeth, he replied: "Not with me." When they were giving him a rectal injection, he urged: "Please add a little soda. I don't like it straight." The day after the operation he asked Red McKenzie, who came to visit, to bring his bathrobe and slippers. When Red told him that he could not get out of bed, he commented: "I've got to try. I just don't like this enameled roadster." He was referring to the bedpan.

In the spring of 1937, shortly after their return from a cruise gig, Condon, Marsala and Bushkin went back to the Hickory House, succeeding a group known as The Three T's. In actuality The Three T's consisted of seven pieces. But John Hammond and others thought so little of the rhythm section—"There have rarely been worse rhythm sections, even at debutante parties," Hammond wrote—that the group might well have been limited to its soloists. These were Jack Teagarden, who was then also playing trombone with Paul Whiteman, brother Charlie Teagarden on trumpet, the inimitable Frankie Trumbauer on C-melody sax, and a remarkable musician named Casper Reardon, who had been harpist of the Cincinnati Symphony at the age of nineteen. (Perhaps the first to make the harp swing, Reardon cut some discs with Jack Teagarden in 1934. He died in '41 at the age of thirty-three.)

But Reardon was not on the job when Marsala and his buddies arrived. Instead, the harp was being manned by an attractive girl named Adele Girard. Marsala raised no objection when Hickory House co-owner Jack Goldman requested that he add Miss Girard to his group. Goldman could hardly have anticipated that he was providing Marsala with a wife as well as "sideman." Four months after they started working together, Joe and Adele were married.

"It was a funny thing," Marsala observes. "Here it was Saint Patrick's Day—March 17, 1937—and we opened that night with a harp in a jazz band. From that time on, we were in and out of the Hickory House for the best part of ten years. We started a series of Sunday afternoon jam sessions, which became a big deal."

Out of the Sunday jams came one of jazz's great drummers, Buddy Rich. In a conversation with Whitney Balliett of *The New Yorker*,

Buddy Rich (drums) sits in with Louis Prima (bass), Sid Weiss (trumpet), Meyer Weinberg (clarinet), and Allan Reuss (guitar) at Hickory House.

Rich told how he began hanging out at a Brooklyn bar called the Crystal Café around 1937. Drummer Henry Adler, later a sideman with Prima at Hickory House and now the owner of an instrument store on West 48th St., invited Rich to sit in with the club's combo. Artie Shapiro, who lived near the Crystal Café and played bass with Marsala's Chicagoans, also sat in occasionally. Shapiro urged Rich to attend a Sunday jam at Hickory House. Adler claims he took him there.

"I went three Sundays in a row," Rich told Balliett, "and never got to play. On the fourth Sunday at about five forty-five—the session ended at six—Marsala summoned me. I played 'Jazz Me Blues' . . . and then Marsala said, 'Let's play something up!' In those days I lived up. I started out at a tempo like this—taptaptaptaptaptaptaptaptap—on a thing called 'Jim Jam Stomp.' People were beginning to leave, but they turned around and started coming back just as if a Hollywood director had given instructions in the finale of some crummy grade B movie. The number broke the place up, and Marsala invited me back to play that night. I called my dad and he guessed it would be okay. I played two sets and Marsala asked me to join the band." Rich went to work for $66 a week, out of which his father allowed him to keep $10.

John Popkin gave Balliett a slightly different version of how Rich came to play at Hickory House: "I brought him in from Brooklyn myself," he said. "He was playing in a little place right on the edge of Washington Cemetery, facing Ocean Parkway. Right on the edge, surrounded by stones. I heard music coming out of there one night—it was eerie—and went in, and this kid was playing. He was sensational. 'How old are you, sonny?' I asked him during an intermission, and he said, 'Seventeen, but I'll be eighteen soon.' I told him I wanted to hire him, but he wouldn't believe me, so later I drove him home and we woke up his father at four in the morning, and he *did* believe me. Then it took me a week to persuade Marsala to hire him." (Rich was actually twenty with a birthday on June 30, 1917.)

And what does Marsala say? "One day our bass player, Art Shapiro, brought in a young drummer who was a terrific soloist and a great crowd pleaser—Buddy Rich. I let him keep sitting in. In fact, I actually had him on salary and kept two drummers for a while, because I didn't have the nerve to tell Danny Alvin I hired somebody else."

However he began playing at Hickory House, Rich was one of several musicians who started with Marsala and then went with Tommy Dorsey. Others include Dave Tough, Joey Bushkin and Carmen Mastren. When Rich left him, Marsala wired Dorsey: "Dear Tommy: How about giving me a job in your band so that I can play with mine?"

Popkin's account of the Sunday jams also differs from Marsala's. "Around 1935," he says, "I started Sunday afternoon jam sessions. Everybody dropped in—Basie, Teddy Wilson, Art Tatum, Hot Lips Page, Chu Berry, Roy Eldridge, the Dorseys, Artie Shaw, Goodman and Nat Cole, who was across the street at Kelly's Stable. Frank Sinatra and Frankie Laine used to hang around in that back booth, waiting for a chance to sing. . . . The customers would be three-deep around the bar, some of them nursing one drink the entire afternoon.

"I stopped hiring horns in the late forties. The food side had become very important, and the horns made too much noise. Since then I've had small, quiet groups, a lot of them led by women, like Mary Osborne, the guitarist; Jutta Hipp and Toshiko [Akiyoshi]; Marjorie Hyams, the vibraphonist; and, of course, Marian McPartland, who's a

Tommy Dorsey, who frequently jammed at the Onyx. *RCA Records*

fixture and who gave Joe Morello his start. George Shearing started here, too, and so did Peter Nero in 1959. He was Bernie Nierow then and our intermission pianist."

To say that George Shearing started at the Hickory is a bit of exaggeration. Leonard Feather, a countryman of English-born Shearing, urged Popkin to book the sightless pianist. Popkin expressed an aversion to hiring somebody with an affliction and, as publicist Joe Morgen recalls, resisted on the ground that he did not want "to expose this man to pity." However, he relented, and as Shearing advises: "My appearance at the Hickory House was confined to one off night." If any club is to claim credit for introducing Shearing, composer of "Lullaby of Birdland" and master of the locked-hands style, it would be the Three Deuces.

Frankie Laine had a longer run at the steakery. But it was under a strange arrangement. As he describes it: "Somebody heard me sing in the Village at Bobby Hackett's place—Nick's, wasn't it? It was trumpeter Red Allen who said: 'Why don't you come up to the Hickory House on Sunday? They have these jams. When I get on the stand, I'll have Joe Marsala get you up.'

"I figured, my God, maybe this is an omen. Joe Marsala was from Chicago. He lived in the same neighborhood as I did, just around the corner from where I went to school. We used to, like, run around with the same crowd, except that he was older than our gang.

"I couldn't wait for Sunday to come. When I got to the Hickory House, Red was already up on the stand playing. One of the things I used to do was what many regarded as a great jazz version of 'Stardust.' Red tried to get Joe to get me up. But Joe kept stalling and calling on other people. I might have been really upset, except that I had never seen a harp in a jazz group. Adele played great and still does, and I was really flipped.

"Finally, there was a lull. Bobby Hackett had gone up, and instead of playing trumpet, he had played guitar, which was his original instrument. Then he switched to trumpet and they had three trumpets going—Bobby, Marty Marsala and Red Allen. Buddy Rich was on drums and Artie Shapiro was on bass. And man, they were winging. Then Joe called me up, and I sang my two wild choruses of 'Stardust.' Joe's eyes kinda opened up, and Red felt real great, like I didn't let him down. 'I want to talk to you,' Marsala said, and I was thrilled.

"I hung around. After they finished, Joe said: 'My budget is such that I can't pay you anything. But if you want to come around, I'll get you up to sing every night. Somebody may hear you and we'll go from there. Maybe if we get enough going here, I can get them to pay you.'

"Well, I spent eight months dressed in a tuxedo every night, from starting time till closing. There was so much activity going on then. Everybody came in, and everybody was a musician who had to be called on to jam. So I'd sit and sit and sit. But I had no other straw.

"I had come from Stamford, Connecticut, where I worked as a shipping clerk for a Du Pont subsidiary that made synthetic leathers. After three months, my money ran so low that I had to write my father. He sent me eight hundred dollars that enabled me to stay another five months.

"Once I think I sat there for a month without being called once. Then Joe promised that he wouldn't miss me on Saturday night. Saturday came and went, and finally I just bust loose inside. As they were playing the closing theme, I jumped up from where I sat in the back and charged out. I was practically bawling. Joe came after me and caught me near 51st and Seventh.

"He put his arms around me and said: 'Frank, I'm sorry. If you only knew what it was like to be up there! But come on back and let's have a drink. I'll see what I can do.' From then on, he called on me more regularly. But nothing happened, and finally, my money gave out, and I had to go home. I guess you might say I was singing for my suppers. But a lot of people got to hear me and I learned a lot.

"I hung around Hickory House from April, 1937, until December.

Willie "The Lion" Smith played the Onyx before Repeal.

RCA Records

I went back home to Chicago for Christmas. After that, it was a long, long road before I cut 'That's My Desire,' the record that sprung me loose in 1947. Probably I was ahead of my time in the Hickory days and people had to tire of the crooning style of Crosby and Sinatra before they could accept my *belting* approach, as it used to be called. Today, I guess they call it soul, blue-eyed, that is, or hard rock."

The soundness of Laine's surmise about the time factor is suggested by a story that Willie "the Lion" Smith tells. "One afternoon in 1937," he reports, "I arrived at Hickory House full of brandy. . . . Bob Stephens, an executive at Decca, came over to where everybody was buying a round and put his arm around my shoulder to start sweet-talking. 'Lion, my boss, Jack Kapp, wants to talk to you over yonder at his table. He's got someone he wants you to meet.'

"So I go over and shake hands with this guy. He's Milt Herth, an organist from Chicago, who's in town to make some records for Decca. Jack and Dave Kapp, the brains at the record company, decide they'd like to get some swing into Herth's music. Before we'd had two rounds, the pens and contract forms were on the table and everybody was signing.

"That's the way things happen. [They didn't for Frankie Laine at that time.] I'd stopped by the Hickory House looking for Joe Marsala to recommend a young drummer by the name of Gene Krupa and walked out with a hundred-dollar bill and a new recording deal."

But the Lion was not too happy. When he read the contract later, he wished that he had insisted on more money. "The next day," he says, "I got a better offer from the Columbia people, but it was too late. I was too busy living it up in those days, getting high with James

P. Johnson and Fats Waller, to tend to business properly. So I was tied to Decca and Herth for a year with an option."

With Willie at the keyboard, O'Neil Spencer from the John Kirby group on drums and Herth on Hammond organ, the trio cut over twenty sides of the hit tunes of '37–'38—among them "The Dipsey Doodle," "The Toy Trumpet," "Flat Foot Floogie" and "The Campbells Are Swinging."

In those swinging years, the Lion recalls seeing "a woman named Polly Adler sitting at a table in the corner. She used to say she had enough material for a book. But a lot of us said that. Polly made it work when she later wrote *A House Is Not a Home.*" In retrospect he notes that he "introduced a lot of musicians to John Popkin. The Lion brought in a singing quartet, The Ink Spots, to meet Popkin, who hired them for $30 a week. That was before they had a hit record. Hazel Scott was another star who had her first important jobs at the Hickory. Popkin couldn't pay enough to have big names working there regularly. The pay was in uppercuts only." In later years he remembers seeing Duke Ellington hanging around Hickory during the afternoons—"it's his midtown headquarters."

In the Marsala era, Hickory House had such a magnetic name that when Roy Eldridge's band broke up in Chicago, due to his illness, Zutty Singleton and his wife walked out of the Three Deuces in the "Windy City," got into their car, and drove steadily to New York. Even before they checked into a hotel, they drove over to Popkin's for a jam session with Joe and Marty Marsala and a steak.

During Marsala's tenure, the steakery played host to three of the era's finest hide beaters. After Buddy Rich came Dave Tough—a mixed-up cat who wanted to write (F. Scott Fitzgerald was his passion) and who died from a drunken fall on a Newark sidewalk. But that did not happen until 1948, after he had played with all the top name bands of the day, including Artie Shaw, Charlie Spivak, Dorsey, Goodman and Woody Herman. Critic Leonard Feather regards him as "the greatest artist ever to work as a jazz drummer." After Tough, Marsala brought in young Shelly Manne, who today is still the busiest drummer on the Hollywood studio scene.

In 1940, shortly after Shelly Manne succeeded Dave Tough, Marsala enlarged his combo to a nine-piece band for which Paul Weston, who later married Jo Stafford of the Pied Pipers, wrote the arrangements. With the big-band syndrome growing apace, Marsala was drawn into the big-money sweepstakes. But two years of experimentation and location dates (Armonk, Glen Island Casino, etc.) were brought to a dismal dead end by wartime exigencies. The rationing of gas and the ban on pleasure driving, not to mention blackouts and swing shifts, reduced the number of customers and destroyed Marsala's hopes, as well as those of other big bands.

For Marsala, the Hickory House era came to an end, with interruptions, around 1947. By then the winds of bop were furiously sweeping through many of the clubs on The Street. Despite his Chicago-Dixieland origins and orientation, Marsala was not unreceptive to the new sounds. Young modernist Neal Hefti worked with his combo in '43 and again in '46. And in an unreleased record session he cut for Black & White in January, '47, his sextet included Dizzy Gillespie on trumpet. In fact, after Marian Margaret Turner, then a trad British pianist married to Dixieland trumpeter Jimmy McPartland, spent an evening listening to the Marsala group, she chided him for his modernity.

But Hickory House was not a haven for bop, big bands or hot drummers so much as outstanding keyboard artists. Joey Bushkin, who worked with Marsala's Chicagoans in '37, was the first of a group that included Billy Kyle in '39, Jess Stacy in '40, and Mel Powell in '41. There were also Hazel Scott, Marian McPartland, Martial Solal, Billy Taylor and others.

Joe Bushkin was an irrepressible prankster. When he and Marsala were rooming together, he once persuaded Joe to help him steal a 6-foot cutout of Louis Armstrong that stood outside the Paramount Theater. They managed to smuggle the papier-mâché figure into their hotel room, where they placed it directly in front of their door to greet and startle visitors.

In August, 1939, *The New Yorker* critic who found Basie's brass section ear-shattering at the Famous Door wrote of Hickory House: "The magnet that draws me is not the trick bar but Hazel Scott, a curly-haired girl who is somewhat of an institution here." By '39 Hazel had actually been paying her dues on The Street for over four years, not all of them at Popkin's *posada*. Joe Morgen remembers first seeing her at Tillie's Chicken Shack, a branch of Tillie's Kitchen of Harlem, which opened in the fall of 1935.

"She was a thin, demure, innocent-looking girl," Morgen recalls, "who never came to the Shack without her mother. They were from Port of Spain, where her mother, who played many instruments, led an all-girl band. Popkin paid her all of thirty-five dollars a week. At the Shack she was overshadowed by a swinging group called the Five Rhythm Chicks, and at Hickory she was just an intermission pianist. Unlike Erroll Garner, she happened only after she left The Street. Café Society did it for her—and by December, '39, she was making records for Bluebird."

Marian McPartland, born in Windsor, England, in the same year as Hazel Scott (1920), began breaking away from the Dixieland orientation of husband Jimmy McPartland in the early fifties. By the time she left the combo and his domicile she was playing the mod style for which she had once castigated Marsala. With interruptions at London House in Chicago, The Composer in New York, etc., Marian served as Hickory's house pianist for about eight years—from the early fifties into the early sixties.

No one remembers Duke Ellington playing The Street, except possibly Marian. "Some of the Hickory House nights are memorable," she says, "because Duke consented to sit in with my trio. This was when I first heard him play 'Chili Bowl' and an extended theme he jestingly referred to as 'Night Creatures,' besides his completely individual performances of 'Perdido' and 'A Train.' Once, in response to a request, he even rattled off a few choruses of 'Soda Fountain Rag.' "

Hazel and Marian were the first of a long line of foreign pianists who manned the Steinway in Hickory's Melody Bar, as the egg-shaped bar was called at the start. Others included German-born Jutta Hipp, a Leonard Feather discovery; Algiers-born Martial Solal, a George Wein protégé; and Manchurian-born Toshiko Akiyoshi, another George Wein protégée, discovered by Norman Granz and Oscar Peterson.

The house pianist after McPartland was Billy Taylor of Greenville, North Carolina, who must have been a Cheshire cat in an earlier existence. Although Billy made his 52d St. debut at the Three Deuces, he is remembered for his pianistics at Popkin's place. Willis Conover of The Voice of America thinks back to the many hours when he sat listening to Billy. In his memory, they were not entirely pleasant hours because "waiters, management and even the audience seemed rather insensitive—talking, shouting and generally paying no attention to Billy's superlative playing." Conover adds: "How he managed to remain so cool was a mystery to me. But he did have an extremely well-balanced orientation toward the condition under which the Negro lives and works in our society. I put it to him once. And do you know what he replied? 'My father was a minister, and he persuaded me that if I kept my own inner strength, nothing would bother me. And nothing has!' "

While Hickory House is remembered mostly for its keyboard killers, also Joe Marsala, at least one distinguished violinist briefly graced its elliptical bandstand-bar. Eddie South could have been a concert violinist. He had the tone, the technique and the touch. But having been born in 1904, he came to musical maturity at a time when there were no black faces to be seen on America's concert platforms and jazz was just beginning to gain acceptance in white America. A comparison of the career of Joe Venuti, who was also a hot fiddler and happened to be born in the same year as South, suggests the advantages that came with being Caucasian. Some critics believe that South was the superior fiddler. But he never attained the renown of Venuti, whose association with the Paul Whiteman Orchestra proved a potent launching platform. South did only limited recording—he can be heard on a rare Remington disc titled "Modern American Musicians"—and made most of his appearances in small clubs. He was at Hickory House in the fall of '42, and Popkin never stopped talking about it.

Hickory House outlived the bop era—Billy played modified bop—as it had the swing era. John Popkin watched all the great music clubs disappear after they hopped from location to location on The Street. He watched the invasion of the strippers during the war and the gradual deterioration in the fifties. For a time, he remained the western outpost of a block that was known as Chow Mein Lane, it housed so many Chinese restaurants. Eventually, as the towers of huge office buildings shadowed The Street, he and Jimmy Ryan's, east of Sixth Avenue, remained the sole vestiges of a golden era of jazz, exuberant entertainment and gentle togetherness.

The opening of the Americana in the late fifties, on the site of what had for decades been the fortresslike Manhattan Storage Company, brought an influx of conventioneers to Hickory House. Popkin made a minimal move of sprucing the front of the restaurant and installing softer lighting. He refused to have the huge fresco paintings on the walls removed or redone, and even an effort to wash off decades of dust was abortively halted—leaving ineradicable smears—when it appeared that the washing would leave the faded colors looking too anemic. Since most customers had such an obviously denigrating attitude toward the crude paintings, Popkin would never confess that he really liked them. But once in a while, when he was in a mellow mood, he would ask the world: "What's wrong with them? They're interesting and they always remind me of a time when life was very good."

When the CBS Building ousted Jimmy Ryan's, Hickory House remained a lone chapel of jazz, its faded frescoes and curling 8-by-10 glossies of celebrities attenuated reminders of the thirties. Popkin still presented jazz in the elliptical bar. But no one came for the music, even after pianist Martial Solal of France had scored a sensation at the Newport Jazz Festival. The steaks, broiled over hickory logs, were still good. But despite the overflow of people from Manuche's next door or the Americana across The Street, Popkin refused to modernize the place or lacked the cash to do it.

According to reports, his betting propensities had thrown him into such debt that no matter how much the restaurant grossed, it was not enough for effective management. A group of bookies who daily occupied a table in the rear, just in front of the shiny white brick fireplaces, were said to have gained possession of the place. Finally, in 1968, the steakery that had contributed so much to jazz history permanently closed its doors to make way for Pier 52, a fish restaurant. Popkin went down to Miami, as Leon Enken and Eddie Davis of Leon & Eddie, Irving Alexander of the Famous Door and Three Deuces, and Ralph Watkins of Kelly's Stable had done. Popkin was said to be looking for a new location. But he was really like a fire horse after the hook and ladders had been motorized. He had no heart for a new place. Like Jimmy Ryan, who died shortly after he left The Street, John Popkin lived little more than a year after he stopped broiling steaks over hickory logs.

Tape 10 . . . SHELLY MANNE

"Fifty-second Street started for me," said drummer Shelly Manne, "when it was still on 51st, when Kelly's Stable was opposite the old Roxy movie palace. That was before it moved to 52d, where Old China restaurant is now situated. I used to go into the Stable to hear Pete Brown's band. My interest was in the drumming of Arthur Herbert. He was the hide beater on that great record of 'Body and Soul' by Coleman Hawkins. I would sit in a corner of the bar, nursing a Coke. The owner, Ralph Watkins, got to know me and was nice enough to let me stay for an entire evening with just one Coke."

Sheldon Manne, better known as Shelly Manne, was then a string-bean kid of eighteen. Born in New York City in 1920, he came from a family of drummers—his father and two uncles. Although his musical education started with alto sax, he soon shifted to the drums, studying not with his father or uncles but with Billy Gladstone.

"One night at Kelly's Stable," he continues, "Arthur Herbert came up to me. The place wasn't that big, and he couldn't avoid knowing that I was all ears and eyes on his drums. When he learned that I was studying drums, he invited me to sit in with the band. Just like that! They did in those days. After that, he'd frequently let me play the last set of the evening. I did for months. And then I got a chance to sit in with the Spirits of Rhythm.

"As a result of all this sitting-in, I finally landed a job. My big break came through Ray McKinley, who led the Glenn Miller band after Glenn's death. Ray heard me drumming one night with Kenny Watts and his Kilowatts. It was an unusual group. Three kazoos and a rhythm section. They played Basie arrangements, copying the solos of cats like Harry Edison, Buck Clayton, Dickie Wells and Lester Young. He told me that Bobby Byrne was forming a new band composed of young guys. I got the job, even though I didn't read that well at the time. Made my first recording with Byrne. In '39, I believe. I used to listen to Davy Tough every chance I got when he was at the Hickory House with Joe Marsala. Once in a while Davy would let me sit in.

"One evening Benny Goodman came into the steak house. I happened to be subbing for Tough who was ill. The following morning I got a phone call. Goodman wanted me for a gig down in Washington. I can't remember whether he told me that it was to play President Roosevelt's birthday party. It might have brought me uptight. He just said something like, 'Kid, meet me at Penn Station. Just bring your cymbals. We've got drums.' On the train to Washington he told me he wasn't 'worrying about my playing.' He could tell that I'd been listening to his records. And so I played with the Benny Goodman band for two nights—there was a rehearsal one evening and the President's birthday party was on the next. What an experience! Here I was just twenty and playing with the greatest swing band of the time! Goodman was a tough, no-nonsense leader. The guys called him The Ray—he had that piercing pair of eyes when he looked at you from the bandstand.

"When we returned to New York, Goodman reached Davy, and Tough went with him. I got the chair at Hickory House. It was a good beginning and a good showcase. I worked with several big bands after that—Bob Astor, Raymond Scott and Will Bradley. Took Ray McKinley's chair after he left Bradley's band. This was around 1941.

"I was in the Coast Guard from '42 on for about three years. Before I got shipped out, I was stationed at Manhattan Beach. Used to travel by subway to 52d St. every night—it was a ride—and sit in until the last minute. Had to check in at six in the morning. I stayed up night after night—who needed sleep then?—to play the drums. I'd play the 52d St. spots until they shut down and then hop over to the Two O'Clock Club for an hour or so. It was around the corner from Charlie's Tavern, upstairs on Seventh Avenue. It opened at two in the morning.

"The Street was really swinging then. You got to see everybody. When they weren't working and between sets, they'd all be up at the White Rose bar on Sixth Avenue. After I got married in '43, we wouldn't live anywhere except on 52d. Our first apartment was across the street from the Onyx—a walk-up in one of the brownstones, above a French restaurant.

"In a way, it was 52d St. that made me want to become a jazz drummer. There was a feeling of camaraderie and a willingness to teach and aid young people. I can never forget one night with Jimmy Crawford, who was the powerhouse drummer of the Jimmie Lunceford band. He was one of my idols. He came up to me at the Hickory House and wanted to know how I did a certain thing with my brushes. He was my idol and he was asking me, a kid! But there was this great exchange and interchange.

"And there were such diversified sounds on The Street! Why, in a matter of an evening, you could walk through forty years of music. The whole history of jazz was there in capsule form. The main object was to swing. And as long as you did that, you could sit in with anybody. Today, styles are so pigeonholed.

"And yet nobody had to stop being himself. I was a clean-living kid. Didn't drink—and I didn't have to, in order to be accepted. I tried it a couple of times. Found that I couldn't think clearly or play as well, and I'd just have a Coke when other guys were hoisting them. I've heard that there were guys who felt they had to smoke pot to be accepted. Maybe it was my personality. But nobody made me do anything or asked me to do anything I didn't want to do. And most of the older guys were protective. And not only for me but about my wife, too.

"When I was shipped out, my wife was working at Radio City Music Hall. Our apartment was on 52d, and Ben Webster would make sure that she got home safely. He'd manage to take five just about the time when she was walking home. He'd see her to the door of our place. But was I miserable while I was away! Not only missed my wife. I missed The Street. The first night after I returned, I was down at the Three Deuces sitting in. It was a Ben Webster trio, with Big Sid Catlett on drums and Al McKibbon on bass. I didn't even bother to take off my Coast Guard uniform. Two shore patrolmen came in and dragged me off the stand. Said I had no right to perform in my uniform. Believe me, these guys were nervous when Ben and Al and Sid followed us out into The Street. They didn't call Ben The Brute for nothing. And Al and Sid weren't small guys either. Those shore patrol guys sure took off in a hurry—me with them. Nothing came of it. When we got to headquarters and I made my explanation about being home on leave and living on the block, the CO told those shore patrol guys off.

"It was late '45 when I was mustered out of the services. I went right into the Deuces, playing with a Johnny Bothwell combo. After that I had a quartet of my own—Allen Eager on reeds, Bob Carter on bass and Ed Finckel on piano. We were there for about three months when I got an offer from Stan Kenton. That was my last job on The Street. I left around February, 1946.

"While I was in the service and home on leave, there were incidents with racial overtones on The Street, particularly where Southern servicemen were involved. I remember one night at the Onyx when a Southern soldier pulled a knife on Argonne Thornton. Can never forget how Ben Webster walked from the bandstand. You know how the tables in those joints were set one on top of the other. Well, Ben paid no attention. He just walked through them. And when he got to the bar, he grabbed this guy, lifted him off the floor with one hand, and just held him there at arm's length. The guy kept squirming until he was ready to pass out. Ben kept holding him and talking to Argonne. Then he just opened his hand, the guy dropped to the floor, and took off like a scared rabbit.

"The tension hit The Street as well as other worlds. But when The Street was swinging, there was no place like it. The pay wasn't good. But anytime I had a choice between working a club gig somewhere or working on The Street, I'd grab the 52d St. job, no matter how much loot I had to give up. Those years, from '39 to '46, were the liveliest of my life and most formative. 52d St. was home if you played jazz. But it was also all the things that made New York City the most exciting place in the world."

After he left The Street, Shelly Manne worked with jazz modernists like Stan Kenton, Charlie Ventura and Woody Herman. In '52 he settled near Los Angeles and participated in the upsurge of West Coast jazz, as the cool, cerebral music of Chet Baker, Gerry Mulligan, Dave Brubeck, Howard Rumsey (at the Hermosa Beach Lighthouse) became known. But he also worked in the Hollywood movie and recording studios and was, before long, the most in-demand drummer in the screen capital. *Encyclopedia of Jazz* estimates that his hide beating may be heard on well over a thousand LP's.

Today, Manne lives on a large estate in Northridge, California, where he raises show horses. Despite his tight schedule of work in the film and record studios, he continues to play with his own combo at the Manne-Hole, a jazz club he owns and has run for many years. His success and wealth have not made him blasé about playing jazz. Weekends, he can be found listening intently to the new jazz groups he books into his club and also playing with his own group. He is still on 52d St. in spirit.

Tape 11 . . . MARIAN MCPARTLAND

"I guess I had one of the longest runs on 52d St.," said Marian McPartland, who was a Hickory House performer from early 1952 until 1960. "Eight years at least on that oval bandstand. I'd take a few weeks or months off to go on the road, but otherwise 144 West 52d St. was my address.

"All kinds of good things happened to me while I was there. Garry Moore came in to hear the trio, and as a result, I was booked on his NBC *Morning Show* for several weeks. I had my own radio show on WNEW every evening, and my trio was also heard via remotes on NBC. Duke Ellington was a frequent visitor—he was a client of Joe Morgen, who handled the publicity for the Hickory House. Once in a while I would persuade him to sit in with the trio, and later I appeared on a television show with the Ellington Band. Stories appeared about the trio in *Newsweek* and *Time* through Joe Morgen's efforts. Birdland came into existence while I was at the Hickory House, and the

Jimmy and Marian McPartland are visited backstage by the great European jazz guitarist Django Reinhardt in 1946.   *Down Beat*

performers used to come over to sit in with us, just as we would go over and sit in with them. I met and became friendly with Steve Allen, who was courting Jayne Meadows at the time. They would sit in one of the back booths at the club, holding hands and drinking martinis. Steve occasionally sat in with the trio, too, and I made a lot of guest appearances on his nighttime television show.

"I lived in a state of great excitement during those years. Every night was a ball with lots of well-known musicians coming in, some of whom I had listened to as a kid in England. I was starry-eyed about meeting people like Artie Shaw, Benny Goodman, Louis Armstrong and others. Dave Brubeck, Oscar Peterson and Bud Powell, who were working at Birdland, were frequent visitors. We had a very good trio—Joe Morello on drums, and Bill Crow on bass. Some of the musicians who came into the Hickory House, I think, had the idea of hiring the two guys away from me. In fact, Joe Morello did eventually go with the Dave Brubeck Quartet, and it was a great thing for him. Later I told Dave, 'I used to flatter myself into thinking that you came to hear the trio, but you really came there to steal my drummer.'

"In that huge room you could get a good rapport with the people who sat at a certain place at the bar. We had our fans who always came early to get these good seats, and they hung on every note we played. A fine pianist, John Mehegan, worked opposite us, and when he played, he'd pound the floor with his foot. One night I sneaked up inside the bar, close to the bandstand, and held his foot down. He couldn't go on playing. John used to needle me by telling me I didn't have enough 'bird' in my playing. Though we kidded each other a great deal, we had respect and fondness for each other. I have always admired the talent that went into putting together the three excellent books on *Jazz Improvisation*.

"I still run into so many of the people I met there: young college kids, now well-heeled suburbanites, who spent their weekends in the Hickory House. I used to jokingly tell these kids that they would never make it through college if it wasn't for the swinging Hickory House weekends. We had students from Princeton, Yale, Harvard, and I got to know many of them. There was one boy from Yale who would come in on the weekends and say to me, 'If my mother comes by during the week, please don't tell her that I was here. I'm supposed to be studying for exams up in New Haven.'

"Jimmy and I came to New York in 1946, just about a year after we were married. We came direct from USO camp shows in Europe, where we had been working together; the trip took us seventeen days on a Victory Ship. The first thing we did was to check into the Victoria Hotel, then we went to a Chinese restaurant, and then we headed for Eddie Condon's Club in the Village. Jimmy wanted me to sit in with the band to show how good he thought I was, and naturally I was dying to do just that, and did. For the next five years or so, I worked with Jimmy's group in Chicago, his hometown, using my professional name of Marian Page. I was born Margaret Marian Turner in Windsor, England; but when I started playing professionally, I took the name of Marian Page because my parents were so aghast at my going into the music business.

"We came to New York again in 1949. But I never really got started with the trio until I opened at the Hickory House. While I was there, my aunt and uncle from Windsor, Sir Cyril and Lady Dyson, came to the USA to attend a Convention of Mayors in Windsor, Ontario. They came to visit me en route. They did not seem to think that the Hickory House was the right spot for me—you know, sitting up behind the bar, playing for such a mixed crowd, and all that. After my set, my aunt whispered confidentially in my ear, 'Marian, does your father know what you're doing?'

"My mother and father were rather class-conscious and wanted me to grow up to be a 'proper' person, as they understood it. But somehow I never was. For one thing, I brought home kids of whom they did not approve, and then music was a trade to them. In fact, my father once tried to bribe me into giving up the idea of going into music, and taking a job in a bank, or something equally dull. But, somehow, I stuck to my guns, I really don't know how. I am sure that poor Daddy probably caught hell from the rest of the family for letting me become a musician.

"I think that what actually happened to my musical career is great. I began making records around 1949–1950, for the King label and later for Savoy. But the first really good record contract came after I settled at the Hickory House. I went with Capitol in 1953 and made five albums. This was one of the many nice things that happened while I was there. But even though I played in the club so many times and for so many years, every time I came back it was like a brand-new opening night, and it would take two to three evenings before I became acclimatized and got used to the sound of the room again. But, of course, knowing the bartenders and waiters and everybody in the place made it a very pleasant time. Mr. Popkin got two new pianos in the years that I played there. That was one nice thing about the room; we always had a good piano.

"Joe Morello, my drummer, was one of the many fine musicians I discovered while I was at the Hickory House. Jazz groups then had a freewheeling policy of letting musicians sit in, and I always did too. It's a shame that musicians don't do this so much anymore. I heard a lot of terrific players that I might have otherwise missed. Of course sometimes you were fooled by appearances. When I first saw Joe Morello, I thought he looked more like a young physicist rather than a drummer. But when he sat in, we were all flabbergasted by this man's tremendous talent. Joe was then and still is one of the great drummers in our business.

"John Popkin, the owner of the Hickory House, was easy to work for, though it depended to a certain extent on how things went at the racetrack. When he was feeling good, he'd come by and give me an enormous slap on the back. But when things weren't going so well at the track, he'd complain that I was taking too long an intermission. He disliked drum solos and he'd glare at Joe Morello, who frequently sat at a back table practicing on a folded napkin. I'd go into the kitchen once in a while to pour myself a cup of coffee, and this would be all right until Mr. Popkin had a bad day. Then he'd growl, 'I can't keep you in coffee,' or he'd tell me I was eating too much. Sometimes I'd come off the bandstand and sense he was in a bad mood, and so I would walk away from him. He'd come after me, I'd quicken my pace, and so would he. If I was lucky, I'd get to the ladies' room before he got to me, and by the time I came out, he'd forgotten all about it.

"In retrospect, I think we all behaved like mischievous kids, but we were having fun, and business was generally good during my months at the club. But you'd never know it from talking to Mr. Popkin. The place would be jammed and I'd say, 'Business looks good tonight.' He would say something like "Oh, they're not a drinking crowd, they're all ordering beer.' Mr. Popkin liked to show off before his cronies, and once in a while he would bawl me out in front of them. But this was all part of his personality, and as I think back, I realize that I was very fond of him and I think he was of me, in a rough and tough sort of way.

"We had so many laughs and little practical jokes going on all the time between ourselves. I remember something we did that we still talk about to this day. You know those big murals of sports events that were on the walls all around the room? I used to nag Mr. Popkin about them and tell him he should do the room over. His retort would be, 'The room was like this before you got here and it'll be like this after you're gone.' He was really quite proud of them and I don't think he wanted to renovate the place; he just liked it the way it was. One of the biggest murals, right inside the door on the left, showed a huntsman on horseback followed by a pack of hounds.

"One night when we were getting ready to leave, we discovered that workmen had left a tall ladder standing. We thought what a joke it would be to add something to this hunting scene. So Bill Crow climbed the ladder, and with my lipstick he carefully added a small appendage to one of the dogs. We laughed a great deal over this, and every evening after that we would take a sidelong glance up at the picture. But no one seemed to notice. As you can see we were capable in those days of doing all kinds of silly things.

"Late one night, when the place was empty and we were ready to go home, we decided to play a tune lying down—Bill had the bass on his chest, Joe held his snare drum the same way, and I lay on the floor and reached up to the keyboard. It was crazy, but fun, particularly when Julius, the headwaiter, came walking around the bar. He could hear the music but couldn't see any of us. Some nights we would pretend we were playing music for acts in a movie or circus. As we imagined different developments, we would play music to fit the movements. The music would get more exciting, with drum rolls and all kinds of effects. The waiters would look at us in bewilderment, wondering what we were doing and why we seemed to be killing ourselves laughing.

"One of the problems at the Hickory House was that we had no place to get away by ourselves. There was no dressing room or any kind of place where you could go to shut the door and be on your own. Unless I went into the ladies' room, I was easily accessible to John Popkin's racetrack-dominated moods and also to the shenanigans of the customers. We would come off the bandstand practically into their laps, and if they were at the bar, you couldn't possibly escape. Of course, I loved talking to the people and spent a lot of time doing this, but occasionally I wanted to be on my own. There was one table directly behind the bar on a straight line from the entrance. It was invisible from most parts of the room, and this was our table and we loved it. More jokes, fun and good conversation went on at that table! Joe brought his drum students there, and various friends came and went at all times of the night. I have a very sentimental feeling for that table, and I have often thought that I should have bought it before the Hickory House was sold and dismantled. I am really sad that I didn't.

"Because of the size of the Hickory House and because of the fact that food was served there, there always seemed to be a lot of noise—although the people at the bar were usually very quiet. When I think about this situation, I think about one of the people I met during this period, a wonderful singer and organist, Joe Mooney. Perhaps you recall the buildup Mike Levin, on *Down Beat,* gave the Joe Mooney Quartet when it opened on 52d St. Joe's arrangements were harmonically captivating and so different from anything I have ever heard—and there was always perfect quiet in Dixon's whenever the group performed.

"A few years ago I went to see Joe in Fort Lauderdale, where he settled. He was playing solo at the time, and he seemed very relaxed and happy on the job. He told me he could wear what he wanted, play what he liked, didn't have to worry about filling the room, and most important of all, he didn't have to smile. Joe is one of the most wonderful human beings I have ever met, besides being a great musician, and I really understood what he meant about not having to smile. I think that's one reason I enjoy playing for dancing—you can sit back and sort of melt into the scenery. You don't have to put on an act, you just play. It's strange—in a concert hall you don't have to smile, but in a club, you are supposed to. At the Hickory House there would always be somebody at the bar who would look up at us after a few drinks and holler, 'Why don'cha smile?' I once had a bass player named Vinnie Burke, who would get furious if anyone asked him to smile. He'd start glaring at the guy and get red in the face and stop in the middle of the tune and shout, 'What's the matter, don't you like music?'

"I have very happy memories of the Hickory House and of John Popkin. Most of the time he'd sit behind our table in his own particular spot with his back to the room, studying the racing form. I realize that underneath all the brusque remarks, he had quite a feeling of affection for me and I certainly did for him too. I was in the club on the last night just before the place was sold and torn down. Billy Taylor was on the bandstand, and he invited me to sit in; but I felt so sad that I just couldn't play. I knew that with this room went almost forty years of jazz history. I never went back, and I've never been in the new place. I don't think I could stand it.

"And now Mr. Popkin is gone, too, and with him some wonderful memories and wonderful music. It's hardly surprising that the Hickory House was like home to him. At times it was like a home for me, too. I'll always think of it with great nostalgia. There has never been another place like it, and there never will be."

Tape 12 . . . BILLY TAYLOR

"I came into New York on a Friday night," said Billy Taylor, the pianist who leads the band on the *David Frost Show*. "It was 1943, and I dropped my bags at a friend's apartment and headed directly for Minton's on West 118th St. I knew about the nightly jam sessions and I was aching to sit in. While I was trying to display my power over the keyboard, Ben Webster came and sat in. After we had jammed for a while, he leaned over, told me he had a combo at the Three Deuces, and invited me to come down on Sunday. I can't remember what I did on Saturday, though I do know I was too uneasy to go near The Street.

"But on Sunday night I found 72 West, took a deep breath, and went into the Deuces. It was a long basement room, a few steps down from the sidewalk, with about three rows of tables on each side of a center aisle. At the end of the aisle, to the right, was the bandstand. As I started down the aisle a girl stopped me. Norma Shepherd was a pianist from Washington, D.C., my hometown. 'Billy, what are you doin' in New York?' she asked. I told her I was auditioning for a job and said hello to the people to whom she introduced me at her table. I was just sitting down at the piano when the name of one of the men to whom I had nodded politely hit me. It came on in capital letters: TATUM. It was rather dark and smoky in the room, but I turned around and tried to spot him. I couldn't. But just the idea that it might be Tatum—and he was on the bill with Webster—paralyzed me. I didn't play well, and I often wonder why Ben didn't change his mind about hiring me. Later, when I got to know Art rather well, he told me that I played a lot of fast things. When I asked, 'Did it sound all right?' he said, 'Not particularly.'

"But that's the way things happened in those days. I arrived in town on Friday night, an unknown with a bachelor of music degree from Virginia State College, and by Sunday night I was part of Ben Webster's quartet. And the way the older musicians watched over

170

you! There were three of them that treated me like a younger brother. Art, drummer Jo Jones, and Big Sid Catlett all went out of their way to guide me. Generally, you hear about older musicians having a bad influence on younger musicians, leading innocent young guys into drinking or dope. I was fortunate to have an entirely different type of experience. I'd be at the White Rose bar on Sixth and 52d where you could get torn up pretty fast for very little. Drinks were twenty-five to thirty-five cents and good-sized. I'd put away a few and begin feeling no pain when Sid would suddenly be at my side. 'See you later,' he'd say. I didn't need a second invitation to know that he wanted me to split.

"Funny thing is that I didn't know these guys that well, except for Jo Jones whom I had met in his Count Basie days. But they kept an eye on me. I got quite a number of jobs through them and didn't even know how they happened at the time. I thought it was because I was such a hotshot at the keyboard. Later I found out that it was Art, Sid or Ben who was responsible. But they never said a word. Working opposite Tatum in those early days of my initiation into the music world, I not only became his friend. I became his protégé. I learned a lot from him, especially when I had an opportunity to listen to him play for me alone at his house. Just knowing that he was interested in me gave me tremendous confidence. And it was one of the most exciting periods in my life.

"Curious thing is that I got fired from my first gig with Webster. Coleman Hawkins was working with Billie Holiday at the Downbeat next door. Erroll Garner was playing for Billy Daniels down the street at Tondelayo's. Then Dizzy opened across the street at the Onyx with the first bebop band—Oscar Pettiford on bass, Don Byas on tenor sax, and Max Roach on drums. Bud Powell was supposed to be at the keyboard—he was underage then and had Cootie Williams as his guardian. Something went wrong, Powell didn't show, and they had to open without a piano player. But then I began sitting in. I was so excited by the new sounds that Dizzy and Pettiford brought down from Minton's that I stayed longer and longer. I'd have to rush to make my sets with Ben. For a few days, I kept getting dirty looks from Sammy Kay and Irving Alexander, the owners of the Deuces. Finally, one night when I really held things up, Alexander just fired me.

"I can't say that I blamed him. Alexander was an ex-musician, a sax player, and a nice, if hard-nosed, guy. There were a lot of short-changers and eccentrics around, and you had to know your way. Alexander did and he certainly was not unfair to me.

"One thing I always remember about the Deuces. The kitchen was in the back of the club, behind the bar. It had a beat-up old upright piano. There were some raucous sessions on that old box. Usually, guys who played other instruments, like Jo Jones or Tiny Grimes or Roy Eldridge—all of them could play some piano—would be there banging away, actually trying to cut one another at the keyboard. Frequently, they would come up with some interesting chord progressions, and they'd be after all the piano players to listen to their 'discovery.'

"After the Deuces gig folded, I went on the road with Eddie South, a giant of a fiddler. When we hit California, I decided to stay put for a while. Art Tatum was living on the Coast at that time, and I remained for about six months until I felt that I was getting into a rut musically, despite my daily sessions with him.

"Returning to New York, I wound up—you guessed it—at the Three Deuces. Slam Stewart had the gig and Erroll Garner was working with him. But Erroll had just hit with his recording of 'Laura,' and he wanted to branch out. And so I replaced him with Slam. John Collins, who was part of my quartet in 1950–51, was on guitar, and Hal 'Doc' West on drums.

"This was 1946, and after I got married, I went to Europe with the Don Redman band. When I returned to New York after spending about eight months in some of my favorite European cities, bop was the new in thing. 52d St. brought the music downtown, but the modern sounds were all over Broadway—at the Royal Roost, where Monte Kay served as midwife to the 'Birth of the Cool' with Miles Davis, and at Bop City, where they tried to serve a musical ragout of bop, pop, and rhythm-and-blues that did not quite make it with anybody.

"But both places showed a concern about bringing jazz to young people. They had bleachers where the Pepsi generation could come in for a low admission charge and soda fountains where they could satisfy their thirst. These innovations proved most successful at Birdland, where I was house pianist for nearly two years. Not only did teen-agers enjoy the jazz of that period, but they knew all the players and their records.

"Eventually I came back to 52d St., even though jazz had largely moved away by then. But it wasn't until Marian McPartland had given up her lease on Hickory House. Her tenancy changed the famous jazz steakery from a Dixieland room to a showcase for piano trios. Even though I worked there steadily for five years, I didn't break her record.

"What made 52d St. was not just the number of music clubs, but the *variety* of the music you could hear and the *interchange* between musicians. There is no substitute for free interchange. 52d St. had it. Color was no hangup. When I took a job, I was free to hire anybody I wanted. I remember Shelly Manne coming into a club in his Coast Guard uniform—it was during the war—and sitting in with a mixed group. Nobody thought anything of it. He was just another good drummer. Of course, there were different pay scales. White musicians often earned more than comparable black men. Even though famous musicians like Basie and Ellington earned more downtown than they did uptown, downtown clubs usually paid black musicians less than white.

"The informality had its negative side, too. You discovered this when you played Barney Josephson's Café Society, uptown and downtown. Josephson was much concerned about the quality of his p.a. systems, his pianos, the lighting, and all the other small things that went into properly showcasing an act. He paid attention to format and thought of his shows as presentations. Consequently, audiences related to the artists who worked for him in a way that they did not relate to them on 52d St. I remember Billy Daniels getting into a hassle with the owner of a 52d St. club because he wanted a pinspot on his face. Why the fuss about a little bit of light?

"But it was the informality and intimacy of all the 52d St. clubs, as well as the interchange between artist and artist, and artist and audience, that gave The Street its character and warm glow and changed the character of American popular music."

9. Tony's and the Yacht Club

When Abel Green made a meticulous survey of 52d St. in 1936, he labeled the north side "the unofficial right side of the railroad tracks" and attributed its "tonier aura" to Jack & Charlie's 21, Leon & Eddie at No. 33, and not alone for the *double-entendre* it invited, Tony's at No. 57.

Robert Sylvester tells the story of the Park Avenue couple attired in tails and mink who came from a posh Metropolitan Opera opening and accidentally wandered into Jimmy Ryan's at No. 53 instead of Tony's. After they made their way past the noisy bar and through the thick, low cloud of smoke, the bejeweled girl turned to her uneasy escort and whispered something he could not hear because of the rip-snorting music booming from the bandstand. But after they were seated at one of the checkerboard tables, he received a repeat play: "I told you," she said, "the West Side would be dreadful!" Obviously, the west side of Ryan's was not the same as the west side of Tony's, even though they hunched side by side.

Like L & E, 21, the Onyx and Yacht Club, Tony's had come out of the era of peepholes, passwords and padlocked doors. As a speakeasy, it operated at No. 59, with which it was still connected by a rear passageway. Tony's was known to be an expensive joint, higher priced than the other clubs mentioned, with the exception of the Iron Gate. What gave it a unique quality on The Street was neither its class nor its prices but its clientele and their way of life—and also one singer.

Among habitués of 52d, Tony's clientele was sometimes dismissed as effete. This was an easy putdown of people who had not only more money but culture, taste and sophistication. Probably the key word is sophistication. To Tony's for a late-hour snack of supper and song came a goodly number of the members of the so-called Algonquin Roundtable. This was the bright group of literary, art and theater people whose jester-in-residence was Robert Benchley and uncrowned queen, the much-quoted mistress of acid repartee, Dorothy Parker.

Reviewing a reissue of Emily Post's well-known book, Miss Parker wrote tongue-in-cheek in *The New Yorker: "Etiquette* is out again, this time in a new and enlarged edition, and so the question of what to do with my evenings has been all fixed for me. There will be an empty chair at the deal table at Tony's. . . ." To the Algonquin crowd, wit was all, and no situation was off limits to well-phrased kidding—"putdown" is today's word. ("Oh, Dottie, if you keep on committing suicide," Robert Benchley commented after one of her attempts, "you're going to injure your health permanently.") Life was a matter of words, and the sublime end was to be clever.

The owner of Tony's, who was a singer—and being a student of yoga, sometimes sang standing on his head—Tony Soma somehow found a performer whose singing style was a perfect expression of the Roundtable life-style. Mabel Mercer was British and came to this country in the late thirties after years of performing at Bricktop's in Paris. There's a paucity of information about Mabel, largely because of her own reticence, but partly because her style is so special that she is omitted from books on both jazz and pop. Even her entry in *Who's Who in America* was compiled without her cooperation. It reads: "b. Burton-on-Trent, Eng., 1900; ed. convent sch. Singer at Bricktop's, Paris, France, 1931–38, in NYC 1941–61; recital at Downstairs at the Upstairs, NYC, 1964; recording artist for Atlantic Records." (It does not mention that when she arrived in this country, she found that she could not rent an apartment except in Harlem.)

The brief entry would hardly indicate the scope of Miss Mercer's influence, or the size, devotion and enthusiasm of her following. "In group" it surely was and is. But it was an in group of influentials like Peggy Lee, Lena Horne, Margaret Whiting, Billie Holiday and Sara Vaughan. "How I love her," Ava Gardner once told her publicist David Hanna as she played a Mercer record. "I used to hear her every night when I was first married to Frank. Sinatra said that more than anyone, she taught him how to handle a lyric." (By the time "The Voice" was courting Ava in the early fifties, Mabel was singing at a small, upstairs, East 52d St. spot, The Byline Room, where they nightly came, and held hands.)

Mabel was not only a singer's singer but a songwriter's singer. Tony's clientele included Bart Howard, who later wrote "Fly Me to the Moon"; Alec Wilder, many of whose songs Mabel introduced; and other sophisticated songsmiths whose work put them outside Tin Pan Alley and even on the periphery of the Broadway musical theater. Edward C. Redding, who wrote "The End of a Love Affair," remembers being taken to Tony's by James Keenan, an architectural lighting expert, who felt that only Mabel could appreciate his smart, then-unpublished torch ballad. (I published it in 1950.)

Sometime after she arrived in New York, Mabel was attracted to Tony's by Cy Walters, a superlative supper-club pianist. The smart crowd was then going to Tony's to hear Walters while they played gin rummy. Once Cy knew the identity of the Bricktop singer, he occasionally invited her to sing with him; and when he left for the chichi East Side, Mabel became Tony's mainstay. Lester Crowley of Ray Noble's orchestra took over as her accompanist until Buddy Barnes arrived. (Bundy Pendleton, who sang and played, was later a Tony mainstay, and Harry Gibson doubled briefly at the Trouville while he was at L & E before he emerged as the "Hipster.")

"One evening I wandered into Tony's," said pianist Billy Taylor. "It was directly across from the Three Deuces where I was then appearing with Slam Stewart. While I nursed a couple of drinks, the stage remained empty, except for a tall stool on which a pin spotlight shown. I was just about to leave when an elderly-looking lady came out, perched herself on the stool, and began to sing or recite. She had an absolutely unique style, not jazz but really beautiful. Her material was as personal as her approach. I used to come back whenever I could. She always had her audiences spellbound."

For composer-songwriter-arranger Alec Wilder, 52d St. was Mabel Mercer. "There was nothing outstanding about Tony's except Mabel," he says. "She made it into a kind of chapel. She gave it an aura of calm and protection. She had magic. People would come in, not just to hear her sing, but to absorb the atmosphere she created—one of great calm and peace and security. Hers was the oddball place.

It didn't swing, as some other 52d St. joints did. She didn't attempt to swing.

"She did dozens of songs that I and others felt impelled to write for her, songs that nobody has since heard. They remain in manuscript. And if they did get published, they seem to get lost on some dusty shelf. Like 'The Olive Tree,' published by G. Schirmer, on which I have never received a cent of royalty.

"But she also did songs that became standards because she did them. 'Wait Till You See Her' was a ballad that was not used in *By Jupiter*. But Mabel liked it. After she began singing it, the magical thing happened. Other singers discovered it. Suddenly, the rejected song became a talked-about song. Peggy Lee added it to her repertoire. So did Sinatra. Bandleaders began putting it into their books. Single-handed, Mabel revived other forgotten songs and popularized songs that would have been forgotten. Mabel was the first to see merit in 'While We're Young,' one of my songs and one of the first she did when she began working at Tony's.

"The Street was like a block party. The area between Fifth and Sixth avenues was total friendship. You felt safe, secure and protected. Everybody seemed to get along with everybody. You talked to anybody and they talked with you. For me, it was a strange experience because crowds generally make me tense. I want to run, to get out. But not 52d St. It was a great big friendly world. It has never happened since. And I don't think it will ever again. There is little trust today among adults. 52d St. was a trusting community. It was good for Mabel. She flourished.

"From Mabel, Sinatra picked a song of mine that I never, for the life of me, would have picked for him. It's a morbid ballad about suicide called 'Where Do You Go (When It Starts to Rain).' It's in his *No One Cares* album. Through Sinatra, Stan Getz found the piece and played it, I am told, at his mother's funeral and also at a concert in Tanglewood with the Boston Pops. But it was Mabel who had the courage to do songs that no one else would dare to touch. She liked sad songs.

"But she also had a marvelous feeling for the lighter and brighter tunes—the smartly worded type that Bart Howard and others wrote for her. You know, where you have to hear every syllable. What enunciation, what beautiful and distinctive enunciation she had and still has! And what attentive listeners! She was really a diseuse in the great French tradition of Piaf. She had impeccable taste and needed a discerning audience, which was what she found at Tony's. She always sensed whenever I was depressed. She would do an entire set of my songs and send me home happy. And she did that to people who didn't write for her. I've never seen such rapt audiences in my life."

Like Tony's, the Yacht Club was a supper club rather than a music room. But that's where the similarity ended—it was brassy, not chichi. Like Tony's, it, too, came out of the Prohibition era, but not without travail. In the period when Texas Guinan and Helen Morgan seemed to be constant police targets, the Yacht Club was raided and padlock proceedings were started. But as with Guinan and Morgan, who kept popping up with new places—when the old were left a shambles by ax-wielding raiders—the Yacht managed to get an acquittal, even though, according to a story in the New York *Times* of January 19, 1929, it admitted that it had sold liquor. Broadway wiseacres had a simple explanation—*ice.* (In those days money given as bribes was maintained on ledger books as expenditures for ice.)

Named after a well-known male singing group on radio, the Yacht Club had at least three different addresses. Shortly after Repeal, it was in the main block at No. 38. According to *Variety* editor Abel Green, only the Onyx, 21 and L & E outgrossed it. The popularity was largely due to Frances "Za Zu Zass" Faye whose stylized piano-vocal version of "No Regrets" and other ballads of unrequited love made her an audience draw. Miss Faye embodied the era's nostalgia for torch songs, a nostalgia that found symbolic expression in Jane Froman's fondling of a large handkerchief as she moaned "Lost in a Fog."

By the time the Yacht was showcasing the talents of the great Fats Waller, it had sailed to No. 150 West, near Seventh Avenue. (A Chinese restaurant, Lum Fong's, later occupied the spot where Manuche's today offers Italian cuisine.) Just west of Hickory House, the club was decorated like a pleasure yacht, and the ceiling represented a night sky ablaze with stars. Fats' appearance in 1938 was his longest in any one place. It was duly noted by *The New Yorker,* whose reviewer was overwhelmed by the "consummate piano playing" of the "monumental man in a derby hat." No mention was made of his comic gifts—his way of leering at the audience and rolling his eyes, his humorous asides and laughable lyric changes—or of his infectious

Fats Waller.

ebullience. (Glaring at the piano stool, he'd ask: "Thomas, is you all on?") The reviewer found space to single out "a wonderful girl who wandered around saying, 'Cigars, cigarettes and Russian wolf-hounds!'"

Recording companies found talent on The Street and music publishers found material. Tenor saxophonist Gene "Honey Bear" Sedric, long an associate of Waller's, recalls that when he played the Yacht, "all the publishers used to go there. They liked Fats and they all wanted his songs. I remember one night when we played 'If I Had You.' He started crying. It turned out that he was thinking about his earlier days and about all the hits he had given away. Jack Robbins, the music publisher, once told me that if Fats had completed all the songs he'd gotten advances on, Robbins would be a millionaire."

(But there were publishers like the current owners of "Ain't Misbehavin'" who could tell you that they had purchased his rights for a paltry $500. In the early days of his marriage, Fats once offered to sell an entire folio of his songs to the QRS piano-roll people for $10. Once he sold nine tunes to Fletcher Henderson for the price of nine hamburgers. When he roughed them out on the spot, Henderson insisted on paying $10 per tune.)

Around 1943 the Yacht moved to the old location of the Famous Door at No. 66 West, just opposite Tony's Trouville. Not long after, Billy Eckstine made what turned out to be a premature stab at becoming a solo singer. "One of the first shows I handled," notes Monte Kay, now producer of the *Flip Wilson Show* and then a publicist producer, "involved Eckstine's debut as a singer. For a reason I never understood, his agent decided that Billy's name should be spelled X-Tine instead of the way it is normally spelled. That's how it appeared on the Yacht Club canopy. But it did not help, and Mr. B, as he became known when he did make it as a singer, went back to leading a big band—the great band that became the most important incubator of bop.

"On the bill with X-Tine, we had two bands. Trummy Young's with Ike Quebec on tenor—this was right after Trummy took his trombone out of Charlie Barnet's band. And Quebec's idol, Coleman Hawkins, with one of the greatest combos of his career. He and Don Byas were playing those breathy, big-toned solos. Little Benny Harris was reaching on trumpet and unable to execute what he was thinking. Thelonious Monk at the piano was a troubled guy and not too reliable. But Hawk would not let either of these guys go. He was always ahead of his time, and he knew that Monk, despite his problems, was into something new and important. That combo was stylistically a combination of Hawk's kind of swing and early bop.

"It was a fantastic group," Kay continued, "and I think of them with warmth and pleasure. But I also have some painful memories of that period—unrelated, by the way, to the new sounds. I persuaded Joe Glaser to let us have Billie Holiday, who was playing across The Street at the Onyx. We doubled her salary and kept her for almost six months, during which she did tremendous business. She was singing at the top of her talent, and no one could top that.

"But whereas my job had been to produce shows, after Billie arrived, my job was to produce Billie. Literally. The problem would start after the first show. She would want to run home. I would try to convince her to go across The Street to Tony's and drink her favorite drink, brandy Alexanders. But she insisted on going home. She had her problems and wanted to take care of them. I was too naïve to know what they were, and I confess that I tended to think of her as antisocial. Once she was home, however, she was lost unless I went and brought her back. I'd get to her apartment and start pacing the floor while she was ostensibly getting ready. I'd have to keep reminding her of show time. It was painful—that's all I can say. But musically, she and Coleman Hawkins' band were delivering some of the best jazz The Street ever heard."

Just about the same time, bop made its first real appearance on The Street in a small, hyphenated combo playing the Onyx. When the Pettiford-Gillespie quintet broke up, it was to the Yacht Club that Dizzy took his splinter group. And so the Yacht, which once had sailed on the adulterated seas of Prohibition booze, became one of the early conveyors of the new jazz. This was shortly before it permanently departed its mooring on The Street. By May, 1944, No. 66 West was the berth of the Downbeat.

Down Beat

Billie Holiday with Mel Tormé.

Tape 13 . . . FRANCES FAYE

Not too long ago, when Frances Faye was at Caesar's Palace in Las Vegas, Mitzi Gaynor reportedly came to her dressing room. "What do you take before you go on?" she asked. "Do you take brandy or something before you say, 'Good evening!'?" Faye does not drink or smoke, never has. "What do you take," Miss Gaynor pressed, "that immediately turns the whole room on?" Faye, who is unpretentious but not without an awareness of her magic, asked me: "Would you call it talent?"

Call it talent or charisma, Frances Faye has been turning rooms on since she was a girl of fifteen and played the Club Richman, near Carnegie Hall. Later, but still in the speakeasy era, she was a fixture at the Club Calais, where she remembers singing "Love for Sale," the Cole Porter perennial introduced in a so-so 1930 revue, *The New Yorkers.* Involved in the operation of the Calais was Hyman Pincus, whose family was later associated with many 52d St. clubs, and Moe Lewis, recently concerned with entertainment at Vegas' Landmark Hotel. Frances Faye paid her dues in Prohibition speaks. But it was the 52d St. scene that brought her stardom.

"I was all over that street," she said. "And they wouldn't let me leave when I wanted to play some of the city's bigger rooms like the Versailles. As soon as I closed the Yacht, I had an offer from Club 18 or the Famous Door. And they kept raising my salary. My first booking could have been Hickory House, right after Prohibition. But the first big booking was at the Yacht Club when it was like across the street from Leon & Eddie. Henny Youngman was on the bill and they weren't paying him very much. But they were paying me like five hundred a week, an enormous figure for those days. And the club was so jammed every night that they kept raising it.

"After that I remember playing the Famous Door for those two fellows, Al Felshin and Jerry Brooks. Al's brother was a rabbi and he married me. In 1942, it was.

"I never had a theme song. But I came on when the room was dark. As the lights went up, I would sing: "Good evening, ladies and gentlemen, how do you do?' Accompanying myself, I sang this in rhythm.

Still do today. And I go off singing, 'I gotta go-go-go,' also to a melodic thing I wrote. These tunes were never published. But Leeds did publish 'Well, All Right,' which I wrote with Don Raye and Dave Kapp and which was recorded by the Andrews Sisters in '39.

"I never was dirty like Belle Barth. But when I was younger, they took everything I said as *double-entendre*. Some of it was. But none of it was dirty. 52d St. was a great starting place.

"In the fifties I played the Interlude on the Hollywood Strip. I was there for nine months, and they had lines that always spilled into the street. I was one of the early stars on the Vegas Strip. Played the Thunderbird when Dave Victorson, now at Caesars Palace, was there, and the Frontier when Bill Miller, who's now head of Hilton entertainment, was there. Broke my hip at the Riviera and was out of action for about nine years. Had to be carried. Was in a wheelchair. Used canes and crutches. Had three major operations. But now, *kaynaynhoreh,* I swing everywhere.

"Since 1961 I've been playing Australia every year, Melbourne and Sydney, and I play The Talk of the Town in London annually. I began recording in 1938 for Decca—'I Can't Believe That You're in Love with Me' was my first side—and I've made records for Capitol and Verve. Have about fifteen albums on the market. It all started on 52d. St."

10. They Came to Be Insulted

One summer night in the late thirties, film star Norma Shearer paid a visit to the Club 18. No celebrity came to New York in those days without pausing at the roistering joint opposite 21. Originally at No. 18 West, it was then at No. 20, just about where the genteel Esso Schrafft's perches today. Miss Shearer was wearing an eye-arresting, floppy, wide-brimmed straw hat. When the trio of rowdy clowns, who seldom worked on stage, reached her, top banana Jack White began with a reference to the "talented actress who has graced us with her charming presence," but ended his introduction: "And here she is, the attractive lady with the whitewall tire around her head." An infuriated Miss Shearer stormed out of the club.

"But she came back the next night," says publicist Jack Egan. "Now she wanted to enjoy the brickbats thrown at other celebrities. And Jack and Pat Harrington, Sr., and Frankie Hyers sure threw them."

"The way I figure it," Jack White told Maurice Zolotow, "these big shots are always being yes-yes-yessed, and it's a pleasure to 'em to be no-no-noed for a change. Also, they figure that tonight they are getting loused up and tomorrow night they can bring a friend in and I will louse up the friend."

When prizefighter Max Baer came in one evening, Jack White shouted: "Hey, Maxie, the folks don't recognize you. Stretch out on the floor, will you?" On another evening, ex-champ light-heavyweight Maxie Rosenbloom refused to take the jab lying down.

"I got this way fighting," he shouted back. "What's your excuse?" Frankie Hyers came in for the kill: "Bettin' on you!"

FBI man J. Edgar Hoover was introduced one evening by White: "Folks, meet a great man—the former President of the United States." As the audience applauded and laughed, Frankie Hyers quickly added: "Not of the United States—this is the bum who invented the vacuum cleaner!"

One evening the celebrated Gish sisters arrived, resplendent in evening gowns and accompanied by writer Quentin Reynolds and J. Braun III, attired in white ties and tails. "Hoddya like that for a couple of high-nosed Park Adden-ya broads!" Pat Harrington commented. "They brought their own waiters!"

The first time that Gordon Jenkins, composer of 'Manhattan Tower' suite, wandered into the 18, he found all eyes turned on him. Suddenly, he realized that White and Company were running toward him, and he heard White say: "Got the tape?" The next he knew, he was seized and made to lie down on the floor. He was so thin that they were measuring him for a coffin!

In one year, according to Maurice Zolotow, White managed to abuse, louse up, give the business to, and/or put down Franklin D. Roosevelt, Jr., Harry Hopkins and Leon Henderson (all part of the New Deal); Marlene Dietrich, Helen Hayes, Errol Flynn, Henry Fonda and Jimmy Stewart; writers Fannie Hurst and William Saroyan; and Lenore Lemmon and Brenda Frazier of high society.

Comic Phil Silvers recalls a night when Brenda Frazier, then the No. 1 debutante, came in wearing a cute hat. "It had a visor," he notes, "and it looked a bit like a cabbie's or a doorman's cap. She looked adorable. But one of Jack White's clowns—I can't remember whether it was Harrington or Hyers—came to her table wearing a shabby cap he had found in their dressing room. He just stood quietly beside her until everyone in the club had spotted him with his beat-up replica. By then the place was in an uproar. He hadn't said a word and he waited until the laughter died down. Then, with a perfect sense of timing, he piped: 'And where'd you get yours, dearie?' The place went to pieces."

Philadelphia was a place that brought out the verbal missiles. "In this contest," White would announce, "first prize is one week in Philadelphia!" One of his sidekicks: "And what's second prize?" Deadpan, White would reply: "Two weeks in Philadelphia."

No one could go to the club washrooms, on the left side, without being seen. White frequently would shout: "Hey, mention my name and you'll get a good seat." Jack Egan tells of an evening when he took Alice of the King Sisters to the club. She was so amused that she stayed for the second show, by which time she had to make a trip to the ladies' room. "She stood it as long as she could," Jack recalls, "and then instead of risking an encounter with White, she snuck to the back, went out and used the powder room in Leon & Eddie's."

A surprising number of celebrities went along with the gags, no matter how rough they got. Once when Alfred Vanderbilt ordered a soft drink instead of wine or a cocktail, a waiter shouted insults at him until the other customers fell off their chairs laughing. When playboy millionaire Tommy Manville arrived one evening, resplendent in one of the first pearly-gray dinner jackets, Pat Harrington approached the table with a pitcher of milk, accidentally tripped on purpose, and splattered the jacket. Then, before Manville could remove the liquid, Harrington proceeded to pour the balance of the pitcher's contents over him. The guests and Manville laughed themselves sick.

In addition to the three comics, Club 18 performers included two girls. The soubrette was Jerry Blanchard, a big, buxom blonde who had worked with White at the Club Ha-Ha, and the ingenue was Lila Gaines, also blonde but leggy. Miss Blanchard sang and Miss Gaines danced, but both were drawn into the comic routines. Many of Miss Blanchard's songs, with gag interruptions by the trio, were slightly off-color. And Lila Gaines, who was easy to leer at, did a waltz clog, after which White would suggest: "Honey, you look tired. Why don't you go up to my room and lie down?"

The comedy cast did not end there. Two waiters, the chef, and even the men's room attendant participated in the shenanigans. Thaddeus Mitchell, who had been a professional fighter, was known as One-Round Jackson because, according to White, "in thirty-eight fights he never answered the bell for the second round." One of the waiters, known as Doc, had an elegant English accent, which hardly seemed to go with his Durante-type proboscis. When customers ordered a bottle of wine, he would do the tasting himself and pour himself a glass. On occasion, after "Happy Birthday" had been sung and the honored guest had blown out the candle, the cake would suddenly be snatched from the table and passed from comic to comic and waiter to waiter until it finally landed back in the kitchen.

Most of the gags that convulsed 18's audiences do not read funny. One wonders why they seemed so funny then; more significantly, why guests permitted themselves, if they did not submit themselves, to be abused. Publicist Eddie Jaffee contends that "Club 18 helped establish that people were valued not for wealth or social position but for their sense of humor. It didn't matter who you were or how big and impor- tant you were. What counted was the good humor you displayed in taking the jibes. That was the exciting part of 52d St.: the premium it placed on personality. It was like the French Foreign Legion of New York. Anybody could fit in. It catered to the eccentricities and the unusual interests of people."

Of course, the tariff at Jack White's was a little higher than at most joints on The Street. To fit in, you had to be willing and able to pay a $4 minimum for beverages only. Once it became the in place, its clientele tended to be a select group of celebrities, visiting dignitaries and the ermine-and-tuxedo crowd. Apart from enjoying the discom- fiture of others who were getting the business, some laughed at the insults, rowdy shenanigans and abusive ploys as superiors enjoying the audacity and hauteur of inferiors. Call it reverse snob appeal.

White, who started out as a show-struck bricklayer, was a superior wit, and so recognized by his peers, other professional comedians. No small part of the club's audiences consisted of would-be comics, as well as the leading comics of the day. In fact, there were so many gagsters around that it was difficult to know who was part of the act and who was just "sittin' in."

In addition to White, Harrington and Hyers, the regulars (at various times) included Vince Curran, Roy Sedley, Tommy Moe Raft, Joe Frisco and Jackie Gleason. Fresh from burlesque and vaudeville but fattish even then, Gleason appeared on the scene shortly before White's passing. Some remember seeing him imperson- ate the men's room attendant. Others recall his playing lead—no lines—in the oft-repeated skit where White flashed the spotlight on a busboy lugging a can of garbage out of the club. "You tell the boys at 21," White would shout, "that we're tired of lending them stuff for their tables."

Of the regulars, derby-and-cigar-smoking Joe Frisco was quoted as extensively in show biz circles as Dorothy Parker among the literati.

Born Louis Wilson Joseph in Rock Island, Illinois, in 1891, he devised the duck waddle known as the Frisco dance, once as popular as
the Charleston. Frisco never told a joke without stuttering, but people
who knew him well claimed that he was not really a stutterer but
merely used it as a timing device.

"But he did stammer," says Peter Lind Hayes, a protégé, "when he
got angry. I loved to bait him about the new up-and-coming comics,
among whom he hated Danny Kaye and Milton Berle. I got on him
one night about Berle. I said: 'You know he's brilliant, articulate, glib
and fast. Sure he takes everybody's material. But he does it better than
they do it.' He took the cigar out of his mouth: 'When they made
Milton Berle,' he said, 'they th-th-threw the shovel away.'

"Frisco got his start with my mother, Gracie, when she was a saloon
singer at Colisimo's in Chicago. She used to sneak Frisco and Loretta
McDermott, with whom he worked, into the place when the old man
went to the opera. Then she'd throw half dollars and quarters as a shill
so that they could walk out with eating money.

"It is true that when Mary Healy and I were booked to play the
Roxy—it had an absolutely enormous stage—Frisco said: 'N-n-n-
never get c-c-caught in the center of that stage without b-b-b-bread
and water.'

"But of the Club 18 wits, Frisco himself picked Vince Curran as
the wittiest. Curran was a paraplegic, who delivered his lines sitting
behind a desk. Most people don't know that Roy Sedley, one of the
other stooges, was Harriet Hilliard's first husband—before she married
Ozzie Nelson. And Pat Harrington, who was a drummer and singer,
as well as comic, had to cope with fainting fits."

An oft-repeated Frisco story deals with his putting up an unem-
ployed comic—it was really a girl, says Hayes—in his hotel room.
When the management found out, Frisco received a call in which he
was advised that he would have to pay for a double room. "Okay,"
Frisco said, "b-b-b-b-but send up an-n-n-nother Bible."

Returning to his hotel room one night, Frisco noticed that the
cleaning women had stacked all the cuspidors in front of an easel
photo of bandleader Abe Lyman. "Abe's got a great b-b-b-band,"
Frisco reportedly remarked, "but I'll n-n-n-n-never believe that he
won all those c-c-c-cups."

Even today one occasionally hears a stand-up comic characterize

Hollywood as the "only place in the country where you can go to sleep under a rose b-b-bush in full b-b-b-bloom and f-f-f-freeze to death."

Comics, as well as customers, were not immune to Jack White's razor-edged ridicule. Once Bob Hope rasped a Bronx cheer into the mike. White spontaneously asked: "Who writes your material, Bob?" As George Jessel sat down one evening after telling some jokes, White commented: "You didn't stop the show, Georgie, but you sure slowed it down."

In a *Variety* anniversary issue, White observed: "The big wits step into our place and we catch them with their puns down—without a script in their hands." One noncomic who got under White was sportswriter Jimmy Cannon. White was an even more rabid Giant fan than actress Tallulah Bankhead. During the season a small blackboard hung over the draw curtain on the stage. When the Giants won, the score was posted; the opposing team always appeared as "Bums." When the Giants lost, the blackboard read: "No Game Today." One evening when the Giants were slaughtered, Jim Cannon came early to the club and changed the wording to read: "No Team Today."

White once admitted to writer Maurice Zolotow that he had been squelched by only three people: in addition to Jimmy Cannon, by Myron Cohen, who was then a Seventh Avenue dress manufacturer, and by dancer Paul Draper. But publicist Jack Egan claims that actress Marie Wilson should be added to the list. Egan was then promoting the supposedly dumb blonde as "The Body." Against his warnings, she insisted on coming to the 18 in an extremely low-cut gown. White and his bananas kept mugging at the cleavage—she sat close to the stage—and shouting, "Wilson, that's all!" after the slogan of Wilson scotch. When they began moving among the audience with their traveling mike, Egan warned Marie not to say anything.

Finally, the trio came over to the Wilson table. White gave his usual warm introduction: "This lovely girl just in from the Coast . . . gracing our joint with her wonderful presence. . . ." Then he handed the mike to Marie. An apoplectic Egan motioned for her to pass it back and say nothing. But Marie took the mike, and as Egan cowered in anticipation of the onslaught, she said very innocently: "Don't drink your own bath water." The trio stopped dead in their tracks. One pressed his hand to his ear as if he had suddenly gone deaf. Marie said a little louder, "Don't drink your own bath water." At that, the three buffoons looked at each other in amusement or amazement and, shrugging, moved on to find another victim. They were lost for a comeback.

In *Notes of a Guilty Bystander* Robert Sylvester tells of an unnamed advertising man who also bested White & Co. They were playing their version of the old "Knock, Knock" game cum audience participation. "Who's there?" someone sang out when White intoned, "Knock, Knock."

"Cohen," shouted the ad man.

"Cohen who?" White demanded.

"Cohen fuck yourself," sang the ad man.

Despite the ridicule, insults and abuse to which he subjected the club's patrons, Jack White was both admired and loved by them. When he became critically ill with TB in 1942—he died that year on July 14 at the age of forty-nine—James Farley arranged for him to enter one of the country's best sanitariums. According to columnist-author Robert Sylvester, he died in the arms of Vincent Youmans, one of the golden era's top Broadway show composers (*No, No, Nanette, Hit the Deck,* etc.) and who also died of TB two years later.

When playwright William Saroyan was introduced to the audience on his first visit to the club, Frankie Hyers supplemented White's encomium by saying: "Oh, I've heard of him. Why, I saw his last play." White turned on his assistant: "You," he growled, "so YOU were the one!" Saroyan appropriately inscribed his book *My Name Is Aram:* "To Jack White, The Biggest Screwball in New York." That year Saroyan wrote an article for the New York *World-Telegram* arguing that White's shenanigans deserved the Pulitzer Prize for the best play of 1941.

Saroyan was one of many luminaries who went to the 18 every night that they were in New York. A group of newspapermen had what they called a *Stammtisch* (meeting table) where they met nightly. Included were John McClain, then drama critic of the New York *Journal-American,* Mark Hanna, Quentin Reynolds, Fini Farr, Bobby Minton, Heff Sage, and Johnno Durant. In 1968 one of the group, Joe Bryan III, who worked in Philadelphia but came to New York for two days a week, privately printed fifty copies of a monograph he called *The Merry Madmen of 52nd Street.* Bryan always spent the evening between the two days at the 18.

The depth of feeling for White is, perhaps, best suggested by the entry in the British *Who's Who* for the late Sir Cedric Hardwicke. The distinguished actor listed his club memberships as "The Garrick Club, The Players Club, The Arts Club, Club 18."

The club did not last long after White's death. The United States was by then involved in World War II, and a midnight curfew worked havoc with nightclub biz. "But in the case of the 18," owner Freddy Lamb admitted, "the curfew was only one factor. Jack's death was the main one. The thing that he had, and that nobody else has had since, was the sure knowledge of when to quit. He could feel just the moment when a customer was beginning to tire of a gag. . . . I'm not sure, though, that we could have kept on much longer even if he had lived. Public taste was changing."

Joe Helbock, who really launched The Street with the Onyx, remembers Jack White as a stage-struck young bricklayer in the Bronx. "It was before World War One," Helbock recalls, "and White hung around this cabaret on Westchester Avenue, where Gene Sennett featured singing waiters who clowned around. He was making good money as a bricklayer, but he wanted to be in show business."

In 1917—he was then twenty-four, having been born on 102d St. in Manhattan in 1893—White was a singing waiter at the Boulevard Inn on 163d St. in the Bronx. During the speakeasy era, he worked at the Château Madrid and the Club Ha-Ha. Percy Hammond of the New York *Herald Tribune* once devoted an entire column to his comic art. At the Club Ha-Ha, located on the second floor of a building near Hickory House, he worked with Dan Healy, the comedian, Jerry Bergen, Lillian Fitzgerald and Jerry Blanchard, whom he later brought into the Club 18. One of the bandleaders was Gordon Andrews, who later led the combo at the madhouse.

The Club 18 started in the summer of 1935 as a jazz-oriented night spot featuring the trumpet playing of Bunny Berigan, a disciple of the great Bix Beiderbecke. By then there were three jazz clubs on The Street: Onyx, Famous Door and Hickory House. Jazz fans were flocking to 52d but not to the 18. A switch from a jazz combo to a guitar quintet did not improve business. After White arrived in the spring of 1936, the club was still not making it.

The formula that brought fame and patrons to the 18 was accidentally discovered one summer night. Acting as MC, White told a few well-received jokes and introduced Pat Harrington, who was an Irish tenor as well as drummer of the Gordon Andrews Trio. As Harrington began his first song, a ringside drunk stood up and became obstreperous. Harrington tried to disregard the interruptions but finally lost his Irish temper and shouted: "Sit down, you bum!"

The audience was shocked. No paying guest had ever been so unceremoniously requested to yield the floor. But the drunk, after glancing jerkily around and wobbling around his chair, plopped into it. "Then came the loudest laugh," Freddy Lamb recalls, "we'd ever had in the club. That night, everything in the show was a hit." And that night, Jack White, who had great empathy with audiences, discovered the gambit that made the Club 18 an SRO night spot and a compulsory hangout of every American comic.

As club habitués remember him, White was a half-bald, bedraggled man who was rail-thin and whose clothes were always rumpled. He worked mostly on the audience floor, rather than on the stage, and used only two props: a Sherlock Holmes deerstalker cap and a cane with which he rapped the floor, ceiling or tables for emphasis or attention. An inveterate chain-smoker who consumed almost three dozen cigars a day, he found it necessary to spit. Correction. Zolotow says, "He liked to spit. When Jack was called upon for a guest appearance [at another club], the first thing he did when he appeared in the spotlight was to deliver himself of a vigorous blob of spit—parking the oyster of mucus right on the polished floor." And Earl Wilson observed: "No saloon entertainer now spits on, or even at, the customers. The late Jack White did. He expectorated freely and ingeniously at the patrons, and many were the minks and silver foxes he splashed." There may have been some psychological connection between this rather unattractive habit and White's penchant and achievement as a comic.

But in addition, he helped make the Club 18 a training ground for comedians, as were burlesque, vaudeville and the Borscht Circuit. In actuality, the 18 was more than that. It was a continuous jam session for comics—and it had all the elements of such sessions at the jazz joints on The Street: free interplay, spontaneous counterpoint and "cutting" contests. The celebrities might have laughed because they thought themselves above the audacious disrespect of White and his clowns. But the clowns and top banana Jack White knew that they were part of the most elite group in the world—the men who can make other people laugh . . . at themselves.

Tape 14 . . . Billy Daniels

Singer Billy Daniels came from his native Jacksonville, Florida, to New York in 1926 to live with his grandmother. The apartment building at 1947 Seventh Avenue was at the corner of 116th St. and Seventh, opposite a vaudeville theater called the Regent. The neighborhood, originally populated by middle-class Jews, was beginning to change its color. Billy went to PS 179 on 140th and Seventh, but spent more time hanging around theaters in the hope of meeting the great black entertainers of the day—Bill Robinson, Ethel Waters, Eubie Blake, Noble Sissle, Fletcher Henderson and Duke Ellington.

Returning to New York for a second time, just before Roosevelt was elected President, he got a job as a waiter at Dickie Wells' when Prohibition went out the following year. The famous club was at 133d St. and Seventh Avenue.

"Dickie Wells didn't have a kitchen," Billy notes. "He had a door in the back through which waiters went to get the food. Everybody thought they were going into the kitchen. But they actually went into an alley, trotted around the corner, and got the chicken and coffee from Tillie's Chicken Shack. While the customers didn't know this, all the moochers in Harlem did. Sometimes you had to fight your way through that alley. This was Depression time—they'd snatch the chicken and run. The first time I lost a plate and reported it, they charged me a buck. I never lost a plate again. Sometimes it was a fight and I'd drop the chicken. I'd pick it off the ground, shake it off, and put it back on the plate. Funny thing was that the customers always seemed to like just that chicken. 'That's the best bird I ever had,' they'd say, about the chicken that fell in the alley.

"I worked there for about a year, going to school in the daytime. But I couldn't make it. So I kept writing my dad that I was going to school long after I quit. Things were very tough in the country then, with all those public works programs inaugurated by Roosevelt to put people to work.

"I found that I got along well with people. I was a pretty good-looking kid. Dickie Wells befriended me. I always thought that he was one of the finest men who ever lived. In those days, you could buy

Billy Daniels was a favorite at Mammy's Chicken Koop and Kelly's Stable.

marijuana in any men's room. Nobody got pinched, except maybe Mezz Mezzrow. But he peddled the stuff like it was Camels. Through Wells I escaped many things that I could have gone into at my impressionable age. And he was an addict, as I learned later.

"In those days, our customers were mostly white guys in the rackets, theatrical people, and high livers among the intellectual set like Gloria Gould, Gloria Vanderbilt, Stokowski, Prince Obolensky, Elsa Maxwell, Talullah Bankhead. Also guys with big bankrolls like the presidents of banks and big corporations. They used to get thrown out and poured out into the street at daybreak. In those years before 52d St., Harlem was the place to go after you dined at the Hurricane, Paradise, Zanzibar, or some other Broadway dinner club.

"I'll never forget the night when Mrs. Gould had some furs stolen out of her car in front of Dickie Wells'. She was quite distraught, but Wells just told her, 'Don't worry, I'll have them back for you.' The following day they grabbed a guy by the throat, and he suddenly remembered where they were. We're talking about '33–'34. Harlem wasn't as tough as it is now.

"From Dickie Wells' I went to the Hotcha and then to the Ubangi— also Mob-controlled—where I became a dancer, as well as production singer. Leonard Harper, a great showman, was responsible for that. In '34 late, I joined Erskine Hawkins as band vocalist at the enormous salary of fifty dollars a week. It was when I went to work in Greenwich Village at the Black Cat in '36 that 52d St. came to life. Suddenly, everybody was talking about the Onyx, Famous Door and Hickory House.

"But the first time I sang on The Street, it wasn't at any of these places. It was at the Club 18. The Jack White funny house had a black boy in the men's room who lived near me in Harlem. I was then working in the Village and went from the Black Cat to Ernie's next door. When I told One-Round Jackson, as they called him, about the hangups, he urged me to sing for White. I did and sang there for about a week. They had a lot of kibitzing going on while you sang, and I couldn't take it.

"That was when Irving Alexander heard me and invited me to go into Kelly's Stable. It was then on 51st, and I worked for a while with Leo Watson and Teddy Bunn—they called themselves the Harlem Highlanders. Alexander was married to Ralph Watkins' sister, Beatrice, who was related to Artie Jarwood's first wife. (His second wife was Betty Buchalter, the widow of Lepke Buchalter.) Beatrice got Artie's first wife to persuade him to lend money to Alexander. That's how Artie was involved in the Stable, which was actually run by Irving and Ralph. Oscar Rubin, who was a Mob guy, also had a piece—the checkroom. Those quarters could add up, especially since the tax people didn't get into them until they knocked out Longchamps with Henry Lustig.

"For a time I alternated between the Stable, the Park Sheraton (then the Park Central) and Mammy's Chicken Koop. When Tillie settled at No. 106 West, she called her place Tillie's Chicken Shack, as in Harlem. Charlie Shavers, later a great horn man, played piano there. But she lost the place and the name, so when Dave Marden—brother of the Riviera's Ben Marden—took it over, he called it Mammy's Chicken Koop. Although he got some financial help from Artie Jarwood, he got into hock to Billy Rockwell, a song plugger at Harms Music, and lost the place to him.

"That's how I came into the Koop. I used to eat there and knew Rockwell from way back. It was a narrow room at No. 60 West, with Reilly's Tavern to the east and the Clover Club to the west. Bob Howard, who entertained at Tillie's in Harlem, started with her when she moved downtown. Rockwell had entertainers like pianist Norene Tate, Gladys Palmer (who is now working in Bangkok), Bob Robinson—and Bob Howard was still there when I came in.

"Funny thing is that I almost bought the building. I had a room upstairs over the Koop, although I lived in Harlem. The old woman who owned the building, a Mrs. Ginsberg, came to me one day. She loved my singing. She said: 'Why don't you buy the place? Someday it'll be worth something.' She was a widow, she was sick, and she had a married son on Long Island who wanted her to live with him. I had about three or four grand, which was all she wanted as a down payment. But my lawyer discouraged me with talk about bad plumbing, a leaky boiler and all that. Bull! I could have bought it and just sat with it, as the other landlords were doing. And do you know what the old lady wanted? Twenty-three thousand dollars! That was low even then.

"When I worked the Yacht Club, it was next door to Hickory House and was owned by Red Murray and the Mob. That was a tough bunch—ooh! They had Fats Waller coming in and booked me just until he arrived. But after Fats showed, they wanted me to stay on. You see I had a following, and it went where I sang—broads, secretaries who worked in the area, faggots and lots of song pluggers. I learned songs quickly, and the pluggers brought in their contacts to hear new tunes. I hung on for a few days. But I didn't like the room. It was a barn, big and cold, and I liked to work close to people. When I finally told the manager I was leaving, he laughed at first and then he got angry. 'You better talk to Red,' he said.

"Now, Murray was known to be tough as steel and had a reputation as a torpedo. An enforcer for the Jewish Mob—that's what they said he had been. But I was nervy and I went to see him. He came at me like a hungry lion: 'What's this about your wantin' to leave. No one leaves until I say so.' I started laughing. 'Well, you musta said it,' I said, 'because I'm leaving. You got Fats. You don't need me.' He was quiet for a few moments. I just sat and looked at him, without knowing what was coming. Suddenly, he started laughing: 'You're OK.' And so I left. He got to be a friend and I went to see him at the hospital when he was dying. Somebody later told me that he was amused that a young kid had the *chutzpa* to buck him.

"When Kelly's moved to The Street, I worked the first bill. And I continued working the Stable all through the war. I got along well with all three of the owners, Ralph Watkins, Irving Alexander and George Lynch. Watkins married Margie, the hatcheck girl. Lynch married a piano player named Vicki Zimmer. He worshiped her, and he liked me because I never took her out. She used to chase me, but I always told her, 'You're George's girl.' A lot of chicks go for the guys that turn them down.

"I got into the war pretty early. Since I had my seaman's papers as a third cook or baker—shipped out of Jacksonville when I was fifteen —I went into the merchant marine. Was twice on ships whose rudders were knocked off by torpedoes and once traveled from Norfolk to Bandar Shahpur in Iran—it took six months. But each time I came back, I'd go into the Stable. Sang, emceed or both. As accompanists, I had the Nat Cole Trio—he didn't sing then; Clarence Profit Trio—he was half-blind and died young; and Nat Jaffe, who also died too young. I appeared on bills with Stuff Smith, Thelma Carpenter, Coleman Hawkins, Billie Holiday, Ida James and Una Mae Carlisle. Una married Johnny Bradford, who went to sea with me. Both of them are gone. I was there so much of the time that people thought I had a piece of the place.

"That was the period in which I began to develop a style, and my individuality crystallized. The first time I realized what style meant, I was singing with Stuff Smith at the Stable. I used to sing 'Intermezzo,' which was originally a violin solo. Stuff would play it, I'd sing it, and then he'd do an obbligato behind me. I also sang it with Eddie South, who was called the Dark Angel of the Violin. (At the Riviera he played behind a scrim, so you saw only his silhouette as he performed.) Eddie took sick then, started coughing, and later died of TB.

"One evening Leonard Joy of Victor-Bluebird came in and talked with me about recording. I was then singing daily on WHN—got forty dollars a week for an across-the-board shot. That's when I cut 'Diane' and 'Penthouse Serenade.' And that's when people started to talk and singers began coming into the Stable to hear me. Up until then I had a cult. Now, I began hitting the general public.

" 'Black Magic' had its start at the Ebony, the club on Broadway that later became famous as Birdland. It was here that I got my first major write-up. It started with Walter Winchell, who called me 'the sexiest singer of the day' in his column. Dicky Wells, who owned the Ebony with John Levy and Al Martin, promoted that.

"In 1945 I played the Spotlite, which was run by Clark Monroe. And the following year, I was at the Three Deuces, where I made noise with a French ballad, 'Symphony.' Irving Alexander was now at the Deuces in partnership with Sammy Krakow, who called himself Sammy Kay.

"All the Murder, Incorporated guys used to come into Mammy's Chicken Koop. Blue Jaw and Abe Rellis and Pittsburgh Phil—their wives and girls hung around the joint. Pittsburgh Phil used to leave his girl with me, go catch a plane, rub out somebody, and come back. He carried a satchel, and believe it or not, I thought he was a salesman. Sweetest guy you ever want to meet. Nice, quiet, slip me a tenner, a twenty to sing something. Once I took his girl all the way to Brooklyn. She didn't want to go home by herself. We never had a bit of trouble with any of these guys. They weren't exactly Beau Brummels, and their eating manners weren't out of the book of etiquette. But then one day I opened a newspaper and I almost fainted.

"There they were—the whole lineup. All indicted and I couldn't believe it. The attorney who knocked them out—was his name Burton Turkus?—used to come into the Koop, too. When I saw all those mugs in the paper, I thought I would faint. They were all good, regular customers. They also hung out at the Famous Door, owned by two of the biggest sharks in the world, big Al Felshin and little Jerry Brooks.

"In those years The Street was jumping. Anything you wanted in pop entertainment was there—jazz, singers, pianists, bands, comics, strippers. And it had some of the most beautiful girls in the world. Girls like Ramsay Ames, who played the Famous Door. She was in her teens and her mother brought her. What a beauty—and I went with her for a time. She's now married to Dale Wasserman, the guy who wrote *Man of La Mancha*. Lucky fellow.

"I played Tondelayo's the year that Erroll Garner was there. John Levy, who was one of the Ebony owners, had the place. It didn't last long, but Erroll's still around—and how. 52d St. was my dues-paying period. Things started moving after I played the Savannah down in the Village. The excitement sent me to the Park Avenue at East 52nd and Park. It was one of the best clubs in the city, with a decor by Joseph Urban. From the Park Avenue, to Café Society Downtown, to the Riviera, the Copa, Mocambo, back to the Riviera, the Copa again—and boom! I was off like a rocket. Played all over the world and made five pictures for Columbia and *Old Black Magic* for Universal.

"There's one club that I keep thinking about. The girl who sang 'He's Just My Bill' was there—Helen Morgan. There was a Helen Morgan club on 52d. It was upstairs around '33–'34 when I was up at Dickie Wells'. Harry Richman's brother, Lou, had the place. Harry came in there occasionally, not often. Didn't seem to get along with his brother. But I saw him there when he was married to Hazel Forbes, the toothpaste chick. I remember singing for them there. Richman used to come up to Dicky Wells'.

"I was all over that street for years, played practically every club you can mention. I guess the Yacht Club was my shortest booking—and did I have trouble getting out? My places were the Stable and the Koop. That street was very dear to New Yorkers. It still is to me."

11. Cats in a Stable

"At Kelly's Stable, sometimes at night," Coleman Hawkins said, "after a couple quarts of scotch, very late, I'd sit down and kill time and play about ten choruses on 'Body and Soul.' And then the boys would come in and play harmony notes in the background until I finished up. That's all there was to it. But then Leonard Joy came in the club and asked me to record it. I said, 'Why? I don't even have an arrangement on it.' "

Bean or Hawk, as musicians called him, recorded "Body and Soul"

Down Beat

In May, 1940, six months after Coleman Hawkins made his famous Kelly's Stable recording of "Body and Soul," Benny Carter corralled him for a Chocolate Dandies date for the Commodore label. All six men had been with the Fletcher Henderson band. Above, John Kirby (bass), Bernie Addison (guitar), Roy Eldridge (trumpet), Benny Carter (alto sax), "Hawk" (tenor sax), and Sid Catlett (drums).

for Bluebird on October 11, 1939. The torch ballad was then a nine-year-old copyright, having made its appearance in a Broadway revue, *Three's a Crowd,* where it attracted attention to a white blues singer named Libby Holman. It had been recorded by Leo Reisman, with Eddy Duchin at the piano, and by others. The Hawkins disc made it a jazz classic. Critic John S. Wilson avers that it "set a ballad mode for tenor sax which is still being followed today."

But on its release, it caused some controversy. "Everybody, including Chu Berry," Bean told Leonard Feather, "said I was playing wrong notes. . . . A lot of people didn't know about flatted fifths and augmented changes. . . . Of course, that sort of thing is extremely common now, but it certainly wasn't before I did 'Body and Soul.' "

Modernist Thelonious Monk later asked Hawkins: "You never did explain to me how these people, these old folks and everybody *did* go for your record. . . . I could understand if you played melody 'cause that's what they like. . . ." The Young Turk of Jazz, as Hawkins has been called, replied: "It just so happened that at the right time it just happened to catch on with the right people, and that's all there was to it—just a lucky thing."

"The lucky thing" was that Hawkins captured on wax the languorous late-hour mood he describes at the outset of this chapter. For this reason, it did not matter that he did not play melody or what chords he evoked. So long as he caught the early-morning feeling of longing, loneliness and lust, he projected the magical mood that attracted listeners to Art Tatum's after-hours harmonies and Billie Holiday's hurting ballads. It was the erotic chemistry of the deserted-street scene on 52d.

As they once came running to the Onyx for "The Music Goes 'Round," to the Door for Louis Prima, to Hickory House for Wingy Manone, and again to the Onyx for Stuff and then "Loch Lomond," so now they lined up for Hawkins' "Body and Soul." But Bean was appreciated by his peers as well as the public. There were nights when every tenorman in town was at the Stable. Art Engler, who was then an active saxophonist and today runs the Vegas office of ABC (Associated Booking Corporation), recalls an evening when he walked along The Street afterward and Georgie Auld turned to him and said: "I'm taking my horn and throwing it into the East River."

Hawkins' necromancy was abetted by the warbling of Billie Holiday for whom the Stable served as showcase through the early forties. Her earlier outings on The Street, at both the Famous Door and the Onyx, had proved unsatisfactory. But Billie now had a long, successful booking at Café Society Downtown behind her. And she had just recorded "Strange Fruit" on Commodore, which was stirring much talk. The '39 stand at the Stable was a triumphal appearance and the beginning of her long, thriving association with The Street. Later she became known as Lady Day. But then they talked of her as the Lady of the Gardenias because she always wore a fresh flower in her hair when she performed.

One evening Billie called manager Watkins to say she was too ill to go on. After considering possible replacements, Watkins had a curious thought. Appearing with Holiday was a new jazz trio whose leader occasionally sang when he was alone in the club. At first, pianist Nat Cole balked. But Watkins was persuasive and Cole went on that evening. This was more than four years before the trio had its first hit in "Straighten Up and Fly Right"—the gifted Oscar Moore on guitar and Wesley Prince on bass—and nine years before Cole broke through as a solo singer with "Nature Boy."

"But he always remembered the Stable as the first place where he sang in public," said Phoebe Pincus Jacobs, a cousin of Ralph Watkins and now associated with the Rainbow Grill. "And that was the last time he appeared on The Street. It was a booking he also never forgot because of Billie. I remember his coming into my office many years later when I was working as Ralph's assistant at Basin Street East. I had a tiny office. Used to be a toilet. You know, they never have space for offices or dressing rooms in high-class saloons. When he came in, or just stood in the doorway, Nat had a handkerchief over his eyes. He had been crying. Peggy Lee was the star at Basin Street and she had just sung 'God Bless the Child.'

" 'I swear,' Nat said, 'Peggy has Billie in her. I've never heard anyone do that song like that, except Billie. It just broke me up. When I closed my eyes, I could see Billie as she sang it almost every night at Kelly's. The gardenia in her hair and the hurt in her voice. She was such a pretty lady then.'

"Ralph came by my office at that point," Phoebe continued, "and Nat took his hand. 'Remember those days in the Stable when I accompanied Billie and you made me sing? Listening to Peggy was just like hearing Billie again.' "

*   *   *

Some writers attribute the name Kelly's Stable to stables that once operated at its 51st St. address and to the practice then of calling someone you didn't know "Kelly." Today, it's "Hey, Charlie" or "Joe." Even though there were stables before garages and Radio City took over, there was also a Kelly's Stable in Chicago before the 51st St. club opened.

Beginning with Kelly's, Ralph Watkins made a notable career for himself as a manager/owner of many jazz clubs, all of them off The Street, except the Stable. His genuine feeling for jazz stemmed from early experience as a performing musician. "Ralph came from an extremely wealthy family," said Phoebe Pincus Jacobs, whose mother was the sister of Ralph's father, Ben. "His father was one of the owners of Kings Beer. They lived on Central Park West in 1930, when it was very fashionable and expensive. Ralph met Irving Alexander, his partner in the Stable, when they were going to school. Irving married (and later divorced) Ralph's sister, Beatrice. At one point they were in the clothing business together.

"But they were both interested in music. They played saxes in a room called The Showplace on Merrick Road, near Long Beach, Long Island. Before he became a club owner, Ralph played in Irving Alexander's band at Ben Marden's Riviera and led his own band at the Frolics Club on Broadway and at the Yacht Club. He and Irving frequently went up to Harlem to sit in with the black combos working at Dickie Wells' and other swinging joints. It was at Clark Monroe's Uptown House that Ralph caught Willie Dukes, a singer who later became a hit at Kelly's. Everybody tried to imitate Duke's rendition of 'Honeysuckle Rose,' and many believe that Billy Daniels modeled his style on Willie's.

"During Prohibition, society folks and white night people all went to the late-hour joints in Harlem. Ralph's awareness of this led to his move into Kelly's, where he presented many Negro artists, starting with the Harlem Highlanders. You might say that he was one of the men who brought Harlem downtown."

When the Stable moved to 52d St. early in 1940, it took over a spot that was briefly known as O'Leary's Barn, after the famous structure that started the big Chicago fire. The sawdust remained on the floor, and carriage lamps on each side of the small stage contributed to the bucolic atmosphere. But the musicians worked in front of a mural depicting a trotter on a racetrack. Singer Billy Daniels moved with the club and for years kept returning in a multiple role of vocalist, host and MC.

The partnership of bulky Pete Brown and big Frankie Newton, who were also on the opening bill, went back to the days of John Kirby's sextet in its breakout at the Onyx. (Frankie led the octet that accompanied Billie on her famous "Strange Fruit" record date of April 20, 1939. It was the only time he recorded with Lady Day, whose favorites on trumpet were Roy Eldridge, Jonah Jones and, especially, Buck Clayton.) The makeup of Newton's combo at the new Stable much impressed *Down Beat*. In a story headlined MIXED BAND IN REVERSE, it noted that the sextet was black except for one man. The ofay was Joseph "Flip" Phillips, a tenorman from Brooklyn, who later played with Larry Bennett at Hickory House but became known through the first Herman Herd in '44–'46.

Not long after Kelly's settled opposite Hickory House, Newton began running Sunday jam sessions. Jams had been a Hickory feature several years earlier under Joe Marsala, and they were to prove a tremendous audience draw at Jimmy Ryan's under Milt Gabler. Despite the popularity of the Stable, the Newton sessions failed to stir the excitement of either of these and were not nearly as provocative as jams run later at Kelly's by Pete Kameron and Monte Kay, two publicists who became successful manager-publishers.

As Monte Kay tells it, their jams had their beginnings in a mailing list given to them by a Greenwich Village *bon vivant,* Ralph Berton. Attending a dance in his native Brooklyn, Monte met "Little Benny" Harris, composer of bop instrumentals like the famous "Ornithology," who was then playing in a combo led by Benny Carter. Harris invited Monte to a Village party given by Berton in honor of writer Richard Wright. By then Kay had become friendly with Kameron, whom he also met at a Brooklyn dance. Both were dedicated jazz record collectors, an interest that so impressed Berton that he gave them a list containing the names of five hundred members of the Metropole Hot Club. With this as a basis, Kay and Kameron began running jam sessions in the Village at Nick's, a Dixieland outpost.

Later, around 1942, they moved uptown and launched the jams at Kelly's. The series, which lasted six to eight months, differed markedly in content, if not in form, from the Village jams. Two factors accounted for the contrast. On the next block, Milt Gabler was running a highly successful series of jams at Ryan's, concentrating on the musicians and sounds of Dixieland. The more significant factor: A new sound was coming out of Harlem.

Up at Minton's Playhouse on West 118th St., a group of angry but inspired cats was experimenting with new harmonies, rhythm patterns and melodic approaches. Among those who participated in the Minton sessions were Thelonious Monk, the inventive pianist-composer; drummer Kenny "Klook" Clarke (to whom Carmen McRae was then married); Dizzy Gillespie; and, of course, Charlie "Bird" Parker. "Little Benny" Harris was an acolyte. On Monday nights Kay and Kameron would journey uptown to Minton's, and on Wednesday they would extend invitations to the new, exciting instrumentalists they heard. Although they also presented top instrumentalists of the Basie band, Ellington, Earl Hines and John Kirby, their emphasis was on the new sounds rather than the traditional tonalities.

Like the jams at Ryan's, the Stable sessions were not advertised. Word of mouth, like signals embodied in slave hollers and work songs, spread the news. The Berton mailing list gave them an in group with whom they started the ball rolling via hand-addressed, homemade postcards. The musicians each received $10 for their efforts. Dizzy, who was working in Philadelphia, frequently commuted to Manhattan, spending $6 of his $10 fee on transportation. With an admission charge of $1 and a cut of the bar, the sponsoring trio of Kay, Kameron and Jerry White managed to gross between $200 and $300 a Sunday, yielding a paltry profit that compelled them to work at other jobs all week.

"But at Kelly's," Monte Kay observes, "we worked with the musicians we liked, the music we liked, and in an atmosphere we liked. There was communication all around, interplay and a feeling of excitement that I have seldom ever again experienced. We needed the little bread we made. But we ran the jams because they made us feel alive. Unfortunately, they ended quite suddenly—and we never knew why.

"Let me put it differently. We were never told why. We arrived one Sunday—the artists booked, the postcards mailed—and there was a padlock on the door. Nobody bothered even to warn us. As we later learned, the police had come into the Stable the preceding evening when Ralph Watkins and George Lynch were locking up, and simply put a padlock on the door. If they gave an explanation, we received none when we began asking. There were just hints—and maybe that's all the police gave to them. Naturally, it had to do with the black-white thing. We drew an integrated crowd. We didn't go asking or looking for it. But the audience for jazz was then mixed. I can tell you that they were beautifully behaved. Our show for that Sunday included Mary Lou Williams, who might have been playing at the Stable at the time, and some of Duke Ellington's soloists. When they arrived, we paid them off, hung around to explain to fans as they showed up, and then went sadly home and got drunk.

"Unfortunately, it wasn't the last time that the color line was drawn on 52d St. At one point I was able to persuade a group of the clubs to run free Sunday matinees. People could go from one end of The Street to the other, listening to all kinds of music for the price of a drink. My work was to publicize not any one club but The Street. For a short time, everybody had a ball. With the Musicians Union allowing the free movement of musicians, real interplay developed between cats of all colors and styles. It had not reached that tight point like today, when musicians play only with their own breed, musically speaking. Cutting added tremendous excitement. It was a scene to behold when three tenormen stood up in a club and each played his ass off to outplay the others.

"But this was short-lived too—I mean, the free Sunday jams. Once again nobody could or would explain why they were suddenly wiped out. As far as I could gather, it was the churches near 52d St. that stirred up the police. Saint Patrick's is at 51st and Fifth Avenue and Saint Thomas' at 53d and Fifth. Presumably, their parishioners were not too pleased by the mixed crowds that came trooping along the avenue on Sunday afternoons. The club owners were not about to start a rumpus with the police, regardless of the legalities, or for that matter, with influential churchmen who might have approached them.

"The funny thing is that we promoted these free Street jams through a radio program called *Tolerance Through Music*. Alan Courtney on Station WOV, later Freddy Robbins, gave us free advertising, and we supplied musicians free for their shows. On each one we had a rabbi and a priest discussing tolerance, and the audience con-

Slam Stewart jams with Roy Eldridge.

sisted of mixed groups to show tolerance in action. Pretty ironic that the churches themselves were so intolerant."

The great years of the Stable were from '39 into '41. With Billie Holiday and Coleman Hawkins as solid drawing cards, the club was able to provide a forum for such outstanding musicians as trumpeters Roy Eldridge and Oran Page, bassist Slam Stewart, saxophonist Lester Young, pianists Nat Jaffe and Clarence Profit, and a long line of singers from Billy Daniels, Lee Wiley, Una Mae Carlisle, Linda Keene and Thelma Carpenter to Dinah Washington, who played the club in its latter days in '46.

Trumpeter Page, appropriately nicknamed Hot Lips, came steaming out of Dallas, Texas, where he was born, via Kansas City, where he paid his dues working with Walter Page's (no relation) Blue Devils, Bennie Moten and Count Basie. Brought up on Texas blues and later the city blues of Bessie Smith and Ma Rainey, he played with an intensity, bite and drive typical of Kansas City horn men. Although he gigged with the Artie Shaw band in '41, he found the 52d St. scene more congenial and worked in a long list of clubs, including Hickory House (1940), Jimmy Ryan's (1941), Famous Door (1943), Onyx (1944–45), Spotlite (1946) and Ryan's again in 1949.

Page never attained the renown of Roy Eldridge, known as Little Jazz, who is generally regarded as the outstanding trumpeter between Louis Armstrong and Dizzy Gillespie, and the horn man who bridged Armstrong's lyricism and Gillespie's modernism, New Orleans style and bop. Like Page, Roy also worked with Artie Shaw. In 1941,

Lee Wiley, who sang at Hickory House and the Stable, performed at a Town Hall jazz concert organized by Eddie Condon and poses here with Condon (left) and Bobby Hackett.

Down Beat

shortly after appearing at the Stable, he joined Gene Krupa's band. His vocal duet with Anita O'Day on the Krupa hit record of "Let Me Off Uptown" made him a name musician.

But his experiences as a black member of both bands led him to say that he would "never in his life work with a white band again!" The guys in the bands were okay. But when the Krupa band played the Palladium in Hollywood, he could not stay at the same hotel with the rest of the men. Performing with Artie Shaw, he had difficulty getting into a "white dance," although his name appeared big as life on a billboard outside. "Man," he told *Down Beat,* "when you're on stage, you're great, but as soon as you're off, you're nothing." Little Jazz relented on his decision and did return to the Krupa band, and later toured Europe with the Benny Goodman orchestra. But he found 52d St. a simpatico showcase for his horn. He started on The Street by "Swingin' on That Famous Door," as an early recording with the Delta Four was called. And he made some notable sides with Billie Holiday during his 1940 stint at the Stable.

Lester Young, who played Kelly's in 1941, also recorded many sides with Billie. Lady Day was more favorably disposed to Young's tenor than to Hawk's, the two representing thermal extremities in the handling of the horn. Bean barked and Lester leaped. Bean's tone was big and deep and throbbing; Lester's was airy and light and legato. Billie thought so highly of Young's playing that she nicknamed him Prez. "The greatest man around then," she said, "was Franklin D. Roosevelt and he was the President. So I started calling Lester the President. It got shortened to Prez." Lester, who succeeded Hawkins in the Fletcher Henderson band in the mid-thirties, worked with Count Basie from '36 through '40, developing the lag-a-long, lyrical style that made him the father of the cool school. When he trotted out with his own combo, he first tied up at the Stable. It was a quiet booking, as were the succeeding appearances of the introverted man who held his sax with the bell facing sideways.

During his brief hitch at the Stable, Young did a record session with Una Mae Carlisle, who worked Kelly's at the same time. Miss Carlisle, an Ohioan, had been discovered in Cincinnati by Fats Waller, whose piano style she imitated. Shortly after Kelly's moved to 52d, Una Mae functioned as intermission pianist. A talented songwriter, she produced two big songs in this period: "Walkin' by the River" and "I See a Million People," both with lyrics by Robert Sour, co-writer of "Body and Soul" and later president of Broadcast Music, Inc. When she returned to the Stable in '41, she sang as well as played the piano. Una Mae, who was dead before her fortieth birthday, may be heard on a Fats Waller recording of "I Can't Give You Anything but Love, Baby" if you can find a copy.

Another and more distinguished singer who played Kelly's in '41 was Lee Wiley, a favorite of many show composers, among them George Gershwin and Harold Arlen. "Lee was a divine-looking girl," says Irving Lazar, who handled her. "She was beautiful in a very unsophisticated way and yet she was a very sophisticated singer." Like Mildred Bailey, Lee was part Indian, and like Mabel Mercer, she was unable to reach out to the larger audiences who spell the difference between fine singing and pop stardom. However, like Una Mae Carlisle, she did write a song hit: "Any Time, Any Day, Anywhere" was a top R & B disc for Joe Morris and Laurie Tate.

Possessing a husky voice that has been described as warm, smoky or erotic, Miss Wiley followed Billie into the Stable shortly after she had completed a series of recordings with Bud Freeman's Summa Cum Laude band and Condon's Dixieland groups. Though her style was not intimate, her phrasing and interpretation were unique enough to benefit from the intimacy of a small club. Yet during the mid-forties she toured with a big band, led by swing pianist Jess Stacy, who was then her husband. She was really in her right setting at the Famous Door with Bunny Berigan in '36, at the Stable, and more recently on wax, eliciting the applause of those who appreciate a subtle stylist.

In its heyday the Stable was a good-luck place for several young arranger-instrumentalists. In 1941 baby-faced Ralph Burns came down from Boston with the Nick Jerret band. Charlie Barnet began

Neal Hefti, for whom Kelly's Stable was a good-luck place.

RCA Records

coming in frequently to listen to vocalist Frances Wayne, who was Jerret's sister. After a time, Barnet offered the keyboard chair *cum* arranging to Burns, launching him on the productive career that bore fruit with the Woody Herman band and, more recently, in composing for the screen.

Neal Hefti, a Nebraska trumpeter who still looks like a lean Midwestern farmer, was not even playing at the club when things began to happen for him. "Since I didn't drink, or have the money to pay liquor tabs even if I wanted to," Hefti notes, "I'd hang outside the Stable or Famous Door and introduce myself to the musicians when they came out between sets. When I got to know some of the guys well, they'd bring me back with them so I could sit in the kitchen or cool it at the bar. The bartenders and the club owners really tried to be helpful. One night, a song plugger who worked for Robbins Music and was a friend of Charlie Spivak came over to me. Within three days, I was on the road with the Spivak band."

In October, '45, when he was playing and arranging with the Herman Herd, Neal and Frances Wayne, who was then singing with Woody, were married. They had met at the Stable. "It was a big study hall," Neal states, "for anyone who wanted to learn."

In 1943 the Stable changed its decor, substituting a collegiate flavor for its original down-on-the-farm atmosphere. Painted black, the walls were adorned with collegiate pennants. At the same time, it opened its doors to the new sounds of jazz, presenting a Kenny Clarke bop group in the early months of the year and a Clark Monroe combo with bopsters Fats Navarro and Bud Powell toward the end of the year. Two years later, Dizzy appeared with a combo that, in the words of *Metronome,* was instrumental in keeping The Street alive. That same year, pianists Clyde Hart and Nat Jaffe played their last chords. Not long after, the Stable ran out of hay and closed its doors.

Tape 15 . . . Ralph Watkins

"Kelly's Stable was in the beginning of The Street, even if it wasn't on 52d," said Ralph Watkins, whose resonant voice and compact stature give him a youthfulness challenging his long career as a club operator.

"The original Stable—I can never figure why some refer to it as Kelly's Stables—was at 141 West 51st. It was next door to the Hotel Abbey and the Barrel of Fun. When I first became interested, the place was owned by Chuck Goldman. I told him about a group I had heard in Harlem called the Harlem Highlanders and offered to go partners if he would let me put them in. I also brought in Irving Alexander as a third partner. The Highlanders did fantastic business. But Goldman wanted out. So Alexander picked up his end of the deal.

"Unbeknownst to us, the place was deeply in debt. Not long after we opened, the marshal came to close us up. We talked him out of it. We didn't have money, but we were doing enough business to take us out of hock.

"After the Highlanders, we tried to promote swing. It was long before Benny Goodman made it with Uneeda Biscuit Show. We brought in a sax man named Pete Brown with a swinging combo. Flip Phillips played clarinet in the group. We played Dr. Sausage, who wore tails, and Kenny Watts and his kazoo band. It was sort of a novelty era. We also used Hazel Scott.

"It was Chuck Goldman who gave the club its name. There never was a Kelly connected with it or any other Irishman. But there was a Kelly's Stable in Chicago, and that's where Goldman got the name. It had a sound and a certain magic.

"We finally tried with a real big band—fifteen pieces. The leader was a great arranger named Jimmy Mundy. We also had a quartet led by Abe Most, who was not even twenty and later went with Les Brown. Billie Holiday was also on the bill. Everybody wanted Coleman Hawkins when he returned from Europe. But I knew the Bean from Harlem, and I got him just by sending a cable to him on shipboard. I put Thelma Carpenter in to sing with him. We lost the club after that show.

"We used to eat in a place called the La Salle cafeteria. It was on 51st and Broadway across the street from Hanson's drugstore. The owner-manager was a guy named George Lynch. His real name was Tich. George had a lot of money, and we frequently talked to him about coming in with us. He just did not like the Stable. But while this was going on, there was a killing in a place called O'Leary's Barn on 52d, across the street from Hickory House. When it was closed down, we decided to take it over. And this time we managed to convince Lynch to join us. We moved the Stable over, with George taking fifty percent and Irving and me sharing the other fifty percent.

"I bought all the talent. Started by bringing over Pete Brown. Had the Nat Jaffe Trio. Nat's piano playing was the closest thing to modern jazz—he was miles ahead of everybody. Our format was to use a trio, a combo and a singer. Billie Holiday played the place pretty steadily for about five years. She was one of our surefire attractions. So was Billy Daniels. Roy Eldridge worked with us frequently.

"I booked Slim & Slam. They were all set and came to the club to rehearse. The afternoon of the evening they were scheduled to open, they had a fight on stage, and Slim walked out. Slam stayed and we brought in another guitarist.

"We moved from 51st after Coleman's 'Body and Soul,' which he hated to play. I went into the Army around '43, and when I came out in '45, I sold out. But Irving Alexander left before I did. He and George Lynch had a fight. Irving urged me to remain, which I did for a while. He went into the Three Deuces with Arthur Jarwood.

"I remember the summer after Irving left because we had one of our biggest periods. First, we had Henry 'Red' Allen. We had the King Cole Trio, Art Tatum, Billy Daniels, Claudia McNeill, Anne Robinson and Baby Lawrence. With all these people, the show cost nine hundred and ninety dollars. When Allen and J. C. Higginbotham left, Benny Carter came in with a combo. That show lasted for about four months. We also had Lena Horne, who was down at Café Society, coming in. But at the last minute she showed me a telegram from the Trocadero in Hollywood offering her four hundred dollars a week. Since I was gonna pay her a hundred and twenty-five, I let her out of the engagement and substituted Thelma Carpenter. What a bill that was!

"For the five years that Billie Holiday worked for me, she was a doll. I never had a bit of trouble with her. When I came back from overseas, she was a changed girl. Before that, the worst thing she ever did was to smoke pot. But everyone did. It wasn't a crime, as it now is. Somewhere along the line, she got married and I think that's when the problem started. That's what I heard anyway. When I saw her after the war, she was on a very expensive habit.

"By then she never had enough money, no matter how much she made. She was borrowing all the time. She was making over a thousand a week, a nut we couldn't carry. When I called Joe Glaser, he said: 'Talk to Billie yourself. Whatever she agrees to is okay with me.' I told Billie the Stable couldn't carry more than three hundred dollars and that's what she worked for. She was a beautiful woman, a great singer and a great gal. What narcotics do to you, I don't know. But afterward she was a completely changed girl. Pitiful! Hers was the greatest talent.

"We had some of the most amazing jam sessions. We'd have like ten great sax players at one time—Lester Young, Sam Donahue, Babe Russin, Chu Berry, Coleman Hawkins, Georgie Auld and others. One of the things that always amazed me. You know how great Lester Young was? Well, he'd go great until the Bean walked in. Then he'd freeze. I never saw anything like it. But the Bean was tough to top.

"Nat Cole worked for me for about nine months. We paid the Trio a hundred and forty a week. They arrived in a broken-down car, bedraggled and without any clothes to perform in. Nat used to sit in a corner and listen to Tatum. He'd be so upset. He was a fine jazz pianist, but he couldn't play like Tatum. But I remember one night when Alec Templeton came in. He and Tatum—both were blind—sat in a corner, staring up at the lights and listening to Cole. I found Nat through a Lionel Hampton record. It was called 'Jack the Bellboy,' and there were sixteen bars by an unknown trio. I tried my darndest to find out who handled them. I finally brought them in through an agent who's now down in Atlanta, Frank Henshaw.

"I didn't know Nat could sing when I booked him. But one day my sister, who was the bookkeeper at the Stable, phoned me and said, 'My God, you've got to come here. Nat's been rehearsing this one number all day. He has sung it so many times I'm going out of my mind.' I told her she must be mistaken, that Nat didn't sing. That's how we found out and got Nat to sing once or twice."

(According to Billy Daniels, Nat did no singing at the time because

In 1943 Billie Holiday presented the *Down Beat* award to J. C. Higginbotham, a 52d St. favorite, who topped the reader's poll for trombone that year, as he did for four years in a row.

Down Beat

he had a speech problem. It was only after he had gotten help from a speech therapist that he acquired the confidence to sing publicly.)

"When I returned to The Street after I got out of the Army," Watkins continued, "the Stable had changed. There were B girls—that's short for shady ladies—all over the place. George Lynch claimed that jazz was finished. I tried it for a short time and even brought Billie Holiday back. But finally, I told him that I wasn't interested in that kind of operation and offered to step out. I won't insult Lynch's memory by telling you what he offered for my end of the club. But I took it just to be out. After I was gone, there was a fire in the Stable. The fire marshal claimed that it started in the wrong place: instead of going up, it started upstairs and went down. That was the end of the Stable.

"George Lynch knew nothing about talent. But I guess that the biggest thing I did for him was to get him a wife. He saw this picture and fell in love with the girl. Once when I was up at Consolidated Artists, I discovered that they handled her. She was a boogie-woogie piano player, and I brought her in. Vicki Zimmer was her name and George couldn't do without her. They were married.

"I never owned or managed another 52d St. club after I left the Stable. I went into the Royal Roost on 47th and Broadway. First attraction was the Jimmie Lunceford band. Opening day in March, 1946, New York had one of its worst blizzards. That was the end of that engagement. Not long after Monte Kay and Symphony Sid [Torin] persuaded me to run a bop concert. I didn't know anything about the new jazz. Such a crowd showed up that we had to call the cops. I turned the spot into a progressive jazz joint. The first show included

Charlie Ventura, who made 'East of Suez' into a big record, Charlie Parker, and Billy Eckstine. From the Royal Roost, I went to Bop City in the Brill Building at 49th and Broadway. Then I had the Embers. After that Basin Street West in the old Roseland Theater building. It gave Birdland a run for its money. When they tore the building down to make way for the City Squire Motel, I opened Basin Street East. That was on East 49th, where Monte Proser had C'est La Vie and went broke. I first called the place Casa Cugat but changed it after he walked out.

"So much of entertainment history! I lost it all one day in Chicago. In the trunk of my car, I had the original menus of many of the places, correspondence with interesting people, and even a book I started. I had a letter from Margaret Truman when she turned down an invitation to sing at the Royal Roost—remember when she tried to become a singer? All of these mementos are gone. They stole the car and everything in it.

"I never had a problem with the Mob. You see, long before I came on the scene, my father owned a brewery. During Prohibition a lot of the fellows got started with a beer route or as pullers. They loved my dad and they never bothered me. They were always good customers and never made any trouble. In fact, they were the ones who would stop trouble before it developed. They never shook me down, never forced me to put anyone on my payroll. And they were beautiful people—maybe not to others but to me. Of course, there was one thing you could never do to them. Apart from not paying back money you borrowed, you could never lie to them—but never.

"I could never stand a liar or a thief. Being in the café business, I knew that everyone who worked for me was a thief—until they proved themselves innocent. When a dear friend wanted to open a place for his son and asked for advice, I said: First, he has to learn to steal; if he doesn't know how to steal, he'll never catch the guys that do. Employees will kiss you and hug you and rob you. And it doesn't matter how much pay they get. They've got to beat you somewhere along the line.

"Waiters steal from customers, which is worse than stealing from the owner. They double-check a customer. When I got back from overseas, I couldn't believe what was going on in the Stable. But George Lynch just didn't know. There was a waiter in the back who had his own bar. He worked with the same check so long it had fingerprints. Many customers are foolish and don't look at a check. If a waiter has a walkout, he's gonna try and hit you with that check. Now, if your check is eighteen dollars and you pay twenty-five, he's started working himself down. And he can keep it going so that he loses only four dollars at the end of the night—or makes a lot more. As for the kitchen, you've got to have a locked door and do the buying or have a reliable steward. It's a tough business.

"Going back, there were four people involved in the Frolics. It was where Hawaii Kai operates today in the Winter Garden Building. Irving Alexander, Chuck Goldman, Artie Jarwood and myself. There were several Goldmans: Jack was involved in the Hickory House; Al went to Florida, where he opened the Fu Manchu; and Charley Goldman was an attorney. The Marty Goldman who had a lease on the Birdland building was not related to the others.

"Chuck Goldman also owned the Pic-A-Rib, east of Hickory House at about No. 110 West. His partner was Harry Goodman, Benny's brother. They opened on New Year's Eve, 1939, and were still there when the Stable came to 52d, though not for long. They had no live entertainment, just a jukebox, but they served great ribs.

"Stuff Smith worked at the Stable for quite a time. This was after his breakout at the Onyx. After I let the trio go, I kept Stuff on as a single. And when his violin was stolen in the subway one night, I kept him on as MC. Later, when I had the Embers, I put him on, at the request of Jo Jones, with a group that consisted of Jo, Hank Jones and Tommy Potter. Then I took Stuff out and brought in Tyree Glenn. That was when the Embers had the greatest jazz in the world.

"Peggy Lee was always one of my favorites, but she never played the Stable. Her husband Dave Barbour did. It was when he left Kelly's that he went out and conducted for her. I think that he was Peggy's real love—maybe her only love—even though they split up.

"The greatest group that ever worked for me was the Spirits of Rhythm. They were like a house band, starting with the 51st St. Stable. I remember one night when Judy Garland, who was just a kid then, came in and flipped over Teddy Bunn. As long as she was in New York, she came in every night. It was a different kind of Stable than the 52d St. place. It had three sections: In one, you'd have all the society people; in the middle, we sat the actors and movie folk like

Gene Kelly and June Allyson; and the third section was for the hippies
—only we didn't call them that in those days—the music people,
colored, guys who didn't want to sit with the others. They had a
camaraderie of their own and they wanted to be segregated; it wasn't
a color thing.

"The 51st St. joint was a big place. You came up a ramp, like in a
stable into the bar area. The bandstand was on the other side. This
was the year of the World's Fair (1938) that I'm talking about. There
was a railing along the ramp and bar area. You know how we caught
on? We had no air conditioning and kept the door wide open in the
summer. Walter Winchell, who was a very powerful columnist, passed
by one night. From the outside, he saw the kids with their kilts—the
Harlem Highlanders—and he gave them a rave. That's how Kelly's
really got going.

"We also had Baby Lawrence, the greatest Negro tap dancer that
ever was. All the dancers of the day used to come to watch him—
Gene Kelly, Fred Astaire, all of them. He worked on this tiny platform, and what he did was unbelievable. He worked with the Highlanders at first—shook a tambourine—but by the time he came into
the 52d St. Stable he danced solo.

"I tried to promote swing by putting in Pete Brown. He was a big,
heavy fellow. I used to watch him coming down the street with his
white shoes and black shoelaces. I could see him a block away. He was
a jolly fellow and had a fine, swinging group. Yet we made no money
with him. Then one day, Ernie Anderson, who was Eddie Condon's
publicity man, said to me: 'Ralph, you're on the wrong track. Dixieland is what sells.' He organized a band for me that had Condon, Brad
Gowans, Pee Wee Russell, Artie Schutt, Davie Tough and some of the
day's finest Dixie men. After Eddie left and went back to the Village,
where he was playing regularly, I brought in another Dixie group.
Could have been Bud Freeman and the Summa Cum Laude Band.
The customers didn't show. Apparently, it was this particular group
that had a following, not so much the music itself.

"In the new Kelly's, I followed a show policy rather than a music
policy. The new place also had a ramp and looked like a stable. We
had mallets and horseshoes and wagon wheels all over the place—
and, of course, sawdust on the floor. We had a small dance floor, but
as soon as the place got crowded, we put tables on the floor. Anyway,
very few people came to dance. We had a hayloft over the entrance to

Two great pianists, Art Tatum and George Shearing, at the Three Deuces. Tatum was headlining; Shearing took over at intermission.

the dining room with fireproof hay. The minimum for liquor alone was two fifty. After a time, your minimum had to cover food as well as liquor. But we didn't serve much food. Kelly's was a drinking spot.

"The Yacht Club across the street and to the west of us was an older club. I had the band there before I opened the Stable on 51st. Could have been 1937. Frances Faye was the star. This was the second Yacht Club. The first was down the street between Fifth and Sixth avenues. Three guys were involved. I remember Sheppy and Red Murray. They might have been tough guys, but they were nice fellows. Red died of a faulty operation. His wife sued the doctors.

"Frances was big and packed the place. She was not much of a pianist, even though she wanted a Steinway when she played Basin Street. She gave a piano a big workout. She was quite a character, exciting, with a cute way of delivering and very likable. She had a way of shouting and made up little tunes. She was not a great singer, not a great pianist, but she could capture an audience. One of her *shtik* was to take the names of people in the audience and put them together in a comedy bit—Mary goes with Jerry and Jerry goes with Tom, etc.

"Going back a lot of years, Frances worked in Lynbrook, Long Island, in a place called The Showplace. It was in 1929. I was in the band and that was the first time I met her. I used to play a jazz solo behind her on the sax. Some hot licks in Dixieland style. The last time I played was when I was overseas, with an Engineers Band. Played the officers' clubs and on the French Riviera.

"The 52d St. performer that stands out in my mind is Art Tatum, above everyone else. Not only his musicianship but the fire in him. He had a way when he was annoyed. When people were talking during his playing, he'd stand up, bang the piano shut, stare in their direction, and tell them off: 'Quiet, you motherfuckers!' he'd shout. And not too many people knew or used that word in those days. He was beautiful. I liked to hear him when we went up to Harlem, and he'd like play for himself on a beat-up upright in some bar. I used to call him Vladimir and he'd call me Gieseking. You know, those were two of the big concert pianists of the day. No matter where he was, if I'd run into him and say, 'How'ya, Vladimir?' he knew immediately who it was. George Shearing always knew me just by the sound of my voice.

"I found a lot of new talent. Claudia McNeill worked Kelly's long before she became a hit in *Raisin in the Sun*. Dinah Washington worked for me after she left Lionel Hampton. She was pregnant with her first child when she appeared at the Stable. Although Billy Daniels worked the Stable over a period of years, the 'Black Magic' thing did not happen until he played the Park Avenue. 'Diane' was his big request number at Kelly's. I think that Diane was his first wife's name. After I left The Street, I found Ahmad Jamal down in Philadelphia. Never forget this group that played with so much amplification and wore suits whose shoulders were also too big for them.

"Not only the history of jazz but the things that went with it are awfully interesting. The Dixielanders were alcoholics. In the swing era, it was marijuana; but people were happy, never noisy and never bothered anybody. With modern jazz, an awful lot of the kids went on hard drugs. But it was confined to a certain number of musicians and colored people. Today, a whole generation seems to be on the stuff.

"You know I named 52d St. Called it the Street of Dreams. It sure was that for many, many artists. . . ."

Tape 16 . . . MARY LOU WILLIAMS

In a field that has been almost exclusively a man's world, Mary Lou Williams is that rarity: a black woman who made her way as both an instrumentalist *and* an arranger. Known for her long association with Andy Kirk (1929–40)—the band's popularity peaked with a '36 best-selling Decca disc of "Until the Real Thing Comes Along," falsetto vocal by Pha Terrell—she also wrote arrangements for Benny Goodman and Duke Ellington. The Kirk orchestra repertoire included such Williams' originals as "Froggy Bottom" and "Little Joe from Chicago," while the Goodman library boasted "Camel Hop" and "Roll 'Em." In 1945 she composed "The Zodiac Suite," introduced that year by her at Town Hall and performed the following year by the New York Philharmonic Orchestra. Born Mary Elfrieda Winn in Pittsburgh, Pennsylvania, in 1910, she remains a deeply religious woman who has at times retired from music to devote herself to religious work.

"I played on 52d with Andy Kirk, of course," she said, "and I appeared with Mildred Bailey and at the Downbeat. When I first left Kirk, I went into Kelly's Stable. Art Blakey, who was a Pittsburgh boy, was my drummer. The Street always reminded me of Kansas City. I once called it a *heavenly city* because it had so much music—fifty or more cabarets in the Negro part of town. Regardless of how much anybody played or where they were from, when they came to Kansas City, they found out how little they were playing. Charlie Parker was there, Ben Webster, Count Basie. 52d St. was like that. It was always a joy to play one of the clubs.

"During the Andy Kirk era, people were so wild about jazz. They showered you with gifts and with love. I usually played with my eyes closed. Once when I opened them, it was dark. I was startled. But I suddenly realized there was a woman leaning over me putting diamond earrings on my ears. She was a rather wealthy woman. People would come up and kiss your hands, and you had to stop playing. This was in the late thirties, and the audiences were young.

"In '52 I came back with a trio of my own to the Downbeat. The owner then was Morris Levy, the man who owned Birdland. He had a brother—the one who was killed at Birdland. Irving was my friend, and I was very fond of him. He was the manager of the Downbeat. I alternated with Billy Taylor. After the Downbeat, I was sent to Europe (in 1952) on a goodwill tour. I was sent to England to break the ban that prevented American musicians from playing in England or English musicians from playing here. I was allowed to play with all the bands and all the musicians there. This had never happened in thirty years. I was supposed to stay there for nine days and I wound up in Europe for over two years: eleven months in England and then in Paris.

"The Europeans had the same attitude toward jazz as the people on 52d St. They respected the artist and loved the music. When I came back to the United States in '54, The Street was gone.

"I am working on a history of jazz. I played through all the different changes. My mother taught me the spirituals and ragtime when I was about three or four. I learned Kansas City-style piano after that. I returned to London in 1969 and played a concert with Miles Davis—the Kansas City sound still broke things up. I'm still writing and arranging, and did most of the songs on my new record album, "Music for Peace," except for the rock. But there's nobody to arrange for now, unless you're with the movies.

"Jazz grows, like everything else in the world. It changes with time. But some people just want to hold it in that other era. I've always welcomed the changes and been able to keep up with the new things. We've lost the kids. Jazz got so far out it lost the beat. So the kids created rock. It has a lot of jazz in it.

"I was on a program with Max Roach. He's a fine drummer. But he said, 'Don't use the word "jazz." That's Uncle Tom music.' Well, it isn't Uncle Tom music. It's true that when I was with Andy Kirk and we were down South, somebody would shout, 'Come on, jazz it up!' And that meant you were Negro. Like I know a white girl who calls herself the Queen of Jazz. I laugh. You can't be the Queen of Jazz because jazz means you're Negro. When you say boogie-woogie, it means that a Negro is playing. Jazz—a Negro playing. That's why middle-class blacks never liked it.

"Like soul: the only thing that was left to a Negro after he was mistreated was his soul, his kind feelings. Soul means Negro, too. By the time I was eight years old, I had heard so many tales of how the slaves were mistreated. My great-grandparents' complexions were very fair. My great-grandfather's hair was blond. He wore it down to his shoulders like a pioneer—like the kids are wearing it today. My great-grandmother was part Indian (Cherokee, I think) and she had straight black hair. I used to hear them tell stories about how badly they were treated. The slaveowners must have had guilty consciences. They thought people would wonder where these almost-white babies came from. Both my great-grandparents told stories about how the slaveowners on the two different farms on which they were raised used to put them in the sun to parch their skin black to escape guilt and the neighbors' talk. It was a question of easing guilty consciences.

"After hearing a number of stories like this, I was really mad. One day I went to school and grabbed a long ruler and hit my teacher who had always been very nice to me. I distressed her. I said, 'You white people made slaves out of us.' She was very upset. She said, 'Oh, you poor child. I wonder who's been telling you all these things.' From that day on she brought me presents every day—little things I liked. She must have told the other teachers because soon they started to write me to come to their boardinghouse to play for them. I used to return home with a lot of money tied up in my handerchief. And the principal used to bring me to hear operas and concerts at Pitt and Carnegie universities. So this teacher was patient with me and took time to bring me through my first shock at hearing that story from my grandparents. We stayed good friends.

"Father Woods told me—and later I found it in a book at the library —that during slavery, the slaveowners would take the slaves to church and teach them their songs (the psalms). As a result, the slaves began writing spirituals. If a slave had a hard time during the day and was mistreated, he'd start a song going while he was working. And for their little functions, they created their own musical things, too.

"What this means is that when the Africans were brought here as slaves, they lost the drum thing and developed a different style. Once I played with eighteen drummers on the stage of Carnegie Hall. They were African drummers. They couldn't play the rhythm of jazz. I had to switch to a kind of African meter. That's how the only American art was born—through the suffering of black American slaves.

"Soul came through the church and suffering. I don't think that any black kid should learn about black history. They shouldn't teach them bad things about white, yellow or anybody. God knows what he's doing, but we don't. He put all those different colors and different people here for a reason. If we didn't have any suffering, it would be a very weak world. The thing is to overcome it and work hard in your music. Then you don't even know someone is mistreating you. That's what I've done all my life. When bad things happened to me, someone had to tell me—I'd be so lost in the music.

"It was a good time, the days with Andy Kirk on 52d St. I wrote a lot of things. I think the first was 'Memphis Stomp.' Then there was 'Walkin' and Swingin',' 'Bear Cat Shuffle,' 'Sax Appeal,' and 'What's Your Story, Morning Glory?' Andy Kirk had a big Decca record on that one with his Clouds of Joy—in 1940, I think it was—and Jimmie Lunceford recorded it. Still in the forties, but late, I had 'Pretty-Eyed Baby.' It was a pop hit for Frankie Laine and Jo Stafford. But I made the original record on Asch soon after I left Andy, a jazz thing I called 'Satchel-Mouth Baby.' In the late forties I wrote the bop fairy tale 'In the Land of Oo-Bla-Dee.' That was a hit too.

"Some funny things happened on The Street. Oscar Pettiford had a great sense of humor. When a musician would play a wrong chord, he'd reach for him with a hook—you know, like the one they use at the Apollo on amateur nights to yank bad performers offstage. But the funniest thing was one night when I got a phone call from somebody: 'You got to come down to the Three Deuces. You won't believe it!' I was getting ready to go to bed, but they wouldn't tell me what was happening. So I got dressed and went downtown. There was Big Sid Catlett on the bandstand all alone, playing all by himself, just the drums. There had been a lot of dissension in the group, and the cats had been coming late. That night he just fired them all. And he went on by himself. He did the shows all alone that night. And the audiences were so great! They sat and listened, and I think they liked it. People were more adventuresome in those days, and they swung for new things. They bought it so long as it was good. And Big Sid was sure good. . . ."

Tape 17 . . . Slim Gaillard

A gangling giant of a man, Bulee Gaillard of Detroit, better known as Slim, always had a mischievous look in his eyes and an ingenuous smile on his face. When he was not clowning—something he found hard to avoid—he seemed to be laughing inwardly. "Carry me back to old Virginny," he would sing and on the spur of a grin, add: "And I'll fight every inch of the way." He had a way of being amused by his own inventions that appealed to audiences. Out of his droll sense of humor came "The Flat Foot Floogie (with the Floy-Floy)," a novelty hit in 1938, and "Cement Mixer (Put-ti, Put-ti)," a noisemaker in 1946.

A natural musician, he was not content just to shine as a jazz performer. He played the piano with the backs of his hands, palms up; the vibraphone with swizzle sticks; and the double bass below the bridge. He could play "Jingle Bells" on a snare drum, producing the pitches by sliding the fingers of one hand along the drumhead as he beat out the rhythm with the other hand. Slim & Slam, Gaillard on guitar and Stewart on bass, were a hot vocal-instrumental duo until World War II broke them up.

"The first 52d St. club I played," Slim said, "was on 51st St. It was just around the corner from the Rivoli Theater, which was and still is across Broadway from the Brill Building. They had Sunday morning concerts with performers like Woody Herman, The Andrews Sisters, Bunny Berigan and Slim & Slam. Martin Block was the emcee. Little Jazz performed. From there we went around to Kelly's Stable, where Irving Alexander ran things. He was a short feller. We played there after 'Flat Foot Floogie' caught on.

"I wandered all over the Brill, trying to get a publisher for 'Floogie.' Finally, I bumped into Lou Levy. I knew him from the Savoy Ballroom in Harlem. He danced with Lunceford, Andy Kirk and Erskine Hawkins, the guy who had 'Tuxedo Junction.' Lou was a champion jitterbug dancer. Used to win all the contests.

"Standing in a hallway, I did 'Floogie' for him. It was mostly a riff with jive lyrics. He says: 'I know just the publisher. Green Brothers and Knight. They're new.' He came along and sold them. They were not only new. They were small. So small, they had to step outside their office to turn around. Bud Green says: 'OK, we'll publish it. We'll give you two-fifty advance against royalties.' I thought he was talking about two dollars and fifty cents. He wrote out a check for two hundred and fifty dollars. I was running into the walls looking at it all the way out.

"Two or three nights later, over the radio we heard: 'Ladies and gentlemen, your Camel Caravan moves on, introducing for the first time on the air Benny Goodman and his orchestra, "Flat Foot Floogie (with the Floy-Floy)." ' Couldn't believe it. 1938 was the year.

"At the club we had to play 'Floogie' a hundred times a night. Slam Stewart was even then bowing his bass and humming along with it. He had perfect pitch. That's a gift.

"The audiences at the Stable were mixed. No problems. Never heard of it. It was a happy time. Just swinging. After you finished your set, you hated to leave because everybody was swinging. If you played a slow ballad, everybody was quiet. If somebody started talking in a corner, everybody would look around and say 'Shh-shh.' In that block between Fifth and Sixth Avenue, they came for music. And you had all types of music.

"First engagement at the Stable was for about a year. Long time we stayed there. Little Jazz was there at the time. Maybe John Kirby. Tatum came in later.

"The *Major Bowes Amateur Hour* was very popular in those days. We used to go on every other week. We'd have a different name each time. It was radio—and the audience never knew. Slim & Slam won every time but each time under another name. We received seven dollars and lunch at Bickford's. And the major would say, 'Where it stops, nobody knows. We have a duo with us from upstate New York.' And we'd come out. 'The Chrysler Corporation presents. . . .' And we'd do our little thing. And then they'd measure the applause . . . and the whole thing. We were on around '37.

"It was right before Martin Block brought us over to Vocalion. As Slim & Slam we made our first recording on February 17, 1938—'Flat Foot Floogie.' Later I recorded with a group I called Slim Gaillard and his Flat Foot Floogie Boys. We did 'Chicken Shack' and some other novelties.

"Streets of Paris came after the Deuces. Let me see. It was across the street from Kelly's Stable. That would be past Sixth Avenue, on

Slim Gaillard with Billie Holiday's Chihuahua, called Chiquita, at Birdland. She also had a boxer she named Mister, who was widely known to 52d Streeters.

Down Beat

the same side as Hickory House. We followed Fats Waller into Hickory House. We played Kelly's Stable when they had wagon wheels there and sawdust on the floor and checkered tables. Tilly's Chicken Shack was just down The Street. That's where Billy Daniels sang.

"Funny things? At the end of the week it had to be funny, salaries were so low. And the club would come up with all these vouchers you were signing and you'd end up owing the club money.

"You'd come into work early. There was a little bar on Sixth Avenue, and you'd go in and buy one beer or soda, and you'd get all the hors d'oeuvres you wanted—pastrami, bologna, salami, pickles, mustard, everything. You'd come out full, and you didn't care whether you got paid or not. The tourists didn't have a chance to get in, the place was always so jammed with musicians.

"For three years I worked Birdland under The Grapevine, a small upstairs bar. I introduced Philly Jo Jones. Brought him from Philadelphia. He was so scared and kept asking, 'Do you think I can make it in New York?' He always gave credit on his albums that I brought him in.

" 'Cement Mixer' was later. I wrote that after I came out of the service. It was after 52d St., but The Street was where you had your schooling. That's where you learned how to handle your ax, like they used to say. I put out a dictionary on jive talk. It had 'groovy,' 'voutsy' and 'rooney.' I had a book out at the same time as Dan Burley.

"At the World's Fair in 1939 they put three songs in a time capsule. 'Stars and Stripes' was one. Maybe 'Rhapsody in Blue' was the other. The third was 'Flat Foot Floogie.' Great honor. I never knew I wrote a historical song.

"When we recorded 'Flat Foot Floogie' for Vocalion, the A & R man broke up when I gave him the title. 'You serious?' he asked. It was Morty Palitz, who later headed A & R at Decca. Well, we did three other tunes, and what happened to them? Nothing.

"Same thing with 'Cement Mixer' years later. We were recording on Sunset Boulevard, right across from a TV station. After we did three sides, the A & R man sent us out for some air. I was glad to get it because I didn't have a fourth song—figured we'd improvise something like 'Floogie.' Just outside the studio, they were repairing the street, and one of these cement machines was going put-put-put-put. When we were back in the studio and the A & R man asked for the fourth title, I says: 'Cement Mixer, Put-ti-put-ti.' Everybody in the place broke up. I started to sing, 'Cement Mixer' . . . That's why the lyric goes put-ti-put-ti, putti-hootie, putty-voutie, macaroonie. That's all it is, ad lib. The other three songs were sleepers and this one took off.

"I liked the Three Deuces because it was a challenge. You'd get a song, a twelve-bar thing like they're playing today. You'd get swinging. One favorite was the anthem—you know, 'How High the Moon.' You take a hundred choruses. OK, you start in the original key G and then you go up to G♯ and you just keep moving, improvising in each key. It was good exercise for everybody, except the drummer, who had no problem. He just had to keep the beat going. Somebody would always come and sit in. It was educational. A lot of the advanced students from Juilliard used to come down and sit in. They'd go back with a few new ideas, like cross-firing chords. Like an E♭ chord and an A♭ chord. It's a wild sound, one chord in each hand. You know who taught me that chord? Duke Ellington. It was the chord of 'Solitude.' There was no solitude on The Street. . . .

"In those days when a traveler hit New York, he'd want to know where Times Square was, the prime rib places, the theaters and 52d St. Here was one block where they'd find all the sounds of the day, yesterday and maybe tomorrow. . . ."

12. Two to the Bar

There is still a Jimmy Ryan's today. It bills itself, not without justification, as the Oldest Jazz Club in New York. Now on 54th St. near Seventh Avenue, it functioned for twenty-two years on 52d near Sixth. Today, Ryan's is a narrower room than the original, red-draped and adorned with paintings, and it has an apostrophe in its marquee, though the original did not. But now, as then, it's a bastion of two-beat jazz, and you can nightly hear such Dixieland standards as "Lazy River," "Fidgety Feet," "Royal Garden Blues" and "Sister Kate."

In its years on The Street, Dixieland faced the onslaught, first of four-to-the-bar, big-band swing, then of *avant-garde* bop. Swing was evolution; bop, revolution. Jimmy Ryans (no apostrophe) remained the fortress of those who were damned as "moldy figs" and who, in turn, tended, like Louis Armstrong, to castigate flatted-fifth music as "the modern malice." Some of the cats who blew at the original club appear at its successor, among them trumpeter Maxie Kaminsky, pianist Cliff Jackson, clarinetist Tony Parenti (until he had a falling out and opened his own club), and drummer Zutty Singleton, who played in the club's very first combo. If the music floating down 54th St. these days has a nostalgic sound, it is not only because Dixieland came roaring out of the dizzy twenties but because the boys always seem to be blowing a requiem for the old club and its hard-drinking founder, Jimmy Ryan.

Ryan, who frequently referred to himself as the Last of the Chorus

Boys, opened his club in September, 1940. It was the year that young Sinatra left Harry James for Tommy Dorsey, *Gone with the Wind* was made into a grandiose film with Vivien Leigh and Clark Gable, who used the word "damn" for the first time on the screen, and 300,000 British and French soldiers were evacuated from the beaches of Dunkirk. Ryan's partner was Matty Walsh, a distant relative who today runs the 54th St. Ryan's. On the north side of the street, about 150 feet east of Sixth Avenue, the 52d St. Ryan's moved only once—and that was to make way for the CBS skyscraper that rises in brownstone splendor between 52d and 53d on Sixth. Ryan lived to see his new place open in December, 1962. Seven months later, he died.

"He died of too much living," says Matty Walsh, who is in his middle fifties and looks more like a bank clerk than a bar owner. "And like many high livers, he died of cirrhosis of the liver." Walsh smiled, and there was a glint in the eyes behind the spectacles. "Jimmy was New York's one-man unofficial host for out-of-towners. He'd start in the afternoon. But he had to keep being the genial host until our closing time at 4 A.M. He held his liquor well.

"He lived in the brownstone next door to the club, at 51 West. A faggy old music teacher lived on the floor above him. Many a morning Jimmy would be pounding on the fag's door because his key didn't open the lock. By that time he was flying and simply landed a floor too high. After a time, the fag didn't bother to open his door. He'd simply call out from his bed: 'Downstairs, Jimmy! Go down one flight!' He really could have lived to a ripe old age. He had a cast-iron stomach. But he simply paid no attention to the warnings. He loved to entertain people and had a real talent for friendship, particularly with celebrities. Sinatra used to come in to hoist a few with Jimmy. So did Phil Harris.

"When Jackie Gleason was doing the *Du Pont Show* at the 54th St.—it used to be next door to where Ryan's is now—he'd be in our joint every Saturday night. He liked Jimmy and they could imbibe quite a bit of liquid together. Once Jimmy invited Gleason up to his apartment. 'Want me to have a heart attack?' Gleason protested. 'You got to be a mountain goat to climb up there.' "

To enter the original Ryan's, you went down one step. The brownstone was 19 feet wide and 100 feet deep. The bandstand was straight ahead. The checkroom and a 30-foot bar were on the right. Ryan's was one of the larger 52d St. rooms, not a "barracuda spot," as the small rooms were called. It could seat about 125 and had a public capacity of about 175.

Before he became a club owner, Jimmy was a lifeguard, as well as a Broadway chorus boy. His partner, Matty Walsh, went to CCNY for two years and worked as a waiter and bartender at his brother's place in Washington Heights. Matty was related to Jimmy through his brother's marriage to Ryan's sister. After the two decided to open a bar, they scoured Brooklyn and Queens for a location. It was a lifeguard associate of Jimmy's who brought them to 52d St. George McGough owned a club at 53 West known as the Troc. Although he featured trumpeter Bobby Hackett and a fourteen-piece band, the Troc did not last very long. McGough sold the place to them. Not the building, which he bought for $46,000 and sold in '62 for $375,000.

Opening night in 1940, a curious thing happened. To attract customers, Ryan advertised a 25¢ martini. September is sometimes hurricane month in New York City, and gusty winds tore the sign from its moorings and swept it eastward down the block. By some quirk of fate, it caught in the decorative grillwork of the tall iron fence surrounding 21. Imagine the shock of the Kriendlers when they arrived the following morning and found a cheap martini being garishly advertised on their fence. They assumed that somebody was playing a practical joke until Jimmy came to retrieve his elusive sign.

Although Ryan's proved one of the most consistent purveyors of jazz, adhering to a music format even during the war years when other clubs found G-strings more rewarding than G chords, the club did not start as a jazz joint. It was just a bar with a trio to provide music. Ryan, who was unquestionably a frustrated singer and had an enormous repertoire of show tunes, "starred" himself. Once or twice an evening, depending on the conviviality of the crowd, he would come forward and sing in a pleasant Bing Crosby type of voice.

"It was Milt Gabler," Matty Walsh notes, "who introduced us to jazz. Milt was then operating a branch of the Commodore Music Shop on The Street, and he was producing jazz records on the Commodore label. One evening he suggested that we put in a small combo. We started with some of the boys who were cutting records for him, Zutty Singleton, Eddie Condon and others. It was a Dixieland combo—and we stuck with the style right up to the present moment. Soon he got the idea of running jam sessions, and these became quite an audience draw for Ryan's and The Street."

Trumpeter Max Kaminsky, who participated in many of the jams, later wrote in his autobiography, *My Life in Jazz:* "There was a moment there, in 1941–42, at the Ryan sessions, when hot jazz seemed at its purest. . . . At Ryan's the music was the thing, and when a musician was building a solo, you never heard a sound from the audience. You could *feel* them listening."

There was no advance publicity or advertising. Gabler simply mailed a handmade flier that he duplicated on his mimeo machine in the back of the Commodore Shop. Those who got the flier—because they were on the Commodore mailing list—spread the word among those who couldn't afford to buy discs. The jams were almost always SRO. After a month, the original entrance fee of 65¢ was raised to $1. At the first jam, the traditional Dixieland front line consisted of Pee Wee Russell (clarinet), Bobby Hackett (trumpet) and Brad Gowans (trombone). Rhythm backing was supplied by Zutty Singleton (drums), Eddie Condon (guitar), Bill King (bass) and Dave Bowman (piano). Of course, the sit-ins outnumbered the so-called house group. Teddy Bunn and the Spirits of Rhythm participated, as did Billie Holiday. The jammers included Joe Sullivan (piano), Albert Nicholas (clarinet), Sandy Williams (trombone), Marty Marsala (trumpet) and many others. All the participants, first-rate or not, contributed voltage to the electricity of the occasion.

Jamming was then hardly a 52d St. or even New York phenomenon. At the Vanguard in Greenwich Village, Ralph Berton, a New York disc jockey and brother of Vic Berton of the famous Wolverines, ran jams before Ryan's. Even earlier, the Javanese jazz critic Harry Lim had conducted a highly successful series at the Panther Room in Chicago's Hotel Sherman. In 1940 there were Sunday jams at the Greenhaven Inn on Boston Post Road in Larchmont, New York, attended by 52d Streeters like Zutty Singleton, Bobby Hackett, Joe Sullivan and Pee Wee Russell. (In the late thirties Gabler himself had sponsored jam sessions for members of the United Hot Clubs of America, organized by him and Marshall Stearns, but these were held at various recording studios as an in-group rather than a public event.) In 1941, *Jazz Information,* an in-group publication, reported jams at the Beachcomber in Providence, Rhode Island—with Hot Lips Page and Hackett—and at the Club Ferdinando in Hartford,

Dizzy Gillespie, Harry Lim, Vida Musso, Billy Kyle, Cootie Williams, Charlie Shavers, John Williams at a Village Vanguard jam session early in World War II.

Connecticut. In March, 1941, jazz critics George Simon and Leonard Feather ran Sunday sit-ins at Café Society Downtown.

But none of these, except possibly Lim's sessions in Chicago, seemed to have the magic of the Ryan's-Gabler jams—and none lasted for as long a time. "In the early forties," Max Kaminsky recalls, "Ryan's was the mecca of jazz fans on Sunday afternoons. You paid a dollar at the door, usually to Jack Crystal [Gabler's brother-in-law], who helped run the sessions, and if you didn't want to drink, you could sit in the row of folding chairs set in the center of the floor and listen without anything to distract you, except the bobbing head of the cat in front of you. The club was small, the atmosphere intimate, and the audience listened hard. The feeling was that musicians and fans alike lived just for Sundays and that Jimmy Ryan, himself, genial, debonair, ex-hoofer turned nightclub owner, was having as big a ball as everybody else."

"Eight tenormen could be around at the same time," notes Art Engler, who is a booker today and was then a musician. "The courtesy that was shown to each man blowing was unbelievable. If you got a groove going, they'd encourage you, 'Take another chorus! Keep going, man!' And they'd start to play little groovy things in back of you to push you on. Forgive me, but with all due regard for contemporary jazzmen, there is no respect, no courtesy. The guys sit there with an attitude of, 'As soon as he gets through, I'll blow mine,' and they couldn't care less.

"I remember a session at Ryan's when all the great tenormen in town seemed to be around—Ben Webster, Chu Berry, you name them. I was there, too, and I was scared stiff. But I *had* to play. I forget the tune, but suddenly, somebody doubled up the time. And with all these great cats around me, I couldn't hold back. I was so excited, I just started blowing and I blew beyond what I could normally play. I could hear Chu, Ben and others urging me on. And soon there were three tenors going like mad, me in the middle. God, you'd come out of a session ten feet off the ground.

"Even the guys from schmaltzy Mickey Mouse outfits like Sammy Kaye's band would come in the jam. They were tired of playing from charts and wanted to be free. And they were welcome. It always ended up as one big, happy party with everybody loving everybody else. It was so beautiful and so exciting. That's why I say 52d was the greatest musical jazz street that ever existed in the world anytime, anywhere. What a street! What a street!"

Not too long after he started the jams, Gabler instituted a policy of using two bands or, at least, two front lines. At the session on February 16, 1941, characterized by *Jazz Information* as "the most exciting of the series," one group was fronted by Kaminsky, Brad Gowans and Pee Wee Russell, while the opposing line consisted of Hot Lips, Sandy Williams, Sidney Bechet and Happy Caldwell, trumpet, trombone, clarinet, tenor sax, respectively. There was overlap in the rhythm sections—Zutty and Bill King worked with both combos—as there was a crossing of color lines. But the two-band format embodied a competitive or "cutting" element that heightened the excitement of the Ryan's jams.

Just as Marty Marsala, drummer Shelly Manne and other cats sat in at this session, so Sunday jams drew sidemen from all over The Street, city, and even country. Max Kaminsky tells of how when he was in the service, playing in the Navy Band led by Artie Shaw, he once received a seventy-two-hour weekend pass. That Saturday he attended a jazz concert at Town Hall and spent Sunday afternoon blowing at Ryan's.

"Bugle Call Rag" became the traditional closer of the sessions,

Courtesy of Milt Gabler

This jam session organized by Milt Gabler at Jimmy Ryan's in 1940 included Eddie Condon (guitar), J. C. Higginbotham (trombone), Charlie Shavers (trumpet), Brad Gowans (valve trombone), Marty Marsala (cornet), Max Kaminsky (trumpet), Pete Brown (alto sax), Pee Wee Russell (clarinet), Billy Kyle (piano), John Simmons (bass).

crowding the tiny bandstand with more sidemen than it could hold. All the horns had to be pointed up—not out, as they normally were—to avoid collisions. "The results, though untidy," according to Whitney Balliett of *The New Yorker*, "were often stunning." Balliett also carries an indelible memory of a Sunday when "a very slow 'Sunny Side of the Street' was played by Coleman Hawkins, Edmond Hall, Eddie Heywood and Frankie Newton, the last of whom also sang. It was an empyrean performance that lasted, I think, over twenty minutes."

Regular attendants at the Ryan's sessions came to feel that they were part almost of a family circle. When Zutty Singleton left for the West Coast in April, 1943, Jimmy threw a farewell party; and when Gabler had a birthday the following month, there was another party at which "Baldy" received a birthday cake and a cigarette lighter.

Trends came and went on 52d St. But Ryan's stuck with Dixieland, establishing a record for the longevity of its bookings and for its willingness to let musicians follow their own bent. Instead of frequently changing his bill, Jimmy held cats over for long periods during which they had the time and freedom to refine their musical ideas. In 1944, for example, Art Hodes and his Mephistophelean smile graced the keyboard from April through December. The following year, drummer Danny Alvin's combo remained on the marquee from May through December. In 1946 trombonist J. C. Higginbotham and trumpeter Red Allen were in residence from February through June, and trombonist George Brunies and pianist Tony Parenti kept the beat from June through November. Honors for the longest tenancy go to the De Paris brothers, Sidney on growling trumpet and Wilbur on sliphorn, who remained on the Ryan bandstand from 1952 (with sabbaticals) until the wrecker's steel ball began knocking the walls down in 1962. Occasionally, when one brother left—as Wilbur did in '57 to make a State Department tour of Africa—the other one took care of "the store."

During 1947 Sidney Bechet played his liquid soprano sax and clarinet at Ryan's for most of the year. Shortly before his death in 1959, he wrote in his autobiography, *Treat It Gentle:* "It's sad to think now that the whole place [52d St.] is pretty well torn down and Jimmy Ryan's is standing there next to a vacant parking lot, I guess about ready to go. . . ." By the end of the forties, according to Max Kaminsky, "52d St. was still holding on by its fingernails. But except for Jimmy Ryan's, where I had a trio for three months in the winter of 1948–49, and one or two other spots, there was very little hot music to be found there anymore."

In January, 1950, after he had performed at a moving Leadbelly memorial concert, Bechet drove back to his hotel with Count Basie. It was a cold and rainy night in New York, and Bechet was leaving for Europe the following day. Although it took them out of their way, Bechet asked the cab driver to go to The Street. He was too worn out to pay a visit, but he wanted just to see the canopy of Jimmy Ryan's. And he did for the last time, in that January rain, from a slow-moving taxi. . . .

Of Georg Brunis, who dropped two *e*'s from his name because of a numerologist's urging, Matty Walsh has happy memories. "Everybody went on calling him George even after the *e* came off," Walsh said. "He always played like it was his last night on earth. And he generally drank the same way. Curiously, he'd come in the next night looking fresh and energetic, and it never seemed to interfere with his playing.

Not unlike Ryan, he was always ready to buy somebody a drink. If somebody at the bar bought him a pony, he'd reciprocate by buying *everybody* a drink. I would pretend not to hear him when I was working the bar, because by the end of the week, he frequently got no pay. Once I talked to his roommate about Brunis' generosity. The word came back fast. 'You live your life and I'll live mine. If Georg Brunis drops dead on the bandstand, nobody can say that he didn't buy them a drink!'

"There were a number of cronies about whom we had standing instructions from Brunis never to give them a tab. One was a ferry-boat captain named Simmons. Georg used to live in Weehawken, New Jersey, and he'd take the ferry across the Hudson River to go home. Simmons occasionally allowed Georg to steer the boat—at 5 A.M. in the morning. To Georg, this was the greatest experience of his life. I always knew about it because when he came to work that night, he'd remind me: 'Don't you let the captain spend any money when he comes in here! The tab's mine.'

"Brunis was a cutup on the bandstand. He had a flair for being funny, and he thought of himself as an entertainer and not just a jazz trombonist. If things were getting too quiet in the club, he'd lie down on the bandstand and play his horn by moving the slide with his toe. While he was stretched out, he'd offer to let anybody stand on his stomach. 'But not over a hundred and fifty pounds,' he'd say, 'and no broads with high heels.'

"On certain numbers like 'The Saints,' he'd go parading around the club. Suddenly, he'd stomp outside with Tony Parenti tootling the clarinet behind him, march across the street into the Famous Door or Three Deuces, come marching back and head for the ladies' room. As the audience howled, he'd go parading in and then come out, holding up fingers to indicate the number of women he'd surprised. Of course, as soon as we saw him go marching out of the club, somebody would duck into the ladies' room and clear the place out. The regular visitors to the club knew that there were no women inside. But the occasional customer would laugh himself sick, thinking that Brunis had actually walked in on several unsuspecting women.

"Wild Bill Davison was almost as much of a cutup as Brunis. When the bar was crowded, he'd sometimes come up to me as I was serving and say loudly enough for everybody to hear: 'Gimme a shot of that whiskey that burns!'

"One night Lee Blair lost two banjos. Well, it actually took two nights. And he didn't really lose the first. He broke it into pieces because he became fed up with his playing. Just raised it by the fret board and brought it down with a crash. (Maybe that's where the new rock groups got their idea of busting up instruments.) He borrowed one for the next evening's gig. But that night he fell asleep on a train. And when the train reached his station, he rushed off without the banjo. We laid out the money for a new instrument, but it took a time for him to reimburse us.

"You remember some things that had nothing to do with the music but now seem typical of the time. At one point Harold Minsky of the well-known family opened a burlesque club next door to us. It was a swank club. After a time, he sold it to Harry Finkelstein, who owned a huge club on Eighth Avenue opposite Madison Square Garden. The Ringside featured B. S. Pully, whose billing read, "The World's Worst Entertainment." In those days, Ryan's used to open in the afternoon, and while Minsky's place was being spruced up, Finkelstein would use ours as his office.

"Once I overheard this conversation between Finkelstein and Pully, who was trying to get a raise. 'You keep promising,' Pully complained, 'but when am I getting that goddamn raise?' Finkelstein countered: 'But I'm paying you fifty dollars a week now.' Pully snorted: 'Fifty dollars! Why, I bet that much in one race at Aqueduct.' After some thought Finkelstein said, 'All right, I'll give you a raise. I'll make it fifty-two fifty a week. BUT you gotta promise me you'll get new material.'

"Even after phone service was restored to the Minsky place, Finkelstein used to come into ours. I guess he preferred to place bets from one of our phone booths than from his. Once Georgia Sothern, the stripper who was then his wife, came looking for Harry. He spotted her out of the corner of his eye and went right on talking as if he had been placing an order for liquor. When he came out of the booth, he greeted Georgia as if he hadn't seen her. Georgia wasn't fooled. She looked right through him and stalked out, with Harry chasing after her, and one of his sidekicks commenting: 'Better he should be married to a tiger!'

"Gypsy Rose Lee once pulled a fastie on Harry. She came into the Ringside one day and told Harry she could get him tons of publicity. It was when she had that novel, *The G-String Murder*. Harry was taken in: 'What do I do?' he asked. Gypsy said: 'We'll tell you as we go along.' The next Harry knew, he was in a deserted theater with her and a photographer. Climbing up to the first balcony, they went out of a fire exit onto one of those outside iron staircases. Then they handed Harry a gun. It was a toy pistol, so he didn't fight it. They told him to put his coat collar up and to pull his hat brim down over his eyes. The photographer took about forty shots. That was the last Harry heard of it until one day a crony phoned him: 'Hey, Harry, you're in *Life* magazine.' Harry ran out elated and bought several copies. And there he was, looking like a typical gangster, gun in hand, with a dead body nearby. For days, Harry was worried that he might be called by the State Liquor License and have his liquor permit revoked.

"One of our maître d's was a personable little man who went by the name of Bobby Dunne. One night a captain from 21 brought a fellow over in tails and asked Bobby to take care of him. Bobby hit it off well with the 21 man—so well, in fact, that he kept coming back every night for five consecutive nights. He was a quiet man who drank moderately and seemed to enjoy the music greatly. On the fifth night, he got up to leave after the first show. 'I'm broke,' the 21 man told Bobby. 'Well, not really broke. But I'm out of cash and I wouldn't think of asking you to cash a large check that I'm carrying.' Bobby doubted that a rubber check was involved, but one never knew. 'Where are you staying?' he asked. When the 21 man said The Waldorf, Bobby urged: 'Then go to the Waldorf, cash the check, and be back for the second show.' The 21 man smiled and left. A few weeks later, Bobby handed me a copy of *Newsweek* and there was our friend on the cover. It was Tex Culbert, then the president of Chrysler. Some months later, Culbert came in one night on a visit to New York, and he and Bobby had quite a laugh about the check-cashing bit."

Ryan's remained a reliable watering hole for two generations of musicians: both the older black pioneers of New Orleans and their white disciples out of Chicago. When high-domed, Oriental-looking Sidney Bechet, who died in Paris in 1959, played the club from '47 to '50, he brought with him the legendary associations of having worked or recorded with the New Orleans Creole Band, the great King Oliver and colorful Jelly Roll Morton—and also the experience of playing for a decade (1928–38) with the Harlem band of Noble Sissle.

Zutty Singleton, another New Orleans pioneer—he was born in

Zutty Singleton at the 54th St. Ryan's.

Davis Quinn

Bunkie, Louisiana, and acquired the name Zutty (Creole for "cute") through an aunt—was a Ryan's resident from the first bill until the last, with time out for gigs in Hollywood and abroad. His performing career went back to the days of the Mississippi riverboats and the legendary Fate Marable. Later in Chicago, he worked in a novelty act with Louis Armstrong, masquerading as a beefy gal who kept interrupting Sachmo's song. He played with Louis also in Harlem when the Savoy Ballroom and Connie's Inn were the uptown rage. Regarded along with Baby Dodds as the most important of all New Orleans drummers, Zutty was active until recently.

Among the Austin High School crowd and other two-beat Dixieland specialists there is hardly a man whose horn was not heard at Ryan's. Unquestionably, the most colorful of this group is the man who always described himself as a "voluntary Negro" and who has been called the Baron Munchausen of jazz. When he played the Grand Terrace in Chicago, he had the guts to lock horns with Al Capone over an entertainer whom the mobster wanted fired. A hip linguist and an acknowledged authority on jive talk, he smoked opium with the notorious Purple Gang(sters) of Detroit, studied sax in a Chicago jail in 1917, and served a twenty-month sentence in the early forties for selling marijuana.

The way he tells it in his peppery autobiography, *Really the Blues,* he laid hold of such high-grade Mexican pot—"it had such a wonderful smell and the high you got was really out of this world"—that everybody in Harlem was after him. "Before I knew it," he opines, "I was standing on The Corner pushing gauge. Only I did no pushing. I just stood under the Tree of Hope, my pokes full up, and the cats came and went, and so did all my golden leaf." In truth, Milton "Mezz" Mezzrow became as legendary a figure as the famous Tree that grew outside "dicty" Connie's Inn at 131st and Seventh Avenue. (When the avenue was widened, dancer Bill Robinson had the so-called good-luck Tree transplanted to the divider in the avenue.) Mezzrow notes without humility that in Cab Calloway's *Hipster's Dictionary* "mezz" is defined as "anything supreme, genuine" and that in Dan Burley's *Original Handbook of Harlem Jive* the same word is defined as "tops, sincere." Also, that Stuff Smith's "Viper" song hit refers to a five-foot-long reefer, "the mighty mezz."

When Mezzrow came out of jail in 1942, he settled at Ryan's, where he played steadily for almost a year. Although he began record-ing with the Chicago Rhythm Kings and Eddie Condon as far back as the late twenties, and made discs for Brunswick and Bluebird in the mid-thirties, Eddie Condon comments on his musicianship (in his autobiography, *We Called It Music*) in such a way as to suggest that "mezz" should not be considered as an epithet in a musical context. But what can you say about a guy who writes of his role as a mari-juana peddler: "Overnight I was the most popular man in Harlem. New words came into being to meet the situation: the *mezz* and the mighty *mezz,* referring, I blush to say, to me and to the tea both; *mezzroll* to describe the kind of fat, well-packed and clean cigarette I used to roll. . . ."

Having weathered the war years when the patronage of servicemen forced many clubs to adopt a girlie format, Ryan's remained "an oasis," in Max Kaminsky's words, for "hot jazz fans" who had no use for bop, cool or hard jazz. Through the fifties the *avant-garde* steered clear of the club. But there were enough moldy figs and Jimmy Ryan had a strong enough personal following to keep it going, despite the relentless invasion of The Street by banks and big business and the overnight appearance of gaping holes where brownstones once stood.

By 1960 it was apparent that Ryan's would have to find another location. CBS was negotiating for the purchase of the building at 53 West. The sale was consummated early in '62. Late in March, William Randolph Hearst, Jr., and Toots Shor had drinks with Jimmy, and a few days later a *Journal-American* reporter came to interview him.

Appearing on April 4, 1962, Nick Lapole's story bore the headline: HOME OF JAZZ GREATS/RYAN'S ENDING SWING ST. ERA. The story was reproduced in full on an ashtray given to those attending the club's obsequies on August 15, 1962.

The sentimental occasion—part of it anyway—is preserved on a 12-inch disc pressed in a small quantity by Nola Penthouse Sound Studios. "I cry every time I listen to it," Matty Walsh admits, thereby establishing himself as a true blood relation of Jimmy Ryan, who had quite a reputation as a weeper. At the farewell party, there were songs by Jimmy Carroll, a speech and songs by Horace McMahon of TV fame, jokes by Peter Donald, two well-sung ballads by Jack Jones (then an unknown), and excessive and unexplained laughter.

Jack Heardle, who was MC, presented Jimmy Ryan with a novelty cigarette box inscribed "From a Few Thousand of His Friends." Sobbing, Ryan tried to make a speech in which he recalled the names of relatives and friends who helped him build the club. Everybody joined in singing an alcohol-soaked "We Won't Go Home until Morning," and the band, with old-timers Don Frye and Zutty Singleton in their accustomed chairs, played "Memories of You." As guitarist Danny Barker, who also played, recalls: "Two days later, the wreckers moved in."

Matty Walsh, now in partnership with John Keveanos, says: "CBS gave us nine thousand dollars to relocate. We looked everywhere before we found the new spot at 154 West 54th St. We opened here in the middle of a newspaper strike in December, 1962. It took a bit of time before our old friends found us. And we now even have Pincus, the 'Doorman' and 'Mayor' of 52d St., back with us. Before they put up that CBS Building, it used to hurt to walk past the spot where the old club was located. One night after they began erecting the brown skyscraper, we were walking on 53d St., and there was a kerosene lamp burning in a watchman's shack. Somebody said: 'Hey, look, Jimmy forgot to turn out the light in the club kitchen!'

"The night we opened on 54th St., Tommy Nola, who runs Nola Studios and who has been a great friend through the years, was one of our first customers. He came in carrying a box that turned out to be a Styrofoam refrigerator. Out of it, he took an ice cube, which he presented to Jimmy. It was a cube that he had been saving since the August night of the farewell party. Jimmy cried uncontrollably. . . ."

Tape 18 . . . Milt Gabler

In 1926 Milt Gabler, an enterprising, teetotaling blond teen-ager, later to become a balding, moonfaced, cherubic cigar smoker, opened a retail record shop at 136 East 42d St., opposite the Chrysler Building and diagonally across from the Hotel Commodore. He called the store, soon known to jazz record collectors throughout the world, the Commodore Music Shop. As the Shakespeare Bookshop in Paris became a gathering place for expatriate American writers in the 1920's, so the Commodore became a hangout for European (and American) jazz musicians, buffs and writers. A list of the store's customers and frequent visitors would include virtually all the illustrious names in jazz. Among the writers: Whitney Balliett of *The New Yorker;* George Simon, author of *The Big Bands;* Barry Ulanov, a *Metronome* editor and author of *A History of Jazz in America;* Mike Levin, editor of *Down Beat;* Leonard Feather, a *Metronome* editor and author of *The Encyclopedia of Jazz;* Wilder Hobson, well-known critic; Frederic Ramsey and Charles Edward Smith, editors of the *Jazzmen* anthology; Marshall Stearns, author of *The Story of Jazz;* and Otis Ferguson, jazz critic of the *New Republic,* who died in the Spanish Civil War. (All the books were written years after the store came into existence.) Among record men: Alfred Lion of Blue Note; John Hammond of Columbia; Bob Thiele of Flying Dutchman; the Ertegun brothers of Atlantic, as well as Jerry Wexler, who sometimes courted his wife, Shirley, in one of the store's record booths. Others who got their basics at Commodore were Ralph Gleason, George Frazier, Gilbert Milstein, Ralph de Toledano, George Avakian and Baron Timme Rosencrantz.

"We got reports," said Gabler, "every day from our customers about everything of note that was happening around town. In the thirties the sounds started coming out of 52d St., and all the talk seemed to be about The Street. Inevitably, after I closed the store for the day, I began migrating uptown. Just a few nights after Riley and Farley introduced 'The Music Goes 'Round,' people were flocking into the Commodore asking for the record cut weeks later by Decca.

"In 1938 I prepared a list of jazz recordings for new collectors for

Milt Gabler at the Commodore Music Shop. Behind him are caricatures by B. Ten Hove.

Courtesy of Milt Gabler

Alexander King at *Life*. [*Life* was then located in the Chrysler Building, and many of its staffers were store regulars.] After the list appeared, we began doing such a terrific mail-order business that I was able to afford a second store. To be right where it was then happening, I leased a place in September at 46 West 52d. It was on the street floor of a brownstone, between a French restaurant and the Drama Bookshop.

"The lady who owned the building was not too helpful. One day I was toeing a nail to keep the record racks against the wall. She came by at just that moment and stiffly informed me that she didn't want me putting any nails into her floors. She also wouldn't allow us to put a sign on the outside of the building. If you were looking for us from Fifth or Sixth Avenue, you couldn't spot us, not with all the nightclub canopies jutting out.

"Actually, during the first year and more of its existence, the 52d St. branch of Commodore was a failure. But it served as a great mailing address not only in this country but internationally. When any of the European jazz critics came to this country—like Stanley Dance, Robert Goffin, Leonard Feather, Hugues Panassie or Charles Delaunay—they inevitably found their way to the Commodore. We did all our mail-order business from there. We became a congregating place for jazz musicians and fans.

"I never renewed the lease after its first three-year term expired. By '41 we were at war and my brothers all went into the service. I was due to go next, but I had two kids who eventually kept me out, due to my age. It behooved us to consolidate in case my dad was left alone with the business. The war made business boom and he could not have handled two stores. So we gave up 52d St. (it was too far from the post office anyway) and remained on 42d.

"I had hardly closed the 52d St. Commodore when Jack Kapp phoned and asked me to come to work for Decca. I told him that I didn't want to give up the retail end." (Kapp had started as a boy in the record business, working in his father's record store in Chicago.) "We came to an understanding that I would put out jazz reissues for Decca on a part-time basis. Later, I quit the retail business entirely—and it's now more than thirty years that I've been with Decca [now a division of MCA, Inc.].

"In 1935 I formed the United Hot Clubs of America in an effort to promote the sale of jazz records, some of which I had previously reissued, on the Commodore label. To maintain interest in the club, I began holding jam sessions—they were the forerunners of jazz concerts—at which musicians would get together and play improvised music.

"I staged them at record company studios on Sundays, when the companies were not using them. I would pay the elevator man who had to work that day, buy a case of whiskey, along with soda and ice, and rent chairs. I would invite all my customers. So I formed a club. You paid two dollars to be on the mailing list for free concerts and were also entitled to buy a jazz record for which you had to pay. But the record cost only a dollar. Jazz records still were not selling, so that it was really a nonprofit kind of thing.

"I ran three jam sessions at record studios. The first was at Decca when they had the studio at 799 Seventh Avenue at the corner of 52d—later the headquarters of Columbia. I remember we had to find drums. It was Sunday. But Roseland was around the corner. So we got Buddy Schutz or Maurice Purtill to lend us his drums, and he sat in. The second jam was at the Brunswick Master-Variety Studio at 1780 Broadway. It was an extra studio built by the company when Irving Mills of Mills Music began making records for them. The third session was back again at Decca. All these were costly to me since we had expenses and there was no admission charge. After the studios, I held one session at the Famous Door. Incidentally, John Hammond was a great help on all these shindigs. He got Bessie Smith for that one.

"As a result of all the publicity the Bessie Smith jam received, the Hickory House began running jam sessions. Wingy Manone was there and he had a radio wire. That session at the Famous Door had prompted WNEW to broadcast the Sunday jams from John Popkin's joint.

"All these concerts and the attendant publicity drew increasing attention to the new music. By this time the word 'swing,' coined to promote jazz, was coming into vogue. *You swing if you're groovin' good.* And 52d St. became known as Swing Street. That happened just about the time that Maxine Sullivan was packing them in at the Onyx with 'Loch Lomond.' It drew the masses because it was a pop hit—not jazz just for jazz lovers. Maxine's success created a market for singers, and Café Society Downtown put in Billie Holiday.

"The increasing interest in jam sessions on The Street soon provoked competition in Greenwich Village. A jazz critic, who shall be nameless, began running jams for which he charged admission. But the rumor was that he did not pay the musicians. I got very upset and decided that the time had come to run professional concerts on The Street.

"Across The Street from my store but a little closer to Sixth Avenue was Jimmy Ryan's. It was just an Irish bar. But they had tried entertainment without too much success. Bobby Hackett's orchestra couldn't compete with the clubs like the Door and Onyx with fat music reps. One day, just on the spur of the moment, I walked across the street and had a talk with Jimmy Ryan. When he agreed that I could have a small cut of the bar to help defray expenses, I was set to go. To increase the club's seating capacity, I decided to put chairs on the dance floor. That was the first time that any club had seats for young people who could hear the music for just the admission charge and without buying drinks. This was the forerunner of all the clubs that later used bleachers, like Basin Street and Birdland.

"I started the jams at Ryan's in 1938–39. Made up my own handwritten advertising circulars. But after a time, the concerts sold out by word of mouth. I ran them for seven years and eventually turned them over to my brother-in-law, Jack Crystal, who is now deceased. When

GUITAR
Eddie Condon
Jack Bland
Teddy Bunn

PIANO
Joe Sullivan
Fats Waller
Earl Hines
Art Hodes
Albert Ammons
Pete Johnson
George Zack
Clyde Hart
Mel Powell
Dick Cary
Eddie Heywood
Kenneth Kersey
Joe Bushkin
Billy Kyle
Cliff Jackson
Sam Price
The Lion
The Beetle
James P. Johnson
Dave Bowman
Don Frye
Cow Cow Davenport
Jack Russin

DRUMS
Zutty Singleton
George Wettling
Kansas Fields
Big Sid Catlett
Eddie Dougherty
Ray McKinley
Danny Alvin
Joe Jones

BASS
Al Morgan
Elmer James
Israel Crosby
Sid Weiss
Earl Murphy
Pops Foster
John Simmons
Billy Taylor
Artie Shapiro
Gene Traxler
Bill King
Jack Kelleher
Pete Peterson

OUR ROSTER OF JAZZ IMMORTALS
They have appeared at previous
sessions and should repeat their
memorable performances this season.
if available — Milt Gabler

JIMMY RYAN'S presents
the 3rd consecutive year!
Milt Gabler's
SUNDAY SWING CLUB
JAM SESSIONS
every SUNDAY from 5 to 8 PM
featuring as usual the
most of the best Jazzmen.
COME EARLY!   COUVERT $1.00

WE'RE READY TO BLOW!
starting SUNDAY-SEPT. 27th

TRUMPET
Sidney DeParis
Bobby Hackett
Max Kaminsky
Henry Red Allen
Roy Eldridge
Hot Lips Page
Marty Marsala
Wild Bill Davison
Emmett Berry
Muggsy Spanier
Jimmy McPartland
Charlie Shavers
Joe Thomas
Dizzy Gillespie
Frankie Newton

CLARINET
Pee Wee Russell
Rod Cless
Buster Bailey
Albert Nicholas
Joe Marsala
Edmund Hall
Doc Slovak

SAXOPHONE
Coleman Hawkins
Sidney Bechet
Scotty
Kenneth Hollon
Benny Carter
Joe Eldridge
Pete Brown
Cecil Scott
Happy Cauldwell
Don Bias

TROMBONE
George Brunis
J. C. Higginbotham
Brad Gowans
Frank Orchard
Benny Morton
Sandy Williams
Vic Dickerson
Claude Jones
Lou McGarity

SINGERS
Billie Holiday
Bea Booze
Ruby Smith
Hot Lips Page

FOR RESERVATIONS - PHONE EL5-9600
JIMMY RYAN'S   53 West 52nd ST., N.Y.

Flier for a 52d St. jam session at Jimmy Ryan's.   Courtesy of Milt Gabler

52d St. was no longer a music street, he took the concerts down to
Second Avenue at the Central Plaza. At the beginning I used my store
mailing list and the United Hot Clubs to build an audience. I always
used two bands. One consisted of members of the Condon mob or
group, like Wild Bill Davison, Pee Wee, Georg Brunis, Joe Sullivan,
Zutty Singleton and other members of the Commodore Dixieland
bands. The other was a Harlem-type band built around Red Allen,
Edmond Hall, Ben Webster or Don Byas. These men attracted the
great black musicians from uptown.

"We mixed personnel right from the beginning. Also audiences.
For that matter, I used mixed bands on my Commodore recordings.
The problem was to get blacks—musicians included—to bring their
wives downtown. They weren't used to socializing outside of Harlem.
But Ryan's was wide open, friendly and had a fine atmosphere. The
shows were great. Where could you get three solid hours of music
for a dollar? And the talent! Stars like Fats Waller, Earl Hines, Nat
'King' Cole, Eddie Heywood—whoever was in town on a Sunday
afternoon—would drop in.

"We paid union scale for a class-B room—ten dollars a man and double for the leader. Sidney Bechet always got double, even when he was a sideman. He wouldn't work for single scale. The closing number was always either 'Bugle Call Rag' or 'The Blues.' Every musician who was in the club sat in for that and sometimes for the set leading to it.

"One Sunday, Norman Granz, who always came to the Commodore to buy records when he was in town, sat through the entire session. Afterward he told me: 'It's a fantastic idea, Milt. I'm going to start the same thing on the Coast.' He went back, and soon after, he launched Jazz at the Philharmonic. We also used to get calls every Sunday from Boston. George Wein would generally phone sometime between 5 P.M. and 8 P.M., the length of the sessions. He would ask: 'Who's in the room that can come up to Boston? I'll pay fare and twenty-five dollars.' I believe he had the Storyville club at the time. We tried not to repeat bands and performers from week to week. And George was able each Sunday to lock up talent for the following week at Storyville.

"These jams were really the start of commercial jazz concerts in New York. There was only one before us. Joe Helbock, the owner of the Onyx, ran one at the Imperial Theater. Our shindigs also led to the John Hammond concerts at Carnegie Hall and the Eddie Condon–Ernest Anderson concerts at Town Hall and Carnegie. Eddie wanted me to collaborate with them, but I bowed out. I was more interested in records by then than in concerts.

"Our concerts were doing so well that we developed competition. Monte Kay and Pete Kameron, who were managing musicians, began running jams with more modern jazzmen. Since they were mostly interested in bop, I stopped using musicians of this school. It wasn't that I disliked bop—I like all types of jazz—but just that I thought there was room for both types of action. I thought the competition was good on a musical level and saw no reason for economic competition. There was only one musician who played both jams: Hot Lips Page. He would play one set in our place and run across the street and play theirs.

"After a while all the big celebrities began coming into Ryan's. I remember Lana Turner, John Steinbeck, playwright Eugene O'Neill toward the end of his life. I also remember a surprise birthday party the musicians threw for me. Ryan's was in such an old building that the wiring system sometimes went out of order. Since I knew a little about electricity, I would be elected to go down into the basement and replace a short-circuited fuse. On the evening of my birthday, my brother and sister-in-law picked my wife and me up at the store (across the street) and took us out to dinner. Afterward, he suggested that we go back to Ryan's and listen to a set. When we got to Ryan's, the place was dark. The steps down to the cellar were right near the checkroom in front of the place. As I started to go down, all the lights suddenly went on, and there were many friends and the musicians who played the jams for me. Some of the bands working around town sent units over. And the biggest thrill was when Duke Ellington walked in with a small group from his orchestra—Johnny Hodges and some of his other great musicians. It was an evening I'll never forget.

"Some of the fun moments on The Street were nonmusical. Joe Frisco used to go to a bar a few doors from my store. No music, no entertainment, just a straight bar—Reilly's was its name. It was a favorite hangout for The Street's musicians, particularly Eddie Condon. Reilly made a good hamburger, but Condon said he liked Reilly's because it was the only place on The Street with clean glasses. Reilly's only entertainment was two canaries that were in a cage near the window and that would chirp when the sun was warm. But he sometimes had unpaid entertainment in the form of Joe Frisco, who would pop into Reilly's between shows at the Club 18. As soon as he came in, somebody would run over to my store. I'd drop everything. Condon, who usually kept a seat warm at the bar, would proceed to act as straight man and throw lines at Joe that got stories out of him.

"One that I recall had to do with a horse player who was so unlucky that he finally decided to cure himself of the betting urge. He went to a doctor who used a weaning technique with incurable betters. He had them bet on seven races the first week, six the next, five the following, until finally, they broke with the habit. 'And where is his office?' the friend asked. Stuttering, Frisco would explain: 'It's ab-ab-ab-about a mile and a quarter from the tr-tr-tr-track!' We had more laughs at Reilly's than at the Club 18—and all for the price of a beer.

"The thing that baffled many owners of competing record shops was how the Commodore got so much publicity. One day a competitor could not resist asking who did my publicity. I told him. It was me. And I really did very little about it. It was just that so many writers, newspapermen, critics and magazine editors hung around the shop. Since the original Commodore Shop was across from *Time* and *Life* and near *Liberty,* the *Daily News* and the *New Yorker,* many of the editors became buddies. And later, when I opened the store on 52d, they were up in Radio City. The shop also attracted many of the columnists and feature writers on the papers and free-lancers on the magazines. It was the music that made friends for me as it did for The Street."

13. War Comes to 52d St.

On the evening of Tuesday, August 18, 1942, 52d St.'s bands came out of the cratelike clubs and performed from platforms erected on the street. The famous thoroughfare was blocked to traffic from Fifth to Sixth avenues. More than 20,000 people crowded the block and enjoyed impromptu appearances by celebrities from the worlds of the theater, radio and nightclubs. The entertainment had a serious underlying purpose: to sell U.S. Savings or War Bonds. More than $1,000,-000 in bonds were bought. The festivities were brought to a sudden end around 1 A.M. when the police halted a striptease performance on one of the platforms.

"Sorry, lady," a cop told Georgia Towne. "The party's over. Don't mean there's anything wrong with your act. But a baby's just been born across the street."

(In '43 War Bonds were sold regularly under the aegis of Gem Safety Razor Corp. at the northeast corner of 52d and Sixth, temporarily christened War Bond Square. Purchasers received seats for a January 18, 1944, concert at the Metropolitan Opera House of the All-American Jazz Band, composed of winners of *Esquire*'s annual jazz poll, almost all of whom were 52d St. regulars.)

And so World War II came to 52d St., bringing not only a curfew, entertainment tax, rationing and an influx of sailors and soldiers on leave, but a rash of striptease joints, tab padding and other sharp practices, fistfights and sluggings, racial conflict, and even attacks on the music. The war made The Street jump in a kind of desperate search for fun and forgetfulness, but it also accelerated its demise.

Rumblings of the war overseas reached The Street in pre-Pearl Harbor days. As in April of '41, when there was talk of the Nazi bomb that killed Snakehips Johnson as it came crashing through the Café de Paris, below street level, in London. And later that month when one of the swing bands donated blood to Britain's war victims.

By October, 1942, *Down Beat* was running a list headed KILLED IN ACTION. Even before the big Bond Rally of August on The Street, bands were getting B-ration gasoline cards, tires were unobtainable, and the difficulty of traveling by bus was playing havoc with bands on the road. Hardest hit, of course, were the black bands, even though the networks, in a gesture of patriotism, began hiring blacks. It was soon clear that NBC's action in adding Billy Taylor to its music staff was largely a token move.

The October *Down Beat* also carried a picture of Glenn Miller at the door of a recruiting office just after he had traded in his baton for the double bars of an Army captain. As he was assigned to morale duty in Omaha, the movement of musicians into the armed forces developed momentum. The Clyde McCoy band enlisted en masse, as did Buddy Clarke and Band. The merchant marines got both the Phil Harris and Ted Weems bands. In March, 1943, Jack Teagarden announced that he had lost seventeen men to the services in four months. By June MCA was sponsoring what it described as a draft-proof band—the sons of celebrities serving the Hollywood Canteen. Hickory House booked a female-led group called Pat Travers and Her Men about Town, in a program of Music for Dancing.

But even before then, a *Down Beat* story averred, SWING STREET JUST AIN'T SWING STREET ANYMORE, and adduced evidence to suggest that 52d St. had become Sucker Street. The wartime tightening of moral codes now became evident in a series of happenings. A narcotics crackdown brought jail sentences to several 52d St. characters. One of the clubs became involved in a Mann Act charge. The doors of the Savoy Ballroom in Harlem were shuttered, throwing three bands out of work, on the charge that servicemen had contracted venereal diseases from pickups at the dance hall.

Westbrook Pegler, then the Senator McCarthy of American columnists, leveled an attack on jazz, swing and even torch songs. Employing epithets like "insult to the American character" and adjectives like "vulgar," "low" and "dirty," Pegler rasped that red-hot singing had originated in brothels on West Madison Street in Chicago. High point of his smear was that the torch song began, ended and remained "a lewd expression of back-room bums."

Among the casualties of wartime emotionalism was a 52d St. boîte known in its brief existence as the Two O'Clock Club. Founded ostensibly by Goldy, headwaiter at the Hotel Edison, it was designed as an after-hours club for musicians. There was talk of calling it the Performers and Musicians Guild, but it was chartered as the Two O'Clock Club. Presumably to insure privacy, it was located on the second floor of 201 West 52d, at the corner of Seventh Avenue. Musicians were supposed to pay a dollar-a-month membership fee, entitling them to a private locker in which they could keep possessions, including bottles of their favorite beverage. As a private club, drinking, listening, and jamming were presumably legal at any hour past curfew.

Art Hodes opened the club with a small trio and was soon succeeded by Clarence Profit. At first, there was talk about The Neem (Henry Nemo) becoming MC. Then Willie Bryant was mentioned. Goldy attended a Harry James opening at the Hotel Lincoln, and its owner, Maria Kramer, returned the compliment by posing for publicity pictures as she accepted honorary membership in the Two O'Clock Club. Less than two months after the opening, the club announced that it was closing. The official reason: collapse of an elevator in the building. Broadway wiseacres claimed that while the Two O'Clock, as a private club, could operate legally after two o'clock under the liquor-licensing law, it could not flout the wartime curfew.

Nevertheless, the club continued in operation for another two months with Teddy Reig, known as Mr. Five-by-Five of the Hotel Forrest, serving as impresario. Apparently, there were evenings—rather mornings—when the jam sessions ran from two o'clock around the clock into the following afternoon. Apparently, also, there was constant harassment from the police. In February, '43, a New York judge declared that the police raids were illegal. But the club had indicated almost a month earlier that in a four-month period it had lost more than $7,000, and was ready to give up the ghost without new financing. Illegal or not, the raids were effective in scaring off potential investors. Whether police avarice figured in the final demise, as it figured in the life of many 52d St. clubs, the wartime atmosphere was not propitious for the launching of a new after-hours spot. The Two O'Clock Club never celebrated a six-month birthday.

Although marijuana was not an unnoticed facet of life on 52d St. and in other pop music areas, narcotics became a headline matter even in music trade papers during 1943. Suddenly, *Down Beat* had a front-page banner that read TEA SCANDAL STIRS MUSICDOM and an editorial, TEA AND TRUMPETS ARE BAD MIXTURE! Perhaps the most celebrated scandal involved drummer Gene Krupa who was arrested and jailed on the West Coast and whose career, fortunately, took only a temporary nose dive. On 52d St. wartime hysteria brought a jail sentence on a narcotics rap for Teddy Reig and an associate.

Race relations became tense during the war and on The Street. Yet there was a tender side that Billie Holiday recalled. "I gave so many going-away parties at the Famous Door and other places," she wrote, "I lost count. It was always the same: three or four young boys would spend the whole night in the joint; we'd lock up, have a final drink, and they'd walk off. A few weeks later I'd get a letter from some damn island where they were fighting the bugs and snakes, the heat and the dry rot. Some of these letters would break your heart. They came from kids I never really knew, or who knew nothing about me, but I was never able to throw them away. . . . Oh, I carried on some torrid long-distance affairs with these kids."

Billie never saw most of these kids again. "The few I did see," she noted in her autobiography, "when they came back, tore me apart. One night in the Blue Note in Chicago, late in the war, a kid came in to see me and started talking about a party a couple years before at the Famous Door on 52d St. I went along with the gag and the reminiscences, and then, suddenly, I recognized him. His hair had turned completely white, and he looked forty years old, though he couldn't have been more than twenty-five when he left."

But the war also created tremendous tension between the races. Despite broadcasting-company announcements about the employment of blacks, in April, 1943, the brother of Lester Young lost a radio job *because* he was black. Drummer Lee Young played one network show with a white orchestra and was unceremoniously fired. There was no secret that color was the cause.

August brought the riots in Harlem that had repercussions in many areas. The following month ballroom operators on the West Coast

A wartime 52d St. gathering—May 1, 1944: Back row: Axel Stordahl (Sinatra's arranger and musical director), Benny Goodman, Mel Powell. Front row: Frank Sinatra, Count Basie.

announced that they could no longer afford to book black bands. They claimed that racial friction resulted in "cold bookings."

As the 52d St. joints filled with men in khaki and Navy whites, black musicians suddenly found themselves facing nightly hazards. Many of the military were from the South. They were not accustomed to the easy mixing of colors among musicians and audiences. And they particularly resented the attention that white chicks showered on black performers. Dizzy Gillespie, Billy Taylor, and many other musicians carry unforgettable memories of the dangers involved in going home after the clubs closed. They felt lucky if they could make the Sixth Avenue subway station without an encounter.

The White Rose bar on Sixth Avenue, where musicians had long congregated, was a near wartime casualty. In the summer of '44 the police swooped down one night and clamped on a midnight curfew. Their allegation: Two plainclothesmen had been picked up by girls at the bar. It was a serious blow to the cats: The low liquor prices and free food had made it a popular hangout. Now musicians had no place to go during the late working hours. A few nights after the ban, pianist Johnny Guarnieri and two black musicians were standing on The Street when a policeman approached them and ordered them to move. "We don't want you niggers on the streets," he reportedly said.

Reporting the incident in a story headlined RACISM MOUNTS ON 52ND STREET, *Metronome* expressed regret that the interracial harmony previously achieved among musicians and patrons was now being jeopardized. It blamed tensions created by aggressive police action and aggravated by white soldiers and sailors who became nasty over the mingling of black musicians and white girls, especially when they were under the influence of liquor. It suggested that the pampering by musicians of "pimps, prostitutes and tea peddlers" was not helping the situation. And it warned that white troublemakers could produce a race riot, which did erupt at about that time—but in Harlem, not on 52d St.

Wartime tensions, frictions and frustrations played a significant role in bringing a new sound into jazz. And it was 52d St. that carried the sound from Harlem into the mainstream of jazz. Known at first as bebop or rebop, it finally became known simply as bop. It revolutionized the sound of pop and jazz music. But it also introduced conflict, musical conflict, on The Street.

Tape 19 . . . DIZZY GILLESPIE

A seminal figure in the history of contemporary jazz, John Birks Gillespie of Cheraw, South Carolina, was one of the fomenters of the revolution known as bop. Among the men who played a vital role in the onslaught on traditional jazz (New Orleans, Chicago, Dixieland and swing), and who contributed to its modernization, Dizzy was the showman or publicist of the movement. When *Life* and other big-circulation magazines became aware of the development, it was Dizzy, with his beret, goatee and oversized black glasses, who attracted the attention. There is historical justification for this lime-lighting. The first bop quartet that played outside the Harlem ghetto was led by Dizzy and Oscar Pettiford, and it appeared at the Onyx in 1944.

"It was Si Baron who had this idea," said Gillespie. "He had just signed Oscar Pettiford to a personal management contract. He called Mike Westerman at the Onyx to hire us with Billie Holiday and the Al Casey Trio. All of us had won *Esquire* awards. But my name wasn't even on the table cards. It's so funny. About a year and a half ago, a guy walked up to me and said, 'I want you to sign an autograph.' And he gave me a table card that I had signed back in those days. He said that he and his wife were together then; that was their first date. Now they had grown children, grown grandchildren, and he kept that thing all that time! Jazz fans are out of sight. Man, they do such spiritual things to make you feel—and they really mean it. Is there any other field quite like that? I mean, the people are really sincere—they're real deep.

"Like when Leonard Feather first came, he completely ignored me. He was interested in Billie Holiday, Al Casey, Oscar Pettiford. The cats that people were talking about, the Gold Award Winners for *Esquire,* he wrote about. So Oscar once asked him, 'Why don't you write something about Dizzy?' Then he did write an article about me. I think it was 'Dizzy Like a Fox.' By that time Oscar and I were swinging together. I had met him out in Minneapolis. We had George Wallington (piano), Max Roach (drums). Mike Westerman hired Don Byas (tenor sax) as a soloist. But we were swinging, and Don just

257

joined in. When we'd come to a rehearsal, there he was. He learned all the arrangements, and he'd fall right in.

"Oscar wasn't a hard drinker. But I remember one night he came from the White Rose bar, and he was *so* drunk. That night he was really missing. I just looked at him. I didn't say anything. I just kept looking at him real hard. And then he opened his mouth: 'What the fuck are you lookin' at?' I said, 'I'm lookin' at nothin', absolutely nothin'. You know what's wrong with you? You're a prima donna.' Oh-h-h-h. He turned on me, and all his Indian came out on him. [Pettiford was born on an Indian reservation in Okmulgee, Oklahoma.] He said: 'My father called me a prima donna, and I quit his band.' So I said: 'Let the doorknob hit you in the back! I was in New York when you came here with the Charlie Barnet band. I'll be here when you've gone.' Well, he quit for a set. Then he came back. But not long after that, we did break up, and I went across the street to the Three Deuces or the Yacht Club.

"I had the same thing once with Don Byas. He'd occasionally get drunk, too. He couldn't play shit when he got drunk, but, man, when he was sober! So I'm sitting and looking at him. He was playing a solo and slobbering all over his horn. I kept looking and going tsk-tsk-tsk. He says, 'What the fuck you lookin' at?' Same words! I said, 'I'm just looking at you.' He says, 'Wha's wrong?' And I said: 'You ain't playin' shit.' He says: 'Well, you're not doin' so hot yourself.' I said: 'Well, I'm doin' the *best* I can, I'm sober.' He says: 'Fuck you!' I said: 'Fuck you.' He says: 'Mother-fuck you.' And I told him: 'Don, if you think for any minute that I won't take advantage of you while you're drunk, you've got another think comin'. You're drunk and if you get up and act like you wanna do somethin', I'm gonna smash you! I'm gonna take advantage of you—you're drunk, you can't do anything. You can't fight.' So he started to cool down. That really was a beautiful group.

"The audiences were something, too. They were aware that something new was happening. We were packed all the time. Jimmy Dorsey came in one night. We were burning so much! He couldn't believe it! The next night he came back—and he didn't get drunk. He was sober and that was an unusual thing from him. He was stone sober! He had a little party afterward at his hotel, Astor Hotel, and invited me up. He was hugging me, going down the street. He said: 'Boy! That shit you're all playin'. I sure would like to hire you for my

Dizzy Gillespie at the Spotlite in 1946.

band. But you're so dark!' I said: 'Well, if I wasn't like this, I wouldn't be able to play like this.' I asked him, 'Do you know anybody who plays like this, your color?' He said: 'No, I'm afraid not.'

"You remember Johnny Carisi? He was the only white boy up in Harlem at Minton's. He'd learn all the tunes. Played all of Thelonious Monk's tunes, all of mine. I'd play a chorus. He'd be right behind me. Roy? Right behind Roy. Right behind everybody. He was welcome so long as he could blow the way he did.

"Things did get rough at times. You remember Madame Bricktop? She was the hostess at Tony's. One night Oscar and I were standing and talking with her—on Sixth Avenue near the subway entrance at 50th St. A sailor came by: 'What you niggers doin' talkin' to this white woman?' Bricktop with her red hair! Under those lights, she did look light. Oscar was drunk. He swung at the guy and fell flat. I said: 'OK, if you can't whip this cat, thass your ass.'

"But I wasn't going to let that sailor kick Oscar. So I straddled him. I had my horn in one hand and a knife in the other—one of those knives with a hooked end for cutting linoleum. Oscar finally got up.

By that time three or four other sailors came along. They all went for Oscar. I swished at them with my knife and caught one. I didn't get him. I just cut his uniform. A little more and I would've opened him up. There were so many of them. We had no other protection. A taxi pulled up and we jumped in. But the cabdriver wouldn't move. He didn't wanna go to Harlem. I screamed: 'Man, can't you see all these guys tryin' to get us? Drive!' He wouldn't move. So I'm sittin' there with my knife waiting for one of the sailors to come into the cab. It was good because they had to come one at a time.

"Finally, we jumped out of the door on the other side, ran across Sixth Avenue, and ducked down into the subway. Going down the steps, I had to drag Oscar. 'Run, you juicehead!' I told him. And he made it down and went over the turnstile. I was left by myself, backing down the steps. And those guys swinging their coats, trying to knock the knife outa my hand. Backing down, I missed the last step and fell and dropped my knife. I tried to reach for it. But as I did, I looked up and saw this sailor come at me in a flying tackle. I raised up and braced myself. When he fell, I grabbed him by the collar and pulled him up—he was dazed—and smashed him in the face with my horn. By that time the rest of them were on me beating me. I was ducking, trying to protect my chops and head. I finally got away and went over the turnstile and ran onto the catwalk. You know, this narrow ledge against the wall, above the tracks.

"They were right behind me. There were about ten of them. But only one could come onto that narrow ledge at a time. And I was waiting with my horn, ready to clobber them. Finally, the SP's came and took them away. And I took the subway home.

"While I was at the Onyx, I got pneumonia—and pleurisy. Running around the corner to the White Rose. I worked right on, never stopped. With the pneumonia and the pleurisy!

"Charlie Parker worked with me later at the Three Deuces. He was always late, always across the street when we were going on the stand. But he was a beautiful player. I remember once when 'Fat Girl'—that was Fats Navarro—and Bud Powell were working together at the Deuces. Bud used to needle Fats. This night Fats couldn't stand the buggin' any longer. He waited until Bud put his hands down on the piano, and then he crowned him on the head. Right on his head, ha-ha, as soon as he had his hands on the piano. But to get back to Charlie. We'd be on the stand playing, and he'd come running in late and I'd get so mad. But then, oh, man, he'd start playing, and I'd forget I was mad.

"Our association—Charlie and me—wasn't a very long association, but it was deep, real deep. It was quick and, you know, like you could draw an analogy—like Hitler. Like Hitler's thing didn't last long, but it was so dynamic and it left such a mark. It's like in music. You don't necessarily play a hundred choruses to make a statement. It's the intensity that counts. We had an association with Earl Hines, with Billy Eckstine, and then with our own group over a course of a few years. You know, Bird was supposed to be at the Onyx with us, with the Pettiford group. We sent him a telegram, and I think we heard from him eleven months later. By that time Oscar and I had broken up, and we were ready to go into the Three Deuces. That's when he arrived—probably just got the telegram.

"In '45 when we went to the Coast, I had a five-man contract. But I took six—Milt Jackson—so that I'd have five men on the bandstand all the time. And then Billy Berg said we weren't heavy enough and hired Lucky Thompson to play with us. We dug that. When we were getting ready to leave, I gave Charlie his fare back to New York. He took it and stayed. That's when he had his breakdown—after we left—and was in Camarillo for a while.

"The Street had its own thing. It had an identification. The groundwork for the music was done up in Harlem. Like at Minton's and Monroe's Uptown House. It was the music that gave it identity. I used to come down before the Onyx gig to play with Joe Marsala at the Hickory House. Just before I went with Ella Fitzgerald in the early forties, I jammed sometimes at Kelly's Stable with Coleman Hawkins. I worked with Benny Carter on The Street—at Kelly's. But I don't think I played between Sixth and Fifth until I went with Pettiford. After we came from California, I played the Spotlite for eight weeks.

"Then Clark Monroe had an idea, and Billy Shaw, the manager, liked it. We started with a small group and built a big band. So we had eight weeks with the small combo and then eight weeks with the big band—sixteen weeks altogether. The small group was the same as the one I brought from California, except that Sonny Stitt replaced Charlie Parker.

"The big band had five reeds and seven or eight brass. Monk and then John Lewis took his place (piano). Joe Harris and Kenny Clarke took his place (drums). Ray Brown was on bass. The money was

Dizzy Gillespie, far left. Third from left, Lena Horne, and next to her, her husband, arranger-conductor Lennie Hayton. Faye Emerson, right foreground.

nothin'. Scale. But I guess we got paid every week and we had a good time. Small place for that big band. They had to take some tables out to put the band in. Made some money after that with the big band. Bought a bus. But then my wife said: 'Either that big band . . . or *me*.' That's when I broke it up the next day.

"There were a few characters on The Street. Moondog, looking like Christ wrapped in that brown Army blanket, used to stand at the corner of Sixth Avenue. And then there was Gilbert Q. Pincus. He was a funny little guy, you know, the doorman. He smoked cigars and I used to get him Cuban cigars. I haven't seen him in ten years. He was just beautiful. Used to laugh all the time.

"Then there was a guy they used to call The Demon. He was a saxophone player. Couldn't play to save his life. But he played with everybody—Lester, Charlie Parker. He was the first freedom player— freedom from harmony, freedom from rhythm, freedom from everything. The Demon was from Newark, and he never stopped playing.

"Then there was a guy named Hoss Collar, an alto player. He was very good. Like The Demon, you couldn't keep this cat out. But he was good.

"We used to have this routine. How'd it go? 'You're an ass. . . .'
No, it went: 'Gimme some skin, man. . . .' No, that wasn't it. Let's
see, you'd hold out your hand and say, 'I'm hitting.' Now I've got it!
When you held out your hand, he'd say: 'I'm hitting. You're an ass.'
You'd reply, 'That's what *you* is.' And he'd say: 'That's what you *want*
me to be.' Right now, I walk up to some of the cats and say: 'That's
what you want me to be,' and they go to pieces. Me, too.

"Come to think of it, Hoss Collar was before 52d St. He was
around during the Savoy when we played the Brittwood at 140th and
Lenox. Charlie Shavers lived right over it. It was before our music got
popular. Hoss Collar played the Yeah-Man on Seventh Avenue and
137th St. I used to make the rounds and play many places—Victoria
at 141st and Seventh, the Harlem Club on 116th between Lenox and
Seventh, places on Eighth Avenue. There were about fifteen places
where we'd go. But we'd have to wait until the union man left. We'd go
in and ask: 'Has he been in yet?' They knew what we meant. If he'd
been and gone, we'd sit in—Charlie Shavers, I, Benny Harris, Carl
Warwick (Bama), Bobby Moore. . . . It was a wonderful time. But
52d St. was better. Uptown we were just experimenting. By the time
we came down our ideas were beginning to be accepted. Oh, it took
some time, but 52d St. gave us the rooms to play and the audiences."

14. They Flatted Their Fifths

In 1945, as World War II was nearing its end, several white jazzmen wandered into the Three Deuces, where a combo led by Dizzy Gillespie was holding forth. Al Haig was at the piano, Curly Russell on bass, Stan Levey at the drums, and Charlie "Bird" Parker on alto. The sounds emanating from the combo were strange to ears accustomed to the predictable diatonics and two-beat drive of Dixieland. So was the song and its chord line. And the tempo was a runaway race.

The visitors mounted the small bandstand, intending to jam a bit. They figured that the first number was an original and therefore strange in its chord line and accelerated, offbeat rhythms. But the next tune proved just as much of a puzzle. (It was a comparatively new show tune, not a pop or jazz standard that was part of the common pool in which jazz musicians had been swimming for years.) The visitors were baffled, but having sensed something of the chord line, waited patiently for the traditional signal that one player gave to another to invite his participation. The nod of the head or the motion of the horn never came. Instead, the Gillespie player who had been soloing just stopped. There was an awkward pause as several measures went by with nothing except rhythm sounding. Finally, one of the visitors came in and tried to fumble his way through a solo. All three of the visitors made an abortive effort to join the ensemble chorus. There was no "ride-out," as the final chorus of a tune was known in the old days. The Three Deuces group simply quit in the middle of a measure the way a car makes a sudden stop. And then Dizzy and his men vanished from the bandstand, leaving three bewildered instrumentalists looking as if their flies had been found open.

"They really scared the shit out of us," one of the visitors later admitted.

Rebop, as it was first called—a derivative of nonsense syllables used to verbalize a triplet figure, *buh-DEE-dah* or *buh-RE-bop*—was aggressive, provocative and belligerent in sound and in attitude. Inevitably, it stirred counterrevolution. In September, 1945, jazz producer Eugene Williams brought an elderly New Orleans cornet player to New York for appearances at Stuyvesant Casino. Bunk Johnson had been found some years earlier slaving in a rice field outside New Iberia, Louisiana. The discovery had come through William Russell of New Orleans during research for *Jazzmen,* the first major American study of jazz, edited by Frederic Ramsey, Jr., and Charles Edward Smith. Early in '45 Bunk played an *Esquire* All-American Jazz Concert as well as a Ryan's Sunday jam. His opening at the Casino became the occasion for a full-scale counterattack on the new jazz. An obstreperous group of critics proclaimed Bunk Johnson's "the true jazz" and his band of old men "the last pure jazz band." The battle lines were drawn. From then on, it was the modern malice vs. the moldy figs, as proponents of New Orleans and Dixieland jazz were dubbed.

The growing controversy elicited comments on bop from men who later regretted them. "This is incredible stuff," wrote critic George Frazier, "for a grown man to produce." Sportswriter Jimmy Cannon, a knowledgeable listener, wrote: "Bebop sounds to me like a hardware store in an earthquake." And even John Hammond joined in the attack: "To me, bop is a collection of nauseating clichés, repeated ad infinitum."

Today, it is an accepted historical fact that bop was the herald of all modern jazz and that it developed at a time when the sound was stagnating. Improvisation had become repetition, and the music was no longer "the sound of surprise." Bop brought new resources into the field of jazz, fresh melodic lines, startling rhythms, complex chords, and new repertoire. But in the latter days of World War II and afterward, it was made the scapegoat for mounting black hostility, increased use of narcotics, and the rise of black nationalism. That black people came out of the war full of resentments and disillusionment is unquestioned. Having fought the perpetrators of racial discrimination abroad, they returned to find that it still existed in blatant form in their own land. Like some of the new black attitudes and movements, bop was itself a reaction rather than a cause.

This fact becomes clear in a glance at the origins of the new jazz. As ragtime came out of the Maple Leaf and other clubs in the black section of Sedalia, Missouri, jazz originated in the black quarter of New Orleans and other cities, and swing developed in Kansas City and other black communities, so bop came out of New York City's black ghetto. Two Harlem clubs contributed the quarters in which experimentation proceeded in the early forties.

One was Clark Monroe's Uptown House, about which the genius of bop, Charlie "Yardbird" Parker, said: "When I came to New York [from Kansas City] and went to Monroe's, I began to listen to that real advanced New York style. I think that the music of today is a sort of combination of the Midwestern beat and the fast New York tempos. . . . That was the kind of music that caused me to quit Jay McShann and stay in New York."

The music moved in a more adventuresome direction in the dining room of the Hotel Cecil at 210 West 118th St., where drinks sold for 20¢ and a deluxe dinner for 60¢. A former saxophonist, Henry Minton, had converted the room into a club known as Minton's Playhouse. The drummer was Kenny Clarke, who had worked with Dizzy Gillespie in the band of Teddy Hill, the manager of Minton's. Regarded by many as the real originator of bop—he went from Kelly's Stable into the Army in '43—Clarke acquired the nickname Klook at Minton's because of a style of drumming that later became the earmark of bop and modern jazz. To maintain time, Klook used the top cymbals (chink-chink-chink-chink) instead of the bass drum (chug-chug-chug-chug) as in swing bands. The big drum became an instrument of special effects. "Dropping bombs," "explosions" and "klook-mop" were the expression for the offbeat accents.

Clarke had begun moving away from four-beat rhythm on the bass drum while he was still in Teddy Hill's band. But at Minton's the experimentation proceeded apace as a group of intrepid sound adventurers began striking out in new harmonic and melodic directions. "I heard Tadd Dameron playing flatted fifths in 1940," Clarke later said. "It sounded very odd to me at first. Tadd was also one of the first pianists playing eighth-note sequences in the new legato manner." Dizzy and Bird were an aggressive duo in the explorations, developing the up-tempo treatment of "How High the Moon" that became as basic in bop repertoire as "The Saints" in New Orleans. With Clarke in the Army, the initiative in the experimentation passed to the two.

The Minton adventurers frankly thought of themselves as a selective clique. "We'd play 'Epistrophy' or 'I've Got My Love to Keep Me Warm,' " Klook told Leonard Feather, "just to keep the other guys off the stand, because we knew they couldn't make those chord changes. We kept the riffraff out and built our clique on new chords." Not surprisingly, the riffraff were more frequently white than not. And it was no secret that part of the adventure was to create something that "Charley couldn't steal." "Charley" meant the white musicians who had reaped the rewards of black-originated swing. "Charley" meant the white musicians who still monopolized the top jobs in radio, in the recording field, in the Hollywood movie studios and in American symphony orchestras. Despite the promises and hopes of World War II, pop and symphonic music were still as segregated as the rest of American society. Many white musicians who were not prejudiced came out of the war to find themselves facing black animus, anger and hatred. Bop was not divisive but expressive of a divisiveness that still existed and had intensified.

The new chord lines, adapted to keep Charley out, were derived from the sophisticated show tunes of Cole Porter, Vincent Youmans, Richard Rodgers and George Gershwin with which the Dixieland and swing musicians were frequently unfamiliar. Discovery of the original sources was made difficult because new titles were calculatingly attached to the chord patterns—"What Is This Thing Called Love?" became "Hot House," "How High the Moon" was called "Ornithology," "Lover" became "Diggin' for Diz," etc. Original compositions were also developed on unexplored and complex chord patterns, like Dizzy's "Salt Peanuts," Oscar Pettiford's "One Base Hit," Budd Johnson's "Bu-Dee-Daht" and Thelonious Monk's famous " 'Round About Midnight."

A number of big black bands also served as incubators for the new jazz. Among these were Earl "Fatha" Hines' orchestra after Charlie Parker joined it in 1943. Before that, Cab Calloway's band when Dizzy became a member in 1940, and later, Billy Eckstine's band of

1944, which included Dizzy, Bird and saxophonist Benny Harris. Many critics regard the last-mentioned as the *first* big bebop band of the era.

Although bop created in-group controversy shortly after it began to be heard on 52d St., it did not become a public issue until 1946. In March of that year Station KMPC of Los Angeles banned bebop on the ground that it "tends to make degenerates out of our young listeners." Singled out for censure were the records of Slim Gaillard and Harry "The Hipster" Gibson, neither of whom had anything to do with the new jazz. But both were then appearing in a Hollywood club—which, of course, immediately began doing SRO business. *Time* joined the fray with an article in which it described bebop as "hot jazz overheated, with overdone lyrics, full of bawdiness, references to narcotics and double-talk." Following the station's lead, it managed to see Gibson as the Mr. Big of the evil movement and Bulee "Slim" Gaillard as the No. 2 man. As an instance of the dangerous impact of the latter, it noted that his "Cement Mixer" had sold more than 20,000 copies in LA alone. As other examples of Gaillard's subversion, it cited the titles "Yop Hock Hearsay" and "Dreisix Cents" (the latter means 30¢ in Yiddish). Perhaps the most curious aspect of this development is that when Barry Ulanov later wrote his excellent *History of Jazz*—and Ulanov was a bop sympathizer—he blamed Gibson and Gaillard for the attack on bop: "Their songs were thick with reefer smoke and bedroom innuendo," he wrote. "Their mixture of this with jazz lingo did all jazz musicians a disservice." (And Ulanov had not yet become a professor of English at Barnard College!) By 1948 *Time* and *Life* took an entirely different tack toward the new jazz; they were snide but not unimpressed.

Apart from Savoy Records and a few other small labels like Musicraft, "52d St. was the proving ground for bop," as clarinetist Tony Scott has said. In its turn, bop temporarily gave new luster to a street that had passed its heyday and was on the downgrade. As the war took a positive turn for the Allies in '44–'45, there were six active music clubs on The Street: on the south side, the Spotlite (opened at 56 West in December, '44), Yacht Club at 66 West, and Three Deuces at 72 West. On the north side, there was Jimmy Ryan's at 53 West and the Onyx, a few doors away at 57 West. In the block between Sixth and Seventh avenues, Kelly's Stable at 137 West looked across at Hickory House, a fixture at 144 West. Of these, four were hospitable to the new jazz: Spotlite, Three Deuces, Kelly's Stable and the Onyx.

By the time the Onyx became a bop sanctuary in '44 it had gone through at least two reorganizations. It was then under the aegis of a group including Arthur Jarwood, Irving Alexander and lawyer Chauncey Olman.

"In 1943," bassist Oscar Pettiford told writer Robert Reisner, "Dizzy Gillespie and I went looking up and down 52d St. for work. We turned down $75 apiece offered by Kelly's Stable. I had worked at the Onyx club, and I was good friends with the owner, Mike Westerman. So I asked if I could be re-engaged. I was welcomed back gladly. I said, 'Make it a Diz group.' And Diz said, 'Make it your group because you got the job.' So we made it the Gillespie-Pettiford group. We wanted Bird to come in with us. But he didn't have a union card."

Originally slated to work as a four-piece combo, one horn plus three rhythm, Pettiford-Gillespie became a quintet with the addition of tenor saxophonist Don Byas, who had been hired by the club as the alternate combo. Accidental though it may have been, the Byas appearance with the group helped contribute a sound that became basic to bop—the trumpet–tenor sax unison duo. With a rhythm section composed of Max Roach on drums, George Wallington on piano and Pettiford on bass, the quintet became the first bop combo to play The Street.

Despite the excitement generated by the engagement—and controversy—the group was not preserved on wax. But saxophonist Coleman Hawkins used four of its members in a big band session cut on Apollo Records in February, 1944, after the Gillespie-Pettiford opening. Bean was then at Kelly's Stable. Only George Wallington was not on the date, whose sides included Budd Johnson's "Bu-Dee-Daht" and Dizzy's "Woody'n You," a number he had originally written for Woody Herman but that was never recorded by the keeper of the Herds.

Saxophonist Budd Johnson became part of the Onyx combo when Don Byas left. Having worked with Dixieland and swing greats like Sachmo, Teddy Wilson and Earl "Fatha" Hines, Johnson wrote bop-oriented charts for the big bands of Boyd Raeburn, Billy Eckstine, Woody Herman and Dizzy. While he played sax on record dates, it was his "maps" that gave vital expression to the characteristics of the new jazz: the polytonal chords, polyrhythmic patterns, and the sweeping, out-of-range figures. Though Johnson had begun moving in the new harmonic direction as early as 1942 with Boyd Raeburn, it was the gig at the Onyx that helped crystallize his adventuring. Johnson had Dizzy write out some of his trumpet solos. The unison performance of choruses by the two served to establish the alto sax–trumpet collaboration that became such an identifiable sound in bop.

Like an amoeba by binary fission, the hyphenated Gillespie-Pettiford combo split apart with the coming of spring. Pettiford remained at the Onyx into the summer, replacing Dizzy with Joe Guy, who had been one of the Minton marauders. And Dizzy took Max Roach and Budd Johnson with him across The Street into the Yacht Club, formerly the Famous Door, and by May, 1944, the Downbeat. Thus 52d Streeters had their pick of two bop bands.

On the bill with Dizzy at the Yacht Club was Billy Eckstine, whose initial venture as a solo singer proved unsuccessful. In June, '44, when Eckstine went back to leading a band—the first big bebop combo— Dizzy served as its musical director.

Dizzy later became the major publicist of the new jazz, exhibiting a kind of crafty showmanship that garnered him and the new music much space in the nation's magazines. When he teamed with Pettiford in '44, he had not yet affected the oversized, horn-rimmed black shades and the jaunty berets (Thelonious Monk–style), the garish goatee, and the *shtik* of conducting with his rump. Not yet in vogue were the nonsense syllables used to identify the new rhythm licks— polysyllables like "oolya-koo," "oo-bop-sh-bam," "oo-pappa-da" and "be-bop"—all devices used by the musicians to indicate accents and suggest durations. But it was with this hyphenated band, identified on the Onyx marquee as Pettiford-Gillespie, that Dizzy first sang the three-note figure that became known as the "Salt Peanuts" triplet.

It was like no other triplet in the history of music—pop, jazz or classical. Even today triplets are traditionally accented on the first note of three. But Dizzy and Kenny Clarke accented the middle note. To achieve this, they employed three notes in which the second was an octave above the other two: "salt PEA-nuts, salt PEA-nuts." Budd Johnson syllabled it as "bu-DEE-daht."

"So many of the rhythmic ideas," Leonard Feather observes in

Oscar Pettiford, who helped launch the bop revolution, in a candid by Leonard Feather.

Down Beat

Inside Bebop, "seemed to end with a staccato two-note phrase, suggesting the word 'bebop,' that this onomatopoeic term soon began to be applied by the 52d St. denizens to describe all the music played by Dizzy and his clique. It was thus, late in 1944, that most of us who were around Dizzy and his contemporaries began to be conscious that there was a musical genre sufficiently distinct to have earned a special name. 'He plays all that bebop stuff,' you would say, or perhaps 'rebop' since either sound was equally representative." During his stand at the Onyx, Dizzy wrote the instrumental later titled "Bebop."

A vital engagement for the bop movement and for Gillespie occurred early in 1945 at the Three Deuces when Dizzy led the combo that included Al Haig on piano, Curly Russell on bass, Stan Levey on drums and Bird on alto. This group created so much talk that their take-home pay was almost doubled after one week, a record company rushed to record it, and promoters sponsored two Town Hall concerts.

On the Manor/Guild label, with Sarah Vaughan handling the vocal on "Lover Man" and Big Sid Catlett manning the hides, the group cut Tadd Dameron's "Hot House" and two Gillespie instrumentals, "Salt Peanuts" and "Shaw Nuff," the latter dedicated to Billy Shaw, his booker, or Milt Shaw, his personal manager. They were brothers. To Leonard Feather and other critics, this session provided "a perfect example of the new 52d St. small-band manner, cleanly played trumpet and alto unison, tricky rhythmic intros and codas, and fantastic solos by Diz, Bird and Haig. It was the new jazz *in excelsis.*"

The Town Hall concerts were the brainchild of Monte Kay, then the dauntless manager of Tadd Dameron and a man who had an open ear for the new sounds. Although he had run jam sessions at Kelly's Stable and was producing shows for Chuck Goldman at the Downbeat, he was worried about finding an audience for the new sounds. With the concert in May, '45, only three weeks off, he decided that he needed help.

"At the suggestion of the owner of Downbeat," Kay recalls, "I went to see Symphony Sid. He had an R & B show on Station WHOM, but he really dug jazz. I offered him half the profits if he would plug the concert. As soon as he began playing the Guild recordings by Dizzy and Bird, tickets began selling. And the concert was almost a sell-out. It gave both of us so much confidence that we ran another a month later, also at Town Hall. We gave the first half of the program to Pearl Bailey or Dinah Washington—I can't recall which. Bird and Dizzy did their thing in the second half. We found a college-age audience that was ready for the new music, also a black audience."

Monte Kay adds: "I got off The Street about that time. It had developed a clip-joint attitude that was rough on the kids, including myself. If you stayed for more than fifteen minutes, they hustled you for another drink. But I was convinced that there was an audience for bop. One night—it was a Saturday—I went into the Royal Roost, a chicken joint on Broadway and 47th St. owned by Ralph Watkins. Jimmie Lunceford was playing. Though he had an outstanding band, the place was practically empty. Watkins was skeptical about the modern stuff. But I managed to talk him into letting me and Symphony Sid produce a concert on an off night. He picked Tuesday, and we did a concert with Bird, Tadd Dameron, Miles Davis, Fats Navarro and Dexter Gordon.

"That night we instituted an admission policy. For ninety cents you could sit in the 'bleachers' and listen to the show without buying a drink of any kind. It worked. We drew over five hundred admissions the first Tuesday. And we did so well on successive Tuesdays that Watkins thereafter ran the Roost on a bleacher admission policy. Tadd Dameron took over the band on a regular basis and was soon making records with the Roost sextet on Blue Note. Bop did not make it in a big way until a year or two later, but the Roost and Tadd played a considerable part in helping develop an audience."

Still another 52d St. booking is remembered as pivotal in the story of bop. The February, 1946, appearance of Dizzy at the Spotlite came just a year after he had recorded "Groovin' High" and several other bop classics with a big band. It came after a tour of the band through the South and an appearance of a small Gillespie combo in Hollywood. Both were disasters.

The Southern tour was a mistake musically and politically. As it progressed the sixteen musicians became more and more embittered by the segregation and discrimination they encountered. But audiences also presented a problem. The band was booked into ballrooms where the kids came to dance. Early bop may not have been concert music, but it certainly was not dance music. An effort to save the tour by playing stock arrangements of pop standards and by adding Ella Fitzgerald to the program both failed.

With his big band out of business, Gillespie accepted a booking with a small combo at Billy Berg's club in Hollywood. He took a star group with him, but the critics were merciless. Audiences sat stony-faced, booed or walked out. The management was critical and then became hostile. Bird, who was, perhaps, more sensitive than the others and who was on drugs, went to pieces and had to be hospitalized at Camarillo State. The rest of the group was happy to call it quits and took off for New York as quickly as the club found a replacement.

Returning to 52d St. was like coming home. Despite news of the Billy Berg bust, Dizzy had no trouble in securing a booking. He was eagerly welcomed with his men of the Hollywood hangup by the Spotlite, a comparatively new club at 56 West. (Oscar Pettiford had played the club early in '45 with a bop group that consisted of "Little Benny" Harris, Clyde Hart, Stan Levey and Budd Johnson.) Not only was Dizzy's stand at the Spotlite an extended one—the group remained from February into July, 1946—but it represented the turning point in the public acceptance of bop.

Until this appearance one could buy bop discs only on offbeat labels like Savoy, Guild, Manor, Musicraft, Roost, Three Deuces, Blue Note, Apollo, Continental and Black & White. But while the Gillespie group was at the Spotlite, critic Leonard Feather was able to persuade the nabobs at RCA Victor that the new jazz was worth recording. Concerned as always with name value, Victor required that Feather use some of the year's *Esquire* Award winners. This brought drummer J. C. Heard and Tenorman Don Byas into a session that yielded four key bop sides: "Anthropology," "Night in Tunisia," "Ol' Man Bebop," and "52d Street Theme." To these four sides were added four by a combo under Coleman Hawkins, who was also playing the Spotlite. (Albums then consisted of eight instead of twelve

A gag photograph tells the jazz story of the forties while 52d St. was still swinging. Left to right, Ray McKinley, Dizzy Gillespie, Claude Thornhill.

Down Beat

sides.) Feather felt that it was hopeless to ask inclusion of the word "bebop" in the title of the album. And so it was released as *New 52nd Street Jazz.*

The change in the public's attitude toward bop—at any rate, the New York public—was immediately apparent. *New 52nd Street Jazz* took off saleswise and eventually finished as the best-selling jazz album of 1946. Its acceptance led to a June recording date with a sixteen-piece big band on Musicraft and a money-making tour with Ella Fitzgerald. Bop was on its way to developing a wider audience than the 52d St. crowd, though enthusiasm did not really manifest itself until 1948, when Dizzy enjoyed the triumph of a successful return engagement to Billy Berg's in Hollywood.

In 1948 *Life* could no longer disregard the new jazz and ran a hokey picture story on Dizzy as the Clown Prince of Bebop. By then bop jokes were the in thing on The Street.

A bopster, watching a cobra bob out of a basket to the vibrations of a fakir's oboe, says to his pal: "Dig that crazy music stand!"

"How come I see you with that beat-up baggage?" a bopster asks of a friend, who is dating a very homely girl. "Where are those slick chicks you used to roll eggs with?"

"What's the matter, man?" his friend asks. "Don't you dig distortion?"

Tape 20 . . . LEONARD FEATHER

Leonard Feather's achievements as a jazz critic, reporter and historian have overshadowed his considerable work as a composer, arranger and record producer. In the last-mentioned capacity, he played a rather large role in putting some of The Street's best instrumentalists on wax.

"In 1941, I believe it was," he told me, "I did a date for Decca with some musicians drawn from the 52d St. clubs. I made Pete Brown leader because I was a tremendous admirer of his, and I took two sidemen out of what was then Benny Carter's sextet at the Famous Door. (I had done several John Kirby–styled arrangements for Benny, including 'Lady Be Good,' his opener). I took his trumpet player, a young man named Dizzy Gillespie, and his clarinet player, Jimmy Hamilton. Sam Price was on piano.

"I first heard Pete uptown at the Brentwood bar, I think it was, next door to the Savoy. Then he came downtown and worked Kelly's Stable on 51st St., moving with it to 52d St. I always thought he was one of the greatest, underrated musicians, and I still think so. I succeeded in persuading Milt Gabler, who was in charge of Decca's jazz recording, to let us put a date together. I was also a great fan of Helen Humes, the blues singer. (When I caught Basie and heard Jimmy Rushing doing all the blues, I thought it was unfair that Helen was shut out, and I wrote an arrangement for the Basie band of a blues, which they recorded with Helen doing the vocal.) Of course, I put Helen in with the group on this Decca date, which was not strictly typical 52d St. music.

"The interesting thing about the Pete Brown–Helen Humes date was that we did not let Dizzy solo. I was as much to blame as anybody. We all felt that he was too far out to be playing a blues date, and all he did was play the parts that were written. It was mostly Pete Brown playing alto sax and Helen singing. We muffed the chance to have young Dizzy on wax.

"The date in '43 of the *Esquire* All-Stars was built around winners of the *Esquire* poll, which I helped organize with Robert Goffin. I was able to get seven of the All-Stars together, and they did include a number of 52d St. regulars: Coleman Hawkins, Art Tatum, Al Casey, Sid Catlett, and Oscar Pettiford. We got thirty dollars each, or whatever the scale was. We cut 'Esquire Bounce,' 'Esquire Blues,' 'My Ideal' and 'Mop, Mop.'

"I was supposed to produce the date for Bob Thiele's Signature Records. But I had a lot of difficulty getting Thiele on the phone. Literally, twenty-four hours before the session, I offered the whole project to Milt Gabler, who took it over. It turned out to be, aside from Billie Holiday's 'Strange Fruit,' probably the biggest-selling record that Commodore ever had.

"The second *Esquire* All-Stars date in '45 was on Continental, and the third in '46 on RCA Victor. And for this one we had the greatest All-Star band of all. On one track, Duke Ellington sat in on piano and Louis Armstrong played and sang. On another track we had Billy Strayhorn and Louis Armstrong doing a thing of mine called 'Snafu.' Red Norvo was also on the date.

"In this period the musicians and I were eager to get together any kind of All-Star situation. In spite of all the music that was being presented on 52d St., it wasn't that easy to get a combination of the greatest guys together. The guys were tied up to different combos on The Street, up in Harlem, etc. The fact that *Esquire* became involved was a tremendous boost to the prestige of jazz. To read about jazz, you had to go to *Down Beat* or *Metronome*. There was nothing in *The New Yorker, Saturday Review,* or even the New York *Times.*

"From '41 to '43 I worked as assistant publicity agent to Ivan Black, who hired me when I was really doing nothing. He offered me fifteen dollars a week and a percentage of any accounts I brought in. Ivan was responsible for getting my byline into the New York *Times* at a time when it was extremely difficult to get an article about jazz in any daily newspaper of consequence. I wrote an article about boogie-woogie because Café Society, where eight-to-the-bar pianists were appearing, was Ivan's account. That was considered quite a rarity and quite a coup for Ivan. To a large extent, jazz was underground—and this, despite everything that was happening on 52d St.

"Linda Keene was one of the great might-have-beens of The Street. She was a singer with a very beautiful emotional quality. Reminded me of Mildred Bailey. And by coincidence, perhaps not coincidence, she sang at one time with Red Norvo. I was very fond of Linda and her singing, and I got her on the *Strictly from Dixie* radio show and had her on one session I made with Joe Marsala, a great clarinetist around 52d St., with whom I made records off and on for several years. Linda was, to my way of thinking, one of the jazz singers that should have made it in a big way. She just did not get lucky. She played the Door, Kelly's Stable and other clubs.

"The Marsala-Keene date was something I did for Black & White Records. It was one of the few labels that were experimenting with some of the more unusual things happening on The Street. The man running it was Paul Reiner. I did a Joe Marsala session for him, also a Barney Bigard session for which I got Art Tatum. I think it was the only time that Tatum played as a sideman, except the *Esquire* date. I used the two Joe Thomases on this session, the trumpet player and tenor-sax man. I wrote a song called 'Sweet Marijuana Brown,' which Joe Thomas, the tenorman, sang.

"Marijuana was pretty much an accepted phase of The Street's way of life. I was not part of it, but I was thoroughly familiar with it. But the whole situation changed around 1945, when one became aware of the existence of heroin and heroin peddlers. Suddenly, you knew about a large number of hooked musicians—not just Charlie Parker, though he was the most celebrated of the many unfortunates.

"You can posit all kinds of theories of how it happened. I think the explanation is the power of organized crime involved in its peddling. Pot·did not represent that much financially, since there was no question of addiction and anybody could just stop it. With heroin, they got a steady customer indefinitely. It became a very disturbing time.

"Billy Eckstine had the problem in his band. Pretty wild band, that one! So much of the development of bebop was hampered by the drug problems of the musicians. Dizzy Gillespie was almost the only major figure that was never involved with any of the hard drugs. Many of the cats got over it very fast. Some of them never got over it. Some of them died.

"The '46 album for RCA Victor consisted of two sessions. One was an All-Star band with Coleman Hawkins, Shelly Manne, and Mary Osborne on guitar. The other was a Dizzy Gillespie session. I caught him between contracts, right after he had left Musicraft and before he signed with a new company. I got to do a series of sessions during the '46–'47 period for RCA, thanks to Steve Sholes, who was in charge of jazz and gave me a free hand. Instead of using Dizzy with his regular group, I got Don Byas—it was the last session he made in the United

States—Bill De Arango, a marvelous guitar player who soon afterward went back to Cleveland, Al Haig on piano, Ray Brown on bass, Milton Jackson on vibes, and J. C. Heard on drums. Heard was not really a bebop drummer but he seemed to fit. It was a great thing for jazz to be able to get a prestige label like RCA for a bop session. Columbia didn't know it existed. Decca did nothing. Generally speaking, the major labels were unaware of or uninterested in the bebop revolution that was shaking up 52d St. In other words, the Gillespie session had historical significance, and it did lead to Dizzy's being signed by RCA Victor for two or three years.

"At about that time, I did several concerts at Carnegie Hall in order to bring the development before a wider public than that frequenting 52d St. I did one with Dizzy, one with Dizzy and Bird, and a third with Dizzy and Ella. They were tremendously successful to everybody's surprise. I had so much confidence in the music that I put up my own money.

"It was a very emotional period for everybody because we were embattled. There were many people who were violently opposed to everything that bop stood for—and incidentally, everything I stood for, because I was a strong proponent of the new music. I remember that at one of the concerts I prepared a speech that had the quality of 'We Shall Overcome': that is, overcome the violent opposition of most of the jazz critics. Barry Ulanov, my associate on *Metronome,* was an exception. He was, perhaps, ahead of me in flying the flag for modern jazz. We were excoriated by critics whose idea of jazz was, maybe, up to New Orleans and a bit beyond. Articles were written—how did I dare to put up Art Tatum, Roy Eldridge, or Oscar Pettiford as representing jazz? Why didn't I present the *true* jazz? and they'd name Jelly Roll Morton or Bunk Johnson. Everything was polarized, and a great deal of animosity was directed at me and Ulanov and the new musicians, who were supposed to be the enemies of the real jazz. Eventually, men like Dizzy were not only accepted but idolized by the same people who had put them down so virulently. Psychologically, it was just opposition to change.

"But there was also the New Orleans myth: the concept that jazz was born down there, and the real true and great jazz musicians were of New Orleans origin. It was a very hard thing to fight because it was perpetuated in books and still is. It's my firm belief that though New

Orleans was a very important center, there were other cities where jazz was developing at the same time. This idea went against the grain of the New Orleans theorists. Also the new sounds of Dizzy and Bird and others were very strange to their ears—in the same way that Pharaoh Sanders sounds strange to many listeners today.

"The opposition to bop was not a social or racial thing. White musicians were involved in the development almost from the start. Dizzy had Al Haig or George Wallington on piano. Charlie Parker had Red Rodney. Basically, it was the product of black musicians, since Dizzy and Bird and Bud Powell and Thelonious Monk and Kenny Clarke were the original creators. But there were white musicians who were working along the same lines and who worked with the black musicians from the earliest. Dizzy told me he had Stan Levey in his band as far back as 1941. The opposition was psychological rather than social or racial. When I got bop on the stage of Carnegie Hall, I felt that I had accomplished something. And the audience was there by December, 1947, and December, 1948.

"At the time of the third concert, December, 1949, I was in the hospital. I had got myself knocked over by a car and was bedded down for three months. Monte Kay helped put it on for me. Apart from these three bop concerts in '47, '48 and '49, I also did the first Carnegie Hall concert of Woody Herman, the first Carnegie Hall concert of Louis Armstrong. I did one or two concerts a year in this period, drawing most of the musicians from The Street.

"It's hard to pick any one club as being most important in showcasing the new music. It varied from week to week, depending on who was on the bill. To me, the clubs never had any identity. Their personality is, perhaps, best described by the word 'sleazy.' I didn't like them as places, and with a few exceptions, I had no use for the people who ran them. I resented the exclusion of black people as customers. I remember one night in 1939 when I was going with a beautiful girl named Louise McCarroll, who was once featured vocalist in the Don Redman band. I wanted her to hear Woody Herman at the Famous Door. We were stopped at the door. There was nothing that Woody Herman or anybody else could do about it. It really was a traumatic experience for both of us. I was from England, and though I knew about things like that, they had never happened in my presence. It was quite awhile before black people were generally accepted as regular customers. The clubs could not exclude black musicians with whom they were familiar. But by and large, they tried to keep as white as they could.

"Of course, later on there were clubs that were black-fronted or black-operated like Clarke Monroe's Spotlite or Tondelayo's. However, in the early forties The Street was very bad in a racial sense. After a time it became wide open. But it started out just as discriminatory and Jim Crow as any place in town, in spite of the number of musicians that were black. At first if there was any tendency at all, club owners would hire white groups over black groups. But then more and more there were mixed groups, and the lines became blurred. Don't forget that 52d St. was jumping when there were no mixed groups, with the exception of Teddy Wilson and Lionel Hampton with Benny Goodman, Roy Eldridge with Gene Krupa. When something like that happened, it was an event. When Joe Marsala hired Red Allen at the Hickory House, it was an extraordinary exception, and when Flip Phillips was the only white in Frankie Newton's outfit, it was one of the very first instances of a white sideman in a black band on 52d St. It was not until 1943–44 that the raised eyebrows began disappearing.

"All the clubs were shaped like shoe boxes, and they had dingy canopies outside, where you found that little man, Pincus, who served as barker, apparently for all of them. Inside, there did not seem to be any difference, though I am sure that the colors of the walls, if you could see them through the cigarette smoke, were different. The tables were three inches square and the chairs were hard wood. The drinks were probably watered. They were miserable places. There was nothing to them except the music.

"The story of the Shearing sound is interesting. I had encouraged George to come over from England in '46. He stayed about three months, did one record date for Savoy, and went back home. When I saw him in London in the summer of '47, he was playing accordion in some band. But that winter he returned and settled in a small apartment in Queens. Since I had helped produce his first records in London, I went to all the clubs on 52d St., telling them about this wonderful musician who had come over. I managed to get him one night at Hickory House. Finally, after George had been here for about six months, I persuaded Irving Alexander to book him at the Three Deuces. He received sixty-six dollars a week. He had John Levy on

Jon Tilmans (top), George Shearing (center), Billy Eckstine (right).

Down Beat

bass at one point and J. C. Heard on drums. He had Oscar Pettiford for a time. Then he had a quartet with Eddie Shu playing the many instruments he played. For a while George was working just with a rhythm section. But he was a fixture at the Deuces. Then he got a job at the Clique, which became Birdland the following year. His quartet consisted of Buddy De Franco (clarinet), John Levy (bass) and Denzil Best (drums).

"I was still trying to get him on wax. Albert Marx, for whom I had made records on Musicraft, started Discovery Records. But after I sold Albert, it developed that Buddy was under contract to Capitol. During '44–'45 I had done a session with a combination I liked very much—vibraphone, guitar, piano, bass and drums. I used it on a Mary Lou Williams date and on a session with Slam Stewart, Red Norvo, Chuck Wayne, Morey Feld and Johnny Guarnieri. One of these was on Continental and one on Victor. In each case, I found the instrumentation very appealing. With Buddy off limits, I suggested that George get Chuck Wayne on guitar and Margie Hyams on vibes. (I'll tell you in a moment about the girl-musician thing.) George liked the idea, and the quintet was organized. I wrote most of the music— 'Life with Feather,' 'Sorry, Wrong Rumba' and two others—because George wanted to save his own material for something important in the offing. He liked the instrumentation so much that eventually it became the Shearing sound. Margie Hyams left about a year later, but the instrumentation remained.

"I produced George's sessions during the first two years of his contract with M-G-M. On the first date, we made 'September in the Rain.' Everything started jumping after that. Overnight, instead of being that blind pianist who was depressing to see, George became pretty much in demand and went beyond 52d St. into some rather good-paying nightclubs.

"Alexander was the only one I was able to sell on Shearing before that. And I probably sold him because I had made money for him with the jam sessions I ran at the Deuces. Also, I had Shearing sit in and Irving had a chance to hear him. There were rumors about Alexander's associations. But I saw in him a former musician who had more sympathy for musicians than most of the guys running joints on The Street.

"To go back to the girl-musician thing, at one time I got together an All-Star Girl Band. To me, sex discrimination was as abhorrent as race discrimination. I had Mary Lou Williams on piano; Mary Osborne on guitar—she was really a beautiful Charlie Christian-style guitarist; Margie Hyams on vibes—she once played with Woody Herman; a girl bass player named Bonnie Wetzel, ex-wife of trumpet player Ray Wetzel in Stan Kenton's band; and as drummer, Elaine Leighton.

"Girl musicians had a very rough time, with the exception of a few piano players, like Mary Lou and Hazel Scott. Barbara Carroll played 52d quite a bit and as the first girl bebop pianist, made the scene with many combos.

"Did I say The Street was finished in '48? As a *Metronome* editor, I must have had good reason. But just about that time Georgie Auld was the operator of a club called the Troubadour. It was on the north side in the block west of Sixth. It did not last long, but a lot of great jazz was to be heard there. And the Deuces, as well as Hickory House, drew a lot of traffic. The time when you felt that The Street was really falling apart was in 1949. That was the year when the opening of Birdland launched a new era and jazz moved to Broadway. Since Birdland was just north of 52d, you could think of it as part of The Street. But gone was the era when you could wander from club to club and spend the whole evening savoring different kinds of jazz.

"I guess the high point of that era were the war years when there was so much money around, even with the cabaret tax and everything. I was lucky, of course, since I was reviewing for some magazine and they'd let me in. But it could be very expensive if you were club hopping. You could spend a hundred dollars a night for a couple without any trouble. Of course, the whole operation of The Street was very dubious, and the musicians were taken advantage of. On the other hand, the clubs were very small and there was only so much they could take in, and therefore, there was only so much they could pay the artist. At least, it was an outlet for a helluva lot of talent. You could more readily understand an artist being underpaid at the Onyx than at the Savoy Ballroom with its capacity of thousands. Scale there was an unbelievable thirty-five dollars a week. Musicians worked for that for years—mostly black musicians, of course. The leader got fifty dollars and I'm talking about 1940, not way back.

"It is interesting that 52d was a divided world for many of us, particularly for musicians. Those of us who were interested in jazz passed by Leon & Eddie as if it didn't exist. By the same token, I was seldom in Jimmy Ryan's. It represented a different kind of music. It was like a foreign territory. To me 52d St. was the Onyx, Three Deuces, Famous Door, Kelly's Stable, Spotlite, etc. Everything else, including 21, was not forbidden territory, but foreign. The only place where the two worlds met was at the White Rose bar."

Born in London, Leonard Feather made his first visit to the United States in July, 1935. He was met at the French Line pier by the ubiquitous John Hammond. His scrapbook contains a menu of the Famous Door at 35 West 52d, green with black printing and red headings, whose top banner reads: SOMETHING NEW UNDER THE BROADWAY MOON. Most of the cocktails sold for 50¢. Feather ate at Maison Louis (67 West 52d) just east of Sixth, where lunch cost 85¢ and dinner $1.25, or the Barbour, outdoor garden and sidewalk café at 1 West 52d, where lunch was 50¢/60¢/75¢ and dinner 75¢/$1.00/$1.25. He stayed at the Hotel President, where many of the 52d St. musicians roomed, paying $2.40 a night.

15. The Three Deuces

One evening at the Three Deuces, bassist Slam Stewart received a last-minute phone call informing him that Art Tatum could not make it. Slam took a walk down the block to Tondelayo's, a small club opposite 21. That night a new, unknown pianist ran back and forth between the Deuces and Tondelayo's playing a set in each club. Not long after, Erroll Garner became a regular member of Stewart's Trio. It was a high jump for an unknown from Pittsburgh.

Of the pianist Garner replaced and succeeded, Eddie Heywood said just about that time: "Tatum plays so much piano it sounds impossible. The more I hear him, the more I want to give up the piano forever and drive a milk truck." And Teddy Wilson added: "He's not only the greatest jazz pianist ever—there are very few concert artists who have his ability."

Nevertheless, Garner made the leap into the glaring limelight with ease and within months, was leading his own trio at the Deuces. In fact, by June, 1945, the unknown of 1944 had generated such excitement that he was a featured performer at the second Town Hall Concert sponsored by the New Jazz Foundation. Even before then, *Metronome* had described his keyboard creations as an "original and fascinating mixture of Debussy, Ravel and Garner" and labeled him "this year's 52d St. sensation."

The kind of motion that Garner made initially between the two clubs remained a characteristic of The Street. "I used to go from one

Oscar Pettiford (bass), Erroll Garner (piano), J. C. Heard (drums) at the Three Deuces in early 1945.

Down Beat

joint to another," says clarinetist Tony Scott, "like from where Ben Webster was playing to where Erroll Garner was, to where Sid Catlett had the band. I'd sit in at each club. I remember one night I'd finished blowing with Sid Catlett, and I walked over to the Deuces where Erroll had his trio with John Simmons on bass and Harold West on drums. Erroll didn't make the set and they asked me to play something. I was in uniform—the war was on. There was a guy juiced who said: 'Hey, buddy, didn't I see you playing clarinet next door?' I could have destroyed him by saying no. Was he relieved when I nodded."

Pianist Billy Taylor recalls that "there was a lot of movement on The Street. Like Don Byas might have an engagement at the Three Deuces as a leader and, at the same time, be a sideman with Coleman Hawkins at the Downbeat next door."

As the fans had once crowded other clubs for breakout performers, now they came running to the Deuces for the parrot-beaked pianist. Garner had a fresh sound, the product of a left-hand that strummed the keyboard as if it were a guitar and that lagged gently behind the beat. He used long introductions that were melodic inventions of his own and that held listeners suspensefully waiting for the familiar opening notes of the standards he played. He also indulged in a bit of showmanship that he might have derived from Slam. He hummed audibly as he played. But more frequently he gave vent to a series of grunts and exclamations—"Oh-ho!" "Uh-huh!" "Ya-hum!"—suggestive of surprised satisfaction that greatly amused audiences and heightened their reactions.

With Garner, the Deuces became the new hot spot, as the Onyx and Famous Door had once been. It was a hegemony that the club was able to maintain into the postwar years with the help of another eighty-eighter, Eddie Heywood, as well as some of the innovators of the new jazz. When Dizzy Gillespie brought a band into the club in April of '45, alongside Garner's trio, *Metronome* observed that it was "the first big opening on The Street since the curfew went into effect." To many, this quintet—Bird (alto), Al Haig (piano), Curly Russell (bass) and Stan Levey (drums)—remains the exemplar of all the combos that promulgated the bop revolution.

Bird frequently played the Deuces from '47 to '49 with a combo of his own. Guitarist Jimmy Raney, a regular attendant, claims that his appearances were always erratic and eventful: "At some clubs he was actually paid by the set, it was that risky a thing that he would show. His horns presented a problem—they were in hock so often. At the Three Deuces, the porter had a job assigned to him, to go to the pawnshop every day and get Bird's horn for the job, and then return it to the shop after the job."

Raney has a vivid memory of one night at the Deuces when "Bird walked in and went right to the kitchen and started to make himself a few sandwiches. He was doing a magnificent job building them very big and garnishing them with all sorts of condiments. The managers of clubs had a very easygoing attitude with Bird. He had a way of stimulating expansive spirits in the hardest people. But this was a hectic evening, and the full bar was waiting for Charlie. The manager came into the kitchen and told Bird that he was on. Bird, his jaws chomping, kept on eating. The manager waited a bit and then said, 'Please, Bird, finish later; the crowd is getting restless.' No response from Bird. This went on until the manager was almost in tears, imploring him to go on, and Bird turned around and said: 'Man, why don't you try one of these sandwiches? They're crazy!' "

But others carry exciting musical memories of Parker and his associates at the Deuces. For one thing, it was here that Miles Davis, the poet of loneliness, made his debut as a small-combo soloist after Eckstine broke up his big bebop band. Though some historians refer to his trumpeting on "Chasin' the Bird," cut on Savoy at this time, as an early example of the cool brand of modern jazz, the "Birth of the Cool" did not occur on Capitol until almost two years later. Unquestionably, Davis was working on the no-vibrato, no-attack style and "the sound of sadness and resignation" that were in evidence at the Royal Roost booking of September, '48. His work at the Deuces was notable enough to earn "young Werther" of the flügelhorn an *Esquire* New Star Award in '47.

Also in the exciting category is a memory that jazz critic Ira Gitler retains of an evening in the summer of '47 when trumpeter Fats Navarro and pianist Bud Powell, regarded as the foremost of bop eighty-eighters, sat in with Bird for one set. Throughout his life, Powell was constantly in and out of mental institutions. Navarro, a mainliner from his early years, died in July, 1950, at the age of twenty-six. But in their functioning periods, both were remarkable performers. The night they sat in with Bird, they replaced pianist Duke Jordan and Miles Davis, neither of whom lacked authority on their instruments.

As Gitler tells it in *Jazz Masters of the Forties:* "The tune was Thelonious Monk's '52nd Street Theme,' played at an intensely fast tempo. Parker and Navarro played well, but what Powell did clearly eclipsed their work that night. For twenty or twenty-five choruses, he hung the audience by its nerve ends, playing music of demonically driven beauty, music of hard, unflinching swing, music of genius." Gitler produces this memorable image of Powell: "Right leg digging into the floor at an odd angle, pants leg up almost to the top of the shin, shoulders hunched, upper lip tight against the teeth, mouth emitting an accompanying guttural song to what the steel fingers were playing, vein in temple throbbing violently as perspiration popped out all over his scalp and ran down his face and neck. . . ."

Of Theodore "Fats" Navarro, who was known as Fat Girl because of his ballooning figure, arranger-composer Tadd Dameron once told Gitler: "I used to try to get other fellows to play with me, and they'd say, 'Oh, is Fats in the band? Oh, no!' It got to the point where I had to pay him so much money that I told him he should go on his own. . . . But he didn't want to quit. He didn't have security because of his habits."

In '49 Bud and Fats played together at the Deuces in one of several jam sessions organized by Leonard Feather. Bud enjoyed needling people and had a way of getting under Fats' skin. This particular evening, as Feather tells it: "The tension between the two was aggravated when Bud chided Fats between sets. At the beginning of the following set, Fats reached the bursting point. While the audience looked on in silent, terrified tension, he lifted his horn and tried to bring the full weight of it crashing down on Bud's hands. He missed, thank God, but the strength of the blow was enough to buckle the horn against the piano; Fats had to borrow a trumpet to play the set." Feather adds deadpan: "The incident, however, failed to affect the close friendship and mutual admiration between Bud and Fats."

Of course, by 1949 The Street was in such a state of nerves and so much on the downgrade musically and morally that at least part of the friction inside the Deuces was, perhaps, attributable to the general atmosphere outside. In fact, in December of '48 Sammy Kay and Irving Alexander, who ran the Deuces, opened a club on Broadway known as the Clique. It was between 52d and 53d on the site of the old Ebony and later the locus of Birdland, more recently Lloyd Price's Turntable. The failure of the Clique brought the two bonifaces back to the Deuces in July, '49, with a bill that featured Erroll Garner and a combo led by trombonist Kai Winding. Controversial, confusing and at times baffling, the bopsters polarized the jazz scene but helped develop a clientele for the latter-day Deuces.

The Deuces hardly limited its bills to the purveyors of the new jazz. In fact, a number of the canopy names were cats without any affiliation. The only time that tenor saxophonist Ben Webster led a combo, it was at the Deuces in August, '43. One of the busiest recording saxophonists in the business, Webster's style was closer to the big-toned tenor of Coleman Hawkins, whom he followed into the Ellington band, than the cool, lyric tenor of Lester Young. But he was always a virtuoso performer who did not belong to any one school.

Another Three Deuces jazzman who was respected by musicians of every school was drummer Big Sid Catlett. Just forty-one when he died of a heart attack in '51, he was the subject of a gag that went like this: "Who's that drummer on the stand?" Someone answers, "He's Catlett." First man: "I don't care what his religion is. He's a fine drummer." And that he was—contributing his inspired stick work to the bands of Benny Carter, McKinney's Cotton Pickers, Fletcher Henderson, Don Redman and mostly Louis Armstrong, with whom he worked for four years beginning in 1938 and again for two years in '47 to '49.

"Sid could play both with Dizzy and with the Dixieland musicians," Billy Taylor observes. "He could play any style, and he could play equally well in a big band or in any kind of small band. He was also

Slim Gaillard and Slam Stewart in 1941.

Down Beat

the first drummer I heard who would play regular choruses, like thirty-two or sixty-four bars, the way a piano or a horn might. If he had two blues choruses, he would take just twenty-four bars, and if you didn't come in on the twenty-fifth, he'd say, 'What?' And he was a really advanced drummer with a melodic approach. Even today, most drummers have the rhythmic approach with no attention to the melodic potentialities of percussion."

Big Sid made his point on The Street, albeit quietly, in the years '44–'46, shuttling between the Deuces and the Downbeat. One of the small combos to which he lent his name recorded under it, but the sides are nowhere to be found. For the sound of his hides, one must turn to recordings of Louis Armstrong, Dizzy Gillespie, Eddie Condon, and Sidney Bechet. Critic Whitney Balliett, who refers to him as "the near-legendary drummer," describes him as an inspired accompanist who was "always conscious of dynamics (a fundamental largely foreign to modern drummers)." Balliett has painted a colorful portrait that many retain of Catlett on The Street: "Well over six feet tall, with enormous shoulders and slender fingers the length of dinner knives, Catlett sat at his drums with Prussian erectness, his trunk motionless and his arms (weighted by hands that made drumsticks look like matches) moving so fast that they seemed to be lazily spinning in slow motion. It was an unforgettable ballet. Once in a while he would twirl his sticks over his head or throw them in the air, allowing their motions to silently measure off several beats. The effect was louder than any shout."

A more subtle type of showmanship was practiced by another frequent resident of the Three Deuces bandstand. The fame of Leroy Stewart of Englewood, New Jersey, better known as Slam Stewart, member of the duo of Slim & Slam, preceded his arrival on The

Street in '43. When the draft took Bulee Gaillard, better known as Slim, Slam was left to pursue a less sensational career as an inventive jazzman. A fine bass player, he won the *Metronome* Poll as top performer on the instrument in '46. What brought crowds to the Deuces, however, was a unique sound that he got on the big fiddle. Instead of plucking, as most jazz bass players did, Slam bowed and produced one of the fattest and richest sounds ever heard on the instrument. After a time, audiences discovered that the man with the heavy-lidded eyes and spread nose achieved this remarkable tone by *humming* the notes of a solo, however complex, an octave above the instrument. It was the combination of the two that listeners heard. They came to watch and marvel.

Pianist Eddie Heywood of Atlanta, Georgia, was a Deuces regular of the war years whose career went into high gear while he was at the club. Heywood actually started at the Deuces as an intermission pianist when the name of the club was changed from the Plantation in the summer of '43. Coming from the Village Vanguard, he was part of the first bill that included a Georgie Auld quartet, Ann Robinson, a sort of female Leo Watson, and Willie Dukes, a male torch singer, who combed his hair in an exotic upsweep. On his appearance the following year, Eddie led a band that elicited rave notices.

"The best music played at any New York location," wrote Barry Ulanov in *Metronome.* "Eddie has polished and refined the sound of his six-piece outfit so effectively since his departure from Café Society that it now compares favorably with bands of any size or instrumentation, and in at least one respect is without compare. The dynamics are astonishing. They range from a spine-tingling, ear-tickling pianissimo to a healthy gland-shaking forte. . . . And delight of delights, all of this without losing the fine beat. . . . Smiling Eddie is responsible not only for his own tasteful piano solos and the band's esprit de corps but for the brilliant arrangements as well."

It was one of these arrangements that brought Heywood to his peak of popularity in 1946. The featured number of a Hollywood biopic of Cole Porter was "Begin the Beguine," the unconventional ballad that had made Artie Shaw's reputation in '38. Heywood devised an arrangement in which he employed a modified boogie beat. The figure opened his presentation and thereafter became an ostinato (repeated pattern) over which the modal melody soared. Night after night, the crowds at the Deuces went wild the moment that Eddie sounded the figure on the piano. The year after he was the talk of The Street, Eddie suffered a paralysis of his hands that seemed to write finis to his career. Fortunately, it was temporary, and four years later, he was back at the keyboard. In '56 he made musical news again with an original instrumental composition, "Canadian Sunset." The hit recording was by Hugo Winterhalter, who employed the modified boogie ostinato used by Eddie on "Begin the Beguine."

While the Deuces was a launching ground for Heywood and Garner, it was just a debut gig for another eighty-eighter. George Shearing spent much of '48 at the club, first as an intermission pianist and then with several combos, though as Tony Scott recalls, "nobody was listening to him at the time." Nevertheless, Shearing treasures "pleasant memories of my appearances as soloist and as a member of cooperative trios that included such marvelous people as Oscar Pettiford, J. C. Heard and Shelly Manne—all this before the formation of the Quintet in January, 1949." This was the quintet that created the Shearing sound.

The Three Deuces had more than its share of outstanding vocalists. Pearl Bailey made what is possibly her only appearance on The Street in '44, conquering most reviewers with her tall, striking good looks, chesty voice and showmanship. Billy Daniels was there early in '46, and Maxine Sullivan late the same year. The great Ella Fitzgerald spent most of the summer of '48 at the club and Herb Jeffries made a fleeting appearance, even as he did on the music scene generally. None of these carried the voltage of Garner, Gillespie or Heywood.

The Deuces was one of the longer-lived clubs among the latter-day establishments. Its pastel-blue door in a white façade remained open at No. 72 until '53–'54. It was memorialized, as were many of the clubs on The Street, in an out-of-print disc by Randy Brooks on Decca. "A Night at the Deuces" was written by John Benson Brooks, no relative. From September, '47, on, it operated in the ominous shadow of Rockefeller Center's Esso Building. After '50 it watched one nearby club after another shutter as real-estate interests took over the southeast corner of 52d and Sixth to erect the Sperry Rand skyscraper.

Tape 21 . . . ERROLL GARNER

The gifted composer of "Misty," the man who grunts as he grinds the keyboard, and the pianist who frequently sounds like a movie-palace orchestra, Erroll Garner is one of a group of giant eighty-eighters who emerged from 52d St. Others were Fats Waller, Johnny Guarnieri and Art Tatum.

"All those stories," said Garner, who was born in Pittsburgh in 1923, "about my bouncing onto The Street direct from Pittsburgh are just not true. I came to New York three or four different times before I stayed.

"The first time I came to New York, I was with a girl I knew. She was a singer. Ann Lewis was her name. Even though I was a youngster, my father let me come with her because she was an older lady. I accompanied her. After I left her, I went back home.

"The next time I came to the big city, it was with another girl singer. I happened to be going with her. And when she left Pittsburgh, I thought that I would just go to New York and visit with her. She talked me into staying. I got to meet a few people. Then I looked up Mary Lou Williams. There wasn't much that she could do or did. She was on the road mostly, traveling with the Andy Kirk band. Then I managed to meet some uptown people, Harlem folks.

"Lucky Roberts—you know, the ragtime pianist who wrote 'Moonlight Cocktail'—owned a club on St. Nicholas Avenue called the Rendezvous. He was very popular and big—a little short guy with glasses. Palled around with high-society folk like the Prince of Wales. I went to work for him.

"After a while, I worked in a place on Broadway called the Melody Bar. Then I came back to a club next door to Lucky's Rendezvous— Jimmy's Chicken Shack. Let's see. It was a few blocks from the subway station and I lived on 153d St. So Jimmy's must have been between 147th and 148th on St. Nicholas Avenue. On my nights off, I used to go down to 52d St. and hear Dizzy, Charlie Parker, Jay McShann, Roy Eldridge. They were all on The Street. Bebop was coming in.

"Then I went back to Lucky's. Just about that time he took in a partner. John Levy, who was later married to Billie Holiday, was then married to Tondelayo. After a time, Levy and his wife opened a club on 52d called Tondelayo's. They were the ones who brought me to The Street. And Tondelayo's was the first spot I played on 52d."

Garner laughed huskily, his small eyes glowing mischievously. "I got to 52d St. the hardest way of anybody you know. But everybody tells me that I blew in from Pittsburgh and just blew right onto The Street. It's not true. Mine was a real roundabout approach.

"There was this situation with the Musicians Union. Three months this and three months that before you could take a steady job. Well, there was this delegate—God bless his soul—who fixed it so I could be out of work only three days. I came in on a year's transfer, and I had to stay in one place for a year. They did it special for me.

"Slam Stewart came into Tondelayo's one night. Several nights later, he came running down The Street, grabbed me, and I doubled that night with him at the Three Deuces. When he [Slam] asked me to come work with him, John Levy let me go without my having to give a week's notice. He knew that it meant more money. And he brought in Gladys Bentley from out of town. She was real hot then with her 'mannish' material. That smart kind of stuff, partly kind of dirty. I was so busy running up and down The Street, I never did get to hear her. I was so glad to be on The Street, I was like a wild man.

"I stayed with Slam for about three and a half years. Not all of them were at the Deuces. We traveled, did theaters and such things. First time I was at the Deuces, I stayed for about six months. Slam was doubling. He had just started in Billy Rose's show, *The Seven Lively Arts,* with Benny Goodman and Red Norvo. He didn't come in until after the theater let out at about eleven thirty. After the show closed, we left the Deuces and went on the road. The package included the Hal McIntyre band and Johnny Desmond, who had just gotten out of the Army.

"But we kept coming back to the Deuces. Sammy Kay, the owner, was like managing Slam. He loved him. And the Deuces was like home to Slam. Anytime he didn't have a job, he just went to work there. Tim Gale was booking Slam and later he booked me. Tim was together with Billy Shaw.

"There was one time when I had three jobs on The Street. I was working at Tondelayo's, doubled at the Deuces and accompanied Billy Daniels when he played the Spotlite. And one night when the pianist didn't show at the Onyx, I played there, too. Four jobs. And

Erroll Garner, who got his start at Tondelayo's.

RCA Records

that was just about making a good week's salary. The clubs sure didn't pay. They were making money hand over fist. But the musicians couldn't get money out of them. Art Tatum and Billie Holiday were the first acts that got big bread on The Street. And Coleman Hawkins when he came back from Europe after he had 'Body and Soul.'

"While I was on The Street, I wrote some little tunes for Slam, things that he could bow on. 'Play, Piano, Play' was later buried in a time capsule in Paris the year [1957] I won the Grand Prix du Disque. When I left Slam, I got Billy Taylor, who had just come back from Washington, to take my chair. And Billy turned his chair over to Beryl Booker. When John Collins got out of the Army, he worked with us, then stayed to work with Billy, after that with Beryl, until he finally went with Nat Cole and the big money.

"The last time I played 52d St. was in '46, the early part of '46. I came to California in the middle of '46. What messed The Street up was putting girls into the clubs. Club owners thought that the girls would make the guys drink more. And they thought they could get all the conventioneers coming into New York. They forget that music brought the conventioneers. They'd have girls sitting in the clubs where a guy could sneak in beside them. Pickup joints they became until the cops got wise. It was the club owners that killed The Street. They can't blame the customers. People came to 52d St. from all over the world. And that was true even after The Street stopped being a music street. They still came looking for the music.

"Now, I come back to New York, and where do you go to hear jazz? Not long ago, I was in the city on a Friday night. At nine o'clock I was standing on a street corner, trying to figure out where I could go to hear some music. I finally thought of the Roosevelt Grill, where Lombardo once used to be and where the Greatest Jazz Band in the World was the house band. I spent the whole night there. Everything in the city is now so strung out. You go to the theater, and by the time you get to a club you're just about in time to catch the last set. But in the days of 52d St., it was right there. All the music you could ask for and more. And not only on 52d St. New York was then a music town, a big music town.

"That's why I laugh at the rock-'n'-rollers who tell you that rock is here to stay. Well, if it is, that's because jazz musicians are playing the backgrounds. You can't go to a symphony cat and ask him to give you a rock accompaniment. But jazz cats can play anything.

"Come to think of it, I did write one thing for or about 52d St. You know the White Rose bar that was on Sixth Avenue. It was our hang-out. You could get a big double drink for forty-five cents—I'm telling you. They had a snack bar. Fresh cheese, fresh salmon, fresh sardines, and little pieces of meat. You bought a drink and then you could nibble all you wanted. That's how I came to write 'White Rose Bounce.' Recorded it for Black and White, along with 'Night and Day.' It was like my second or third record date."

16. Onyx III

In the spring of 1942, not too long after he became involved in the management of the Famous Door at No. 66, Irving Alexander noticed that an English basement across the street at No. 57 was becoming vacant. Alexander was then part of a group—partly a family group— that included Jack Colt (and while he was in the Army, his wife Beatrice Watkins Alexander Colt), former liquor salesman Mac Rosen, Arthur Jarwood and lawyer Chauncey Olman. The enterprising group was involved in varying degrees in the management and/or ownership of Kelley's Stable, Downbeat, Three Deuces, as well as the Door. (The latter-day ownership of clubs is difficult to determine, partly because the Mob controlled unregistered percentages of some clubs and partly because liquor licenses were registered in the names of bartenders and others "clean" enough to pass the scrutiny of the State Liquor Authority.)

With the assent of his associates, Alexander took a lease on the premises near Jimmy Ryan's and announced that they would reopen the spot as a new Onyx. Immediately, Joe Helbock, the original owner and founder of the Onyx, brought a lawsuit against Alexander and Jarwood. Asserting that he was planning to reopen the club he had launched in the speakeasy era and maintained into 1938, Helbock claimed ownership of the famous name. Chauncey Olman, who represented Alexander and Jarwood, countered with two technicalities. He contended that when Helbock had taken in guitarist Carl Kress as a silent partner, he had turned the name of the club over to the corporation they formed, and that on leaving the venture after a falling-out with Kress, he had left the name with the corporation. Olman also dug up an old police regulation that required club owners to notify the police department of any change of address. It was Olman's contention that having failed to register the new address when he went into partnership with Kress, Helbock lost the right to the name and could not have then legally turned it over to the corporation. Unfortunately for Helbock, the court upheld Olman's arguments and ruled against him in July of '42.

By the following year the Onyx was, in *Metronome's* view, "once again a magic name," and it maintained its popularity as a jazz club through the war and into the postwar years. Although its span of life was not as great as Ryan's or Hickory House and though it changed hands, it remains the most important of The Street's music clubs. Even when it metamorphosed in 1949 into a strip joint with snake dancers (Black Orchid), it employed top jazzmen like Sol Yaged to accompany the peelers.

The "magic" was performed by a bill that offered the Cozy Cole Trio and Billie Holiday, who had used Cozy on drums during the first two years of her recording career. The Cole Trio, doubling a full schedule at CBS, included Hank D'Amico on clarinet and Johnny, the pipe-smoking, piano-playing Guarnieri, at the keyboard. Billie, who remained a mainstay of the club during '43 and '44, was to say later: "I spent the rest of the war on 52d St. and a few other streets. I had the white gowns and the white shoes. And every night they'd bring me the white gardenias and the white junk." It was a comparatively uneventful period for her. The bouts with the law came, as she explains in her autobiography, only when she tried to get off the stuff. It was a period when she was singing extremely well and when wartime audiences could not get enough of her. (The Petrillo record ban kept her off wax during '43, as it did all recording artists.) In some ways, Billie's tortured style, the sense of hurt and longing, may have been a perfect expression of what servicemen and their loved ones were feeling.

By 1944 Onyx III had achieved the distinction via the Gillespie-Pettiford quintet of being the first club to bring bop onto The Street. Though the bopsters thereafter seemed to gravitate to the Three Deuces and the short-lived Spotlite, the former "Cradle of Swing"

Billy Eckstine and Charlie Parker at the opening of Birdland on August 31, 1949.

Down Beat

remained hospitable. But it devoted much of '48 to separate bookings of Gillespie and Charlie Parker combos.

During one of these appearances, pianist Duke Jordan found Bird lying across a large garbage can, rolling himself back and forth. "I rushed forward," he recalls, "saying, 'Hey, Bird! Are you all right? Are you sick?' But he just smiled and said, 'Hey, Duke, hey, Jimsey, everything's cool, everything's cool.' He was just trying his in-between-sets experience experiments." Jordan goes on to explain: "Bird always came on with a new musical line that would make my hair stand on end. He used to say to me: 'If you do something out of the ordinary between sets, when you come back to play, you will have a different thought, and it will come out in your playing.' "

Jordan also recalls what he characterizes as one of Bird's "impulsively generous acts." He was in a cab one day with bassist Tommy Potter when the door opened and Bird shoved a good-looking girl inside, saying, "Duke, here, she's for you." Jordan continues: "A present, like. We took her to the hotel, and she laid out for us." Wherever they traveled, Jordan found that Bird called his mother in Kansas City quite regularly. "I once saw him phoning her during a terrible thunderstorm. He opened the window and stuck the phone out for a minute during the thunder, and then he said, 'Mom, do you hear God talking?' "

Wherever they went, Jordan adds, "the pushers would be with us. The grapevine, as far as drugs is concerned, is very quick, very swift; and as soon as Bird hit town, someone would contact him. . . . As years went by, Bird started cooling. He went to a doctor during the Onyx date in 1948 and was told he had about six months to live unless he took a complete rest for a few years, which he never did."

Historian Ira Gitler remembers Bird as a witty man who introduced the trio playing opposite him in a way that "put on" owner and audience. "The management has gone to grrrrrrreat expense," he would half-chant, "to bring you the next group. Let's bring them on with a rousing round of applause." And as Gitler describes it: "The last line would be delivered with rapidity in a descending arc. . . ."

By 1950, when the Onyx had become the Orchid or Black Orchid, and the new club was going the way of all flesh, it nevertheless played host to a stellar bop group consisting of trumpeter Miles Davis, tenorman Wardell Gray, saxophonist Sonny Stitt and pianist Bud Powell. It was, in Gitler's words, "a last gasp for the modern" since jazz had by that time largely moved off The Street onto Broadway.

It would be inaccurate to describe the jazz policy of Onyx III as exclusively modern. Through the six years of its existence, it presented nonschool groups like those led by trumpeters Roy Eldridge, Hot Lips Page and Red Allen, fiddler Stuff Smith, saxophonist Ben Webster, pianist Jimmy Jones, and drummer Cozy Cole. These were bookings of men who were more or less steady residents of The Street and who moved from club to club.

The palpitating Paganini, as some called Stuff Smith, did not generate the same electricity as he once had at the original Onyx. But his performances were still inspired and led to reviews in which he was described as "really one of the few true geniuses of jazz." Working at the piano with Stuff was Jimmy Jones, whose inventive and lovely chording made him a true descendant of Art Tatum, then playing at the Downbeat. Jones later accompanied Sarah Vaughan in her triumphal '47 appearance at the Onyx.

Where Onyx III proved inventive was in the vocal area. Its receptivity to black female singers, also male, may well have been advanced by the long and profitable stands of Lady Day on its bandstand. None of the black singers who followed Billie, with the exception of one, developed the kind of following she had. But each was outstanding in her own way and betokened a fine sensitivity on the part of the Onyx management. In 1945, there was Etta James, who was an R & B rather than a jazz singer, and who came to wide public notice almost a decade later when Georgia Gibbs, a white singer, covered her record of 'Dance with Me, Henry.' Miss James did not attain her real public acceptance until the late sixties, when a series of hit records placed her in the select company of *Billboard*'s seven Top Female Artists for '69.

In 1947 the club presented Savannah Churchill, who had sung with Benny Carter but made a name for herself on the indie Manor label vocalizing with Don Byas and J. J. Johnson. The following year, the Onyx tried with Hadda Brooks, a stunning girl with a tart delivery, who never lived up to her promise.

But there was one singer who did, and for whom Onyx III proved a launching pad. Sarah Lois Vaughan first made herself known through Harlem's Apollo Theater where, like Ella Fitzgerald before her, she came in first in three Amateur Night contests and won a week's booking. After her October, '42, debut, she sang with the bands of Earl "Fatha" Hines and Billy Eckstine. In the latter days of '44, she made some recordings with Teddy Wilson, Billie Holiday's initial record mentor. Almost from the week of her Apollo appearance, the Divine Sarah or Sassy, as she came to be called, was in danger of remaining a coterie singer. Endowed with remarkable vocal equipment, she could gracefully do with her voice what jazz instrumentalists did with their horns. The gift of inspired and complex improvisation was more impressive to musicians than to record executives. At a Musicraft session, one of the A & R men listening to the perfectly executed but involved turns of her vocalizing reportedly wailed to an associate: "For God's sake, tell her to sing the melody, or we'll lose our shirts." He was unintentionally prophetic about Musicraft's future: It did go bankrupt. But Sarah's artful handling of melody—later, "Broken-Hearted Melody," a song which I published —eventually brought her wealth and fame.

It was the unrestrained enthusiasm of innovators like Dizzy Gillespie, who knew Sarah's work from the Eckstine band, that gave the Onyx management the willingness to book her as a star soloist in '46. Obviously, their enthusiasm was guarded, since they paid her the munificent sum of $75 a week. But the in-crowd reaction was tremendous. From the Onyx, Sarah went to a neighboring citadel of jazz, the Downbeat at 66 West, which was within the orbit of the Jarwood-Alexander-Olman operation. The next stop, and exposure to a different kind of audience, was Café Society Downtown. (Here she met George Treadwell, a trombonist to whom she was married for some years and who continued to manage her even after their marriage went on the rocks.) When she returned to the Onyx about a year after

George Shearing, whose Street debut was a one-nighter at Hickory House, plays for Sarah Vaughan, who made her debut at the Onyx. The year: 1951.

Down Beat

her debut, her weekly salary soared to almost ten times what it had been.

For Billy Eckstine, as for Sarah, it took two appearances on The Street to hit pay dirt. The '44 debut of X-Tine, as he was billed at the Yacht, yielded rather dismal reviews. Ulanov in *Metronome* was, perhaps, the most unkind with references to a "shattering tremolo and a pompousness in phrasing not unlike that of operetta performance." Even the positive comments seemed negative: "Eckstine is a pretty good-looking boy with a mesmerizing way of contorting his face that seems to get the girls." Reversing Gillespie's movement, X-Tine crossed The Street from the Yacht to the Onyx. Changing his name to its original form did not help either.

But when Billy played the Onyx again three years later, it was a new ball game. By then he had received a plaque from the New Jazz Foundation naming him the Outstanding Male Vocalist of 1945. It was presented to him on the stage of the Apollo Theater by Monte Kay, who also happened to be a publicist-producer of some of the 52d St. clubs. The plaque was promotion rather than recognition. Record releases on the National label to which he was signed in '46 also helped build an audience. Though none of these discs was as big as "Sophisticated Lady" or "Fool That I Am," both '48 best sellers, or of his later hits on M-G-M—"My Foolish Heart," "My Destiny," "I Apologize"—they created an awareness of the "Sepia Sinatra," as *Time* called him in a '49 story. In 1947 he was not yet the hit singer known as Mr. B. But he excited so much interest during a September appearance at the Onyx that the club brought him back in December.

The success of the original Onyx was in large measure due to founder Helbock's savvy in finding talented jazzmen who were also engaging entertainers and showmen. If bop represented an adventure in the realm of the esoteric for the new management, it demonstrated that it, too, had the common touch with Sarah and Billy. Miss Vaughan was unquestionably more of a jazz singer than the man with the throbbing vibrato who had popularized "Jelly Jelly," "Stormy Monday" and "Water Boy" as vocalist with Earl "Fatha" Hines. But both had fat jazz backgrounds—and Mr. B had sex. The knack of mounting entertaining as well as stimulating bills undoubtedly made it possible for the Onyx to remain a music club long after competitors had become strip joints and turned to peddling sex.

Tape 22 . . . JOHNNY GUARNIERI

"We got little sleep that year—1943, it must have been. We'd finish at the Onyx around three in the morning. We had to be at CBS at seven for rehearsals of the Raymond Scott band. The three of us, Cozy Cole, Hank D'Amico and me would find some place at CBS— the Music Library, a studio, a couch in an upper-floor lounge. During the day we managed to sleep a bit now and then. We didn't mind it. We were young. But even if we did get dragged once in a while, we never thought of giving up the 52d St. bit.

"When we took the Onyx gig," said Johnny Guarnieri, a descendant of the Guarnerius family of violin makers, who was born in New York City in 1917, "we knew we'd have to give up some sleep. It wasn't the money. We couldn't have gotten more than seventy-five dollars for all the hours we put in. And we were making good bread at CBS. We just couldn't stand the vise of Raymond Scott music. He set tempi with a metronome. Being good friends, we decided that no one would be leader on the job. But we gave Cozy the job of collecting the bread.

"At the end of each week, the owner would pull out a bunch of bar bills. Hank and Cozy got clipped. I would come out with the full sum. I think it bothered the owner. But I wouldn't touch a drop on the job. To me it was the music. I got drunk on that. I was sociable. I loved my friends. But I knew that if I did any drinking, I'd never be able to work for Scott in the morning. I don't know how they did it. But they did.

"During this gig I also accompanied Billie Holiday. The first night she handed me some tattered lead sheets and said, 'Give me four bars.' I played four bars. But she didn't come in. Figuring that she hadn't heard me or just missed her cue, I started over again. Suddenly, I felt a tap on the back of my head and I heard her say: 'Don't worry 'bout me—I'll be there.' She added that she liked to come in behind the beat, as I discovered, and that I didn't have to bother to make her look good.

"Looking back, I would say that few performers had such solid judgment about tempi as she did, particularly when it came to doing

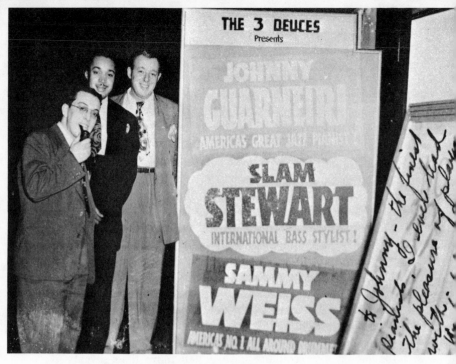

Johnny Guarnieri, Slam Stewart, Sammy Weiss at the Three Deuces.

Johnny Guarnieri

certain tunes in a very slow tempo. Most performers who try the slow-temp bit do it for effect, not because it's right for the tune. Billie Holiday was the greatest tempo singer that ever lived. When you heard her do 'I Cover the Waterfront,' you had to say that her draggy delivery was perfectly suited to the song. But on the piano, that temp didn't work at all. She made a timeless tune out of 'I Didn't Know What Time It Was.' To me, her greatest quality was not the one that everybody fixes on—the expression and the feeling—but her innately and absolutely perfect sense of timing. No other singer ever approached her on this.

"Frank Sinatra came into the Onyx frequently. He was the vocalist on the Raymond Scott program. One night while he was listening to us, some guy started talking loudly. He tried to get the guy to pipe down. Maybe the guy talked back or just didn't lower his voice. The next he knew, he was on the floor and Sinatra had a few sore knuckles.

"My earliest recollection of 52d St. is not of a jazzman but of Mike Riley, who wrote 'The Music Goes 'Round.' The tune focused a lot of attention on The Street, and overnight, music clubs popped up all over the place. In time, I played most of them. Regular engagements at some. Fill-in at others, like one night when Red Allen's pianist didn't show. When I worked at CBS, I'd take the subway at 50th and Sixth Avenue to go home. Always walked through The Street. There weren't too many nights that I made it through the block without stopping somewhere. As long as there was an empty piano stool, or anything going on, I'd always get involved and jam until they closed the joint—and that happened hours after the paying customers were gone.

"I played the Three Deuces for longer engagements than most of the clubs and had the greatest little trio there: Slam Stewart on bass and Sammy Weiss on drums. I took Slam away from Art Tatum. And I hired Weiss, even though he once brought me up before the union for missing a club date.

"Also working the Deuces with us was Tatum himself. He had Tiny Grimes on guitar. Grimes had a trick of playing licks from well-known tunes during breaks. Like in the middle of some ballad, he'd play the opening phrase of 'The Campbells Are Coming.' Another favorite of his was a snatch from 'Yankee Doodle.' Every time he'd interpolate one of these, the audience would go wild. It bugged me that he'd get a bigger rise out of the crowd than anything the great Tatum did.

"Also on the same bill was Eddie Heywood with a twelve-piece band. How all the guys got on the tiny bandstand of the Deuces is still a puzzle to me. Always made me think of a hilarious movie scene—the Marx Brothers in that sardine-packed elevator. Eddie had just recorded his hit arrangement of 'Begin the Beguine' with that infectious rhythm figure: Boom—ta-da-ta-da-a . . . Boom—ta-da-ta-da-a. All that he had to do was play that vamp and the place would become a madhouse. There'd be an outburst like Sinatra provoked just by turning his head, or Presley stirred by knocking his knees together.

"Between sets you'd see the cats go streaming up the block to Sixth Avenue. The White Rose bar just around the corner was a neutral meeting ground for all the guys, including those who weren't working. Most of us never went to Jimmy Ryan's to listen. The cats there were interlopers who played strictly Dixieland. Today I don't look down on Dixieland the way I did. But to us, jazz was four-beat pulsation and the two-beat thing was old hat. Harmonically, too. We were listening for new sounds and looking for the guys who were coming in with fresh ideas. But at the White Rose everybody loved everybody, including the Dixieland cats at Jimmy Ryan's. I went there—though I didn't drink—just to be with everybody. It was a wonderful feeling. This was our world and there was love in it.

"Well, it was at the White Rose bar one evening that I met this excited kid. He just came into town from Pittsburgh. 'Man,' he said, 'I gotta get in and hear you guys play!' It was Erroll Garner, and he obviously didn't have even that proverbial pot. I snuck him in, though this was strictly verboten. The room was so small the owners didn't want any freeloaders. But I do love people. Music is my communication. But people are my life. 'Man,' he said to me, between sets, 'I can't read like you guys. Have to make it some other way. All you guys have nothing but left hands.' He was very personable, very likable and completely genuine.

"After I was finished for the evening, I walked with him toward Fifth Avenue. There was a place on the same side as the Deuces and the Famous Door, almost directly opposite the 21 Club. It had practically the only good piano on The Street. Guys who wanted to play for themselves, for friends or for a tip usually found the place. Though Garner was in his early twenties, he had already developed that spread-chord, ten-finger style, and he was doing that bit of strumming with his left hand instead of striding the way we did. And he was coming in behind the beat with his right hand, almost the way Billie Holiday sang. We played all night together. And for many nights after that, I'd be playing for nothing with Garner while I was being paid at the Deuces.

"Soon Garner was coming into the Deuces pretty regularly. There were three pianists in the club—myself, Heywood and Tatum. He just couldn't stay away. And he was anxious to show what he could do in competition. In his autobiography, Willie 'The Lion' Smith tells of how in the twenties in Harlem and other places, a guy just couldn't get off his piano stool, not even to go to the bathroom. Once he did, some young kid raring to get started would grab the stool—and that was the end of your job! Well, that was the way it was with Garner and the three of us. The moment we got off that piano stool, he was ready to go! Eventually, he got started professionally at the Deuces."

Johnny's father was the last of the famous family of Guarnerius violin makers, and he fervently wanted his son to be a concert violinist. "Unfortunately for my father's hopes," Johnny says, "when I was fifteen, a friend played me some Fats Waller records. I can't recall the titles. The strict upbringing under which I grew up? And believe me, it was strict—more like for an Italian girl. But once I heard Fats, you couldn't hold me down. I *had* to play like that. As the kids say today, it really *turned me on*. I could think of nothing else and I could hear nothing else. I got those Waller records and began copying his style, including his singing. I wasn't the only one who was mesmerized by him. By the time I was known locally as the Fats Waller of Tremont Avenue [in the Bronx] a cousin of mine, Frank Barker, was the Fats Waller of Burnside Avenue, and Harry Raab, later known as Harry 'The Hipster' Gibson, was the Fats Waller of Fordham Road.

"Shortly after that, I met Fats and shook hands with him. His paw reached up to my elbow. He listened to me and got a charge out of my imitation of him. By the time I was nineteen I had met all the other great colored piano players. I couldn't stand the society-style players or the Dixieland cats. My pianists were Tatum, Waller, Basie, Mary Lou Williams and Teddy Wilson. Overnight I learned how to play like all of these. And that's where my trouble started.

"Possibly I would be better known today if I had sat down and devised a few little tricks so that I would have what would be known as a recognizable style. But I believed that you played music the best way possible for the sake of the music itself. If I found myself with a swinging rhythm section and a good guitar, I played like Basie. And if I found myself with a fine clarinet player and drummer, I played like Teddy. And if I were all alone, I played like Fats or Tatum, since these guys could play by themselves and sound like a complete orchestra, which Basie couldn't do.

"And so I preferred the sounds of all these great piano players to sounds that I could create, although I never had difficulty when called upon to devise something original and distinctive. Invariably, some detractors would say I sounded like Tatum or Wilson or Fats, which was like saying, in those days, he's an imitation of Babe Ruth because he hits sixty home runs.

"When I worked with Benny Goodman in '39–'40, he was very perturbed because I sounded like Teddy Wilson with the trio. And I said: 'Mr. Goodman, you play your dotted eighths. Teddy plays his dotted eighths. And you can never interfere with one another. It's perfect music you make. It's a perfect marriage. So where do I come off—being a young punk of twenty—where do I come off trying to do something other than the best that can be done?'

"Now, Artie Shaw, with whom I worked in '40 and '41, gave me a lot of liberty. He generated enthusiasm and stimulated my thinking. It led to my playing the harpsichord with the Gramercy Five, and I became the first jazzman to jam on harpsichord. I helped put a lot of those Gramercy Five things together.

"I started earning my living professionally when I was seventeen. By the time I was twenty I was working at the Hotel Taft on Seventh Avenue with George Hall and Dolly Dawn. We were jamming even then. I remember a gig we played at the Hotel St. George in Brooklyn, where there was a Battle of the Bands between George Hall and Claude Hopkins. Between sets, we jammed—Tony Mottola on guitar, Doc Goldberg on bass and Nick Fatool on drums.

"Not long after that, I played the Stanley Theater in Pittsburgh with George Hall's Band. The second night we were there, I discovered that the Musicians Union, Local 60, had a social hall on the second floor of a building. It stayed open all night, and there was a piano on which they could jam. And so I jammed all night. All the time we were at the Stanley, after I finished with George Hall, I'd spend the night jamming at Local 60. I met some fine musicians there—Eddie Safranski, the bass player, and Dodo Marmarosa, the pianist, who was still in short pants. When I came through six months later with Mike Riley—a comedy band and really not for me—I did the same thing. The musicians at Local 60 were so impressed that they gave me a scroll, making me an honorary member of the local. Dave Garroway was one of the members.

"Six months later, a funny thing happened. I was with Benny Goodman, and our first stop was the Stanley Theater. We opened without any advance notice, except maybe a squib in *Down Beat* about my joining the band. When Goodman introduced the members of the band—Charlie Christian on guitar, Davie Tough at the drums, Lionel Hampton (vibes), Artie Bernstein (bass)—each guy got some applause. Finally, he said: 'And now my new piano player, Johnny Guarnieri'—and the whole theater stood up. All the guys who used to listen to me jam at the Local 60 had packed the theater. Benny was dumbfounded at the hand I got. 'Why, I thought you were from the Bronx,' he said. Then I explained that I was an adopted member of the Pittsburgh local.

"All that week, I'd go from the stage shows to the local's social hall and jam right through the night. It was like riding a glory wave. Of course, I couldn't do it now. But then it was exciting, it was my life, and I was young.

"And that was the way 52d St. was. When I was at the Onyx one time, Stuff Smith was at the Famous Door. We would interchange. When I was between sets, I'd work at his place. And when he was between sets, he'd work at mine. I have a classical background and knew many of his violin selections. We'd jam on them and put them in four/four meter. And then there were the dark nights to dawn with Coleman Hawkins, Roy Eldridge, Dizzy, Charlie Parker. We were always sittin' in with each other and jamming after the club closed. It was a bubble that never broke.

"But there were also serious moments. Once when I was working the Three Deuces, a well-known actress of that time, whose name escapes me, got loaded and began making anti-Semitic remarks. I got more and more provoked that nobody was doing anything to stop her. Finally, I asked Tatum, who was on the bill, to sit in for me. My brother, who happened to be in the club, and I went outside and found a cop. When we came in with him, the owner got mad at me, but I said that I wanted to prefer charges. The cop managed to get her into his prowl car and we drove over to the 54th St. station house. We were told to appear in court the following morning. It meant that I had to cancel out of the Sinatra and Milton Berle shows, which I did from the police station.

"We were there at 8 A.M. in the morning, my brother and I. Waited around for several hours. When we finally asked about the case, we were told that it had been quashed in chambers. Now I really got angry. Went down to the offices of *PM* in Brooklyn and talked with the people on the New York *Post*.

"Those were the two most liberal papers of the day. I explained that if I were Jewish, my outrage would be understandable and personal— her saying things like Hitler is gonna come to this country and kill all the Jews and make the USA a nice place to live in. Since I wasn't Jewish, I thought it might do a little bit of good to point out that Christians don't like to hear this kind of talk. Well, neither paper would carry the story.

"One of the men I remember with affection was little Harry Lim, who acted as A & R man for Keynote Records. He was a dapper little man with a great feeling for jazz. He was Javanese. We made many recordings together. The most famous was the Lester Young date that included 'Sometimes I'm Happy' and 'Afternoon of Basevite.'

"There were bad and phoney people on The Street as well as good. It was my good fortune never to be caught up in the swirl of the dope peddlers. They'll always be around, I suppose. But they did prey on some of the greatest musicians that ever lived. And when these cats got high, they thought they were playing great. But this was just when they weren't playing well at all. There are a number of boys who would be living today if not for the pushers—Charlie Christian and Jimmy Blanton, Duke's bass player. They weren't very strong, and they allowed bad cats to take advantage of their weakness.

"There were also men who took economic advantage of the 52d St. performers. I'm thinking of a man who recorded much of the talent you heard on The Street. He cut one of my compositions which sold over half a million. I think he gave me a pipe for a Christmas present. His maneuver was to grab the publishing rights to all the original material he recorded. At the height of a recording session he would come in with a piece of paper and say, 'Hey, you gotta sign this.' Later I found out that I had turned over all my music to him. Not only that. There was a clause that said that he could take my name off a composition if he chose—and all this for a consideration of one dollar.

"Oh, he helped a lot of bop guys get off the ground. But he took advantage of everyone that came near him. I love all people, and mind you, I got along with him.

"The Street also was a natural habitat for characters. A number of them were double-talk artists. Like Harry 'The Hipster' Gibson, a very clever man with words, who mixed jive and bop and blue talk. Then there was Nemo, a talented songwriter who wrote some very tender ballads. But he could be a flip, a wild man. He was like fifty years ahead of his time, especially with jazz talk. A very hip, very modern, very groovy type of cat, and he helped create atmosphere for jazz.

"Maybe it was the oddballs that drew crowds to The Street. But the audiences were generally great. When Billie Holiday sang in that slow, slow tempo, they listened—how they listened—and they loved and were inebriated. I don't think that any performer today can get that degree of attention, with the possible exception of Sinatra. Except for the soldiers who came for a binge—because they heard The Street was a wild place—people came to 52d to hear music. They surely didn't come to show off their clothes or be seen, and they had a genuine respect for performers.

"And the musicians, inspired by the respect they commanded, reacted to audiences. Unlike today, there was very little format in the presentations. When Tatum sat down to play, his sets weren't prepared—and we weren't prepared. We reacted to how audiences made us feel. And there was a lot of challenge stuff going on. You didn't hesitate to play the same number another guy played. It wasn't considered professional discourtesy or, as it would be today, bad programming. It was just that you loved the tune and did it differently and maybe wanted to show that you could do it better.

"I liked to make it a challenge. I could play as fast as anybody—and I had the fastest drummer and bass player around. I could do Basie or Fats. And I could do classical things, like Bach-style choruses on different standards.

"But with the challenge, there was love. The musicians on The Street were a compatible bunch. After-hours jamming was an expression of mutual feeling. We were a brotherhood. But like every period in history, it had to come to an end. My dad is the last descendant of the greatest violin makers of all time. It's hard to believe, but all those violin makers lived together at the same time and not in a big city. Cremona was a small Italian town. There must have been forty or fifty violin makers. And there couldn't have been more than a hundred and fifty people all-told in Cremona. But they all worked together and challenged one another. This never happened again in the history of the world. In the same way, musicians creating together and challenging each other made 52d St. It was not the proximity of the broadcasting studios or frantic antics or wild broads or odd characters.

"By 1947, as I remember it, The Street was already beginning to decline. Walking to the subway from CBS, you could see the girlie shows coming in. Now there were fewer places to jam. Soon I stopped walking through the block. It hurt when I did. And the next I knew, there were tall buildings."

17. Cracks in the Door

In February, 1943, the police swooped down on the Famous Door, then at 66 West 52d, and arrested Zorita, the exotic snake dancer, manager Irving Alexander, and the club's maître d'. All three were charged with violating the Mann Act: transporting women across state lines for immoral purposes. The trade papers reported that the crackdown was motivated by the efforts of the city fathers to reduce and eliminate the mingling of female "performers" with servicemen, not only at the Door but at other clubs along The Street. By mid-April all three were cleared of the charge. But the incident helped give 52d an odor that did not bode well for The Street's musical future. As for the servicemen who were flocking into midtown Manhattan on weekend passes, the incident may well have served to suggest that one could find action on The Street. It was symptomatic of the tenderloin atmosphere that was beginning to envelop and eventually to destroy a once-great music thoroughfare.

But The Street and the Door were still to enjoy some unforgettable moments, even though *Down Beat* was then saying SWING STREET JUST AIN'T SWING STREET ANYMORE. In fact, the Door was at that very moment playing host to Red Norvo, who had proved such a fabulous draw the preceding summer that he was back again in April. During the summer of '42, The Street was suffering not only the traditional seasonal slump but curfew jitters. Not the Door! Alternating with pianist Herman Chittison—"Chit's stuff is subtle but it

Henry Nemo, 1937.

Down Beat

swings," said *Down Beat*—the Red Norvo septet kept the Door swinging with customers. The amiable xylophonist-vibraharpist was such a solid click that manager-booker Joe Glaser reportedly shelled out a four-figure hunk of cabbage to buy Red's contract from the William Morris Agency. Norvo's reappearance in April, '43, led club manager Alexander to switch the character of his bill from a seamy strip show to a jazz concert. As Norvo's stay lengthened, Alexander brought in Hot Lips Page and his driving horn.

The Door did not splinter easily. When it reopened in its third incarnation, owned and managed by the Jarwood-Alexander-Mac Rosen combine, it tried to revive the big-band policy that had brought fame to the club with Basie, Barnet and Woody Herman. Through the year of Pearl Harbor, it presented the bands of Benny Carter; tenor saxophonist Babe Russin, acclaimed for his work with Goodman and Dorsey; and Andy Kirk. None provoked the furor that Basie or Kirk and His 12 Clouds of Joy had once aroused on The Street. Part of the explanation for Kirk's so-so appearance may lie in the tension that had developed between the Kansas City bandleader and his longtime pianist-arranger, Mary Lou Williams. In actuality, during the engagement at the Door they were only months away from the '42 breakup that ruptured a ten-year-old partnership.

In December, 1942, the canopy of the club carried the name of Henry Nemo and his Orchestra. It was one of the strangest "band" bookings in the history of the club but perhaps indicative of the search for an audience—a problem that the war helped solve, though not in too healthy a style. Nemo was a successful songwriter whose hits included " 'Tis Autumn" and "Don't Take Your Love from Me," but Nemo was a character.

Publisher Lou Levy, who tried managing The Neam before he became the fourth Andrews Sister, recalls *shtik* that went back to Nemo's days as a social director in the Catskills. "He had colossal ideas," Lou observes, "but always on the weird side. Once he asked the owner of the hotel for a wagonload of apples. When they were delivered, Nemo had them piled on the stage of the social hall. Then he asked for another wagonload. The owner knew that The Neam was *meshugge* but he got him more apples. Came show night and Nemo had the band play 'Limehouse Blues.' To the melody, he sang his own words: 'An apple a day keeps the doctor away. An apple a day keeps the doctor away.' As he ran up and down the stage repeating the line, he began throwing apples at the audience. Soon the entire cast joined him in singing and throwing apples.

"For a time, I did a vaudeville act with The Neam. And he himself played the Nut Club down in Greenwich Village. In the vaudeville act, he would dress up as Aunt Jemima and we did the lindy hop together. You know how big and heavy he was, and you can see that I'm much shorter and lighter. But I was quite muscular. And we sure got a big hand when I would lift and twirl him around. Incidentally, he was the first comic to hand a newspaper to guys in his audience and say, 'If you don't like my jokes, read!'

"One of the craziest offstage *shtik* he pulled took place at Sing Sing prison. With lyric writer Sammy Cahn and another character, he once went up to Ossining to put on a show for the prisoners. I think they did the thing in connection with a movie being produced by Vitaphone Studios in Brooklyn. Well, when they were leaving the prison after they did their act, they had to be counted out. Without telling anybody, Nemo doubled back on the line. Naturally, the tally showed one man too many. In seconds, their bus was surrounded by armed guards, who went through it foot by foot. Even after it was clear that there was no escaped prisoner on the bus, they were held up for hours as a search was made of the prison. Finally, they were allowed to leave. Only then did Nemo break down and confess what he had done. The producer fired him on the spot."

Woody Herman, who once approached Nemo for a special song, remembers him as "a wild but talented man and an irrepressible prankster. Some of his cutups were quite innocent—fun for the sake of fun. Once he and a stooge went to R. H. Macy and began measuring the floor. One of them went down on his knees with a tape measure and called out numbers to the other guy, who carefully entered them in a notebook. With all the traffic in the store, it created quite a commotion. But nobody stopped them.

"At some point Nemo left New York and went to the Coast in the hope of breaking into the movies. I believe he did appear in one or two films. But I heard from movie people that funny as he was off-stage, he would freeze when he went before the camera. To get to Hollywood, he traveled across country in a dilapidated, secondhand car. Riding with him was Maurice Duke, now a well-known Hollywood manager and agent. On the second day out, Duke began complaining that there was no sun on his side of the car. After he had repeated this several times, Nemo suddenly swerved the car, made a sharp U turn, and started driving furiously back in the direction from which they had come. 'What the hell are you doing?' Duke demanded. 'You wanted sun,' Nemo shouted. 'Well, now you've got it!'

"On the second day out, Duke, who was lame and walked with a cane, also began complaining that he was having trouble walking. The following day, he seemed to have more difficulty. Nemo listened and said nothing. The next day, when they were going to breakfast, Duke almost toppled over. After a time, he confessed that he thought his legs were really going bad on him. Nemo just went on eating his ham and eggs. But later that day, as they were driving along, Nemo finally told him what he had been doing. Each night after Duke fell asleep, he had been cutting a half inch or so off his cane! Can you imagine that? Funny but kind of cruel, too. Duke took the news rather well, even laughed about it, probably because he was so relieved."

When he appeared at the Door, The Neam was not advertised as a comic. "He did sing some of his songs," Jackie Mills, who played drums on the date, recalls. "But his forte was long comedy monologues when he wasn't making with a fast and furious line of jive. I remember one skit, the closer, which went on for at least ten minutes. He played the judge—also all the characters who came before him for sentencing. He worked hard and he was funny. But the band?" Nemo hardly enhanced the reputation of the Famous Door as a music club. His appearance was the forerunner of other nonmusical bills.

By the spring of '42, as clubs began veering toward a skin policy, the major attraction at the Door was Zorita, the Snake Charmer. Working with a live snake, she stripped until she was wearing little more than the snake. Only when Red Norvo made his record-breaking stand in July, '42—astonishing as it may seem, the septet at first accompanied Zorita in her strip routine—did Irving Alexander decide to throw out the snake-charming bit and bring in a jazz pianist. Later he brought in singer Linda Keene and still later, singer Blue Drake, an ex-Benny Carter chirper.

But as one note does not make a chord, so one or two hot bookings do not a successful club make. By November 1, 1943, the Door had moved out of its quarters at 66 West and located on the northwest corner of 52d and Seventh Avenue, above the House of Chan. Mac Rosen, listed in *Down Beat* as the owner, had come to feel that wartime attendance might fill a club seating five hundred. The opening bill consisted of a John Kirby combo and the Lionel Hampton Orchestra, the latter reportedly being paid the highest fee ever given to a black band in a downtown spot.

During the initial period, the new Door looked like a winner. Even though there were complaints that the Kirby combo had too light a sound for the large room, the Hampton drive pulled the crowds in. The favorable omens were unfortunately premature. The enlarged Door never made New Year's Eve. The management was slow in paying the musicians. When the union yanked the Hampton band, Kirby took his combo into the Riobamba, owned by Arthur Jarwood, and as *Down Beat* put it, "the Door closed with a bang."

Although there were constant rumors of Mob control of clubs, evidence of gangster interest became apparent only when some hood tried to muscle his way into ownership. Musicians claim that a small-time hoodlum named Frankie Carbo made several attempts to take over the Door. One time there was a holdup, a rare occurrence on The Street, engineered, it was believed, not for the take but to exert pressure. On still another evening, a fistfight started in the club. Waiters ran to find a cop. But as was apparently traditional in those days, as soon as trouble started, the cops seemed to vanish. By the time the waiters returned some guy was lying on the floor bleeding from a head wound inflicted with a bar stool. Since an ambulance could then be summoned only by a policeman, the victim had to be taken by cab to Polyclinic Hospital.

When the fight was over and those responsible for starting it were gone, detectives appeared at the club to question onlookers. For the next few weeks, the detectives came periodically looking for possible suspects. It was a blessing in disguise. A number of hoods who occasionally visited the club preferred not to be around when the detectives appeared. They would call up in advance, and when they were told that the cops were still active on the case, they made themselves scarce.

One of the club's employees vividly recalls the evening that a Carbo stooge shattered the bar mirror with a stool. A fight started between Carbo and another racket guy named Arnie Johnson. Club procedure was to push guys who were fighting out onto the street. Outside, as the two continued swinging at each other, a crippled fellow came by. He had no feet and no legs, just a torso on a skateboard. He propelled himself along by pushing against the sidewalk with his hands. Somehow he got entangled with the fighters. He tried to maneuver around but could not. One of the guys kicked his board and almost turned him over. In desperation, he tried to run the guy down. At that point, a bodyguard pulled a gun and began aiming it at the cripple. But the cripple kept twisting and turning his board about so that the bodyguard could not take a shot. By then a crowd began gathering, and the fighters, who never liked witnesses, decided they had had enough.

With the demise of Famous Door III in December of '43, the well-known name disappeared from The Street for about three years. Early in '47 a new Door opened at 56 West 52d with trumpeter Red Allen as the first attraction. It remained in action for about two years, benefiting from the drawing power of established Street jazzmen like Ben Webster, Roy Eldridge, Stuff Smith, Art Tatum, and Dizzy Gillespie. The great Ella Fitzgerald made a stand in September of '47, followed by lag-along tenorman Lester Young.

In the spring of the year trumpeter Max Kaminsky played as part of a sextet led by Jack Teagarden. Drummer Big Sid Catlett led the alternate combo. Kaminsky recalls that the moment the combo finished its set, Big T would amble out the Door with his horn and wander into the Three Deuces, a few doors to the west, or across the street into Jimmy Ryan's and sit in with whatever combo was in the competing club.

After a time, the manager of the Door caught on to what was happening. "You're supposed to be appearing exclusively at the

The end of the Famous Door.

Arnold Shaw

Famous Door," he would remonstrate with Teagarden. "That's why your name is on the canopy—so that people who want to hear Jack Teagarden will patronize us."

Big T's composure could not be ruffled. Looking at the furious manager through half-closed eyes and with a little, self-satisfied smile on his lips, he would drawl, Texas-style: "Jes' bein' neighborly."

The five musicians in Big T's combo had their own problems with their leader. Big T could not resist a hard-luck story told by an out-of-work musician. As a result, the sextet would expand to a septet, octet or nonet. Came the end of the week, and T's musicians had the trying task of informing their new associate(s) that there was no green stuff for the additional men. They were each receiving the munificent sum of $75 a week, and it frequently took a bit of pressure to extract even that pittance from the management.

With occasional lapses, the Door existed into the heyday of the strippers. And having offered such stellar attractions as Camille, the "Six-Foot Sex Girl," it had the doubtful honor of being among a group of clubs closed down by the State Liquor Authority in January, 1950. The charges were that performers were permitted to mingle with (read "solicit") customers. By February of '50 *Down Beat* noted that there was only one music club left in Swing Alley, Jimmy Ryan's. But the name of the Door was too magical to stay permanently out of sight so long as there was an available store or cellar on The Street. It cropped up again in the sixties on a nondescript club, this time on the north side between Sixth and Seventh avenues, just about where a well-known discount record-radio store, Rabson's, was situated in the thirties and forties. When the New York Hilton was being erected a block to the north, the site of the final Door was torn up to make way for the J. C. Penney skyscraper. In some incongruous way, the demolition crew left only the lintel of the doorway resting on its two vertical supports. Over piles of brick rubble, through this inverted U, one could see the skeletal structure of the Hilton as it went up. Clearly visible on the lintel spanning the void, as in an *avant-garde* movie, were the words "Famous Door."

At various times, there have been Doors in Boston, New Orleans, Baltimore and Toronto. Unrelated to each other, they remain a lingering reminder of the club that was originally launched by a group of radio musicians who wanted a place of their own to jaw and jam. Through the years, I have wandered into these remembrances of things past, hoping vaguely that I might find the original door that was autographed by musical and other celebrities of the mid-thirties. No such luck. But sometimes you hear a strain that brings back with a rush the sound of Basie or Woody as it echoed through 52d St.

Tape 23 . . . ARTHUR JARWOOD

Today, Arthur Jarwood is in the wholesale clothing business with an office in the Sperry Rand Building on Avenue of the Americas between 51st and 52d streets. "My street address," he says, "is 52 West 52d. But my office is right over where the Famous Door was in the days of Swing Street at No. 66. I really haven't moved too far.

"I began as a club owner," Jarwood recalled, "with a little club on East 50th known as The Vogue. I had a good advertising sense and publicized the place with a line that read, 'Life begins at 40,' and lower on the ad or flier, it would say, 'East 50th St.' That was the address: 40 East 50th. It was a successful operation. I used to sell motion pictures of prizefights as well and disposed of The Vogue when it became necessary for me to spend time in California. I sold it one night in Dave's Blue Room.

"Later I was involved with the Frolics Club on Broadway. It was around 1938, and the club was situated directly over the Winter Garden, where Hawaii Kai is now located. I brought Louis Prima up from New Orleans to play the opening show. We had Joe E. Lewis, a singer, Fox and Ames, a dance team, and Oshins and Lessy. Unfortunately, Prima couldn't play a show. His was a performing band, a jazz band, not a 'pit band.' We persuaded the Famous Door to book him and we hired Ralph Watkins, who later became the well-known club owner, as the show-and-dance band.

"I was involved with the original Kelly's Stable on 51st St. near Seventh Avenue. It had a huge bar. So long as there were enough standees, we were in the black, even when the tables seemed empty. The Harlem Highlanders started at the joint. Baby Lawrence, a great tap dancer, made them.

"I built O'Leary's Barn on 52d St. It was opposite what once was the Hickory House and now is Pier 52. The decor of O'Leary's Barn came from the Twentieth Century-Fox picture about the Chicago fire. After a time I sold out to Ralph Watkins and George Lynch. That was when O'Leary's Barn became Kelly's Stable.

"One night I went into the Famous Door, then owned by two fellows, a Mutt and Jeff team, Felshin and Brooks. They had a girlie show and the place was empty. 'How can you expect to do business in a famous jazz joint with girls?' I asked. They were obviously fed up. And so I bought it. And I was associated with it from 1940 through 1943.

"Those were the years of Red Norvo and Mildred Bailey, Andy Kirk and the Clouds of Joy, Billie Holiday and Linda Keene. I guess the strangest booking was Zorita working with Red Norvo. She was not a stripper, mind you, but an exotic snake dancer. We had Art Tatum, whom all the musicians called God. We had Morgana King, a singer who had Mildred Bailey in her and a bit of Billie. We never had Peggy Lee, but she came in night after night to hear Billie. Every singer in the world came to listen to Billie.

"Billie was a fantastic performer in this period, with an enormous following. We didn't have to advertise. We didn't need publicity. Word got around and the club would be packed. And she was musically at her peak.

"Chauncey Olman, a knowledgeable show business attorney, was handling Billie at this time. I guess she went to him for advice, and he became her manager after a time. He represented some of the best talent of the day—Pearl Bailey, Thelma Carpenter, Lionel Hampton, Teddy Wilson, and later Eartha Kitt and Tony Bennett.

"In addition to the Door, I had an interest in the Onyx, Three Deuces, and Pick-A-Rib. The Onyx was a name that was floating free at the time. When an opportunity developed to acquire a room across the street from the Door, we decided to call it the Onyx. The name had great jazz associations. After all, it really was the 'Cradle of Swing.' Eventually, I sold out to Mike Westerman, who ran the club for us.

"The Three Deuces was next to the Famous Door. We called it the Plantation Club after a time. Off 52d St. I had the Riobamba—and this eventually led to my leaving The Street.

"The Riobamba was on 57th St., practically next door to Hammacher and Schlemmer, between Lexington and Third avenues. We opened with Jane Froman, who gave us a great start. Then business was so-so until we booked a new kid named Frank Sinatra. He came in an unknown and went out with a weekly paycheck of fifteen hundred dollars. It was in the Riobamba that the fainting thing really started, and it was our press agents, Gertrude Bayne and Irving Zussman, who coined words like 'swoonatra' and shortened his tag to The Voice. He came in as an extra added attraction—a comic named Walter O'Keefe was the star—and went out The King.

"After Sinatra, business dropped. It was 1943, and clubs had a tough time finding customers as we got deeper into the war. That was when I gave up my 52d St. rooms. But before I did, we moved the Famous Door to the corner of 52d and Seventh. For our first show, we booked Pearl Bailey, one of Chauncey's clients, as our star. We had Nemo Roth write special music. And the band was Lionel Hampton's, another Chauncey Olman client. Incidentally, we paid Pearl Bailey, star of our show, just thirty-five dollars. We raised it to seventy-five when business shot up. Pearl was dynamite. But it was Hampton that broke things up. Every time he did 'Flying Home,' we had a visit from the Chinese. The whole building bounced to the beat of the band!

"This was the only Famous Door that had any room. We could seat three hundred easily, where the old Doors could crowd only one hundred, but tight. We raised the minimum from a dollar fifty to two dollars. There still was no cover charge. That was 52d St. style. We offered two shows a night. But there was continuous music. And the shows! Hampton didn't know of so many minutes on and so many minutes off. When that band got going, they played until he collapsed. That Door was a great, great club. And it did great—for a while. Unfortunately, it was a short while.

"But 52d St. always did great—at this time anyway—even if some of the clubs had the miseries, as some always did. I think that pub crawling really started on The Street. Patrons seldom went to one club. You just went to The Street. And then you wandered from club to club, depending on whom you wanted to hear. We didn't push people to drink, though our doorman would gently suggest another when the entry was getting overcrowded. Excitement spilled over into The Street itself. It was always like a festival night in Greenwich Village's Little Italy. Half of the action was on the sidewalk.

"Harold Minsky had a club directly opposite the Door when it was at 66 West. He offered the kind of fare with which the family name Minsky is associated. It was in good taste. So The Street combined music, burlesque comedy [at the Club 18], and good, raucous entertainment [Leon & Eddie's]. You know there was once the Gay White

Way. That was when Broadway was the big attraction in New York City. But in this period, Broadway didn't mean a thing. It was 52d St. that was known throughout the world.

"It was one of the first downtown streets where the racial thing didn't mean a thing. Audiences considered it a privilege to be with black musicians, to try to understand what they were doing. They couldn't care less whether a cat was black or green. They were carried away by the music. They lived the music in a way that reminds me of Freddie Finklehoffe.

"Freddie, who was co-author of *Brother Rat,* was married to Ella Logan. One night he came to the Riviera on the Jersey side of the Harlem River carrying two huge boxes. Each contained a mink coat. He was bringing them for Ella to select the one she liked best. A friend who was at the Riviera asked Freddie: 'You could have any of those great-looking show girls in the line here. What do you see in Ella?' And Freddie replied: 'Are you kidding? Did you ever hear that girl sing 'Take Me Out to the Ball Game?' And see the way she flips her hair back when she sings. Man, that's the living end! What else is there?'

"Well, that's the way 52d St. people dug the music and the musicians. They couldn't begin to think of color. On weekends, the crowd was a young college group. During the week you had every show business personality in town. There were tourists, of course, who gravitated toward Leon & Eddie's. But The Street's *aficionados* were knowledgeable, sophisticated, generally well-fixed people who came for the music. You take the gambling out of Las Vegas and keep the high-salaried star performers, and you still wouldn't have the excitement on the Strip that we had on The Street.

"Basically, twenty-five to thirty percent of the week-night customers were people who knew the performers, knew the club owners, and who felt themselves part of a big family. It was an in group, but an in group that did not necessarily live in New York. You could live in Chicago, San Francisco or even Europe, and still be *in*. It was a question of how you felt about the music and something that you shared with others who felt as you did, and whom you got to know just by sitting crushed next to them at one of the mini-mini tables. You dug anybody who dug the music, and they immediately became part of your family as you were part of theirs.

"It's lamentable that it's gone. But 52d St. was economically and physically outclassed. We went to bigger rooms—like the Door with the three hundred seats—to try to absorb the increased cost of performers and employees and the mounting cost of food and liquor. But even the bigger rooms that prospered for a while lost out when performer costs became astronomical because of what Vegas and Miami were paying. Performers are transitory. But when they're hot, they take the business with them. You can have a great club—attractive decor, good food, excellent service, good location—but without the names that glow, you won't get the business. 52d St. was priced out of existence.

"Today, you look in *Cue* if you're planning to spend the night out in New York. Things are spread all over the city. But in those days, you just got in a cab, told the driver to take you to The Street, and then you just walked from Seventh Avenue east or Fifth Avenue west, and crawled into places that had people you wanted to hear. Sometimes it didn't matter whose name was on the canopy. Performers were constantly sitting in. Name guys would sit in with unknowns, and unknowns were always trying to sit in with the stars. And the stars didn't complain. What counted was your talent.

"You see The Street got started with musicians. And musicians remained customers. You couldn't fool them. When they heard something good, they spread the word—and fast. It was a time when guys lived to discover new talent. It became theirs when they could say, 'I heard Garner before anybody knew him from the black keys.' And from the musicians and show people, the word spread to the columnists, and the next you knew, there was a line outside the club. Anything new was shopped, shopped by the in people, the very people who really wanted to keep it for themselves."

Sybil Olman, widow of Chauncey Olman and sister of Mac Rosen, had this to add about the demise of The Street: "I think that the Rockefellers had a little something to do with destroying 52d. Arthur and Chauncey frequently talked about buying the brownstones. But the Rockefellers were paying good prices. They obviously had far-ranging plans, whose fruit you can now see. Instead of small clubs, excitement, great music, what do we have now? Tall buildings and banks. How excited can you get about that?"

Phoebe Pincus Jacobs, who is the Rainbow Room's talent buyer, adds: "A woman was safe on 52d St. in those days. The clubs closed at four. Artie Jarwood's Pic-A-Rib closed at five. And Dave's Blue Room never closed. They served liquor in coffee cups after curfew—I think it got Dave into hot water at one point. 52d St. was like a big, beautiful matronly woman embracing all people. This was the only street in the world where you could walk alone and never be lonely. You could talk to the first person you met. It was like one big house party. Where else could black and whites get to know each other, work together, and form lifelong friendships? There was no other place at that time.

"I knew The Street, or at least my family knew it, from Prohibition on. I was just thirteen when my father owned a brownstone speakeasy called The Calais. Frances Faye pounded the piano so hard it had to be tuned every week. In time, it was the clubs that became the stars. A room like the Famous Door could introduce an unknown, and if he had talent, he could become a star overnight. And this happened in rooms that were hot and smoky, crowded and packed, with out-of-tune pianos, crummy stages and lousy service. But who cared when you heard somebody great? The Street was a street of greats. . . ."

18. Wartime and Postwar Clubs

The doormen of 52d St. were much like Lindy waiters, particularly in the latter days of The Street. They refused to restrain their creative impulses. One lapel grabber, after enumerating the sundry strippers on the bill, would add: "And we give green stamps!" Whether it was a matter of abbreviated leases or not, the life expectancy of the 52d St. clubs grew shorter during and after the war. And quite a number came and went like ephemerids.

In May, 1944, the Downbeat popped up at 66 West, where a late model of the Yacht Club had been moored for little more than two months. (The Yacht had berthed at a spot vacated by a Famous Door.) One of the longer-lived of the latter-day clubs, the Downbeat enjoyed a life-span of more than three years. Dizzy Gillespie, having been the star attraction at the Yacht when it sailed, remained and was joined by Coleman "Bean" Hawkins, who became one of the Downbeat's steadiest tenants.

Bean was a good vis-à-vis for bop potentate Gillespie since he was both a modern and a moldy fig. He had grown up with the New Orleans and swing styles, playing first with Mamie Smith's Jazz Hounds ('21–'23) and then for more than a decade with Fletcher Henderson ('23–'34). But just before he opened at the new club, Bean sponsored and played with the first bop combo recorded on wax, a group involving Dizzy, pianist Clyde Hart and drummer Max Roach. Inevitably, the Hawk was caught in the crossfire between the moderns and the figs, regarded as too old by some of the bopsters and with suspicion by the Dixieland and New Orleans crowd.

Originally a jazzman who improvised by "running changes"—using chord progressions as structures from which to select notes—Bean moved in time in the modern direction of rhythmic and thematic improvisation. But even after Lester Young became the popular leader of the cool school—the introspective, soft-textured, behind-the-beat style of tenor—Bean continued using hard reeds and an open mouthpiece to produce the lush, throbbing, ballsy sound he made famous. "Stuffy" was one of the notable sides he recorded during his stay at the Downbeat. Later, in '47 he cut "Picasso," a highly original, five-minute bravura selection in which he was entirely unaccompanied.

It is interesting that when people think of jazz musicians, they inevitably associate the art with the more flamboyant, destructive and unstable performers. Hawkins was a family man, who took care of his mother and grandmother and lived quietly with his wife and three children. And after a night of blowing at the Downbeat, he was content to return to the family apartment on West 153d St. in Manhattan. In a sense, 52d St. was for him almost as long a gig as his eleven years with Fletcher Henderson.

For Billie Holiday the Downbeat was home through most of '44, '45 and '46; and when she was not at 66 West, her name was on the canopy of the Spotlite, another wartime "baby," at 56 West. Although in its weekly listings *The New Yorker* kept referring to her as "moody" and suggesting that she could not be depended on to show up, *Metronome* found her "the best buy" on The Street in March, 1946. Perched at the Downbeat when Billie settled for an extended, if interrupted stay in August, 1944, "Hawk" was back in January when Jay McShann brought a big band into the place early in 1945.

McShann's was the first big band to play The Street almost since the days of Count Basie and the Herman Herd at the Famous Door. The Army had taken out of circulation the Oklahoma–Kansas City leader whose band had made a stir in '41 with "Confessin' the Blues"—an unheard-of sale of 81,000 on Decca—and whose sidemen included blues shouter Walter Brown and the then-unknown Charlie Parker.

Bird was not part of the group that McShann brought into the Downbeat in January, 1945, after his medical discharge from the military. It was a hastily assembled ensemble, and McShann could not find his original library. Nevertheless, *Metronome* found it "a re-

markably powerful outfit, one which jumps as few others in the business do, one which provides hour after hour of moving jazz, of driving
solos, of top-notch blues singing and piano." Though Bird was not in
the lineup, the original confessor of the blues was. *Metronome* characterized Walter Brown as "perhaps the most persuasive of carollers
of the exploits of wastrels, wanderers and the woes of uncontrolled
drunkards and illicit lovers. He's still bending notes and breaking
phrases with the imperious nasal enunciation which springs from a
wonderful sense of rhythm or maybe a bad sinus."

Lloyd Grimes, better known as Tiny Grimes, was a sideman for
whom wartime 52d St. provided an opportunity to front his own
combo. A self-taught guitarist from Newport News, Virginia, Grimes
encountered Art Tatum and Slam Stewart at a jam in Los Angeles,
where he became part of a trio who worked together from '41 to '44.
Largely to amuse themselves during long evenings, they developed a
trick of interpolating odd quotations in their improvisations. The
more incongruous the quotation, the more pleased they were—like a
phrase from "Yankee Doodle" in "Embraceable You," or a quote
from "The Campbells Are Coming" in "Body and Soul."

The opening of Tondelayo's (where Erroll Garner got his start) in
September, 1944, found Tiny fronting a trio that included pianist
Clyde Hart and bassist Oscar Pettiford, who was in between jobs of
his own combo. The gig came at almost the same moment that Grimes
landed a date on Savoy Records and called in Charlie Parker, who
used to come into Tondelayo's and jam with him. For students of
Bird, these are the earliest small combo sides made by the supremely
gifted improviser after he left the Jay McShann band.

From Tondelayo's, a comparatively short gig, Grimes moved to the
Downbeat, where he joined Hawk and Lady Day. During the next two
years, he played the club almost as frequently as Holiday and Hawkins. In the course of these engagements, he dropped the device of
making cute (to some) or annoying (to others) quotations during his
solos. In 1946, during an almost six-month stay at the club, he was
briefly reunited with his old boss, Art Tatum, who also performed
frequently at the Downbeat in '45 and '46.

Playing opposite Tiny in the fall of '46 was Trummy Young, a
trombonist with such jug ears that you had the temptation to grab
hold and lift him by them, as LBJ had once done to one of his cocker

spaniels. Born in Savannah, Georgia, and raised in Washington, D.C., James Osborne Young played with three distinguished big bands: Earl Hines ('34–'37), Jimmie Lunceford ('37–'43) and Charles Barnet ('43–'44). A singer as well as sliphorn player, he attracted attention on a hit record of "Margie," recorded with the Lunceford band in 1938.

In a sense, most of these were interim bookings for the Downbeat, despite the distinction of some of the music delivered. Coleman Hawkins brought the crowd in '44; Tatum rang the cash register in '46; but Billie Holiday, in good voice or bad, always was a draw. During 1947 the club presented Eddie Heywood early in the summer, Dizzy in July and August, Ella Fitzgerald in September, and Lester Young in October and November. It was a good, eclectic lineup of names and sounds. But by 1948 the Downbeat name was gone from the brownstone at 66 West, and in its place was the Carousel, a club that traded on skin, not music, and the unbuttoned humor of B. S. Pully.

The name Downbeat appeared again, not on The Street but on West 54th, where in '52 someone established Le Downbeat (no less). Studious-looking pianist Billy Taylor and mallet-murdering vibraharpist Terry Gibbs occupied the small bandstand during much of its two-year storefront existence.

"Spotlite" was the title of an instrumental recorded by Coleman Hawkins and the 52d St. All-Stars in February, 1946. It was also the name of a wartime club situated at 56 West 52d that led a bright, if brief, boppish two-year existence. It presented some of The Street's standbys like Billie Holiday, Harry "The Hipster" Gibson and Billy Daniels. Coleman Hawkins occupied the bandstand for much of '46, as did Dizzy Gillespie. But its fleeting claim to fame seems to be based on the first appearance of two modern jazzmen.

Drummer Stan Levey contends that the Spotlite was the scene of Charlie Parker's "first gig as a leader, and it was also the first time I really had a chance to hear him play. Oh, I'd heard his record of 'Swingmatism' with Jay McShann. My first impression of Charlie's playing was that he was a sort of Pied Piper. I'd never heard anything like it. I didn't really know what he was doing, but it made me feel good to listen to him."

Trombonist J. J. Johnson is not nearly as well known as Parker.

But when he left Basie in '46, he frequently sat in with Dizzy's quintet at the Spotlite. Musicians were amazed at a dexterity and precision that hardly seemed possible on a slide instrument. Soon J.J. was fronting his own combo at the club, performing with an old felt beanie hanging on the bell of his horn.

The general public reacted more strongly to the antics of Harry Gibson, the hipster humorist, then enjoying the notoriety of a *Time* attack as the bop misleader of American youth. A forerunner of pianist-satirist Victor Borge, Gibson was the creator of such timeless, and harmless, ditties as "I Stay Brown All Year 'Roun," "Get Your Juices at the Deuces," and "Who Put the Benzedrine in Mrs. Murphy's Ovaltine?," his most popular number.

To some observers of the 52d St. scene, the Spotlite was something of an enigma. Clark Monroe, in whose Harlem club the bopsters did much of their woodshedding, was the manager and acknowledged owner. But over the Spotlite's running expense—in '46 it presented two bands with a personnel of thirty musicians—lurked the sinister shadow of the Mob. Although its ample treasury helped tide clubs over seasonal slumps, the vice from which it drew its revenues was a time bomb.

"Jazz in New York stinks," said Norman Granz, producer of Jazz at the Philharmonic, after a '46 visit to the Spotlite. "Even the drummers on 52d St. sound like Dizzy."

Of all the short-lived clubs, it was Dixon's that enjoyed the greatest excitement during a less-than-a-year run and briefly revived memories of The Street in its days of musical glory. Dixon's was the old Club 18, managed by Freddy Lamb, and relocated at 131 West between Sixth and Seventh avenues. Refurbished with thick rugs and orchid-colored lights, it presented an unknown quartet whose main achievement was that it played Sandy's Bar & Grill in Paterson, New Jersey. The Joe Mooney Quartet brought a stream of eager customers who kept the joint jumping during the fall of '46.

It was the enthusiasm of *Down Beat,* specifically of an editor named Michael Levin, that started the commotion. What impressed Mix, as Levin signed himself, was the modern, fresh-sounding harmonies explored by the group—an exotic mixture of Debussy and Prokofiev. Led by accordionist Joe Mooney, who was lame and who sang à la Nat Cole, the quartet consisted of clarinet, guitar and bass.

The Joe Mooney quartet created a furor at Dixon's: Jack Hotop (guitar), Gate Frega (bass), Andy Fitzgerald (clarinet), and Mooney (accordion).

Down Beat

SRO audiences vigorously applauded the Mooney versions of "Just a Gigolo" and "It Might As Well Be Spring." During the engagement, its popularity led to a thirteen-week program on ABC. *Time* magazine welcomed its subtle sounds as a delightful contrast to the "screaming" of the preceding years.

Once the Mooney Quartet departed, Dixon's failed to maintain its box office. By the fall of 1947 the sign at 131 West read Club Troubadour. Saxophonist Georgie Auld led a swinging combo and brought in outstanding jazz performers like Mary Lou Williams, Anita O'Day and possibly Mildred Bailey. But the existence of the Troubadour was even briefer than that of Dixon's. Apparently, a Louis Jordan booking proved a disaster. And before long, the premises were occupied by a Chinese restaurant, Ben Yee. By then many of the clubs east of Sixth Avenue were featuring striptease while the joints west of the avenue housed so many Chinese eateries that the area became known as Chow Mein Lane. When Ben Yee took over the Troubadour address, a columnist wrote: "52d St. is being strangled by a G-string dipped in soya sauce."

One of the fastest in-and-outers of the postwar era was a club called the Keyboard. At the beginning of the summer of '46, it opened at 54 West with a Wild Bill Davison combo. Drummer Danny Alvin, another Jimmy Ryan's regular, crossed the street and settled briefly at the Keyboard. It was like a summer resort. Came Labor Day and it was gone.

Longer-lived were two clubs of the early fifties. The fate of La Zambra, a three-year-old at 127 West, was linked with one performer, guitarist Vicente Gomez. Typed a Latin or Andalusian Eddie Condon, Gomez not only was proficient on his instrument but possessed Eddie's gift of gab.

The New Yorker encountered problems in classifying La Commedia, a shorter-lived club near Jimmy Ryan's. Located at 59 West, La Commedia went from "small and cheerful" to "supper club" and back to "small and cheerful." In actuality, it was much more of a music club than La Zambra. During its brief existence, it presented a succession of fine, if somewhat offbeat, black singers. These included fat-mama Sylvia Sims; "tiger-lily" singer Thelma Carpenter, who recently came out of retirement; and Alberta Hunter, the blues singer-songwriter, who was co-writer of Bessie Smith's debut disc, "Downhearted Blues." It is not an inappropriate note on which to end this tale of The Street's latter-day clubs.

Tape 24 . . . Sherman Edwards

Composer-lyricist of *1776,* the Broadway hit musical, Sherman Edwards played piano on 52d St. before and after World War II.

"When I returned after the war," he said, "The Street was going to the strippers. I'm talking about the late forties and early fifties. But even though the emphasis was on dames and not music, good music was being heard. It was the jazz combos that played for the peelers. You played different numbers, things like 'Temptation,' that were good for bumps and grinds, with a lot of tom-tom stuff.

"I worked quite a lot with Sol Yaged, the clarinetist. He was the living epitome of Benny Goodman. It was just as if a Dybbuk of Benny had moved into Sol's body. He even looked like Benny and, of course, played like him. He would think nothing of phoning you at six o'clock in the morning, just about the time you were bedding down after a long evening's work, and asking you to listen over the phone to a Goodman record that had him all charged up. He was absolutely out of his mind when it came to Benny—and he still is.

"When we came back to the clubs after the war, the influence of the underground criminal element was rather strong. I remember a club where we used to go into the kitchen between sets. There was a table where we played cards. The show here was always greater than out front. The cook was a faggot who was a fine chef and very amusing. Occasionally, the strippers, some of whom were lesbians and exhibitionists, would do each other.

"One night a prowl car pulled up as we were getting up to leave—after a private after-hours show—and we all went back so the dicks could see the exhibition. There was another social phenomenon taking shape at this time—the disappearance of the professional prostitute. In their place, you had young actresses and models, really legitimate chicks, who needed the one hundred dollars a night so they could keep going.

"But what stands out vividly in my memory is a night when our card table was occupied by four or five hoodlum types. They were sitting and talking very quietly. It was very controlled, almost like an overdone movie scene. And it was evident that they were talking about a contract to kill somebody. I remember hearing that the hit would be made in the Williamsburg section of Brooklyn under the bridge—'And we'll leave him there in the car,' one of the hoods said. We got out of the kitchen as quickly and as quietly as we could, despite our curiosity. Sure enough, about a week later, the papers carried the story of a Greenpoint Mafia guy who was found full of bullets in an abandoned car under the Williamsburg Bridge. What we heard never got out of the club. We didn't talk about it to anybody, not even among ourselves.

"There was another strange scene in some of the clubs. Sometimes in the course of an evening, big cartons would arrive. They could be brought in only by passing them over the heads of customers, with the customers holding them up and passing them from hand to hand until they got to the kitchen. After the club closed, we'd go into the kitchen, and there'd be an auction. The cartons contained merchandise consigned to Fifth Avenue stores. One night I was able to buy a fabulous Balenciaga creation for forty dollars. It must have been priced at five hundred or six hundred dollars. In other auctions, I picked up watches and jewelry.

"I won't name a certain madame, since she's happily married now. But her headquarters was in one of the clubs. She sat at a corner table that had a phone. Visiting firemen were steered to her by hackies and others. She would call Bar & Grill on 49th, near the Van Cortland Hotel, where her girls were waiting at a table. As soon as the call came in, the girls would leave and meet the guys at the madame's apartment, which was on 58th St.

"One time when I played the Three Deuces, Zorita was the headliner. She did this weird strip with a snake—a live snake! She used this cockamamie script that was delivered by Kiki Young, who was very elegant and sounded more British than Noel Coward. In dramatic Shakespearian tones, he would narrate this legend of a young prince who had been changed into a snake and could recover his human form only when some maiden fell in love with him and allowed him to give her a good bang. Zorita did this wild dance, writhing on the ground and carrying on erotically. Sometimes there'd be just a half-a-dozen guys in the joint, loaded to the ears and spending all kinds of money while the other gals made up to them.

"In this era, the clubs were selling skin. Music was secondary. You might say that The Street was 'stripped' of its greatness."

19. Stripty-second Street*

"I brought nudity to 52d St.," says Harold Minsky of the famous family whose surname is a synonym for stripping and who is today still producing burlesque shows in Las Vegas. "But it was done in good taste—like the club I opened. Believe me, I know the difference."

A number of celebrants of the rite of undressing-to-music would challenge this priority claim. For one, Leo Bernstein, owner of the Club Samoa, who also boasted that the South Sea island knickknacks in his establishment at 60 West cost more than $30,000. (In the mid-fifties he also owned the Pigalle.) For another, Danny del Rio of the club of the same name. Leon and Eddie merit consideration, though they would be ruled out as latecomers. Still another contender for the doubtful honor would be Albert Gilbert, who fitted the interior of a brownstone at 9 West with banisters shaped like girls' legs, order bells cut like female breasts and a bar designed like a bed. If Gilbert had not been estopped from opening his Chez Burlesque by Mayor Fiorello La Guardia's ban on burlesque, he would probably have taken the prize since he was building his strippery early in 1937.

As it is, Harold Minsky is doubtless on solid ground with his claim of priority. He established the 51 Club in 1937–38. Stripping was, in short, part of the 52d St. scene almost from the beginning and flourished for years before it turned into a destructive virus. The 51 Club was on the north side of The Street, just about where the saturnine CBS Building stands today. It had, in fact, the same number as CBS's

* Columnist-author Louis Sobel's colorful phrase.

mailing address. At the time of its founding, Harold was running the theaters for the Minsky family. (They controlled three of the five burlesque houses in the Times Square area alone.) He wanted to do something on his own.

There is also the possibility that he was reacting to the fulminations of New York's "Little Flower," who succeeded in outlawing the word "burlesque" in 1937. After a time, burlesque houses were permitted to reopen under the umbrella of a word popularized by the great Ziegfeld—"Follies"—with the understanding that there would be no vulgar stripping or dirty comedy material.

"I had the decor designed in the best of taste," Minsky states, "by a prominent decorator who was responsible for the polished interiors of Hampshire House in New York and the famous Camellia Room in Chicago. When I opened, Louis Prima was down the block with Martha Raye at the Famous Door—right next to Leon & Eddie's, who didn't bring in a stripper until I sold my club in '40 or '41. Dave's Blue Room was across the street.

"I used girls appearing in our theaters, the more attractive and refined of them. There was Charmaine, a stately stripper, who did her act to the music of 'Sophisticated Lady.' I featured Georgia Sothern, who did six minutes of bumps and grinds to the fast music of 'Hold That Tiger' and generally came offstage needing oxygen.

"There is no burlesque without comedy. And I presented many comics who went on to make their mark on Broadway and on the screen. Phil Silvers, for one, and Hank Henry. Tommy Moe Raft is still working in Las Vegas at the Silver Slipper. I used a duo then known as Pully & Gump. Until then, they had never performed in public—only at private parties. That was B. S. Pully's first club job.

"Whatever anyone may say about burlesque, it was a great training ground for the comedians—like vaudeville, like the Borscht Circuit. Audiences were tough, since they were just waiting for the strippers to come on. To make them laugh—just to keep them quiet—you had to be good. A comedian learned the art that made for great clowns like Bert Lahr, Jack Benny, Phil Silvers, Jimmy Durante, and Jackie Gleason. All of them came out of burlesque. Sure, you had to take pies in the face as the third banana. But you played in the sketches, and when you finally became top banana, you were schooled, you were a pro. Not like the kids of today that become stand-up comics overnight.

"At the 51 Club, we could present only a capsule version of a burlesque show. The size of the stage was confining and forced intimacy on us. No broad scenes—no pun. We used a five-piece band—no jazz. The girls stripped to things like 'The Mooch.' Later they'd use 'The Man with the Golden Arm' or 'The Theme from Dragnet.' Nowadays, they use 'The Theme from Mission—Impossible.' Bumps and grinds require music with strong accents.

"I operated the club for about four years. But as we became involved in the war, the entertainment tax, the curfew and all that jazz—and Mayor La Guardia got tougher and tougher—I sold Club 51 to Harry Finkelstein. He was Georgia Sothern's husband. I went down to New Orleans after that to look over theaters that the Minsky family operated in the South."

About the time that Harold Minsky was leaving for New Orleans, Leon and Eddie added Sherry Britton to their regular bill of fare. Like Eddie Davis' *double-entendre* song parodies, Sherry's act was only mildly risqué and gave no offense to the family-type audience that frequented the club. L & E were not troubled by the police, even though Sherry remained at the joint all through the war years when a tightening of morals led to an all-out war on burlesque. Sherry's seven-year stand makes it clear that it was not stripping in itself that brought the downfall of The Street.

By the time Sherry was moving to the Club Samoa in '47–'48 *Time* noted that "the town hadn't seen so many strippers since Fiorello La Guardia sent them packing." Actually, the word "stripper" was no longer in use, certainly not among the peelers themselves. The La Guardia onslaught had motivated the substitution of "exotic dancer," "veil dancer," "snake dancer." To publicist Eddie Jaffee, H. L. Mencken suggested "ecdysiast."

One of the first jazz clubs to react to the wartime search of servicemen for something more spectacular than music was the Famous Door. Jaffee recalls that stripper Zorita had a habit of poking her live snake in the face of customers, which was not difficult to do, considering the size of the club. One patron became so upset that he pulled a gun and threatened to shoot the snake and Zorita. Only the cool of owner Arthur Jarwood, who happened to be in the club, prevented a catastrophe. Columnist Danton Walker's comment on Zorita's act: "The problem is that she has taped both ends of her snake instead of herself."

The new emphasis on stripping made problems for singers. "If you wanted to keep an overheated guy cool," says Morgana King, who had to compete with the peelers, "and hold his interest, you had to have a hypnotic sound—calming but interesting. Like putting a baby to sleep. I had to compete with the B-girls too."

Among the strippers, Eddie Jaffee thinks of Lili St. Cyr as "a great star who could have made a lot more money than she did. But she seemed to have a special deal going at the Samoa, where she stripped for almost as many years as Sherry Britton did at Leon & Eddie's. After she became a high-bracket performer, I went to see her about handling her publicity. I told her I would get her a write-up in *Vogue*. She wasn't interested. I mentioned *Life*. No reaction. I pitched *Look* at her. Still no interest. Finally, in desperation, I asked her what I could do to get her as a client. She had a quick response: 'Introduce me to Marlon Brando.' "

Variety shared Jaffee's enthusiasm for Lili. In its knowledgeable view, "she rubbed a bit of much-needed glamor on The Street" even in the days of its decline. Possessed of the lovely figure of a model, she reversed the strip act, putting things on instead of taking them off. A bathtub sequence was her starting point, and she thereafter slowly got dressed.

Although there was a certain amount of policy switching, with some clubs returning to a music format, after 1948 G-strings were more and more used for stripping. In February, 1949, *The New Yorker* observed: "Jazz is hard to find in midtown. On 52d St. it has given way to a discouraging collection of stripteasers."

In a door-to-door survey, which I personally made around 1951, the strip joints outnumbered the jazz clubs by seven to three. On the south side, where many of the eighteen brownstones were already shuttered, there was the red-canopied Flamingo at No. 38, "No Cover or Minimum at Bar" and pictures of no-name strippers in white frames. Club Nocturne at No. 54 was noncommittal. Club del Rio at No. 60 featured a shot of Kathryn Case in tiger garb, holding her hair in the air. Club Samoa at No. 60, with a yellow front and dirty yellow canopy, offered a bill headed by Winnie Garrett, the Flaming Red-head, and Georgia Sothern, the Wow Girl; it also displayed garish pictures of strippers whose names could be meaningful only to cognoscenti. Huddling near the corner of Sixth was the Famous Door at No. 64, separated by several shuttered spots from the Three Deuces at

No. 70. While the Door advertised Jimmy Valentine & Band, there was a shot of Janeen holding her breasts, along with faded photos of some no-name strippers.

On the north side of the decadent Street, Club Ha-Ha, with a yellow canopy and façade at No. 39, featured Sherry Corday and Toy Carol Lowe. Between the Lido at No. 41 and Harem at No. 57 (with a special-shaped canopy), sat the red-canopied Moulin Rouge, whose boast was Melba, the Toast of the Town. Only Jimmy Ryan's, behind a black-marble façade, offered jazz—The Six band and pianist Don Frye.

By '52 *Variety* changed 52d's label from Swing Street to Strip Row. It described the girls as "fat, flabby and in their forties." What it objected to more than the sleazy stripping was the tawdry atmosphere and uncouth treatment of customers.

In succeeding years, the reputation of The Street tumbled steadily, even though a few clubs struggled to keep jazz alive. Complaints mounted. The police department constantly received reports that girls were brushing against customers and seating themselves at tables uninvited. Though menus were required by law, some clubs had none. Others were so dimly lighted that the exorbitant prices were not visible until the waiter flashed a light on checks that were recklessly kited and padded. The minimum at many clubs rose to $3.50 for liquor alone, and the drinks were heavily watered. (Champagne was sometimes made by funneling ginger ale into an authentic champagne bottle and adding a dipper of grain alcohol.) Sidewalk barkers were known to be pimping and shilling, while hackies engaged in "steering." Pushers of hard drugs operated openly in one or two clubs.

One trick for padding a check was to turn extra champagne bottles upside down in an ice bucket. A drunken customer could then verify his tab by counting them. The story is told of a customer who suspected the trickery and, on a second visit, carefully put the corks of opened bottles into his pocket. Of course, when he got high enough, the waiter managed to slip some additional corks into his pockets.

Columnist-author Robert Sylvester reports another, somewhat less legal means of stealing. Occasionally, when a club knew that a patron was loaded, the maître d' would indicate that a "check was most acceptable." When the patron, who was in his cups by then, wrote a check, the maître d' would tear it up on the ground that the signature was illegible and request that a new check be written. This check would be destroyed, too, and the procedure repeated again. Of course, none of the checks was torn up. They were palmed—and the next morning, the club owner hurried to the bank to cash them before the patron realized what had happened.

Pianist-composer Sherman Edwards tells the tale of a big spender "who made himself so obnoxious that a waiter slipped him a Mickey Finn. By then the club was empty. When his pockets were checked for the money he owed, a wad of twelve thousand dollars was found. A taxi was called, and the driver was paid to drop his fare miles away. Within the hour, carpenters and decorators were called in. By ten o'clock the next morning, the bar had been moved, the bandstand was in another spot, and the drapes were changed. Sure enough, the spender was back in the afternoon with a detective, who began asking questions as to where he had sat, the location of the bar, etc. Of course, the guy gave wrong answers to everything, and the detective kept suggesting that maybe it was another club. Soon the guy admitted that he was no longer sure and reluctantly took off. Part of the twelve thousand dollars found its way into the dick's pockets."

Curiously, two men who are among Broadway's current successful composers worked in combos that accompanied strippers. In addition to Sherman Edwards, responsible for the lyrics and music of *1776*, in the '56–'57 period Charles "Buddy" Strouse and his Orchestra (sax, bass, drums and piano) created the sound for the strippers at the Club Samoa. Strouse is the composer of the music for Broadway hits from *Bye Bye Birdie* to *Applause*. He recalls that all the peelers had a particular love for "Harlem Nocturne" as a strip piece and that the owner of the club discouraged the musicians from hanging around the bar, while he urged the girls to do so.

Through the fifties, the police and other authorities waged a war of attrition against offending clubs. Once an inspector asked a peeler at the Moulin Rouge the difference between a burlesque striptease and an exotic dance. When she confessed that she did not know the meaning of "exotic," they shuttered the Moulin Rouge. On another occasion they raided the Three Deuces. A stripper named Titza, who did a wine dance, was given a citation by the city health department on the ground that the colored water used in her dance was unsanitary. The SPCA stepped in at one point and insisted that Zorita stop using a live snake in her act.

"They're slapping us to death with suspensions," Winnie Garrett, a well-known stripper of the day, complained to reporters. "It's such a lousy little street. Why can't they leave us alone?"

Despite constant harassment, the end was slow in coming. But come it did on July 4, 1960, when in one fell swoop the State Liquor Authority walked into seven clubs and yanked their liquor licenses.

Tape 25 . . . AHMET ERTEGUN

Ahmet Ertegun is a co-founder and currently president of Atlantic Records, the flourishing black-oriented label. As Nugetre (Ertegun spelled backward) he wrote and produced many of the early record hits of R & B groups like the Drifters and the Coasters. At this late moment in the 52d St. story, rapidly drawing to its dismal close, his memory of The Street's early days offers a stirring and stunning contrast. I have somewhat reduced the breathlessness of his delivery. Ahmet is a rattling fast talker, the words spilling out in a vain effort to catch up with the rush of his thoughts.

"When I was a young boy and first came to America, my brother Nesuhi and I were jazz fans. We were very excited when our father, who was a diplomat, was assigned to the USA because we thought we were coming to the land of jazz. It was very hard to find any jazz in Washington, D.C. All the record shops had was Ray Noble and Hal Kemp. Then we started to hunt around and began to find records in nooks and crannies, on U Street in secondhand record shops. There we found old blues records, and we started going from house to house in our quest for jazz.

"We were aware that the Commodore Music Shop in New York was a center for jazz and the blues. They were just starting to make their own records, and so was Steve Smith, who had a store on 54th St. and Seventh Avenue. He called it the Hot Record Society. It was a society with members reissuing records that were cutouts from catalogs and unavailable. When I first came to New York to listen to jazz—because Washington was a wasteland—we were terribly hungry to hear the groups that we had heard on records in Europe. America wasn't very jazz conscious at all then. The swing era had come in, and Benny Goodman was famous and Tommy Dorsey, etc. They had some very good jazz players in the bands. But they were playing arranged music, and arranged music was antithetical to our idea of jazz at the time.

"In New York we stayed at a small hotel. We really didn't want to spend money on anything except jazz and jazz records. Hanging around the Steve Smith Record Shop, we ran into a fellow named

Herman Rosenberg. He's died since. He was an elderly chap then who seemed to know everything that was going on. He knew who was playing where and had very definite ideas of what was good and bad. We were quite impressed by this man, who befriended us in the shop one day. He offered to introduce us to Joe Marsala, who was one of my favorite clarinet players from Chicago. I liked New Orleans jazz, but I really loved Chicago style—the way Leon Rapollo, Rod Cless, Pee Wee Russell and Frank Teschemacher played the clarinet.

"That led to our first trip to The Street. Herman Rosenberg took us to the Hickory House. Marsala had his brother, Marty, who was a great Chicago-style, rockhouse trumpet player. He had Dave Tough on drums, who had just left the big Goodman band. It was a swinging band. There were a couple of drummers who used to sit and listen to Tough. Buddy Rich was one, and Shelly Manne, then sixteen or so years old, was the other.

"I used to hang out with Dave Tough. He was my idol. He looked like Jean Louis Barrault sitting behind the drums. At the time I knew him, he was disgusted with the bands he had been playing with. He wanted to play jazz, and he wanted to play with black people. And he had started a book on F. Scott Fitzgerald. He loved Shelly, and Shelly loved him and learned to play drums from him. I guess Dave Tough and Big Sid Catlett were then the best drummers around—Gene Krupa, too, I suppose. Then came Buddy Rich, who took Dave Tough's place with Joe Marsala. Also of course, Lionel Hampton, who was a great drummer as well as good vibes.

"I spoke English a little bit and didn't know my way about. It was Herman Rosenberg who took us around. It meant so much not only to hear the music but to be able to meet musicians who had been idols of ours. Another person who took us around was Harry Lim. He was later A & R director of Keynote Records and made a lot of very important jazz records. Lim was very much with the scene and a good friend of musicians like Illinois Jacquet. He took us to hear Count Basie at the Famous Door. At that time, Basie's band looked like Bennie Moten's or Hot Lips Page's band. Hot Lips was one of The Street's greats. Leo Watson was the pivot of the Spirits of Rhythm. You could hear Fats Waller at the Yacht Club. There were great tenormen like Herschel Evans and Chu Berry—until I discovered what Lester Young was about. They were all children of Coleman Hawkins. Lester was a child of Coleman's in his drive, but he was light and started the whole modern school of jazz. Modern jazz was based on him—King of Elegance—and to an extent, on Roy Eldridge.

"I used to sit and listen to Charlie Parker in the early forties and Billie Holiday, and I think of those as my greatest moments in music. Milt Jackson had what looked like a toy set of vibes. Man, it sounded better than anything I've ever heard! It was a tiny little set, like a traveling set. Dizzy would sit in sometimes. And Charlie was with Gillespie. And Dizzy had a swinging band with Bags and Charlie Rouse from Washington on saxophone.

"I remember when Billy Eckstine sang. We'd go outside and stand in The Street between sets because it was stuffy in the clubs. He was a great inspiration to many of the jazz players because he stood up for them. He was a very cool and marvelous person. He was like the beginning. All of these people were not only great jazz players—Dizzy, Bird, Miles, Eckstine, Milt Jackson, John Lewis—but they were also men who started the new attitude of black people. They established principles of pride.

"In the beginning 52d St. was Jim Crow in the sense that bands were either white or black. There were no white players in Count Basie's band. If you had an all-star group in one of the clubs—say, like Bud Freeman's—you'd have Pee Wee Russell on clarinet, Billy Butterfield or Max Kaminsky on trumpet, Brad Gowans or Jack Teagarden on trombone—that would be a white band. The Chicago guys had no prejudice as such—like Bobby Hackett, who was another great luminary of the 52d St. scene. But that band played the kind of music that was white music trying to sound like early black music. Bud Freeman, Eddie Condon, Red McKenzie, Mezz Mezzrow—they came from Chicago. Mezzrow carried it to an extreme where he idolized Negro musicians. Like Louis Armstrong was the beginning and the end of music. But the music they played didn't come out the same. It was white music.

"Benny Goodman started mixing. It was still Jim Crow, but he had some black musicians, like Lionel Hampton and Teddy Wilson. There were mixed audiences after a time. Not as much in the thirties as during the war. 52d St. was really buzzing in the war years. That's when the bebop guys came in. Before that, crowds came to The Street for what? Well, there was Fats Waller. He had a great sense of humor. He was a great blues player. He could sit down and play church organ, blues organ, blues piano, and sing blues. He was one of the great, great performers. He was the king of the stride pianists like James P. Johnson. He was a clown, and he did make fun of everything because in those days you either had to do that or just break down. So many bad things were happening.

"I enjoyed Fats' band because he had two groovy horn players: Herman Autrey on trumpet and Gene Sedric on tenor. Another great band that played 52d St. in the pre-bebop days was Stuff Smith's. He had a fantastic trumpet player who later became a big star on Capitol Records—Jonah Jones was a bitch. He played with drive. He was like a modern Louis Armstrong wailing. He had a little bit of Jabbo Smith.

"Now, what jazz were we hearing at that time? We couldn't hear King Oliver's band, though we were all King Oliver freaks and Jelly Roll Morton freaks. When we lived in Washington, we found Jelly in a tiny joint over a tearoom. When he came to New York, he used to play Nick's in the Village. It was an extension of 52d St., but it was a Dixieland extension. On Sundays Jelly Roll had a fantastic band: Sidney Bechet on clarinet, Sidney De Paris on trumpet—oh, man—he always had fine players on trombone like Zu Robertson, or Roy Palmer, and, most of the time, Vic Dickenson. I remember we were looking for Geechie Fields, who used to play trombone with Jelly Roll. He had Wellman Braud on bass, later Duke Ellington's man, and Big Sid Catlett on drums. And, man, we used to drive every Sunday all the way from Washington, straight to Nick's just to hear a set. Unfortunately, Jelly Roll didn't play too much. He loved to talk about how he invented jazz. All the younger guys would come in and laugh and get angry because he'd say that he taught everybody how to play jazz back in 1902. Guys like Albert Nicholas, a great New Orleans player who was in the band, used to sit and smile. It was a great world. It was an inside club in those days. We all knew each other. And those great kicks when Bunk Johnson arrived from New Orleans and played those sessions in the East Village with Baby Dodds and Wild Bill Davison sitting in.

"Like John Hammond made records in 1932 with Bessie Smith that I collected, and now he's the one who recently discovered Aretha Franklin. Between, he found a lot of other talents. Pretty terrific, impressive person. When he said that 52d St. was Jim Crow, he was probably right because the Dixieland guys played with each other. Sometimes there'd be little crossovers, like Lips Page would sometimes play with Joe Marsala.

"But actually the place they crossed over was Jimmy Ryan's. They had these jam sessions run by Jack Crystal, who ran the Commodore Record Shop for Milt Gabler. The Sunday afternoon jam sessions were thoroughly integrated. This was the groovy music that we all went to hear. It really was improvised jazz, and you never knew who was going to be there. And the greatest people played. You could hear a set with Wingy Manone playing trumpet, Coleman Hawkins on tenor, Red McKenzie singing—and it would sound like a record made ten years before. McKenzie was a great singer in the Bing Crosby mold. All these guys dug Crosby because Crosby swings. They liked Johnny Mercer, who used to hang out with the Bob Crosby guys.

"Now there was a whole other thing—the big bands. We went to hear them. I used to go to the Camel Caravan broadcasts, you know. Herman Rosenberg got me into these so we could hear Eddie Miller, my other favorite tenorman, Nappy Lamare, Ray Bauduc, Bob Haggert and Muggsy Spanier. When Muggsy left Ted Lewis and came from Chicago, he brought George Brunies with him, who played trombone with Lewis. They got Rod Cless, who was not that well known on clarinet, and they formed a group that broke up New York. It was a tear-assed Chicago-style band.

"Then we went uptown to the Savoy Ballroom to hear Chick Webb in a battle of jazz against Benny Goodman's band, later Harry James' band. These things used to be a ball! The toughest band to beat was Lunceford, who had the greatest reed section in the world. The way they played together they were unbeatable. Sy Oliver did the arranging.

"You couldn't beat Count Basie's band, too. It was like a machine, a blues machine. Talk about a young exciting band playing the blues! There was nothing like hearing Herschel Evans and Lester Young trading choruses. And Dickie Wells on trombone might have been one of the greatest jazz musicians who ever lived. And great trumpet players like Harry 'Sweets' Edison and Buck Clayton. Man, we lived in those days! It was unbelievable to us to see and hear those guys in person!

"There used to be a place in Harlem called the Plantation Café, which was only for white people. In '36–'37 I heard Hot Lips Page's band when he had just come from Kansas City and had half of the Bennie Moten organization that later became part of the Count Basie band. I didn't know very much about anything, except that I thought everybody played other people's numbers and all of them must be very good friends. I went up to Lips Page and I said—I was wearing short pants and was just thirteen or fourteen years old—'Would you, please, sir, play for me "Satchelmouth Swing"?' That was a number that Louis Armstrong had put out a few months before. He looked at me and laughed. He said: 'No, but I'll play Lips Page's special message to young ofay. . . !' All the jazz musicians were very nice. They weren't used to having that many jazz fans around them. Like Sidney Bechet befriended me and told me a lot of stories.

"52d St. was an incredible gas for the jazz fan! I never thought of anything except music in those days. We would start at one end of The Street, and the thing was just to go with one bottle of beer. We would sit and stand with that for two and a half hours until the bartender or the bouncer threw us out unless we bought another. We had just enough money to buy one beer each at eight different clubs. You'd stand at the bar and hope that some of the musicians would come to the bar and talk to you.

"52d St., man, was Roy Eldridge, Coleman Hawkins, Stuff Smith, Fats Waller, Spirits of Rhythm. You'd walk into a place and run into Willie Bryant, the world's greatest MC. If he'd been white, he probably would have been one of the great actors on Broadway. He had a big hit with Ethel Waters in *Mamba's Daughters* when he was about sixteen years old. Then he didn't have any roles. He had a good little band for a while, for a hot minute.

"What we used to do was go and sit and hear our favorite bands. When I say 'we,' I mean myself and my brother, Nesuhi, and jazz collectors like Dan Qualey, Jerry Wexler, Sidney Martin, Bob Thiele, Ralph Gleason, Herb Abramson. All these guys were real diggers. Having listened to the band, the idea was to catch the musicians as they went out and go around the corner with them to the White Rose bar, where there was free lunch. You bought a beer for a dime and you could pick up on a little bit of cheese, stale pickles, etc. They had little alleyways. Like Wingy used to run out and sit between sets in the parking lot behind the Hickory House. You know everybody felt a little better after they came back from there. The Street was wide open. Everybody was groovin' . . ."

Though it has only a peripheral relationship to the 52d St. story, I cannot omit Ahmet's observation about the blues. It is one of the most beautiful and probing I have ever heard, and not irrelevant, considering how many of The Street's tremendous artists were black.

"We always dug the blues," he said. "The blues is the soul of jazz. There are all kinds of blues, not just the big-city blues like Bessie Smith sang. There are country blues where it all started. It's a funny thing. Everybody knows that the more down home you get, the funkier you get, the more pigs' feet you get—these are all expressions for getting close to soul. But red clay. What are they talking about? Where does it all come from? It all comes from being black. From being black, that's where this music emanates. Go to the very blackness of being black. It's the trouble that the black people have had in being brought over here. And those black people grew up in red clay mud up to their knees, working all day on some plantation. That's why it's referred to as 'pigs' feet music' and 'funky music' and 'real home music' and 'gritty music.' It's real black music in terms of black environment under the worst possible conditions.

"It's sad music and it's happy music. It's also secret-language music. It has two things: By the fact that it's a lament, it has the dignified beauty of the black people expressed in it; and because of its obvious innocent sincerity, it captivated the world. It isn't because it's got a drum that came from Africa. It's because it's got a soul that came from suffering.

"That is the reason, I believe, that this music has become the music of the world. That is the music that today's kids are imitating to a great extent. Of course, they add their own thing. But there is a basic core there. And jazz is certainly a development from the blues.

"In the thirties and forties, a jazz player would not play blues changes. And if they did, they tried to hide it. They must have felt that the blues was retrogression. It was with the advent of people like Ray Charles—who is not only a great blues singer, not only a great blues player, but also a great jazz musician—that black people came to understand that this was their heritage. There was nothing wrong in loving their own heritage, which is beautiful. The blues is undeniable. If you like American music, you must love the blues because the blues is the most important thing in American music. And jazz phrasing has come from blues phrasing and gospel phrasing. The looseness of rhythm that a white or black rhythm section has, is the result of subconscious imitation of the rhythm of Negro gospel and Negro blues singing."

20. Death of a Street

On May 1, 1948, *The New Yorker* devoted its cover to a cartoon comment on 52d St. The drawing by Getz viewed The Street from Sixth Avenue looking east. On the north side (left) of the seedy brownstones, you spotted such names as Tony's, Onyx and Jimmy Ryan's. On the south (right), you could make out Famous Door, Samoa and Carousel. Bright yellow rays of what had to be a morning sun arrowed from the gap of eastern sky toward which the two sides of The Street converged. But for 52d St., it was really a setting sun, or sunrise on a dying street. Cartoonist Getz was giving visual embodiment to obituaries that had already appeared in *Time* and *Collier's.* The obsequies had unquestionably been initiated by *Metronome,* whose April issue carried a story headed THE STREET IS DEAD: AN OBIT.

Convinced that The Street was "headed for oblivion," Leonard Feather of *Metronome* tried to find a way of halting the downhill toboggan. In his assessment of causes, he enumerated the following: lack of talent with sufficient drawing power; exorbitant demands of talent with a following; rotten liquor and clip-joint attitude toward customers; and "low-life reputation of The Street acquired through its fringe of dope addicts, dope peddlers, pimps, prostitutes and assorted characters."

Contending that The Street had degenerated from a healthy meeting place for musicians and fans into something paralleling the notorious Barbary Coast of San Francisco, he noted: "The Street's reputation has been blackened by reports of dope raids and arrests, by items in newspaper columns and by the associations of some of the musicians. . . . The truth is that today marijuana is kid's stuff compared to what's been going on. . . ." Feather was not unsympathetic to the plight of many musicians: "The depressing professional condition in which many are forced to live nowadays, the failure of the public to accept the kind of music they believe in, drives them more and more to artificial escapes from their neuroses. All this, whether you want to face it or not, is an essential part of the 52d St. story. . . ."

"An era was all but over," *Time* echoed. "Swing was still there, but it was more hops than horns. Barrelhouse had declined. Burlesque was back. . . ." And it added: "There was little jazz left on 52d St. Even the customers had changed. There were fewer crewcuts, pipes and sports jackets; more bald spots, cigars and paunches. . . ."

In all this soul-searching, no mention was made of two groups that had a large stake in The Street and contributed to its demise as an entertainment center: the city's landlords and the hoods. The former were not content to see a tenderloin threaten real-estate values in an area that could yield immeasurably greater revenues than the rundown brownstones. And the hoods who came as customers and stayed as partners demonstrated the relevance of Gresham's law about bad money driving out good. Only it was vice, not money, that spread like an inkblot and eventually blotted out the greater profits that came at first.

Robert Sylvester adds the probing comment that while the hoods were crafty club owners—with planned closings and reopenings—they were ineffective. "It is impossible," he observes, "to recall a single hoodlum nightclub that had more than a brief spin on the dizzy whirl of success." His curious explanation: Clubs are "a foot in the social door" for hoods, but they are easily "taken" by the knowledgeable craftsmen on the scene.

The year 1948 may have seen the end of an era. It did not bring an end to The Street, whose last club did not disappear until the late sixties. However, the downward upcurves, as in the earlier years, sent a number of the 52d St. club owners and promoters investigating locations off The Street. Symptomatic was the abortive effort of Irving Alexander and Sammy Kay, longtime bonifaces, to establish a club on

Broadway between 52d and 53d. *Metronome* memorialized this development in a story headed: JAZZ IS DEAD ON 52ND STREET AND VERY MUCH ALIVE ON B'WAY.

From this time forward, the story of The Street became a tale full of headlines signifying decay and death: THE STREET JUST A DEAD ALLEY AGAIN (*Down Beat,* February 24, 1950). "Reopening of the Deuces last July," John S. Wilson commented, "combined with a police clampdown on the strippers who had taken over the street, brought hopes that music might make it on the alley again. However, the only other club to try a music policy was the Orchid room, which lasted a few weeks. The Deuces held on, using Erroll Garner most of the time, until mid-January when he moved over to Birdland. With the pianist's exit, Clark Monroe took a bunch of girls into the 52d St. club."

Just about the same time Hickory House dropped its live-music policy and substituted a disc jockey, who played records over WINS from midnight to 3 A.M. Although the steak house later returned to a piano-trio format in January, 1950, live jazz could be heard only at Jimmy Ryan's.

In *Variety* of March 11, 1952, byliner Herm Schoenfeld reported: "New York's 52d St.—more specifically that moldering midway of strip and clip joints clustered off the corner of Sixth Avenue—isn't going downgrade anymore. This sector of the street hit bottom several years ago and has stayed there ever since—a casualty of puritanism, the police and its own putrid talent."

In *Variety* of April 14, 1954, byliner Joe Cohen observed: "There's a new sense of urgency among the operators along New York's 52d Street. Feeling is heightened by the fact that wreckers are now already tearing down the defunct Leon & Eddie's, and demolition crews will start on the southeast end of the block sometime in August, thus killing off a few more joints along the thoroughfare."

By this date The Street was a shambles. In a survey that I personally made in '54, I found six strip joints and only one jazz club operating between Fifth and Sixth avenues: Pigalle, Flamingo and Club Samoa on the south side, and Club Ha-Ha, Moulin Rouge, Harem and Jimmy Ryan's on the north. But there were parking lots and shuttered and boarded-up joints all over the street: on the north side, Lido Club and French Quarter; on the south, Club Nocturne and

A last view of the 52d St. Jimmy Ryan's.

Arnold Shaw

Chez Lina, as well as such hallowed jazz hangouts as Reilly's Tavern, Famous Door and Three Deuces. It was apparent that the wreckers were waiting for two closings before they tore down everything on the south side from the corner of Sixth halfway down the block. In this chunk of property, later the site of the Sperry Rand structure, only the Club Samoa and Nedick's on the southeast corner—closing Saturday, March 13—were holding up the wrecker's steel ball and bulldozers.

Six years elapsed before the decadent clubs were forced to close. A small story on page 2 of *Variety*, dated July 20, 1960, reported that the State Liquor Authority had rejected a plea of the Musicians Union for restoration of licenses to seven padlocked clubs, which had been raided two weeks earlier on the most historic of American holidays, July Fourth. The refusal to restore their licenses meant that The Street was dead, but stone dead. That the real-estate interests should have been behind the SLA's move seems only fitting since it was the same interests that had originally opened The Street to business in 1926 and made Swing Alley possible.

The passing of what was the next-to-the-last club on The Street, Ryan's, was a quiet thing, noted in only one metropolitan newspaper. But the New York *Times* memorialized the event in an October, 1962, story that appeared, appropriately enough, in its Real Estate section: SKYSCRAPERS OVERWHELM 52D ST., ONCE A HOME OF JAZZ AND BARS.

Nobody but nobody seemed to notice the 1968 inundation of Hickory House by a music-less fish shanty. After all the great and magical sounds that had filled The Street with awe-struck crowds for so many years, 52d ended not with a bang—and hardly a whimper.

Tape 26 . . . THE DOORMAN OF 52D ST.

As the Cadillac vacated the pavement in front of Al & Dick's, a steak house on 54th St. near Seventh Avenue, a stocky little man with a cigar in his mouth scooted across the street, lugging a large garbage can. He set the tin down where the front end of the car had been. Recrossing the street, he ducked into a garage, came out trundling another large garbage can, and placed it where the rear of the car had been.

"It's his own private parking lot," laughed Matty Walsh, the genial owner of Jimmy Ryan's, the Dixieland jazz joint across from Al & Dick's. "He's our doorman, as he once was on 52d St. in the old days. But I let him pick up tips all over the block. He'll get a cab for anybody. And he can tell just by the way you walk when you want one. He's fast. And he knows how to put on the act, with the bows when he opens a door for you, and the big gestures when he's directing your car into a tight spot. He actually services three other restaurants, though he works for us: Santa Lucia, west of us, La Scala, a few doors to the east, and the steak house across the street. But he's established his own parking lot only in front of Al & Dick's. I guess the best tippers go there—and he holds the place for his favorite clients with those garbage cans."

The little man with the big cigar was a scant five (sore) feet tall, with a large, bald head that sat heavily on a barrel chest. His name was, surprisingly, Gilbert J. Pincus. Once in the forties, when he had worked on Swing Street, he had been named mayor of The Street. It was a publicity stunt dreamed up by press agent Eddie Jaffee.

"Yeah," says Pincus, "I was the mayor once. The mayor of 52d. I was in *Look* . . . in *Life* . . . in *Esquire* . . . in *Cue*. That was in, I'll say, 1944 or '45 and all that."

As we stood talking outside Jimmy Ryan's, Gilbert J. Pincus' black eyes carefully scanned the cars moving into 54th from Seventh Avenue. "I was always outside. All them big stars started on 52d. Every one—Henry 'Red' Norvo—with those things there—Billy Daniels, Dizzy Gillespie . . . yeah." Suddenly, he darted away from me, shouting, "Pardon me."

Gilbert Pincus
the MAYOR
of 54th St.

Gilbert J. Pincus, once "Mayor"
of 52d St., now of 54th. He
moved when Jimmy Ryan's did.

Davis Quinn, from the collection
of James K. Makrianes, Jr.

Nodding to a thin man who came out a doorway, Pincus waddled off the sidewalk, moving more like a sandpiper than a duck, flagged down a cab with big arm motions, opened the door with a flourish, and as the thin man passed him, deftly accepted the proffered tip.

"I get aroun' pretty good, don't I?" Pincus asked when he was back at my side. "I'm tellin' you, I feel good, thank God. I feel good. My feet—once they were awful bad on me. I couldn't hardly walk. Happened to me, oh, about eight or nine years ago. So they took out a vein. And since then I walk good. I walk fine, thank God, so everything is real good."

As Pincus smiled brightly, the oversized nose seemed to grow longer. "Being a doorman ain't bad," he mused. "I brought up a family. My son had a baby boy, you hear, so I'm a granddaddy now for the first time. So I went down to 14th St.—that's where my wife got her glasses—I went down there and I need glasses. I mean reading glasses, you understand. When I told the doc I was sixty-three, he couldn't believe it. I'm tellin' you somethin'. He thought I was forty, maybe forty-five. You wanna know? That's because I'm always outside. In the rain, in the snow, in the sleet."

Pincus shook his head unhappily from side to side. "In the 52d St. days, you could park on both sides of the street. Now, on the south side only before twelve and on the north only after seven. The cops won't listen today. In the old days when 52d St. had all that music, you could talk to anybody. People got along better. Even the cops. And they grab cars now! People come from outa town. They go in a restaurant—and BOOM! the car is gone. The other day, ten minutes, a guy had the car parked here just ten minutes before seven—and they pulled it away. You hear me? The guy comes out. 'Where's my car?' So I had to send him over to the 54th St. station.

"And the tips were better in the old days. Everybody made a good dollar then. So many clubs! And one on top of the other. I worked Jimmy Ryan's, the Moulin Rouge. I worked the Samoa, where Lili St. Cyr, Sherry Britton, all them big stars, Winnie Garrett, Lois De Fee. I worked them all. Lois De Fee, the one with the big boobies. 'Member she married a midget, a small midget? That was nothin'—yeah, nothin'."

Pincus charged across the street as two people came out of Al & Dick's. By the time he reached their car it was moving off. "I'll be seeing you, Jack," he called, watching the car disappear down the street. "There'll be another day, Jack."

Returning to my side, he said: "I like everybody. I liked all the musicians on The Street. Pretty nearly all of them. But there was one man I'll never forget. You 'member Tommy Manville—he was that crazy millionaire. Well, some people said he was crazy. I opened the doors for him and his wife. And Georgie Raft—I met him when he went in the 21 Club. The day he was there, he was in a lotta trouble. The income tax and all that. Whatta nice guy! Used to be a hoofer, a dancer. And the first picture he ever made—*Scarface*. You 'member that *Scarface* picture with the coin? I'll never forget that."

Pianist Johnny Guarnieri remembers Pincus at the Three Deuces. "He was a huckster," he recalls. "Everytime the three of us would come out of the club, he'd start shouting: 'Come and hear Johnny Guarnieri, America's Greatest Jazz Pianist! Slam Stewart, International Bass Stylist! Sammy Weiss, America's No. 1 All-round Drummer.' He was just repeating word for word what was on the tent billboard in front of the club. And it was all for our benefit. But he'd always add his own clincher. Like: 'Come and hear this great jazz trio before this building comes down!' "

"All I wanna do," Pincus continued, "is just make a livin', pay my rent, pay my bills. A millionaire I can't be—that's for sure. One time I was broke. I says to Dizzy Gillespie, 'Let me have ten dollars.' He give it to me just like that. I always give him a little extra service when I saw him. He always had a tip ready. But I wouldn't take it. Well, maybe once outa four or five times. But there was this singer—I ain't mentionin' no names. I once went to see him when I needed some money. 'I'm busy,' he says, 'don't bother me.' What a stifferoo! But Dizzy, that's one fine man. I always liked Dizzy. I like everybody. Like when I see that singer, I say hello to him anyway.

"The greatest of all those guys? You know who? 'Member Charlie Parker? Everybody said he was the greatest. 'Boid,' they called him. He was a very good friend of mine, a real good friend. If he wouldn'ta fooled aroun' with that stuff, he would be all right today. But they all take that dope—and all that. And it kills them. Isn't that somethin'?"

Milt Gabler, the Decca Records executive who ran the jams at Ryan's and owned the Commodore Music Shop, remembers Pincus as a fellow who wore a long overcoat and a beat-up doorman's cap. "Except for 21 and Leon & Eddie," Milt recalls, "the clubs didn't have doormen. But they did well if one is to believe the rumors about the apartment houses owned by Red, the 21 doorman. As for Pincus, he elected himself doorman for four or five clubs. No one knew who paid his small salary, if anyone did. In all kinds of weather, he ran up and down the block, opening car doors, calling cabs, and holding an umbrella bigger than himself to protect the ladies from the rain and snow. He never offended anybody and later attained a certain kind of stature. In the beginning, people fluffed him. But after a time everybody knew Pincus and liked him."

"I went away from 52d," Pincus said, "oh, about 1960 or '61. I stayed all through the girlie days, after the music was gone, and the tips weren't so good. From 52d I went over by the Peppermint Lounge—you know, the twist place on 45th. What a madhouse that was! You never saw such crowds, not even when 52d had all those clubs. And the celebrities! They came to watch the kids. It was really a nothin' place. But everybody wanted to get in. The lines outside! But the big tips were inside. The excitement didn't last—maybe six months. Then it got quiet like on 52d after all those big buildings came up.

"But I go on working. Pincus always works. I used to get to The Street around six o'clock. In the winter it was already dark. And I'd get done about three thirty or four o'clock in the morning. Used to go home by subway. But not now, no, sir! One of the hackies that works around here picks me up every night. He takes me home on the West Side."

Jackie Mills, former drummer and now manager of Bobby Sherman, says, "Some of the guys used to call Pincus Yiz'll because he'd tell people blocking a club entrance, 'Yiz'll have to move on.' We all loved him. The last time I was in New York, I ran into him on 54th St. He hadn't seen me in at least fifteen years. But when I walked over to him and said, 'Hey, Pincus!' he took one look and said: 'You're Jackie Mills. That's who you are. Pincus never forgets a face.' Somehow I always remember him with a folded newspaper sticking out of the pocket of a long, black-gray overcoat. He wore a doorman's cap that sat on his nose. He was a landmark like the White Rose bar."

"I came here to 54th St.," Pincus said, "after Jimmy moved here in 1963. Jimmy died right away. I guess maybe he really died when they tore down the old place. Just imagine, he was in that spot for over twenty years! It musta been hard for him to leave. You know, some of the old-timers that played there are still playing here. The same kind of music! It's a happy sound when you hear it on the street late at night. Not so loud or fast like Dizzy, or noisy like Joey Dee with that twist. It's good work music.

"All I wanna do now is make enough money to take care of my wife. My son, he's got a good job with United Parcel, thank God. Everything fine! He lives out on the Island—Long Island. We go out there to visit. I get to work aroun' cocktail time here. The music don't start until about nine thirty. That gives me time to take care of my customers at Al & Dick's and La Scala. What a business they do! The music goes until after three, and I stay. It's work. But I enjoy it. And I like the music. Pardon me!"

Pincus was in the middle of the street in a flash, motioning to a station wagon. Waddling to the spot where he had earlier placed two barrels, he quickly moved them aside to free a parking spot directly in front of Al & Dick's. With vigorous arm motions, he guided the station wagon into the place, opened the right door for the woman, and dashed flat-footed around to open the other door for the driver. As he flung open the restaurant door for the pair and bowed them in, a wide Ernest Borgnine smile lit his face. You could hear Art Tatum's rippling piano arpeggios, Billie Holiday's slow, bittersweet balladry, Coleman Hawkins' vibrant, after-hours tenor, and all the music going 'round and 'round and 'round. . . .

Acknowledgments

The story of 52d St. would have lacked much in color and detail had it not been for the personal recollections, taped and/or written, of the following: Paul Ackerman of *Billboard;* drummer Henry Adler; Willard Alexander; Larry Bennett of National Campus Concerts; Barbara Belle; violinist Harry Bluestone; Sherry Britton; Joey Bushkin; Sammy Cahn; Benny Carter; Mrs. Jack Colt; disc jockey Ira Cook; Billy Daniels; Eddie Davis of Leon & Eddie; Joe Delaney, Las Vegas columnist, radio-TV commentator; Sherman Edwards; Art Engler; Ahmet Ertegun; contact-man Johnny Farrow; Frances Faye; Leonard Feather; Bud Freeman; Joel Friedman of Warner Bros. Records; William Frost, formerly of Capitol Records; Milt Gabler; Slim Gaillard; Erroll Garner; Stan Getz; Dizzy Gillespie; artist-manager Martha Glaser; Harry Goodman; record retailer Art Grobart; Johnny Guarnieri; Peter Lind Hayes; Lennie Hayton; Neal Hefti; Joe Helbock; Woody Herman; the late George Hoefer; Eddie Jaffee; Arthur Jarwood; Gordon Jenkins; Quincy Jones; Murray the K; Monte Kay; Richard Kirk of BMI; Manny Klein; Burt Korall of BMI; I. Robert Kriendler; Frankie Laine; Irving P. Lazar; Lou Levy; TV producer Richard O. Linke; Herman Lubinsky of Savoy Records; artist manager Lee Magid; Shelly Manne; Wingy Manone; trumpeter Howard McGhee; Marian McPartland; Johnny Mercer; Jackie Mills; Mills Brothers; Harold Minsky; Sy Oliver; Mrs. Chauncey Olman; Red Norvo; Gilbert J. Pincus; Louis Prima; banjoist Davis Quinn, whose paintings hang in Jimmy Ryan's and who has given photographs for the book; songwriter Edward C. Redding; Joe Reisman of RCA Victor Records; composer-conductor Henri René; former contact-man Charley Ross; Russ Sanjek of BMI; George Shearing; publicist

Gene Shefrin; Phil Silvers; the late Charles Edward Smith; songwriter Robert B. Sour; Charles Strouse; Maxine Sullivan; Billy Taylor; Sam Trust of Capitol Records; Ralph Watkins; Alec Wilder; Mary Lou Williams; publicist Maximillian Wolkoff; and publicist Irving Zussman.

In the area of the printed word, I owe a debt to the autobiographies of Pearl Bailey, Sidney Bechet, Hoagy Carmichael, Eddie Condon, Benny Goodman, Billie Holiday, Max Kaminsky, Wingy Manone, Mezz Mezzrow, Artie Shaw, and Willie "The Lion" Smith. Other books that provided valuable information were *ASCAP's Biographical Dictionary,* Frederic Ramsey, Jr., and Charles Edward Smith's pioneer study *Jazzmen,* Ira Gitler's *Jazz Masters of the Forties, The Big Bands* by George Simon, John C. Wilson's *The Collector's Jazz,* Barry Ulanov's *A History of Jazz,* Stanley Walker's *The Night Club Era,* Robert George Reisner's *Bird,* Leonard Feather's *Encyclopedia of Jazz* and *Inside Bebop, Variety Music Cavalcade,* Nat Shapiro and Nat Hentoff's *Hear Me Talkin' to Ya,* the volumes of Shapiro's Annotated Index of American Popular Songs, and *Show Biz from Vaude to Video* by Abel Green and Joe Laurie, Jr., and Whitney Balliett collected pieces on jazz.

The columns of Bob Considine, Walter Winchell, Danton Walker, Leonard Lyons, Ed Sullivan, Earl Wilson and Louis Sobol—also books by the last two—offered insight into The Street's legends and happenings. In this regard, two of columnist Robert Sylvester's books, *No Cover Charge* and *Notes of a Guilty Bystander,* are particularly noteworthy.

Quite a number of people helped to locate or make available pictures, people, programs, memorabilia, out-of-print records, defunct publications, old songs and information-arcanum. I would be remiss if I did not mention Bob Altschuler of Columbia-Epic Records; Charles Berns of 21; Willis Conover of the Voice of America; publicist Jack Egan; Leonard Feather (who possesses the only bound file of *Metronome* west of New York); Mrs. Eleanor Follick of Great Falls, Montana; Dan Franklin of Warner Brothers' music department; Milt Gabler; Arnold Gingrich of *Esquire;* Gilbert Goldstein of Life of Virginia; Robert C. Grant of Nedick's Stores; *Variety* editor Abel Green; Johnny Guarnieri; John Hammond; Herb Hellman of RCA Victor-Bluebird Records; Charles M. Hurley of Springfield, Massachusetts; Phoebe Jacobs of the Rainbow Room; Les Koenig of Contemporary Records; James K. Makrianes, Jr., of Young & Rubicam; Mercurio's Restaurant in New York; Irving Mills; Judith K. Mulvey of Rockefeller Center, Inc.; columnist Jack O'Brian; June Paramore of the Clark County Library of Las Vegas; Maury and Muriel Stevens of the Las Vegas radio-and-TV scene; Matty Walsh; Sam Weiss; and Shirley and Jerry Wexler.

A special word of thanks to Dan Morgenstern, editor of *Down Beat* who made the magazine's picture file available; to Judy Pierro, whose typewriter helped me make a deadline; to Ellis Amburn, vice-president of Coward, McCann & Geoghegan, who saw the importance of the project; and to Peggy Brooks, who is that rare editor—she reads with care and understanding.

52d Street Music

Records (*Singles and LP's*)*

"52nd St. Theme": Kenny Clarke and His 52nd Street Boys in *The Bebop Era* (RCA Victor LPV 519)

"52nd St. Theme": Dizzy Gillespie (RCA Victor LPV 530)

"52nd St. Theme": Thelonious Monk in *Fats Navarro Memorial Album* (Blue Note 5004)

"52nd St. Theme": Charlie Parker in *Bird on 52nd St.* (Jazz Workshop 501, Fantasy 6011)

"52nd St. Theme": Oscar Peterson in *At Newport* (Verve 8239)

"52nd St. Theme": Oscar Peterson in *At the Stratford Shakespearean Festival* (Verve 8024)

"52nd St. Theme": *Bud Powell* (Blue Note 1503)

"New 52nd St. Jazz" (Victor HJ 9)

"52nd Street Scene": Tony Scott and the All-Stars (Coral CRL 57239)

"Swing Street" (Epic SN 6042, 4 Vols.)

"46 West 52": Chu Berry (Commodore 20024)

"Knockin' at the Famous Door": Charlie Barnet (Bluebird)

"Swingin' at the Famous Door": Roy Eldridge and Delta Four (Decca)

"At the Hickory House": Jutta Hipp and Her German Jazzmen (Blue Note 1515)

"At the Hickory House": Marian McPartland (Capitol T 574)

* Many of these are not currently available.

"At Storyville—At Hickory House": Marian McPartland (Savoy 12004)
"Swingin' at the Hickory House": Joe Marsala (Bluebird)
"The Onyx Hop": Frankie Newton and His Uptown Serenaders (Variety 647)
"Onyx Club Spree": Stuff Smith (Decca)
"Pic-A-Rib": Benny Goodman Trio-Quartet-Quintet (Victor LPM 1226)
"Spotlite": Coleman Hawkins' 52nd Street All-Stars (RCA Victor LPV 544)
"Night at the Deuces": Randy Brooks (Decca)
"Get Your Juices at the Deuces": Harry (the Hipster) Gibson (Musicraft)
"Tillie's Downtown Now": *Gems of Jazz* (Decca DL 5133, Vol. 1)
"White Rose Bounce": Erroll Garner (Black & White)
"Yacht Club Swing": Fats Waller and His Rhythm (RCA Victor 939)

Songs

"The Music Goes 'Round and Around": Mike Farley and Eddie Riley in *The Original Hit Performances, The Late Thirties* (Decca DL 4000)
"You'se a Viper": Stuff Smith and His Onyx Club Boys
"Isle of Capri": Wingy Manone and His Orchestra
"Let's Have a Jubilee": Louis Prima and His New Orleans Gang
"Loch Lomond": Maxine Sullivan and Her Orchestra
"Flat Foot Floogie": Slim & Slam

all in *Swing Street* (Epic SN 6042)

"Body and Soul": *The Hawk in Hi-Fi* (Victor LPM 1281)
"The Fourth Deuce": George Shearing (London LL 1343)
"I Love It So": Tommy Dorsey (Victor 27-392 A)
"51st St. Blues": Charlie Mingus (Bethlehem 6019)

Films and Broadway

52nd St., A Walter Wanger production (1937)
Fifty Second Street Follies, a revue (1939)
52nd St. Special: Wingy Manone (RKO short)
52 St., a song, with words by Sammy Cahn, music by Saul Chaplin, from the Vitaphone Brevity "Sound Defects." Copyright 1937 by Harms, Inc.

Index

Figures in italics refer to pages on which photographs occur.